MRS GANDHI

DOM MORAES

JONATHAN CAPE
THIRTY BEDFORD SQUARE LONDON

First published 1980
Copyright © 1980 by Dom Moraes
Jonathan Cape Ltd, 30 Bedford Square, London WC1

British Library Cataloguing in Publication Data

Moraes, Dom
Mrs Gandhi.
1. Gandhi, Indira
2. Prime ministers—India—Biography
954.04'092'4   DS481.G23
ISBN 0 224 01601 6

Printed in Great Britain by Ebenezer Baylis and Son Ltd
The Trinity Press, Worcester, and London

MRS
GANDHI

For Leela

Contents

Illustrations

ACKNOWLEDGMENTS

The author and the publishers would like to thank the following
individuals and institutions for permission to reproduce the photographs in this book: B.B.C. Hulton Picture Library, 10; Jawaharlal
Nehru Memorial Fund, 2a and b, 3, 4a and b, 5, 6, 7, 8, 9, 11,
12; Keystone Press Agency, 16, 20, 22, 23, 29; Popperfoto, 13,
14, 15, 18, 19; Raghu Rai, jacket, 1, 17, 21, 24, 25, 26, 27, 28.

Preface

This was a difficult book to write in many respects. It involved a lot of research, and the deployment of a considerable amount of diplomacy, a quality for which I have never been famous. Also, it took me nearly two years to finish. I do not consider these two years wasted, for during them I studied at close quarters the life and mental movements of one of the most remarkable people in the world. In that sense I transformed myself, for months, into a mirror, though sometimes the image that stood in the mirror was not beautiful. When it was not, I have tried to reflect it. But I hope the mirror never cracked.

I am most thankful to Mrs Indira Gandhi and to members of her family both in Delhi and in Allahabad, for their co-operation; to Mr Jag Parvesh Chandra and Mr Khushwant Singh of New Delhi for their help and advice; to Mr Raghu Rai whose photographs provide many of the illustrations to this book and who has followed Mrs Gandhi closely with his camera since 1966, not only for his own photographs but for the help he afforded me in choosing photographs of Mrs Gandhi's earlier life from museum collections. I am also grateful to my wife, Leela, who took notes and helped me in the research period; and to Peter Grose, my agent and friend, who came from London to India in 1977 to help me through a difficult situation at the beginning of all these words.

New Delhi
January 1980

DOM MORAES

Prologue

SHORTLY AFTER MRS GANDHI was defeated, in March 1977, in the Indian elections she had called after she ended her emergency, my wife, Leela, and I went to see her in New Delhi, at 1 Safdarjang Road, the house where she had stayed since she first became Prime Minister in 1966. She was supposed to remove from it shortly, since her successor, Morarji Desai, who had a perfectly good house of his own in Dupleix Road, wanted to take 1 Safdarjang Road over as his official residence. It was a petty prod at Mrs Gandhi: but it must have hurt.

Mrs Gandhi sat in a large chair, her feet curled up under her. 'Thank you for coming,' she said. 'I'm sorry the house is so disorganised, but I'm supposed to move soon.' She looked terrible, worse than I had ever seen her even when as Prime Minister she followed her father's habit of working eighteen hours a day. Then the pouches under her sharp eyes had been those normally caused by tiredness and lack of sleep: now they were something else, they were black pouches, and she seemed physically to have shrunk. She was also, though very quiet as usual, not as watchful as usual, not as alert or as wary. She repeated, 'Thank you for coming,' and to my horror Leela burst into tears. Mrs Gandhi, courteous by nature, affected to be unaware of this, turned her tired eyes to me, and said, 'We've all the furniture and things to move, and we don't have a lot of time.' Leela, having somewhat recomposed herself, said, 'If I could help you pack ... ' and Mrs Gandhi blinked, smiled, sneezed like a little cat, and said, 'No, no, Leela, don't worry. Don't worry so much. I'm all right.' I then said, 'You look awfully tired.' To this, unblinking, but her hands curled in her lap, she replied, 'I'm better than I have been for a very long time. I feel as though an enormous weight has been lifted off my shoulders. Do you understand what I mean?' She later said this, perhaps less spontaneously, to several other people, including David Frost.

There was then a considerable silence, during which Leela dried
her eyes and Mrs Gandhi and I stared past each other into the
middle distance. Finally she said, 'I had lost touch with the people.
Halfway through the election I felt here,' and with a typically
unemphatic movement of her hand touched her chest, 'that we
would lose. Well, we've lost.' There seemed little more to say. At
length Mrs Gandhi said, 'They're setting up all these tribunals and
commissions, so I suppose I'll have to face those.' With some
asperity she added, 'I don't know why they want to waste so much
money.' This was one of those conversations which proceed by
stops and starts. 'Are you going to go back into politics, ma'am?'
I asked. She said 'No. I told you I feel as though a burden has been
lifted from my shoulders. I will never return to politics.' At that
moment I didn't doubt what she had said.

A few days later I revisited her at Safdarjang Road, this time alone.
Apart from her small grandchildren, the son and daughter of Rajiv,
her elder son, and his Italian wife, Sonia, and a large and stately
wolfhound, she was also alone. Moreover, even the furniture of the
house, solid and palpable entities which can act as company to a
lonely person, had vanished, or most of it had: it was being packed
for transfer to 12 Willingdon Crescent, where she was now to live.
This house had formerly been the home of Mohammed Yunus, an
old family friend and at one time the Special Envoy of Mrs Gandhi.
He had given it up so that her family could inhabit it.

So, amidst an absence of furniture and pictures, she sat, smiling
only when the high voices of the children carried into the desolate
house. It was the first time I had seen her with no aide or secretary
hovering about. Even the telephone seemed dead: its birdlike cries,
which had so often interrupted our conversations in the past, stilled,
its chilled body lying black on the table.

I had come to broach a topic that I had raised on our last visit.
In 1971 an American publisher had approached me, asking me to
write a biography on what he called 'the most powerful woman in
the world', Mrs Gandhi. The firm had approached Mrs Gandhi and
she had expressed herself to be willing to co-operate. But at that
time I was the editor of a magazine in Hong Kong, and I had a
responsibility to it. I couldn't, therefore, write the book: anyway,
I did not feel very strongly about the idea of a biography of a

politician in power: an article, yes, a book, no. Somebody else wrote
the book: 'I gave him,' Mrs Gandhi said with a faint smile, 'fifteen
minutes of my time.'

I now thought, possibly, that Mrs Gandhi out of power would
be far more interesting for me to write about than Mrs Gandhi in
power. When I had asked her, at our previous meeting, if she would
like me to write such a book, she had replied, 'Why not? If it wasn't
you it would be someone else,' not a surpassingly modest remark.
Today I said, 'Ma'am, do you really want me to write this book
about you? I'd like to.' She shrugged a little. 'Then,' I said, 'you'll
have to help me. I shall have to have much more of your time than
fifteen minutes. Are you willing to spare me quite a lot of time?'
She said, 'From now on I shall have a lot of time on my hands. Why
not? Phone me next week, when we have moved.' I patted the
children on the head, smiled weakly at the wolfhound, and left,
thinking that this should not be a difficult book to write. Little did
I know.

The next time I phoned, Mrs Gandhi had completed her move.
The new government were actually in process of making their first
positive steps, neither of which, granted the economic state of the
country, seemed strictly necessary: they were forming commissions
to try Mrs Gandhi and those concerned with her in the emergency,
and they were busy banning the manufacture of Coca Cola in India
and in thinking up some indigenous substitute. Mrs Gandhi, when
I spoke to her, seemed rather dreamy: yes, she said, I could come
the next day.

I arrived, found crowds of people outside 12 Willingdon Crescent,
which I hadn't previously visited, tentsful of people on the lawns,
Congressmen on the veranda, and, in the reception room with
which I was to become increasingly familiar over the next year, two
persons, one of whom was an old friend of my father's, G. Partha-
sarathi, known to his intimates as G.P., who had been an excellent
cricketer and had nearly played for India. He had later become an
outstanding diplomat, had been Vice-Chancellor of the Jawaharlal
Nehru University in Delhi, and most recently, head of the Planning
Commission. The other person, a short and affable person, was
Mr D. P. Singh, a famous lawyer. 'We,' said G.P., 'are protecting
Mrs Gandhi's interests. On the matter of this book, we want to
know what exactly you have in mind.' Being entirely unprepared

for this, I stuttered somewhat. 'You see,' said Mr Singh in his affable way, 'the party may not like it if you print certain things she tells you.' I was surprised: 'I thought she wasn't in politics,' I said. 'What has any party to do with this?' Mr Singh shook his head. 'No, no,' he said patiently. 'Who has said she is not in politics? Who is to lead our party?'

These discussions lasted several weeks. Sometimes Mrs Gandhi was present, frowning a little and scribbling notes: sometimes it was only G.P., Mr Singh, and myself: sometimes our numbers were increased by Pupul Jayakar.* At one point, utterly mystified by what was happening, I flew to London to consult my agent. He was as mystified as I by the proceedings and shortly after I flew back to Delhi he came over to try and sort the matter out. He returned to London even more perplexed than before. There were, according to Mr Singh, certain aspects of Mrs Gandhi's life I could write about, certain aspects the party would not like me to write about, certain matters she would help me with, certain matters she would not be allowed by the party to help me with, and so on and so forth.

One day Mrs Gandhi asked me to come and see her, and when I did, she said, frowning, hands folded in her lap, 'I don't see what all this fuss is about. I'm not authorising this biography, am I? As you see, I am now trying to help the country, in my own way.' What she meant, obviously, was that she was now back in politics. 'I won't have the time I thought I'd have,' she added, 'when we first talked about this book of yours. But I'll help you as much as I can. I can't promise you anything, but I'll try.' After so many deaths, as Herbert† said, I lived and wrote. But the extraordinary chain of circumstances that led up to my writing this book seem to me worthy of record, if only because they confirmed my view that in all the ground around her, advisers bulge up like mushrooms after rain, sometimes because she wants them, sometimes not, and that in the end she tends to disregard all the advice and to do exactly what she thinks or feels is most sensible.

* A woman writer, once head of the Handloom and Handicrafts Export Corporation in India.
† The poet, George Herbert, 1573-1633.

PART ONE

The Inheritance

The High and the Flat Land

INDIA, ROUGHLY SPEAKING, is shaped like a carrot, with a tuft at the top. The carrot lies more or less flat, except for a few knobbly parts in the middle, beneath the enormous creamy mountains of Central Asia. The green tuft brushes those multiple breasts: eastward its borders abut upon Tibet and China: westward lie the dry, vicious peaks of Afghanistan, brooded over by Buddhas that came from the chisels of artisans now forgotten. For centuries past they have looked down at wild tribesmen, part animist, part Muslim, who paid no homage to the huge entities in the hills. Beyond Afghanistan is the gigantic mass of Russia, from which, some thousands of years back, a Caucasian race which Hitler was to call the Aryans started to trot their hairy ponies south, crossed the high passes, and entered a new country. Here they became the forefathers of the race that now inhabits northern India, a race fair of skin and hedonistic of habit.

The tuft of the carrot, the northernmost part of India, is called Kashmir. The creation of Pakistan in 1947 added to the welter of borders that surround it. It is now famous not only as a place of remarkable scenic beauty but as an area of dispute between India and Pakistan, and both these claims to fame arise from the same cause. Kashmir consists of a large valley surrounded by high snow-helmeted mountains. These mountains form a defensive barrier difficult to surmount, which is in part the reason for the dispute. They also form a superb backdrop to the valley, its green coverlet patterned by vividly painted flowers. The landscape is dotted with lakes and ruined temples. In prehistory, however, the whole valley is supposed to have been one vast lake, formed by the melted snow and ice from the mountains. The recession of the water over thousands of years brought men to the valley. Most of the lakes which exist now were, ironically, made by men.

But they were made in comparatively recent years. Excavations amidst a peculiar complex of menhirs at Burzahom, started in 1935 but shortly afterwards abandoned, yielded evidence of neolithic man. The excavations were recommenced in 1960, and much has now been discovered. For example, there are pit dwellings, which were probably thatched with straw, dated, tentatively, at 3000 B.C., stone axes, polished black pottery, hoes, pestles, and various implements of stone and bone. It is possible that the people who used these materials came down from the bitter plateau of Ladakh, or up from the plains, over the steep and difficult passes. But after them trotted the Aryans, to occupy the valley.

Physically and linguistically, some ethnologists say, the Kashmiris are closer to the pure Aryan stock than any other of the races of India. This is despite the fact that in later years Persians, Greeks, Turks and Tibetans entered the valley and settled there, and that the Kashmiri rulers varied racially from Huns to a solitary Tibetan.

The isolated nature of the valley may partially account for this, in that the difficult approaches prevented the arrival of newcomers in any very considerable numbers: but also the Kashmiris obviously had peculiar powers of racial assimilation. Nevertheless, even in the past, they cannot be said to have been a wildly popular race, however pure their blood. A Buddhist pilgrim from China, Huen Tsang, who arrived in Kashmir in A.D. 631 and was the guest of the king for the next two years, wrote, rather ungratefully, of his hosts, '[They] are good-looking ... but they are crafty'.

A peculiarity of the state was that women often played a fairly prominent part in politics. 'Broadly speaking,' Jawaharlal Nehru wrote, 'women had greater rights [in Kashmir] than in other parts of India.' There were queens who ruled the state, though they came to power after their husbands died. One such was Diddarani, in the tenth century, described by one writer as 'cruel, suspicious, unscrupulous ... ' though he also says that she possessed 'statesman-like sagacity, political wisdom, and administrative ability'. Whatever her failings, she was in power, first as queen consort, then as regent, and finally as queen, for half a century before she died in A.D. 1003. Three hundred years later, at the very end of Hindu rule in Kashmir, another queen, Kotarani, widow of the Tibetan ruler Rinchin, came to the throne. She became a folk heroine of sorts when she had to surrender her power to her former minister, Shah Mir, who had started a revolt.

One of the conditions of the surrender was that she should sleep with Shah Mir. She arrived in his bedroom splendidly clad. Before he could remove any of this raiment, however, she produced a knife, stabbed herself, and in a highly dramatic fashion, died.

These women actually ruled: but there were very often others who, even if they weren't rulers, were the power behind their unlovely husbands. Mountain societies are very often matriarchal: Kashmiri society, in a disguised way, apparently was. Women of the poorer classes may often have done most of the work: but it could be said that this established their ascendancy over the males. Women in ancient Kashmir owned private property, and they managed their own estates. They went unveiled: in Harsha's court in the eleventh century women counsellors sat with the men when important decisions were to be taken. These were women who had been educated in diplomacy and statecraft.

There may have been freedom for women, but there was certainly not freedom for everybody. Kashmir was potentially a rich state. It grew saffron, a commodity much in demand in the plains, and it was the only state in India to do so. Its fruit was famous; the raw wool imported into Kashmir from Tibet was woven into shawls and blankets, and, as such, advantageously exported. But the profits from all this never came back to the poor: indeed, they were taxed at a preposterously exorbitant rate. They also had to submit to a system of forced labour, and if they did not appear when summoned, they were heavily fined. Wavelike the dynasties broke upon one another, spreading war across the valley. Jewels flashed on the costumes of the courtiers: elephants caparisoned in silk rolled from foot to foot in royal courtyards. All this splendour was confined to the few, but it was heavily subsidised by the many.

There were thus, in effect, two disparate races in the valley, the rich and the poor, even though ethnically they came from the same stock. They dressed and ate differently. The poor wore robes of coarse wool known as *pheran*, and woollen caps. The Mogul Emperor Jehangir remarked that an ordinary Kashmiri, due to his poverty, could only afford to have one *pheran* at a time, which he wore until it fell to pieces. The rich wore costumes woven of silk or the finest wool, and their wardrobes were anything but scanty. As regards diet, rice was the staple food: barley was considered edible only by the poor people. Meat of various kinds, cooked with vegetables and fruit, spiced with saffron and asafoetida, was served at the tables of the rich: they drank perfumed wine, rose petals afloat in the cup. Poor men settled for rice or barley, with some kind of vegetable, or meat when they could afford it. The rich ate what they liked when they liked: the poor ate what they could when they could.

Quite often they could not eat at all. The irrigation canals in the valley were fed by melted snow brought down from the mountains through a slow summer thaw, for there was not much rain. Sometimes, however, when heavy summer rain fell, the snow on the slopes melted quickly, and tons of water roared down, drowning people and crops. The result was famine, usually not alleviated by outside aid because of the difficulty of ferrying food over the passes. Early snowfall also destroyed the crops at harvest, and this caused famine as well. Kashmiri history is scarred with recurrent floods and consequent famines. Sometimes the rulers filled granaries in case of emergency, and initiated flood control methods: sometimes they didn't.

Whenever the granaries were empty, the cemeteries were full. In 1746-7, for example, three-quarters of the valley population died of starvation and disease following floods that ruined the crops. The dead lay all over the fields, one chronicler says, and the crows and vultures fattened.

The people were menaced not only by water but by fire. The availability of timber all over the valley naturally led to the construction of wooden houses. These were sometimes five storeys high, with sloping wooden roofs to act as snowslips. The roofs were sealed with birchbark, which was covered with earth to hold it in place. When spring came, lilies, violets and tulips sprouted from this earth. This was all very idyllic, but less idyllic was the fact that if a house in a city street caught fire, every house in the vicinity was likely to burn. The inhabitants lost their possessions and sometimes their lives: if it was winter, they were exposed, roofless, to the cold. The fires spread more quickly in winter, because of the wind fanning them into unselective fury. In the Kashmiri order of things, the houses of the poor burned more quickly than the houses of the rich, since they were not thatched with wood, but with dry reeds or straw, fodder on which the flames throve.

In the first years of the seventeenth century, when Jehangir was Emperor, a tremendous fire destroyed a quarter of the capital, Srinagar. This was a very old and very cluttered city: the original town is supposed to have been built by the Emperor Ashoka, who reigned in the third century B.C. According to a chronicler, there were '96,000 dwelling houses resplendent with prosperity' in this city, which was actually sited at Pandethran, four miles south of the present Srinagar. In the sixth century A.D., a king named Pravarasena built a second city, known as Pravarapura, on the present site of the Kashmiri capital. Ashoka's city must still have existed: Huen Tsang calls Pravarapura 'the new city' in contradistinction to Puranadisthana, 'the old city'. These would have been cities of wooden houses, populated by families from all walks of life: but a very important section of the population would have consisted of the scholars, the Kashmiri Brahmins, who were known as Pandits.

The valley, for a thousand years before Pravarapura was built, had been a nest and cradle for Sanskrit scholarship. How Sanskrit came to Kashmir is not quite clear — possibly through the Indo-Aryans from the south — but what is certain is that it found an excellent home there. Great scholars developed, and lesser scholars came to learn from them, not only Indians but scholars from China. There were enormous libraries of Sanskrit manuscripts in the temples, and some of the Pandits had private libraries of considerable size and importance. Huen Tsang, who arrived some years after the foundation of Pravarapura, spent his two years in Kashmir studying in these libraries. The tradition of Sanskrit scholarship continued unabated: indeed, what is perhaps the greatest piece of Kashmiri literature in Sanskrit, the *Rajatarangini*, a verse history of Kashmir from its earliest days, was not written by Kalhan until 1148.

Shah Mir ascended the throne in 1339, under the title of Sultan Shahabuddin. It was a historic year in that it marks the transition of Kashmir from a Hindu to a Muslim state. From then on until 1819, when Kashmir was conquered by the Sikh armies, there were always Muslim rulers: those of the Sultanate which Shah Mir established, the Chaks, the Moguls, and the Pathans. Many were unwise and unscrupulous men: they intrigued as much as the Hindu rulers had done: but, curiously enough, the quality of life improved for the common people. Some of the crippling taxes exacted by the Hindu rulers were lifted, and irrigation and flood control schemes were implemented at last. Nevertheless, the initial shock of finding themselves under Muslim rule sent many Hindus flying south across the passes, among them a number of the Pandits. Those who remained prudently applied themselves to the study of Persian.

Under Zain-ul-Abidin, the most enlightened of the Sultans, who came to the throne in 1420, the flood of Pandits through the passes reversed itself. He offered them complete religious freedom, security and equality, and they returned. However, the Brahmins who had stayed in Kashmir were rather contemptuous of them, and the two sets of Pandits separated themselves in terms of nomenclature. Those who had returned called themselves Banamasis; those who had stayed were known as Malamasis. The tradition of scholarship was now a dual one: the Pandits studied both Sanskrit and Persian. Zain-ul-Abidin then lifted the tax imposed on any Brahmin who refused to embrace Islam, as well as the tax on cremation, and banned cow-slaughter. He renovated old Hindu temples and built new ones. He travelled to various Hindu shrines as a pilgrim, read the Hindu classics and did yoga exercises. Goodwill could go no further: though it is possible that some of his subjects, both Hindu and Muslim, thought him slightly mad.

He seems, however, to have been an eminently sane man. He extended the irrigation systems in the valley, thereby enabling the villagers to bring more land under cultivation. He sent to Samarkand for papermakers and started the production of paper in Kashmir, thus creating a new industry. Kashmir paper was apparently of fine quality and much sought after in the plains. As late as 1783, George Forster wrote, 'the Kashmiris fabricated the best writing paper in the East'. By that time the craft was already dying. Zain-ul-Abidin encouraged woodwork. He also whisked more workmen down from Samarkand to instruct the Kashmiris in the craft of making papier mâché. He thus unwittingly provided the peccant pedlars who now, five hundred years later, accost unwary tourists in Srinagar with their two main sources of income.

The subsequent Muslim rulers were nothing like Zain-ul-Abidin. Some were exceptionally unpleasant. Eventually, in 1586, the Mogul Emperor, Akbar, proclaimed himself overlord of Kashmir. The Empire was then at its zenith. After the death of Shah Alam in 1712, however, it began to crumble. Jahandar Shah, the eldest son of Shah Alam, succeeded his father. He had reigned for less than a year when his brother Farrukh Siyar had him murdered by a minister called Zulfiqar Khan. Farrukh Siyar installed himself as Emperor. Almost his first act as a ruler was to have Zulfiqar Khan murdered. This Mogul Macbeth now launched himself on his royal career. Like a snake, he hissed and struck this way and that. The biggest mistake he made in his short life was to antagonise a pair of influential brothers, the Sayyids, who struck back, and shortly became as powerful in the court as the Emperor himself.

In 1716, perhaps finding Delhi too hot for him, Farrukh Siyar decided to visit Kashmir. One would hardly have thought him the sort of person to take an interest either in scholarship or literature, but apparently he did: most of the Moguls were rather dilettantish when they were not being patricidal or fratricidal.

In Srinagar, at this time, lived a Brahmin family named Kaul. The head of the family was a famous scholar, both in Sanskrit and in Persian.* He was probably a fairly prosperous man, his tall wooden house, with its latticed windows, set amidst trees and flowers. In any event, he seems to have met Farrukh Siyar, who was much impressed by him. The Indian courts, from time immemorial, housed poets and scholars, so Farrukh Siyar was not doing anything extraordinary when he invited the Pandit to come to his court. An invitation from the Emperor was in effect an order: however unwilling the Kaul family may have been to leave Kashmir for Delhi, they had to leave.

The Kaul family had been connected with Kashmir for centuries. The green body of the landscape, the blue blood of the lakes, had bred them. The snow-sky, blackening between the high white peaks of winter, they understood, as well as the carpets of colour that spread over the slopes in spring. They were highlanders, and now, at the whim of a mad monarch, they had been dragged down to the

---

* In a note on his family history written in 1916, Pandit Motilal Nehru says that his elder brother had told him that the name of the Kaul who was invited to Delhi by Farrukh Siyar was Pandit Raj Kaul. He adds that this information was 'mainly based on family tradition'. I can find no record in any book on Kashmir of a famous scholar of this period called Pandit Raj Kaul. However, around 1716, there was in Srinagar an extremely famous scholar and historian, erudite both in Sanskrit and Persian, named Pandit Narayan Kaul. In 1710 he published a history of Kashmir, *Tariqui-Kashmir*, which was a standard work of the time. I have deliberately omitted the first name of the Pandit Kaul who went to Delhi in 1716, because of the absence of any records, but I would think it very likely that it was Pandit Narayan Kaul.

plains. They probably crossed the pass to the south on horseback, and from then onward travelled by cart and palanquin towards the capital. To cross the pass in winter, on a slippery unmade track, the snow spiralling around them, the horses blind in the mist, would have been suicidal, so they must certainly have crossed in the summer, when the heat in the plains is at its worst. The red earth exhales it, it is breathed from the trees, the sun makes the rocks shimmer, the wind, a fire-wind from the deserts to the west, brings no comfort. Most of the rivers are dry, swallowed by the earth, undigested, to be spewed out in winter.

The wayside water is warm: watermelons are best for quenching thirst. Even today, driving towards Delhi in summer, every mile-stone seems an eternity away from the next one. For the Kauls, moving snailwise between Mogul wayposts, the distance between each of these stunted stone towers, washed over by the red and yellow dust, must have seemed not only an eternity but an eternity of torture. The plains were studded with Muslim monuments: as they came towards Delhi a scatter of houses showed slowly through the dust. They must have seen the great walls of the Red Fort, out-side which the fire-wind snarled, inside which Farrukh Siyar and the Sayids were snarling at each other.

The Pandit was probably called into the Fort for an audience. Farrukh Siyar granted him what was called a *jagir* or fiefdom over some villages, and a house of his own. The Moguls, when short of actual cash, were accustomed to pay people in this way. The Kauls settled down.

There had been five Delhis, set up by various kings, around the area where the city stood in 1716. One after the other, for one reason or another, each had been abandoned. The city to which the Kauls came was the sixth Delhi, which is now called Old Delhi but which must then have been thought of as a highly modern capital. As was common in India from Aryan times each trading community lived in its own area: the silversmiths in one quarter, the barbers in another. The heart of the city was an area known as Chandni Chowk, which had a large canal flowing through its central square. It was built in 1650 in front of the massive façade of the Red Fort. When the moon was up, trailing its light over the canal, it turned the water to beaten silver: hence the name Chandni Chowk, Place of Silver. The canal flowed between two rows of sentinel trees.

By 1716, however, when the Kauls came to Delhi, the canal, like the Mogul Empire itself, had fallen into disrepair. But the area around the square had become one of the most remarkable commercial centres in the world. Not only were there shops fronting the square, but shops in the narrow lanes which led off it into residential areas: a huddle of shops: a babel of shops. They sold gold, silver and precious stones, ornaments and weapons: songbirds whistled in cages, monkeys and bears stared dolefully at the crowds of people teeming by: there were shops that sold perfumed wine, shops that sold fresh and dry fruit, some of which came from Kashmir, and shops that sold antiques. Most shops had agents, who flittered through the crowds, inducing people to patronise their employers. The salesmen came from all parts of India and some from foreign countries: so, indeed, did their customers. Besides the shops there were a number of coffee houses, where writers and poets used to meet, as was the custom in England at the same period.

All this was a far cry from Srinagar. The Kauls must have shopped in Chandni Chowk, though scarcely on the scale of the Mogul nobles who came there, resplendent and lazy, their minions thrusting the crowds aside to allow their masters passage. A story which is certainly apocryphal none the less reflects something of the way in which these nobles spent money. A Mogul noble, says the story, died, leaving a widow and a son. One day the boy asked his mother for some money with which to shop in Chandni Chowk. His mother burst into tears and said that her husband had left so little that it would be difficult for the boy to buy anything much, 'but,' she said, 'here is something which will buy a few trifles,' and she gave him a hundred thousand rupees. This is not to say that Chandni Chowk was only for the rich: everyone in the city went there at one time or another. Huge and sinister, the Red Fort loomed over chowk and canal: few of the busy shoppers could have imagined the intrigues which went on behind those colossal walls.

About a thousand yards from the Red Fort was the great mosque, the Jama Masjid. Like most of the other main buildings it rose in red sandstone, high over the crowds below. Every day at the appointed times for prayer, muezzins cried to Allah from the high points of the mosque, and every Muslim within earshot prostrated himself with his turban pointed in whatever direction it was he thought Mecca lay. The planned nature of the city was demonstrated by the fact that the mosque was surrounded by poor-houses, orphanages, and hospitals for travellers. The mosque was not yet old: its foundation stone had been laid in 1650. Indeed, the whole city of Delhi, sprawled out under the strident sun, indolent, unaware of the future, was still in its first youth: the Red Fort itself had only been completed in 1648. When the Kauls arrived in it Delhi was little more than seventy years old, and a long history of plunder, bloodshed and treachery still lay ahead of it.

But the masses knew nothing of what was to come. They were the inhabitants of a new city, and they had plenty to do. Apart from Chandni Chowk, a spectacle in itself for someone with time on his hands, there was a huge open fleamarket not very far from the Red Fort, which was rather more than a market. As in Chandni Chowk, there were birds and animals for sale (the people of Delhi seem to have had a predilection for pets) as well as foodstuffs and weaponry. But the place also swarmed with tumblers and clowns, astrologers and necromancers, and, everywhere, winesellers. Perhaps the Prophet had forbidden wine, but the inhabitants of Delhi (or most of them) had conveniently forgotten this. If excessive bibulation made them feel ill they could always consult one of the puissant physicians who wandered around the market, though the main items sold by these medical men appear to have been aphrodisiacs, and perhaps later to the same patient, cures for venereal disease.

This in itself is somewhat indicative of the interests of the male population. Even more indicative is that a popular attraction consisted of troupes of dancing boys. 'There were boys in such numbers,' wrote one delighted visitor to the market, 'that if one looked up, the eye was caught by some attractive face, and if one stretched out an arm, it encircled a graceful neck.' It did not mean that most Muslims were homosexual, merely that they were Muslims. The inaccessibility of women to the unmarried was one reason: in any event, one cannot be physically attracted to what one cannot see, and Muslim women in those days, when they went out at all, looked less like women than like black Bedouin tents on the move, robed from head to foot and so heavily veiled that it is difficult to imagine how they could see. Muslim sexual conventions naturally affected women, too: not only was the world cut off from women, they were cut off from the world: Lesbianism flourished in the harems.

It was, in one way, this relaxation into sexuality that weakened the Mogul Empire and eventually led to its collapse. Already

Farrukh Siyar sat insecurely on a swaying throne, and though the city he could hear through the thick walls of the Red Fort seemed a busy and prosperous one, it was actually at the beginning of a prolonged and painful death. Within the court the Sayyid brothers were vulpine at the Emperor's heels, and gained more followers day by day. There was actually little to choose between Farrukh Siyar and the Sayyids: all three were depraved, dishonest, and more than a little mad, though Farrukh Siyar was probably the maddest of the three. The Sayyid brothers could at least see what they wanted and how they could achieve it: Farrukh Siyar does not seem to have known what he wanted except to be a despot, and he did not know how he could achieve even this. Nor does he seem to have worked out why he wanted to be a despot, a mistake.

All successful despots have been hard men. Farrukh Siyar was inwardly, like nearly all the later Moguls, a soft man: his viciousness came out of weakness, the sudden violence of a thwarted child. In some ways his city reflected him: thefts and murders took place surreptitiously in dark alleys. There was something rather fantastic about the people who defended the ordinary citizens against such attacks, for the Mogul watch seems to have been ineffective. These defenders of the public could well have created a Round Table of their own, despite their lunatic appearance and eccentric habits. They were called the Bankas, and were not so much a caste as a confederation. The word Banka literally means a dandy: but the Bankas were hardly that.

Each of these men cultivated some individual oddity of dress or appearance to mark himself out from his fellow Bankas. One, for example, would shave off half his moustache, but allow the other half so to grow that he could wind it around his ear or plait it, as the fancy took him. One would shave his head but allow his beard to waterfall to his waist. Another would wear trousers one leg of which was full length and the other cut off at the knee. Each Banka adopted some legendary hero of the past as his model, and strove to emulate the feats of his hero. In some respects they were like the samurai: to harden themselves they wore suits of chainmail in the full blaze of summer, and in winter went around in fine muslin clothes, proving their desire for discomfort by pausing from time to time to pour buckets of icy water over themselves. Perhaps they liked it.

These Bankas practised various forms of violence. Like the

samurai, they swaggered in the streets, carrying their various lethal weapons like talismans. Ridiculous though their appearance was, they were however unquestionably the protectors of the public. They patrolled the streets out of pure philanthropy, though it may be questioned whether they were not also anxious to shed a little blood, which they could not have otherwise done except in time of war, when they filled the front ranks of the Imperial Army.

There is a very curious story about one member of this clan of vigilantes. A gang of rapists was active in Delhi, and this particular Banka dressed up as a woman, climbed into a palanquin carried by four other Bankas, and was ferried out into the dark streets of the city. The gang promptly appeared and seized the supposed lady. Thereupon the lady and the palanquin bearers turned into five ferocious Bankas, and beat the rapists up severely.

This should be the natural end to a moral story, but few stories at this period of the Mogul Empire had natural ends. The Banka who had dressed up as a woman liked his costume so much that he wore women's clothes for the rest of his life, and was known as 'Begum', or lady. It was in this attire that he was killed in battle, faithful to the cause of his Emperor and to the cause of transvestitism. There were many peculiar people around in Delhi at this time, but, outside the Red Fort itself, the Bankas were probably the most peculiar. It is significant that as the Mogul Empire slumped further and further into an unpeaceful senility, the Bankas (who were partly dependent on court patronage) disappeared. Not only had the court no money to pay them, but somehow the melted muscles of the Empire were reflected in those of the large, eccentric warriors who once swaggered the streets of Delhi.

The Kauls probably had plenty of leisure to observe these novel places and people, since it is unlikely that the Pandit had much to do at court. Farrukh Siyar was preoccupied with problems more immediately important to him than Persian literature. In the marble courtyards of the Red Fort fountains dappled the air: the women of the royal household, their bodies firm and white as marble, splashed one another in the spacious baths of the harem: afterwards they sipped perfumed sherbets, freshened with ice from the palace cellars. Prayers were said as usual, huge meals eaten as always. In the Red Fort life seemed to be normal, but it was not. The ghost of his murdered brother behind him, the menacing reality of the

Sayyid brothers before, Farrukh Siyar paced the balconies, aware too late that everything was nearly over. The year was 1719. There were British and French troops in India, but Farrukh Siyar was not concerned with them, only with what was going to happen to him.

The capital was not particularly concerned with what happened to him, though the bazaars were probably rustling with rumours. At this last hour, as the Sayyid brothers readied themselves for the final stroke, Farrukh Siyar must have felt utterly alone. As the current of life in the Red Fort stayed steady, so also did the current of life in the city. The Emperor, a microcosm under the enormous night sky of India, studded with cold stars and the trails of comets, waited for the end. From the balconies on one side of the fort he looked out over open country. From the ramparts on the other side he looked down over the city. But he could not cool his eyes with the silvery water of the canal: the canal, like himself, was out of commission: and soon he had no eyes to cool. The Sayyid brothers had him seized and blinded, the traditional Mogul torment for a deposed monarch. They kept him alive for a while, the better to savour his terrible pain and even more terrible humiliation. Then, tiring of this, they had him killed.

This was the end of Farrukh Siyar's brief and not very noble career, and it was also the end, for the Kauls, of imperial patronage. They had, nevertheless, the fiefdom of a few villages, and their house, the grants made to them by the dead ruler. The French traveller, François Bernier, who visited Delhi in 1656, described the kind of house the Kauls probably lived in, for the styles of architecture could not have changed very much in sixty years: 'Very few [houses] are built of brick or stone, and several are made of clay and straw, yet they are airy and pleasant, most of them having courts and gardens, being commodious inside and containing good furniture. The thatched roof is supported by a layer of long, handsome, and strong canes, and the clay walls are covered with a fine white lime...' Nobody knows where exactly the Kauls' house was, except that it stood by a canal. This canal was to play an important part in the future history of the family. The word for canal in Persian is *nahar*, which in Urdu, the common language, became *nehar*. The local people called Pandit Kaul 'the one who lives by the canal'. They called him Nehru.

❧ 2 ❧

Fires on the Ridge

THE NEHRUS SAT by the canal and watched their livelihood slowly flow away. Farrukh Siyar was followed by two rulers, both, in the Mogul tradition of the times, so consumptive and syphilitic that each died within a few months of his accession. The Sayyids were the real power in the land and they used their powers with a casual ruthlessness which eventually was used on them. In 1719, a year which had already seen the deaths of three kings, Muhammad Shah ascended the famous Peacock Throne of the Moguls. He was to reign for twenty-nine years. Like his predecessors he was something of a dilettante: he wrote and admired bad verse, sniffed flowers in the gardens of Shalimar and anointed them with unnecessary verbal praise. He was also, like anyone who does everything badly, a very weak person. He did not really stand up to the Sayyids: and when in 1720 one of them, Hussain Ali, was stabbed in the side and decapitated by a court official, the Emperor not only praised the assassin but condoled with the surviving brother. This brother, Abdullah Khan, was a somewhat forceful character. Lesser Muslims might have bowed to the Emperor and accepted his condolences, but since his brother's head was being paraded around on a pole in the place where he was killed, Abdullah Khan attacked the imperial tent pitched there. Muhammad Shah was so terrified that he sheltered with his mother in the harem quarters: one of the Sayyid faction, however, veiled himself and, in the transvestite costume that seems to have been so popular at the time, entered the harem and forced the Emperor to come out. Surrounded by soldiers, Muhammad Shah was conveyed on an elephant to the public market where Hussain Ali's head was on display. The Emperor was urged to enjoy the spectacle, one very different from that of the roses of Shalimar.

The bloodstained head, its bulging eyes feasted upon and quarrelled over by flies each of which made a noise like a minute airliner as it fed, seems to have made Muhammad Shah, for once, take positive action: perhaps because being delicate in his tastes he did not want his own head to be displayed in a similar state. He sent his armies out, conquered the Sayyid forces (he himself played no very notable part in the fighting), and brought Abdullah Khan to Delhi. Here the last Sayyid was killed by poison. This was a Mogul tradition for political prisoners, and it was a horrible way to die: the prisoner was not, like Socrates, handed a cup of hemlock which he had to finish and which would in turn finish him. Every day his delicately spiced food would be politely laced with poison, not enough to do more than make him, on the first day at least, feel mildly sick. As time went on, however, he would feel sicker and sicker, and be in acute pain for some days before he finally died. Muhammad Shah, smiling over the deathbed of Abdullah Khan, may have now thought himself a free agent, but, partly because of his own diluted and dilapidated character, he was not. The power in court was held by his officials: from the corner of his eye he could see the colours of foreign uniforms, still far away but moving nearer: his ear was filled with the rumble and thunder of French and British guns. The Marathas, wiry little guerrilla fighters on thin, speedy ponies, harassed him in the west. They even started to show a desire to trot northward towards Delhi. The Red Fort was, to understate the matter somewhat, a comfortable place to live in: Muhammad Shah obviously did not want hostile horsemen camped in his courtyards while he was composing what he thought of as poetry. He had to take action: at least his generals did: the Marathas did not visit Delhi. But the rise of such powerful opponents demonstrated the weakness of the Empire.

It is rather uncertain what became of the Nehrus while all this happened. One known fact is that the properties granted them by Farrukh Siyar were considerably reduced, and their rights over the surviving property curtailed, so that in the end they ceased to be *jagirdars*, that is to say owners of land under royal grant, and became *zamindars*, landlords of property which they had themselves purchased. This buying of land suggests that they still had some money, and the money may have come from the property they possessed in Kashmir. But this is pure speculation: the facts have been lost in the hazy horizons of Nehru family history. Indeed, even Pandit Motilal Nehru, in 1916, did not seem to know the names of his forefathers from the first Pandit in 1716 to the Nehrus

of around 1816, only forty-five years before he himself was born.
Their actual whereabouts during the reign of Muhammad Shah,
and even later, are not known either: whether or not they retained
the house by the canal which renamed them is a mystery, though the
way in which Pandit Motilal referred to the house implies that the
family had not lived there for some considerable while before his
own birth in 1861. In any event, the Nehrus lived somewhere in or
around Delhi and they must have had other Kashmiri friends, for
after the persecution of the Pandits in Kashmir restarted in 1724,
when the Governor forbade them the right to worship, many of
them fled south once more. Delhi, the centre of power, was obviously
the place to flee to, for there the laws which spoke of Hinduism as
an outcast religion were relatively mild. Another reason for the
exodus from Kashmir was the prevalence of famine and the absence
of opportunity for material advancement. The Sanskrit and Persian
books and manuscripts rotted peacefully in the temples of Srinagar:
but there were only a few Pandits left.

Detached from the affairs of the court, the Nehrus probably led a
fairly quiet life. Presumably the elders studied, read, and instructed
others, while the younger members of the clan looked after the land.
Their habits of life were probably rather austere. This was a contrast to the life style that prevailed in the court of Muhammad Shah.
Grapes from Kashmir and Kabul wreathed themselves around
golden plates, nibbled at by nobles. Huge meals, scented with
Kashmiri saffron, were served: beyond all this were the innumerable
women of the harem, and the boys. 'Across the river,' said a poet
of this time, 'is a boy with an arse like a peach. But, alas, I can't
swim.' Hawks wrenched at the wrists of the noblemen: released for
flight, they slew some humble and amiable animal, some wretched
beautiful bird, for no particular reason: there is nothing observably
aesthetic about death, but by this time death was an important
feature of the Mogul empire. It was pervaded by the odour of death:
death flashed over the marble of the audience hall where Muhammad
Shah listened to his petitioners: death shone in the Kohinoor diamond fixed to his turban: death was reflected from the Peacock
Throne upon which he perched, a rare bird, not listening to his
advisers. The Peacock Throne was not a throne in the western
sense: it was a kind of portable fourposter bed, but it glistened
with precious stones and gold.

Under and within this canopied chariot the Emperor sat. He waited for the next petitioner, for the next visitor. The next visitor who came to Delhi was undesirable in the extreme. He spun the Peacock Throne from under the Emperor, and the Kohinoor, plucked from the imperial turban, flashed fire from his palm. His name was Nadir Shah.

Nadir Shah, like Alexander of Macedonia whose unfortunately memorable deeds he longed to emulate, was basically an adventurer. After him other adventurers, notably Napoleon and Hitler, proved their anxiety to lay waste the world they knew. Nadir Shah, like Napoleon and Hitler, though not like Alexander, came from what might be called humble parentage: various chroniclers described his father as having been either a shepherd, a tanner, a peasant, or a cameldriver, to which a poet of Nadir Shah's court replied: 'A good sword owes its existence to the way it was tempered, not to the mine from which the iron that forged it came.' Nadir Shah was a Turk, and his original name was Nadir Quli Beg. He was kidnapped, in childhood, by Uzbek warriors: he was taken to Iran, where, in manhood, he turned into a percipient and somewhat vicious leader of armies. He became the Shah of Iran after a number of brutal victories over invading Russians and his own countrymen, the Turks, and then cast his long, shadowed, covetous eyes eastward. He took his armies into Afghanistan. Herat, Balkh and Kandahar shuddered to the beat of his advancing drums, tottered, fell: he found himself and his armies in the throat of the Khyber Pass, well on the way to the gold of the Indian temples, the golden women of the plains, the Eldorado of Alexander, of Timur, and of various other violent and colourful leaders of armed men. He advanced, and he advanced further than Alexander had done.

Muhammad Shah quivered, as the Afghan cities had done, under the avalanche and earthquake that had descended upon him from Persia. He welcomed Nadir Shah and his armies and Nadir Shah became the Emperor, at least for a while. He would probably have stayed on the Peacock Throne but, like many other later rulers, he seems to have decided that the enormous and turbulent country called India was too much for any one man to handle. As a proof of his power, however, he sent his soldiers out on a killing mission in Delhi. Thirty thousand people were killed in five hours: Hindus and Muslims were not discriminated against in their dying. 'Many women,' says a historian 'drowned themselves in the wells of their

houses to escape a shame worse than death ... but many more were
outraged and dragged away as captives ... ' After this Nadir Shah,
wishing to sit upon the Peacock Throne, but not necessarily in this
troublesome country, adopted a logical line and took the Throne
back to Persia to sit on. He also took the Kohinoor from Muhammad
Shah's turban, and when he left Delhi on May 16 1738 his soldiers
were burdened with more than thirty million pounds sterling in
cash, 'besides jewels, plate ... and other valuable property ... also ...
a thousand elephants, seven thousand horses, ten thousand camels,
a hundred eunuchs, a hundred and thirty writers, two hundred
builders, a hundred masons,' and then, rather anticlimactically,
'two carpenters.'*

What happened to the Nehru family during this period is
unknown. If their women threw themselves down the household well
when Nadir Shah's soldiery exploded, grunting like armoured
elephants, into the byways of Delhi, whether the men 'slew their
own wives and daughters to save them from dishonour by the
Kizilbash soldiery and then rushed on the enemy's swords or cut
their own throats ... ' is unrecorded. Whatever may have happened,
the family appears to have survived. Survival as a family, in those
times, was in itself a considerable feat.

Nadir Shah had, almost as an afterthought, re-crowned the
Mogul Emperor, but any charisma Muhammad Shah may have
had was now dead. He, ghostly as Farrukh Siyar, wandered around
the Red Fort. The marble pavilions, the splashy fountains, the resilient flesh of women and boys, the huge banquets, could not have
been a comfort. For all effective purposes (and of course there was
more treason, more rebellion, more intrigue, more war) Muhammad
Shah, as an emperor and as a person, had died and would stay dead.
So, in fact, would the Mogul Empire which Babur had founded in
1525. It foundered amidst its red sandstone ruins, as, to this
unarmed and hopeless ruler, the British, their faces red sandstone
against the sun, on horseback and by palanquin, curiously and
covetously came.

In a small, tumbledown town called Ajmer there is a plaque,
possibly erected by the Government of independent India, to
commemorate the fact that Sir Thomas Roe, an envoy from the
court of Elizabeth I, the queen with red hair and no breasts, came
to visit the Emperor Jehangir. Roe must have been rather amazed

* Sir Wolsely Haig (*Cambridge History*, Vol. IV).

by the size of the court he came to. The courtiers must have been
rather amazed by him: doubletted, waistcoated in velvet, purple in
the sun. After him, however, came others, in red coats, guns in their
hands, cannon behind them. Not only were there white soldiers,
but brown ones: mercenaries recruited from the Maratha and Jat
people: paid, policied, purposed. Guns spat and flashed on the
enormous horizons of India. The Portuguese, the French, and the
Dutch fled from the British. The East India Company occupied
much of India. Though Delhi was the Mogul capital, Calcutta,
occupied by the British, was basically the centre of power. Here
William Hickey, whose main monument today is a gossip column,
lived in a relatively modest manner, with sixty-seven servants. The
number of servants employed by richer Englishmen ran into
hundreds. A strange development, however, was that the British of
the seventeenth and eighteenth century, though they employed
many Indians in menial posts, did not think of them as inferior.
With these enormous households to maintain they were heavily
dependent on Indian moneylenders to finance them, and on Indian
women for other, equally pressing reasons, since there were few
English damsels around. It was only when these damsels, who on
account of their desperate angling for husbands were known as
'The Fishing Fleet', began to arrive towards the middle of the
nineteenth century, that the attitude of the British altered. The
change was mostly for sexual reasons. The British seldom abandoned
their Indian mistresses completely. These women had elegant bones
and full breasts, and features more delicate than those to be found in
London. However, the British equally did not want Indian men to
have affairs with Englishwomen. The jealousy of the newly come
memsahib for their Indian sisters, the distrust of Englishmen
towards Indian males, were the main contributory causes for the
change in British attitudes.

By the 1850s, therefore, there was an overpowering sense among
the Indians that they were considered, by the invaders of their
country, an inferior race. The East India Company ran about half
of India. Bahadur Zafar Shah, who was to be the last Mogul ruler,
spent his time writing verse and fondling his various wives. The
great empire founded by hard, armoured chieftains out of Central
Asia had virtually ceased to exist. The British were in Delhi, and the
Emperor danced to the strings they pulled. Meanwhile, the Nehrus
seem to have risen from a temporary obscurity into the mainstream

of events. Lakhsmi Narayan Nehru became the first vakil or scribe
to act for the East India Company at the Mogul court. This would
have been in the early years of the nineteenth century. His son,
Gangadhar, was a police officer in Delhi in 1857, a calamitous year
for the country.

This was the year of the sepoy mutiny. Since the influx of the
memsahibs the Indian soldiers employed by the East India Company
did not have the same rapport with their British officers that they
had previously had. When, in 1857, the Company issued a new type
of cartridge, the end of which had to be bitten off before it could be
fired, the Hindu soldiers were told by intelligent agitators that it
was greased with beef fat: the Muslims were told that the unguent
employed was pork fat. Both Hindus and Muslims would have been,
so to speak, excommunicated from their religions, had the Hindus
eaten beef or the Muslims pork. They did not believe their British
officers when they were told by them that no animal fat was employed in the greasing of the new cartridges. What subsequently
took place was, in microcosm, typical of the entire history of India.

The sepoys of the East India Company did not believe their
officers, but they did not really know whom they should believe.
India was used to conquerors, Persians and Greeks, Afghans, Turks,
and now Europeans. The point was that not all these people had
achieved their conquests through military power. The smiler with
the knife was present in every Indian court: rippled whispers of
rumour passed to and fro between the marble walls. The idea that
an intelligent man should be an excellent liar was prevalent. India
was not a country, it was a disorganised mass of fighting states: the
rulers combated one another with propaganda as well as steel, and
most were ready to sell out to the highest foreign bidder if the
invader would be of help in the overthrow of the enemy in the
neighbouring state. Their officials were ready to sell out their
rulers if the invader could then help the official concerned to mount
the throne. Lies, deceit and treachery were an essential part of
Indian politics. The British had realised this early: they bought out
kings and court officials, and the states came over to them without
too much trouble. The British political scene in the eighteenth
century was not all that different from the political scene in India:
so the British knew what to do. They understood India more than
any previous conqueror had done.

What they did not understand, however, was that popular gossip in India plays a very important role in the politics of the country. The rumours and whispers among the sepoys were disregarded because by this time Indians were regarded as a lesser breed. Meanwhile, a confederation of rulers, none of whom much liked the other, had collected to drive the British out of India. It was from their employees that the rumours and whispers came: unheard by the East India Company: heard loud and clear by the sepoys. The word that came was that they should rise and slay the British: they rose and slew: Delhi fell to the mutineers: the Emperor cowered behind what was no longer the Peacock Throne and agreed to be, at least nominally, their leader. In September 1857 the British troops were sitting on what is known as the Ridge, a rise in the land above the old city of Delhi. The reason they were sitting there was largely because of the political dissension between the rulers who led the mutiny: the Indian forces were numerically much superior to the British, but, badly led, and not knowing which leader to follow, they crashed into cannonfire and died: or, captured, were fired out of cannon. The British troops, after a few days on the Ridge, descended and took Delhi. They had seen their hero, John Nicholson,* killed by the sepoys. They had seen massacres of British women and children in various cantonments scattered around India. They were paid a shilling a day: loot formed much of their additional income, rapine most of their sex life. When they came down from the Ridge, they looted and raped for all they were worth. There were not only British troops who dropped down on the city, but Indians, mainly Sikhs, who had remained loyal to their salt.† The Sikhs were even more bloodthirsty than the British. Thousands of people fled from Delhi, amongst them Gangadhar Nehru, his wife Jeorani, their two sons Bansidhar and Nandlal, and their daughters Patrani and Maharani. They did not flee all that far: they stopped in Agra, the previous Mogul capital, where the Taj Mahal stands grotesque amidst its gardens. In Delhi, meanwhile, the house they occupied, and all the family records, were destroyed, like many other houses and many other family records. The three sons of the Emperor were shot: the Emperor was arrested and ushered off to

* Administrator and soldier, he conquered the Punjab for the Empire, and rescued Delhi from the Mutineers. He was remembered with terror in Northern India as Nikal Seyn, maker and breaker of kings.

† *Namak khana*, to eat salt: rather like the Anglo-Saxon tradition that to eat bread and salt with someone makes you his debtor.

Rangoon. The corpulent body of Queen Victoria sat, by proxy, on the throne of India (which she never visited). In 1861, Bahadur Zafar Shah, surrounded by the manuscripts of piteous poems concerned with exile, and a few nubile wives, died in Rangoon, the Shwe Dagon, rather than the Red Fort, the last image scrawled upon his eye. With him the Mogul Empire died. In the same year Gangadhar died in Agra, leaving his wife six months pregnant. The son was called Motilal Nehru.

With everything left behind in Delhi, Jeorani Nehru was penniless. The two boys, Bansidhar and Nandlal, rescued her: Bansidhar found employment as a scribe in the Agra Court and became a subordinate magistrate: Nandlal became a schoolteacher, and later the chief minister of Khetri, a small feudal state in Rajputana, west of Agra. Bansidhar had to be moved from post to post: Nandlal, less mobile in his habits, looked after the family, including the boy Motilal. In 1870, when his brother was nine, Nandlal moved out of Khetri. He became one of the first Indians to be a qualified lawyer under the British system of education, moved back to Agra, and there established a practice. Motilal, in the meantime, had been learning Arabic and Persian from the tutor of the Khetri ruler, and by 1873 he was proficient in both languages. The High Court was shifted to Allahabad, then the capital of the United Provinces, now known as Uttar Pradesh: Nandlal shifted with it, so, of course, did Motilal. The boy passed his matriculation examination in the town of Kanpur, a northern town full of trees and these days of riotous students, then moved southward to Allahabad where he became a member of the Muir Central College. This was run by the British, now the rulers of India: from his teachers Motilal learned about England and its culture, and developed a great admiration for the colonisers of his country.

In 1883, back in Kanpur, he received a degree as a lawyer and set up practice there, but in 1886 he moved back to Allahabad and became a partner of Nandlal. Nandlal died a year later, aged forty-two: Motilal took over the practice: he was twenty-five. He married: in 1889 he begot a son, Jawaharlal Nehru. It took eleven years for the next child, a daughter, Swarup Rani, later known as Mrs Vijayalakshmi Pandit, to appear, and it was seven years after this that another daughter, Krishna, who was usually called Betty, was born. By this time Motilal was an exceptionally successful lawyer.

In 1900 he bought a house called Anand Bhavan, or the Abode of Bliss, in Allahabad, redesigned it, introduced English governesses and the habit of using knives and forks to eat with, acquired his clothes in Paris, and so legend says, sent his shirts to a laundry in London, which suggests, since ships in those days took a considerable while to chug and flap between the shores of India and those of the British Isles, that Motilal had quite a lot of shirts.

Motilal himself was heavily built and thickly moustached: he looked like any other Victorian squire: his watchchain spread over his waistcoat, itself amply filled. His son, Jawaharlal, was slight, and not tall: he had a feminine delicacy of feature: his skin was pale, a Kashmiri complexion. Born three decades after the flight of the family from Delhi, from the guns and dead John Nicholson and the furious British troops, he knew nothing of hardship or terror. His father had numerous English friends and intended to send the boy to Harrow. Their own house in Allahabad was commodious and normally filled with people: there were two meals every mealtime, one cooked by Brahmins in the Kashmiri style, the other by Goan cooks from Portuguese India in the Western style. Whoever happened to be invited could choose to eat one or the other, according to his or her taste. The women of the household were confined to their quarters: the sweepers and other people of low caste had a separate stairway to the house, in which porcelain and silver shone on the tables. There were carriages in the stables, horses, ponies for the children. Every day Motilal's phaeton took him to the High Court. Unlike some of the other Indian lawyers who went about unbecomingly clad, between their dhotis and turbans, in long black coats which had a dusty look about them, Motilal went to court in raiment more splendid than that of any British lawyer. He has been described as leonine in appearance: and certainly in his youth he was a handsome man. He talked well and with humour, and his laugh was loud and resonant. Few Indian princes entertained and lived on the scale of the Nehrus. Few Indian princes were admired by their friends: Motilal was by his. His lordly lifestyle was extraordinary when one considers that his was a family which within his own experience had seen poverty and stress. A man who has once been poor is likely to be careful with his money when he makes it: Motilal was an exception to the rule. According to one writer, he earned, towards the end of his legal career, Rs. 685,000 a year (£100,000 by the exchange rates prevalent before 1920) and spent it all instantly and without difficulty. This generous and convivial side of him was not always the side he showed to his family. As the patriarch of the household he seems to have been formidable: his tempers were frequent, but short-lived. One doesn't know about his ancestors, but this is certainly a trait handed down to his descendants.

For a man of his domestic habits Motilal had some very surprising interests. He was, for example, involved in the theosophical movement. This, a relative of his told me in Allahabad, was not so much because of its spiritual value but because it had become fashionable in the West. He also had some contact with the Indian Congress Party, newly born and still unformed, but in the early days he was more interested in his practice than in politics, and moreover he was an admirer of the British. This was all to change, but very slowly. To his wife Swarup Rani, a gentle, simple, and orthodox woman, he must have been an enigma. While he ate all sorts of European dishes, she adhered to vegetarian food cooked by Brahmins. While he wore European clothes, she dressed in modest saris. She had been married at fourteen, when Motilal was already an adult set in his ways. 'She was,' her daughter Mrs Pandit writes, 'an extremely beautiful person – dainty like an ivory carving with lovely hazel eyes, exquisite hands and feet and thick chestnut hair that fell in waves far below her waist and which we loved to brush and play with.' This chestnut hair was apparently the cause of some controversy in the family, for whenever they visited Europe, Motilal ordered his wife to adopt what Mrs Pandit calls 'the hideous Western coiffure of the day'. Mrs Pandit remonstrated with her mother about this, saying that she should do what *she* liked, not what she was told to like. 'My dear,' said Swarup Rani, 'I *do* like what your father likes, and anyway he knows best.' To so passive, so submissive, so Hindu a wife, her children must have been as much of a mystery as her husband. She spoke no English, though she was by no means uneducated: her Urdu was fluent and she knew Persian and Sanskrit poetry. Everyone else in the house, however, spoke English, and her children behaved like English children: her son dreamt his dreams, occasionally floating down from the clouds into a fury about some minor irritation: her daughters were mischievous, lively, talkative, a side of their nature probably inherited from Motilal. The quality of absence and reserve within Jawaharlal must have come from her, though he was by no means a passive person. This paradoxical quality in all the Nehrus since Motilal, and perhaps before him, has persisted in the family: they have not been people who could, as it were, be catalogued and fitted into shelves.

The Congress movement, when it started in 1886, was not precisely a movement for Indian independence. There were a number of British members, and many of the Indian ones had received an education of a British type. This education of Indians, recommended by a solicitous Lord Macaulay some time before the Mutiny, was eventually to prove the downfall of the British in India. What the Congress initially wanted at the time of its foundation, was a kind of political equality, a representation of Indian opinion in the legislatures of the country. But there were some Indians who wanted more than this: at the Congress session at Surat in 1907 the hall was stormed by Lokmanya Tilak, a national leader, and his followers; and Tilak and the Congressmen threw chairs at one another. Tilak wanted to see the British out: but the whole history of a country divided into feudal states fighting one another, on a larger scale, not unlike the Congress meeting at Surat, pointed towards the necessity for a powerful centre, and this the Congress at the moment was not able to provide. The concept of rule by a democratic party, brought in by the British themselves, instead of rule by a king and his courtiers, was as yet an unclear one to many Indians. At the time of the Surat meeting, Jawaharlal, Motilal's son, was starting to clarify it in his own mind at Harrow. In between his more pensive moments, he wore the school uniform, played cricket, and with his colleagues, chanted the faintly imperialistic Harrow songs. As with his father, his was a somewhat paradoxical life, but one supposes, like his father's, a full one. If the British Empire was built on the playing fields of Eton, its collapse was probably initiated on the playing fields of Harrow. Of this Motilal probably knew nothing. In Allahabad life was secluded and exclusive. The tall houses of rich families, many of them Kashmiri lawyers, rose amidst flowered, tree-lined lawns. Hooves clattered in the streets as the barouches and phaetons went by. The beehive drone of the poor in the older part of the city went unheard.

Only once a year was the peace of the city disturbed. Despite its Muslim name, Allahabad, for the Hindus, was a holy place. It stands at the confluence of two sacred rivers: the blue waters of the

Yamuna and the brown waters of the Ganges, slouching south from
the Himalayas, meet and mix in the broad river bed by which the
city was built. Early each year a *mela* or fair takes place here:
pilgrims come to splash themselves in the murky water for purifica-
tion, or swallow it thirstily for the same reason. Surprisingly few
die of cholera, or of any other disease connected with the ingestion
of these liquids, but, every ten years or so, there are deaths from
other causes. Every twelve years, when the swimming stars have
adjusted themselves in auspicious positions, there is what is called
the Kumbh Mela, the great fair. At this time pilgrims come to
Allahabad from all over north India to purify themselves. Their
campfires flicker on the shore: limp flowers and toy boats containing
lights are floated out on the current as offerings to the deities.
Millions of people arrive and settle down by the riverside, and if
there are stampedes, as there not infrequently are, thousands are
trampled underfoot or drowned.

It is likely that the Nehru family attended these occasions, for
though Motilal was very Westernised, certain beliefs were obviously
in his blood. He was not a Western man: his Westernisation was an
inlay upon the tradition he had been bred to. Gigantic banquets,
regularly thrown by a single individual, were not really a feature of
English life: but they had always been a feature of the lives of Indian
aristocrats. The real Westerner was to be Jawaharlal, who, far from
the confluence of the holy rivers, sat by the blue ripples of the
summer Cam and let them wash tradition out of his blood.

Meanwhile, in South Africa, a Gujarati lawyer named Gandhi (the
propensity of Indians towards a legal education was perhaps due to
their propensity for litigation) was collecting his thoughts about
India, to which he was shortly to return. He was to be the most
powerful force in the lives of Motilal and his son, but anyone less
like them would hardly have been found had they searched for him.
Gandhi was not an aristocrat, but a commoner, though his father
was the chief minister of the princely state of Porbandar. Though he
had lived away from India for years, the philosophy of life he had
evolved was not Western. A traumatic experience in his youth seems
to have played an important part in the formulation of this philosophy. He was married young, and though he was a small, weedy
person with bat ears and spectacles, and his wife was no beauty, his
sex drive seems to have been considerable, not to say inordinate.

In fact, according to his autobiography, the only minutes he did not spend leaping about in his wife's bed were spent happily visualising the moment when he could leap back into it. His father was ill, and Gandhi, dreaming of ecstasies to come, was in the habit of massaging the paternal calves to relieve them of pain. During one such occasion, he suddenly felt his husbandly impulses getting the better of him, excused himself, and rushed to his own bedroom, where he made love to his wife. Through the door, a servant informed him that his father had died. Gandhi appears to have been overcome by remorse.

He therefore decided that he would not have any more sex for the rest of his life and apparently never did, though in later years he used to sleep with naked young women in order to test his willpower. The psychological effect of this on the young women doesn't seem to have concerned him: in fact, despite his gentleness and kindness and his undoubted possession of a sort of saintliness, he implemented his theories, as a rule, without very much consideration for the effect they could have on others. Thus his abstention from sex ran parallel with abstention from any foods that could perhaps rouse unwholesome desires, such as eggs, meat or fish, and abstention from any form of alcohol. He evolved, therefore, a diet for himself which consisted of goatmilk and various not always easily procurable vegetables and fruits. Mrs Sarojini Naidu, a poetess of sorts and a follower of Gandhi (she used to call him Mickey Mouse), once remarked on how much it must cost the Congress to keep the Mahatma in poverty. Gandhi spent a while learning law in London, where his life style must have cost a lot: then he went to South Africa and ran an Indian ambulance corps during the Boer War. Meanwhile he evolved various ideas about how to obtain Dominion status for India, and the rehabilitation of villagers and other poor people by making them produce their own food and weave their own clothes. This, he felt, would enable them to lead independent lives as they had done in the golden centuries of India before the shower of invaders fell upon it. Industry to him was anathema: in this he differed completely from Jawaharlal Nehru.

With this armoury of ideas Gandhi returned to India. Saints are widely accepted in that country, however impractical their ideas, and he quickly became an acknowledged leader. During Gandhi's initial years in India, Jawaharlal also returned. It was 1912: Jawaharlal had wended his way through Harrow and Cambridge,

and had taken silk, but he was still only twenty-three. Motilal must
have looked forward to his return. He idolised his son, as many
writers have reported: he wanted to take him into partnership, as
he himself had been in partnership with Nandlal. He had visited
Jawaharlal in England, but it is doubtful if he knew entirely what had
happened and was happening inside the handsome head of his son.
The petulance, the intelligence and sensitivity, the mixture of shyness and fire, the endless inward inquiry, he must have known would
still exist: but he perhaps did not know how these had coalesced to
make a person, to make a man, a very young man, true, but unmistakably a man.

The collision of these three great comets, Gandhi and the two
Nehrus, burning above the British in the vast night sky which once
provided so dark a pall for the Moguls, took time to occur. Jawaharlal
came back to Allahabad, to the relaxations and rigours of an Indian
household. By this time there had been a swimming pool installed,
to add to the other amenities: Motilal was somewhat averse to
paddling about in this pool, preferring hot baths, but Jawaharlal
loved it. In the garden outside Motilal watched the household
servants wrestle with one another: wrestling is an old Indian pastime,
which Motilal had liked watching since his youth. With his son, he
breakfasted on the back veranda, and the horses and ponies were
brought up to it to be fed with lumps of sugar. After breakfast
father and son, grave in their robes, climbed into one of the carriages
drawn up outside the front door: whips cracked, orders were issued,
the carriage moved away towards the court: the children of the
household, who included Jawaharlal's two small sisters, shouted
and waved. Motilal may have frowned a little at this disorderly
conduct: Jawaharlal was probably in an absent mood: but it is fairly
certain that at some time or other, perhaps over breakfast, perhaps in
the phaeton that took them to the British court, Jawaharlal started
to tell Motilal about his ideas for an India that would be forever free.

Motilal, in the meantime, was formulating his own ideas. He had
thought of himself as Westernised, but this boy was Western.
Perhaps he was too Western: how was his father to make him
realise his Indian identity? Marriage was one answer: a marriage that
recalled Jawaharlal to the traditions of his fathers: a marriage to
someone like Motilal's own wife, Swarup Rani, an orthodox Kashmiri
Brahmin who would obey her husband, love him, look after him,

and teach the old traditions to him once more. The books in Motilal's library were nearly all books about law: he did not know about the books Jawaharlal had read and talked of. Marriage was the best answer to all these new ideas: a grandchild: grandchildren. His wife would like it. The carriage drew up outside the steps of the court: father and son climbed out and a little whisper of accolade rose from the lesser lawyers around the steps, waiting to be called. It would not be easy for him, Motilal thought, but there were laws to all life: Jawaharlal would be all right in the end.

❦ 3 ❧

Of Money and Matrimony

AT THE END of the nineteenth century a family known as Atal lived
in Delhi, in a house which had once belonged to the treasurer of
Bahadur Zafar Shah, last of the Moguls. They were Kashmiri
Brahmins: but like the Nehrus, migrants from the mountains.
Pandit Kishan Lal Atal, the head of the family, had grown grey in
Jaipur, a Rajput state west of Delhi, where he had been private
secretary and principal adviser to the ruler. He had obviously
acquired money during his lengthy spell as a courtier, for his Delhi
house cannot have been a small one: it accommodated, as well as
Kishan Lal and his wife, their seven sons, each with his own family,
and their daughter. The accumulated assets, however, must at
times have run a little short, since the fifth son, Jawaharmul, had
been adopted as a boy by wealthy but childless family relatives, the
Kauls. These Kauls do not appear to have been related to the
Nehrus. When the head of the Kaul family died, Jawaharmul
returned to the Atal house but retained the surname of Kaul. He
seems to have been less educated than the brothers he left behind
him, and so decided to enter the world of business, for which he
subsequently proved to have no flair whatever. His enterprises were
hardly on a grand scale: he owned a cloth shop in the old city and
set up a midget flour mill in the yard of the house 'to supplement the
family income', which suggests that the family income was not large.

Rajpati, his wife, was a prudent and thrifty woman who managed
the money for her husband, which was as well, since both cloth shop
and flour mill collapsed, soundlessly and permanently, within a very
short while. The family nevertheless survived: each brother, with a
wife and children, occupied separate quarters. The women of the
family lived inside the house during the day, chattering like squirrels,
unseen by the eyes of strange men. The male children were sent to
school, the female ones were not: they were taught Hindi and the

scriptures at home. One harsh August, a month when Delhi is swept alternately by dust and rain, a month not only sometimes moist but always hot, Rajpati Kaul produced a daughter, her first child: she was called Kamala. The year was 1899. Three more children were still to be born, but the house was already full of Kamala's cousins. It was also full of courtyards and alcoves where all these children could play. Kamala may have been, temporarily, the only child of her parents, but she was never lonely.

Still it was an enclosed life. The females of the family seldom went out of the house: when they did, it was in a palanquin carried by male attendants. So the child cannot have seen very much of Delhi, a changed city since Gangadhar Nehru fled from it in 1857. The red faces of British soldiers and civilians were seen in the streets, the masters and rulers, whose firm clipped language seemed hard against the elided liquidities of Urdu and Hindi. But more and more people spoke English, though Kamala did not. The appearance of the city had changed too: the old flea market had been pulled down and had re-formed its ranks around the great red mosque, the Jama Masjid. A noteworthy feature of this cluttered area of shanties and shops was the appearance of itinerant cooks, who mostly made and sold kebabs, cooked on iron skewers above charcoal fires. Some of these cooks were famous, and not only for their cuisine: one particular kebab seller was known for his style of speech. Asked about his health one day as he grew old he pointed to a large stone nearby, and said, 'Twenty years ago I could not lift that stone. Nowadays I still can't lift it.' Pet birds and animals were still sold. In the maze of lanes off Chandni Chowk, which still prospered, though not in the incredible way of its Mogul days, poets in Urdu and Persian read their verse to each other: silver coins clashed together, thrown by the audience at the feet of female singers and dancers. If the British ran the administration, the cultural and social life was still run by the ghosts of Moguls: Farrukh Siyar, Bahadur Zafar Shah, wringing their hands on the ramparts of the immense fort, were still present. Of this aspect of Delhi life the small Kamala probably knew and saw nothing. Her own life was hermetic, sealed, inside the walls of Atal House, inside the rickety sway of a palanquin, inside the drone of the Brahmin teachers who instructed her in religion and language. Even as a child, however, she was not entirely complaisant. Around 1909 the family paid a visit to Jaipur, where Kishan Lal had once been so important. The female members of the family were strictly instructed to observe *purdah*, to lock themselves up indoors, and this dictum included girl children. Kamala acquired a small turban, concealed her hair under it, and slipped out of the house to play with her male cousins: an independence of attitude and of action which later echoed itself in some of her descendants.

Marriages, among the Kashmiri Brahmin exiles in Delhi, were partly an excuse to formulate other marriages. During the actual marriage parties, where the groom arrived on a white horse, splendidly caparisoned, the parents of a boy and the parents of a girl could meet, peep and pry into each other's family history and horoscopes, eye each other's children, and make a deal. As the married couple walked, hand in hand, around the sacred fire, flower petals scattering, incense burning, and priests mumbling, other conflagrations were planned for the future by anxious parents. The youthfulness of engaged couples in India was looked on with some anxiety by the British, for by the early 1900s (prior to this the betrothal could take place when the children concerned were infants) children of twelve or thirteen were often engaged to be married before they had reached puberty. Such marriages, or engagements, had not been all that uncommon in Europe when it was a predominantly agricultural society, which India at the turn of the century still was, and which it mostly still is. These engagements did not mean that the children slept together as soon as they had arisen from their respective cradles: they meant, first of all, that the two families had some kind of bond and could help each other in times of hardship: and secondly, it was thought to ensure the chastity of the children, thus locked together early in life. Thirdly, as children, the engaged couple could acquire some knowledge of each other's personal characteristics, the more easily to tolerate them in the adult future still to come. These early engagements were by no means such a bad idea, at least in a traditional Indian society, as they were thought to be by the British.

Motilal had sleuthed around for a daughter-in-law for a while before Jawaharlal returned from England. At some time in 1912, at a wedding in Delhi, the eye of a member of the Nehru family was caught by the face and personality of Kamala Kaul, then aged about thirteen. Inquiries were made and negotiations began. Jawaharlal was still in England and apparently he had not been, exactly, consulted. There followed a rather strange exchange of letters between father and son, strange in the sense that these letters could have been written in reverse: the letters of the father are eager and somewhat boyish, those of the son verging on the pompous and a bit tutelary. However, Jawaharlal, even in England, seems not to have been wholly averse to the idea of an arranged marriage. 'You express a hope,' he wrote from England in 1911 or 1912, 'that my marriage will be romantic. I should like it to be so but I fail to see how it is going to come about. There is not an atom of romance in the way you are searching out girls for me and keeping them waiting till my arrival. The very idea is extremely unromantic ... ' In the same letter, none the less, he remarks, 'On the subject of my marriage ... [I] have left the matter entirely in your hands.' Motilal replied: 'The day after I wrote last I suddenly made up my mind to go to Delhi for a day and see the little beauty.' She was also described, by another member of the family, as 'a desirable acquisition'. This kind of talk could not have been thought of as very romantic by Jawaharlal, and he replied: 'I am not in a matrimonial state of mind at present.' Having, however, seen a photograph of Kamala, Jawaharlal wrote a letter which lends some credibility to the fact that on his return from England he called himself 'a prig': 'As for looks, who can help feeling keen enjoyment at the sight of a beautiful creature? And I think you are quite right in saying that the outer features generally take after the inner person. And yet sometimes this is not the case. Beauty is after all skin deep ... ' This short and misinformed lecture from son to father, containing a large internal contradiction, led to the marriage of the younger Nehru. Motilal decided that the marriage would happen, and he brought Kamala to Allahabad, with the rather patronising idea that he would educate her to be a wife worthy of his son. His elder daughter, Swarup, or Vijayalakshmi or, as she was called within the family, Nan, did not like her: his younger daughter, Betty, did. Kamala spoke no English at the time, and they spoke it fluently: they flew around like butterflies in English clothes: they ate English and French food and Kamala, in her neat cotton saris, did not. Swarup thought Kamala was not, and would never be, a worthy wife of a brother who was basically Western. Betty, a more lively sort of person, obviously thought of her as another girlfriend in the household. There were other aunts and cousins and nieces around, and the house was full of children.

Betty wrote of Kamala at the time they first met: 'She was 16 and very lovely: slim and rather tall for an Indian girl, with the typically fair skin of Brahmins of Kashmiri descent. Her hair was dark brown and she had large brown eyes and a very gentle disposition ... She was one of the most beautiful women I knew or ever have known ... ' By this time it was around 1915, and Jawaharlal used to escort Kamala through Allahabad in one of the three cars Motilal had recently acquired: in these tall, creaky machines, the couple was accompanied, not only by a uniformed chauffeur, but by a chaperon. Eventually this chaperonage ended. In February 1916 they were married in Delhi, in a house near where the Atals lived. A special train brought people from Allahabad to celebrate the event, but since the available accommodation was inadequate a town of tents was erected outside the walled city. Written (in flowers) on the outer wall was the legend 'Nehru Wedding Camp'. The ceremonies went on for a week. Jawaharlal wore a brocade coat and turban: Kamala a sari dotted with pearls. On the porticoes of the great house in Allahabad tailors had been occupied for months in the sewing of this elaborate costume. The sari, and Kamala, then returned to Allahabad with the rest of the family. 'Lunches, teas, dinners, music recitals, poetry recitations, and tennis parties kept the family occupied ... for many weeks after the wedding ... ' Swarup may have played tennis: Betty certainly: Kamala probably not. An Indian wife, she ate separately from her husband, but fed him first: demure in her cotton saris, speaking only Hindi, somewhat looked down upon by the other women of the house for these reasons, she was married to an elegant young man who not only thought and talked in English, but, as somebody who later shared a prison cell with him and heard him talk in his sleep once said, also dreamt in English. She was also the daughter-in-law of a man who, up to a point, lived an English life. She probably played, in her own gentle, not unintelligent way, a greater part in the Indianisation of these two men than anyone except Gandhi.

By the time of his marriage, Jawaharlal was much involved with the Congress Party. But this was a new kind of party. It was a democratic party and it was making demands for democracy from the British. Because of the involvement of his son with this party, Motilal had also become involved. So had Mahatma Gandhi. In December 1916, in Lucknow, a small town not very far from Allahabad, the

Congress met: so did the two Nehrus and Gandhi. The Nehrus were resplendent, their glow from Savile Row: Gandhi was clad in the shabby costume of a court scribe, turban, black coat, dhoti. He did not make much impression on either father or son. 'All of us admired him for his fight in South Africa,' wrote Nehru, 'but he seemed very distant and different and unpolitical to many of us young men.' He changed his mind rapidly (and so did the other young men) after his discovery in 1917 of the oppression of indigo workers in Bihar. Gandhi moved, in his gentle fashion, into the fray: and Jawaharlal wrote: 'and then Gandhi came. He was like a powerful current of fresh air that made us stretch ourselves and take deep breaths; like a beam of light that pierced the darkness ... he did not descend from the top; he seemed to emerge from the millions of India ... ' At about this time, in November 1917, with soldiers of many nationalities fertilising France with their bones, and Russia roaring for the blood of its princes, Kamala had a child. The child was born on November 19. She was called Indira. Shortly after her birth, when the household servants came to pay homage, an old servant, misled by her swaddling clothes, congratulated Jawaharlal on having produced a son.*

The appearance of a child seems not to have made much of a difference in a household where children were hardly a phenomenon, except that Indira was the first child of the beloved heir of Motilal. The beloved heir, however, seems at times to have been in some difficulties with his father, who, somewhat alarmed by his views, was of the opinion that he might become a terrorist. At one point he threatened to throw Jawaharlal out of Anand Bhavan. Nevertheless Indira used to sit on his desk while he worked: his pet: not yet his foundling. He still wore English clothes and he clad his granddaughter in English frocks. She also received English toys from friends abroad. Meanwhile things kept happening in the country called India.

In 1919 a British general named Dyer ordered his troops to open fire upon unarmed Indians in a garden called Jallianwala Bagh in a town called Amritsar, in North India, a place holy to the Sikh people. Unmemorable as a man except for this episode, Dyer then ordered all Indians to crawl down a certain alley leading off this garden, on all fours. The result was to incense Indians all over the

---

* Many years later, when Indira Gandhi was first Prime Minister, she was described as 'the only man in a cabinet of old women'.

country: one of them was Motilal. And to incense him was an
enormous mistake: he rose like a lion in fury, shook a prospective
lioness off his lap, and called his male cub home. The Nehrus rose
up together: Gandhi met them: the three comets had fused in the
fiery sky, under which a child sat, reading gruesome Scandinavian
fairy stories. Meanwhile a very quiet, entirely ungruesome man
was talking to her grandfather and father.

To analyse the extraordinary and particular charisma Gandhi
exercised over those who were associated with him is like trying to
analyse the action of the wind upon trees. He was not, as Nehru was,
physically attractive: as a public speaker he was not exceptionally
powerful. But whatever the flaws in his philosophy of life, and these
were not unplentiful, he carried conviction because he could draw
something intangible out of his inward self, and something equally
intangible from the inward selves of those he met, and make these
invisible elements fuse in the air between himself and other people.
Thus he exerted a particular, rather astonishing influence not only
upon his followers but upon tough foreign correspondents, and even
upon British officials who were entirely opposed to his aims and
policies. Churchill once called him 'a naked fakir', but there is no
record that Churchill and he ever met. Had they done so Churchill
might have revised his opinion: Churchill admired men of power,
and Gandhi, for all his frailty of voice and physique, for all his
mildness, was a man of power, expressed from within himself in a
whisper which was heard by millions of Indians, one of them
Jawaharlal.

Motilal was slower to associate himself fully with Gandhi. He
was sixty years old and for most of his life had been a lawyer. He
believed in the British constitutional process, however long a time
it might take. Jawaharlal believed in rapid change, and in a more
rapid and radical change than Gandhi did. In 1920 he took Kamala
and his mother, neither of whom was well, to Mussoorie in the
northern hills, for a holiday. An official delegation from Afghanistan,
which had come to bargain for a frayed peace after the third Afghan
war, was staying in the same hotel as the Nehrus. Jawaharlal had no
occasion to meet them but the local District Magistrate was afraid
that he would, and asked him to promise not to do so. This turbulent young lawyer, the British thought, would be a bad influence
on the mountain men. Jawaharlal refused to make any such promise
(though he had no desire to meet any Afghans, at least not at that

time) because, he said, 'it went against [his] grain.' This manifestation of the typical Nehru stubbornness led to his being thrown out of Mussoorie.

This unexpected experience of bureaucracy, added to the fresh echoes of the guns of Jallianwala Bagh, caused Jawaharlal's admiration of the British in their own country to be intermixed with a certain resentment and dislike of the British in his country. On his return to Allahabad he encountered a delegation of poor peasants from a backward area of the state of Oudh, seeking redress for certain wrongs. He then started actively to seek out the peasantry, to visit the starved, scruffy villages around Allahabad, and to try and ascertain their troubles. Their condition horrified him: the broken children, the scarred and ruined adults, living at subsistence level in hovels where an English farmer would not have sheltered his pigs, on food at which an English pig would probably have turned up its snout. Then, perhaps most importantly, there were his encounters with Gandhi, and their talks together.

These three factors, his resentment of British bureaucracy in India, his sudden, shocked realisation of the state of the Indian peasantry, and his astonishment at the existence of such a person as Gandhi, probably combined to rush him from the flat, boundaried plains of the law up to the precipices of politics. Yet, curiously, even while he venerated Gandhi he disagreed with him on many points. Gandhi, like other saintly persons in history, thought poverty was beautiful, which it may well be if one is able to choose to be poor. Jawaharlal thought poverty was hideous. What was common between them was the idea that in some ways the British had created the poverty which burdened India. The fact was that from the time of the Hindu rulers in Kashmir, when the peasants suffered frequent famines under brutal taxation and a system of forced labour, through the Mogul days when the people of the plains starved in a silence enforced upon them by the knowledge that they would not be helped, the bulk of the Indian nation had been engulfed by an apparently endless poverty, from which there was no way to escape. Gandhi's idea of a solution was that the poor peasants should stay in the villages, spin their own clothes, cultivate their own food, and thus become solvent: Nehru's was that they should travel to cities where new industries would be set up to provide employment, where the style of life of the Indian peasant would be changed for the better, and thought not so much of the continuation of village

India as of the construction of an urban, technologised India. Both
Gandhi and Nehru, over the years, were to quarrel on this score,
but they always made up: it is extraordinary that two men so
different in character and philosophy should have remained so
close for so long. It was also extraordinary that Motilal should have
succumbed to the charisma of Gandhi, for while Jawaharlal had a
streak of austerity in his nature, Motilal did not. At least it was not
manifest in him for the first sixty years of his life. The association
of her grandfather and father with the freedom movement had
considerable influence on the character and life of the child Indira.

Nearly sixty years after her birth in Allahabad, Jawaharlal's child
sat opposite me on a sofa in her New Delhi house. Until a few
months before this, as Prime Minister of India, Mrs Indira Gandhi
had been the most powerful woman in the world. Her government
was defeated and fell after the elections of March 1977. Now she
looked a little lonely; but, I reflected, even when surrounded by
crowds, she always had. Her face, so much like her father's, sensitive,
tired and with hooded eyes, but full of presence, under the dark hair
with a thick white streak in it, was impassive: she has, in fact, two
main aspects of countenance. One is impassive, almost bored. But
sometimes, suddenly and unexpectedly, like a mobile rainbow after
a hermetically frozen and suspended storm, she smiles, and becomes
radiantly alive. Now, after the suspended storm, came the smile.
She looked up from her hands, fingers plaited. 'Go ahead,' she said,
'I'm listening.' The smile disappeared.

　　She had a sari on in some pastel colour, and sat in a typical posture,
elbows on knees, hands locked, and now her handsome head bent
itself forward so that she could survey her hands as though they were
her only friends. I said: 'An aunt of yours in Allahabad told me that
you were very spoilt as a child, and that everyone made a pet of you.
Would you say you were a spoilt child?' She said in a crisp and final
voice, 'No.' The monosyllable hung in the air between us for at
least a minute. Then, as I began to despair of any further amplifica-
tion, even though used to these silences, she added, 'I certainly
think I wasn't spoilt. On the contrary, I felt rather deprived of
everything.' Another lengthy silence followed. 'My aunts and other
relatives,' she eventually said, 'had a very carefree, happy childhood
in my grandfather's house, but, by the time I was three years old,
life there was very austere and very unsettled, at least for me. My

first memory was of burning foreign cloth and imported articles in the courtyard of the house: the whole family did it.' These presumably included her own clothes and toys: since most small female children have a fixation about pretty clothes and dolls, I understood why she should recall this so vividly, the lace of her own clothes and the wax of her dolls flaring and melting away under the flames. Afterwards, like the other members of the family, she dressed in clothes of *khadi*, handspun cloth.

Later, when she was four years old, in 1921, she balanced on her grandfather's large, solid knee, in the dock of a court where she listened inquisitively, not sure of what it was that she was listening to, as he and her father were each sentenced to six months imprisonment. From this time onward Jawaharlal was to spend more than nine years of his life behind British bars. These were also nine years of his only daughter's childhood and adolescence, very important years.

'So, you see,' she continued, on this Delhi afternoon, miles and decades from her childhood, 'it was really all very unsettled. There was no regularity about meals, and I never knew where my parents were or when or if they would come home. By that time my mother was also involved in the freedom fight. I used to want to be with them whenever they went out, but I was never allowed to.' Her right eye blinked several times in rapid succession. It does this whenever she is moved about something, or nervous. 'It wasn't too bad for my father in prison,' she said. 'He conditioned himself in a way. But for my grandfather, who was used to a fairly luxurious life, it was very difficult. When he wasn't in prison, and all the rest of the family were in prison, or on demonstrations or pickets, he would worry terribly about them till they all came home from wherever they were.'

There was another pause. I have learnt to allow these silences to fill with the words she wants to find. Eventually she said, 'My grandfather used to like to take me up into the hills with him, when the other people in the family weren't at home. I used to—you know —scurry ahead of him when we were walking. He was a man people were afraid of, for his temper, but his tempers never lasted.'

While out with her grandfather on these submontane excursions, she used also to ride hill ponies, not in those days, the practice of female Indians of any age. She would have learnt to be independent, leading the life that she did, or so I would suppose, and also learnt, like any other lonely child, not to confide her trust in more than a very few people. Today, looking beyond me towards the balcony outside, where Congress personnel in white handspun clothes swarmed, awaiting an audience, she said nothing, but the impassive and detached look reappeared on her face. Eventually she said, 'I think I have to see somebody else now.' Then that extraordinary smile came back for the space of about a second. 'Oh, and you know, my first school, when I was little. It was run by two ladies called the Misses Cameron, in Allahabad.' I inquired if she had liked it. 'All the other girls wore—well, other kinds of clothes,' she said. 'I had to wear *khadi*, homespun cloth. It was very rough and stiff, and very uncomfortable. And I always felt out of place.'

'Jawaharlal,' an old friend of his once told me, 'educated himself in prison. He never had much time to read or write while he was outside it. Inside, he read all kinds of writers and he wrote the better part of his own books.' Despite his daughter's concern for him, Nehru appears to have led a tranquil life in prison. As a political prisoner he had a considerable amount of freedom within the political compound. He spent his time, during his first imprisonment, sweeping the barracks (of his own volition), spinning cloth, washing his father's clothes and his own, and giving lessons in Hindi and Urdu to other prisoners. Indeed, according to one writer, 'prison became a second home to Nehru.' Obviously, however, he must have missed his wife and child: to Indira, over the prison years, he wrote a sequence of letters about world history which he later edited down and published as a book.*

As to Kamala, he had rather specific worries. After his commitment to politics and his abandonment of a legal career, he had little or no private money and certainly no income. Kamala, Indira and he were totally dependent on Motilal. It is true that the old lion loved his only son, and the wife and daughter of that son, but it must still have depressed Jawaharlal somewhat. Kamala wore very little in the way of ornaments, and she dressed, unlike her sisters-in-law, in simple cotton saris. This led to some of the Allahabad household feeling, and indeed expressing, a certain amount of scorn for her: particularly Jawaharlal's older sister, Swarup or Vijayalakhsmi, who according to other relatives resident in the house at that time, had always felt that her brother had married beneath him. On one

* *Glimpses of World History*, Kitabistan, Allahabad, 2 vols, 1934.

occasion Swarup discovered a diamond ring, one of Kamala's few items of jewellery, left behind in the bathroom. She produced it in front of the rest of the women, and someone said, 'That's Kamala's.' Swarup said contemptuously. 'Has she ever seen diamonds before?' Life in the house must have been hard for Kamala, especially when Jawaharlal was away or in prison, and her health suffered: she started to lose weight and suffer from migraines. All this started in 1919, when Indira was two years old, and in that year the complaint was diagnosed as tuberculosis. Then the doctors, as doctors do, changed their minds. They said that Kamala had uterine trouble and treated her for it. She got better, but the house was hardly a haven of rest: the police constantly raided the place. In 1925 she became pregnant once more, but miscarried, and her weakness led to a slow but persistent rise in her temperature. This, some doctors said, was tuberculosis: others said it was not. Kamala did not improve.

She was now sent to hospital, and, on her emergence, ordered complete rest. This being impossible in Anand Bhavan, Motilal, who was deeply concerned about her health, arranged for her to spend time in a house on the riverbank, where the wind was fresh and the peace palpable. Here, beautiful and fragile, like some romantic heroine, she lay and looked out over the blue Yamuna to where it locked itself with the muddy Ganges. Her temperature stabilised itself but the doctors were still dissatisfied. They recommended that she be treated in Switzerland. Jawaharlal, recently released from his last spell in prison, decided to accompany her. There was also Indira to consider. At nine years old she was shy and coltish and deeply dependent on her mother. The constant turmoil in the household, the absence of her father and other relatives in prison, so that there were few faces she saw every day, naturally made her insecure. This insecurity had been added to by the illness of her mother and Kamala's disappearance into hospital. Normally speaking, she could have stayed in Allahabad, where there were plenty of people to look after her, but Jawaharlal and Motilal both felt that a prolonged separation would harm both mother and daughter. Accordingly Indira sailed from Bombay with her parents. With them was Swarup, and her husband, Ranjit Pandit, who made some valuable translations of the Indian classics before his premature death. The Pandits were on holiday: the Nehrus on a solemn and difficult mission. They arrived in Geneva at last, found a flat,

deposited Indira in a school at Bex in the Alps, and doctors started
to whir around Kamala like dragonflies.

Unlike the doctors in India, the Swiss consultants concurred that
Kamala did have tuberculosis. The treatment was expensive, so was
life in Geneva, and Jawaharlal was not personally rich. Kamala at
one point had to sell her few pieces of jewellery to maintain the
family. When Motilal heard about this (it happened very shortly
after the arrival of the family in Geneva) he wrote: 'I was much
pained to read your letter advising sale of Kamala's gold bangles ...
you ask me not to worry but it is you who are worrying over the
expenses of a most necessary trip ... I see signs of this in your not
providing yourself with an overcoat until you have actually caught
a chill and giving to Kamala some very inferior stuff ... ' A short
while later his solicitude expresses itself once more: 'I have received
the snapshots you sent. They do not show very clearly how Kamala
and Indu look. Indu is as thin as ever and Kamala looks like an old
woman.' In fact the treatment did not seem to work, and the doctors
advised Jawaharlal to take Kamala to Montana in the Alps. This had
the advantage of being close to Bex and Indira. Jawaharlal was
probably a little restless: he had nothing to do except sit with his
wife, and he did not like having nothing to do. He took off on short
trips to other European capitals to investigate the political situation
in each. When Kamala was better he ferried her over to London
for a holiday. Here Kamala apparently felt there was a lot of colour-
consciousness, and became a feminist. She wrote back to India:
'We have degraded ourselves beyond limits. Women are even less
enlightened than men due to lack of education. When I think of the
plight of my sisters my heart bleeds because they are indifferent to
the question of their own rights. Day by day I am getting more and
more determined that on my return home I shall take my sisters
along with me. I shall urge them to place their trust in God and
fight for their own freedom, educate their daughters so that they
are not in trouble like us and join the struggle for independence so
that we do not have to spend our lives in shame.' Kamala was now
no shy Indian bride: some of her husband's social awareness had
rubbed off on her. Unluckily she couldn't do all the things she
wanted to. Even by that time she was dying.

In 1927 Motilal arrived in Geneva and swept the family off to
Paris and Berlin, where Jawaharlal made a contact which was to be

one of the most important in his life. He encountered some Russians who invited him to visit the Soviet Union. Kamala went with him. Jawaharlal was a socialist, but a theoretical one: he had never seen socialism in action before, and this was a peculiarly exciting time in Russia. The Revolution was only ten years old: it was still possible for a Russian to be idealistic. Jawaharlal, himself an idealist, was carried away. He saw how industry had developed, on farms as well as in cities. He did not, or was not allowed to, see the long shadows behind the light. This Russian experience played a vital role, twenty years later, in forming his economic policies and targets as Prime Minister of an independent India. Through him, Indira developed many of her ideas: through her, the 1927 visit showed its effects on Indian policies fifty years after it was made. Jawaharlal must have talked to her about this visit, so must Kamala: Jawaharlal also made her read a book called *The Life Of The Ant*, which she recollects vividly today. 'My father used to try and force me to read books which were too advanced for me,' she says, 'like H. G. Wells's books. But I really enjoyed that one.' It is perhaps significant that a colony of ants lives under much the same working conditions as prevailed in the Soviet Union in 1927.

Kamala was also impressed, but, curiously enough, what seems to have impressed her most were the prisons, which she thought far superior to those run by the British in India. It is very doubtful that she knew what had happened, and would happen, in the prisons she saw. Prisons are not really the first priority for display to visitors: it is possible that the Nehrus were shown these prisons so that they could later defend the Soviets against foreign criticism of the Russian penal system, already widespread. Nehru himself, incidentally, does not seem as delighted with these prisons (if he was he never said so) as his wife. An ironic touch was that Kamala, for the purposes of this visit to the socialist world, had equipped herself mainly with saris of coarse *khadi*: it was with some surprise that she noted that at parties the socialist ladies arrived for their vodka and caviar splendid in rustling silk.

In December 1927, Jawaharlal, Kamala, and Indira sailed for India. Motilal, perhaps to turn his last taste of Europe over his tongue and savour it fully, did not. Kamala now seemed better: but there was some further confusion about the nature of her illness when, in Paris, a Dr Bernard said that she wasn't tubercular and never had

been, 'and that her troubles were largely uterine'. Nevertheless,
though in fairly reasonable health after the family returned to India,
in 1928 she developed appendicitis, which must have further
weakened an already fragile system. Meanwhile Jawaharlal and the
entire Indian political scene were moving into a period of change.

A Congress session had been held in Madras in early 1928, and
the main question raised was who should be the party President.
Motilal was now sixty-seven. He felt the rough kiss of *khadi* on a
skin more used to silk and expensive wool: he had also decided to
shave off his magnificent moustache. Apparently the society ladies
of Allahabad, believing this moustache to be one of the glories of
the city, begged him not to, but, as he was accustomed to, he did
what he wanted. Whiskerless, he looked older: shriven of his suits,
he nevertheless continued to be elegant, a shawl of fine Kashmiri
wool draped over his *khadi*, like the toga of a Roman Senator. But it
now seemed that his years burdened him. He had always stood for
moderation: now he felt that this was not the right policy for the
Congress. On July 11 1928, he wrote to Gandhi, eight years younger
than he was, about the Congress presidency, which he had been
offered. 'The hero of the hour is Vallabhbhai* and the least we can
do to appreciate his public services is to offer him the crown.
Failing him I think that under all the circumstances Jawaharlal
would be the next best choice. He has no doubt frightened many of
our goody goodies by his plain talk. But the time has come when the
more energetic and determined workers should have their own way
of guiding the political activities of the country.' Gandhi, like Motilal, was at this time a moderate, and they both thought Jawaharlal
was pushing ahead too fast. The next sentences of this letter are
sad ones, the reflections of a sunset: 'There are I admit points of
difference between this class and the one to which you and I belong
but there is no reason why we should continue to force our views
on the former. Our race is fast dying out and the struggle will sooner
or later have to be continued by men of Jawahar's type. The
sooner they begin the better.' Then, in a sentence completely out of
character in the days before this letter was written: 'As for myself
I feel I have lost much of the confidence I had in myself and am more
or less a spent force ... '

However, as regards his immediate family, Motilal had plans
which were not political. He built a new house next to the old one,

* Sardar Vallabhbhai Patel, a veteran Congress leader.

amidst his trees and lawns in Allahabad. The new house was also called Anand Bhavan: the old one renamed Swaraj Bhavan. On the top floor, Jawaharlal and Kamala had a kind of suite. Indira had a separate room with a bath. Today the house is a museum, belonging to the nation: the rooms that were occupied by the three Nehrus are sealed off, but surrounded by windows through which the visitors can peer. On a hot rainy afternoon in 1977 I was admitted to these quarters. The museum authorities, apologetic, told me I would have to be locked in. Consequently I spent three hours in a sort of zoo situation, stared at through the windows by hundreds of tourists, as I ploughed about in the shelves of the library that still inhabit the dead and empty rooms. Motilal's books seemed mainly to be legal: Jawaharlal's displayed an extraordinarily catholic taste. He possessed copies of Balzac and Dickens, Koestler, Waugh, Ernst Toller, Somerset Maugham, amongst numerous other novelists: copies of 1930s books of verse: Left Book Club editions: books about China, Spain and Russia, about gardening, cameras, and palmistry: he seems to have wanted to know about almost everything. Indira's books were not numerous, and in some the leaves were uncut. As I laboured through the library, the crowd pointed through the windows and tittered. Seldom have I better understood the emotions of a caged tiger: part embarrassment, part a desire to slay my unwanted audience. Overhead the ceiling fans, their tongues clicking at every revolution, dislodged warm, wet, slightly musty air and dropped it on my sweaty shoulders.

'The house was always full of activity,' Mrs Gandhi said, plaiting her hands together. 'It was full of people. But I preferred Swaraj Bhavan to Anand Bhavan. It was more like a home. Still, Anand Bhavan *was* full of activity. We used to hide Congress party workers on the run from the British. One night we had some who were wounded. All the women of the house acted as nurses. Including me.' She looked up and smiled. 'One of my earliest memories was when I saw Chandrasekhar being shot.'

Chandrasekhar was an Indian revolutionary involved in a plot to kill a British official. He now looms in bronze in an Allahabad park, the place in which, surrounded by British police, he was killed and became a sort of instant martyr. 'I don't think I actually saw the last shot,' Mrs Gandhi said. 'But I saw the flashes and heard the shots. Violence is terrifying you know. I saw all this from the house,

and I felt numb, as though I had been dropped in very hot water or
very cold water.' It had been a hard day for her, and her hooded
eyes looked tired. 'You know,' she said, 'I have no particular feeling
for Allahabad, even though I was born there and lived there for
years. It wasn't that I was lonely: only I felt that my key people
were never there and I felt people didn't understand me. I saw how
my mother was hurt by people, and I made up my mind never to
let people hurt me.'

❧ 4 ❧

Death of a Lion

TO ANALYSE THE causes of the hurt inflicted on Kamala it is
necessary to explore the history of the state then called the United
Provinces and now known as Uttar Pradesh. This included several
provinces collectively known as Oudh and ruled by a Nawab.* The
successive Nawabs, as the years went by, were in the patriarchal
habit of handing out tracts of Oudh to favoured courtiers. The
courtiers collected revenue and tithes from the villagers who inhabited their land, and not unnaturally waxed fat, for the soil was
extremely fertile. Admittedly the villagers themselves thinned down
considerably, but this was no concern of the Nawabs. Until 1857
they held absolute power in Oudh. Then, with the outbreak of the
Mutiny, the ruler of the time threw in his lot with the rebels. The
landowners supported him. They may have felt some loyalty
towards him, though this is debatable: certainly their interests lay
with him. The brief, bloody rebellion ended with the death of the
Nawab and a British victory. The landowners who had supported
their ruler must have bitterly regretted their decision: several of
them were executed and their lands were taken away. Those people
who had supported the British or who at any rate had not supported
the Nawab, now became rich, rewarded by their new rulers with
vast tracts of land containing many helpless and milkable villages.
These talukdars, as the landlords were called, were a very mixed
bunch, most of whom had never known wealth before. They lacked
trained minds, to say the least: there were continual squabbles over
patrimony and property. Most of these people did nothing but
collect rents and loll amidst concubines, sycophants, and rapidly
emptied bottles. Prostitutes were presented with land: gambling
debts gnawed the fields away. In this curious and unique situation
litigation was constant and ferocious. Oudh therefore became a

* This was the Muslim equivalent of a Hindu Maharaja.

3

vernal soil for lawyers, and, naturally, the better the lawyer the more he made.

Motilal never actually qualified as a barrister. He was what Indians called a pleader, which was not difficult to become. The force of his personality, his native sharpness, and his undeniable charm, all combined to take him to the top, and he took care to stay there. He was one of the great Indian lawyers of his time, he lived in Allahabad, not far from Oudh, and so it was natural that talukdars in trouble should hire him to fight their somewhat dubious causes. Some of these men were enormously wealthy and could afford colossal fees. An accumulation of such fees speedily made Motilal as rich as any of his plutocratic clients.

The Nehrus had never been what one might call truly wealthy before. The nearest they had come to it had been in the three brief years before Farrukh Siyar's death in 1719, when they had been granted land by the Emperor. Motilal had been poor in his time: and his association with the talukdars must have opened his eyes to a new world, a world he wanted. Some talukdars were educated men, involved in politics, interested in poetry, music and the arts: these were the exceptions. Most of them were only partially literate, and exceptionally uncouth in their personal habits and tastes. Every talukdar, however, was highly skilled in transforming himself into a different person for the benefit of the British, for he was entirely dependent on his masters. What the Crown had given, the Crown could take away. When a British official came their way the talukdars trembled, and transformed themselves.

A veteran officer of the I.C.S.* told me of one such encounter between a talukdar and the British. The Collector of Oudh, an Englishman, was on tour, and was to pass through the estates of an elderly talukdar, with whom it was decided he should dine. The day before the arrival of the Collector, my friend was sent on ahead to tell the prospective host of his commitment. He was dismayed by what he found: both the talukdar and his residence were decrepit and unclean in the extreme: my friend perched on the only chair in the house, which had three legs and was infested by fleas, sipping tea from a chipped cup, the only one in the house, while the talukdar, clad in a simple loincloth, squatted on the floor swigging whisky from the bottle. It was too late to amend the programme and my

* The Indian Civil Service, manned by Indians as well as Englishmen, which looked after most aspects of administration.

friend returned to the Collector's camp, too nervous to warn his senior officer of the horrors ahead. Next day the Collector's party set forth.

When they arrived they were welcomed by the talukdar, but a talukdar transformed. He had attired his wizened person in a turban, a long coat, tight trousers and slippers, all made of expensive brocade studded with pearls and diamonds. At his waist, hanging from a brocade belt, was a curved sword in a brocade sheath. He led the Collector and his entourage, not to his own house, but to a large field, in which tents and wooden pavilions had suddenly sprouted. Crystal chandeliers clinked and flashed on the ceilings of the pavilions: damask and silver adorned the tables: bottles of champagne froze themselves to death in ornamental ice-buckets: there were seven brands of Scotch awaiting consumption in cut-glass decanters: pheasants, peacocks, wild boar, venison, and various kinds of fish lay, dead but delicately cooked, in silver dishes: Persian carpets covered the floor. From this ornately furnished field it was possible to see the talukdar's own house, which though extremely ramshackle, was undeniably large. 'Who,' inquired the Collector, 'lives there?' The talukdar, whose English had not risen to the occasion as had his arrangements, shrugged his shoulders, 'Not knowing, *huzoor*,' he said. 'But must be some bastard with no money.' My friend later discovered that the tents, the pavilions, the food, and the liquor, had all been brought in overnight by a contractor from Lucknow.

The kind of hospitality the talukdars felt it incumbent upon themselves to offer, particularly to the British, was not only lavish but extravagant to the point of vulgarity. It differed widely from their own style of life, but they felt it was expected of them. The British may have been flattered by such hospitality, but they were not impressed: it was too ostentatious. But Motilal was impressed: very. Like the talukdars, he had only recently come into the possession of large sums of money, though unlike the talukdars he had earned it. The talukdars and he shared the opinion that when it came to hospitality, personal wealth should be displayed. Motilal, however, thrown by his profession into close contact with the British, made his style of life as extravagant as his hospitality and showed more taste than his clients, though not very much more. His meals were served off Dresden china, his liquor decanted into Czech glass. His servants, his carriages, his cars, his horses, were all acquired in inordinate numbers. Perhaps in an effort to compensate for his childhood poverty, he gave his two daughters anything and everything he thought would please them or was asked for. Growing up in an ambience of newly acquired wealth, and encouraged by their father to pursue Western ways, they had little time for the quiet, orthodox Kamala, though Betty had more than Swarup. Jawaharlal, moreover, they had always idolised: their possessive instincts were stirred by the presence of what they thought of as an unsuitable young wife in the household. They didn't understand her: possibly she didn't understand them.

The family money and the family style seem to have made a totally different impact on Jawaharlal. He returned from England, as did nearly every Indian who went there at the time, as a theoretical socialist of the Fabian variety. The way in which his father lived probably shocked him somewhat: what may have shocked him even more was the necessity to defend talukdars, whom he considered enemies of the people, in court, in order to help provide the family with wealth he did not want. This may have precipitated his entry into politics, combined with the reasons proposed in the last chapter. In any event, he seems to have made a sort of mental withdrawal from the normal life of the family, and this probably added to Kamala's troubles: his sisters may have attributed this to her.

But the withdrawal eventually led to the entire family, including the sisters, becoming involved in the free for all of the Indian nationalist movement. It is conceivable that Jawaharlal's love of huge crowds, when he addressed the public, stemmed from a sort of guilt at being born with a large silver spoon in his mouth, so that he wanted the presence of many poor people around him to prove to himself that he was not what he had supposedly been born to be.

There is a rather touching story, told me by the same I.C.S. officer mentioned earlier, which relates to Nehru's first entry into politics. 'Jawaharlal was barely thirty. He was to address a meeting in the park at Lucknow. A friend of mine from college, P. C. Joshi* and I heard about this. We knew of Jawaharlal's reputation as a supporter of the freedom movement, so we went there early to avoid the crowds we were sure would turn up. Jawaharlal was already on the platform. He was in *khadi*, but he had a beautiful gold chronometer—I remember this because he kept consulting it. He was awaiting an audience, but two hours after the scheduled time

* Later the head of the Communist Party of India.

there were only twenty people there. Then Jawaharlal started to speak. He was obviously not very pleased. He was much less pleased after his speech, when he found out that because there was no loudspeaker, nobody had heard a word that he had said.' Having told me this story, he said: 'Years later, after Independence, I was posted to Delhi. Jawaharlal had to inaugurate some kind of memorial early in the morning. I went with him; it was about nine o'clock. At certain points on the road we passed huge crowds. Jawaharlal obviously thought they had come to see him, and he was delighted. He said, "X——, what brings these crowds here? Whom do they want to see?" I am afraid I am a bad courtier. I said, "Sir, it is the fault of the Delhi transport system. At this time in the morning, thousands of people are trying to reach their places of employment, and there are very few buses. None of these people wants to see anybody, they simply want to reach their offices." I hadn't realised what my answer should have been. I was astonished that he was so angry.'

It runs in the family. Of them all, only Kamala shunned crowds.

By 1928 the whole family was in politics. Kamala, despite her spirals between illness and health, started, with other members of the household, to make salt in public, in defiance of the British tax laws which considered that Indians should be supplied with salt from the mother country. Indira at this point also became involved in the nationalist movement. There were numbers of Congress workers in the leafy city of Allahabad, none of whom knew, from day to day, when they would be arrested or their homes searched by the British. To give them information on these unpleasant facts, a kind of children's corps was organised in the city, headed by Indira. This organisation was rather coyly called 'The Monkey Brigade'. Indira's function was apparently to make speeches to children: other children did the actual donkey work of running around to warn people that they were about to be arrested and should vanish into the underground system of the Congress party, which would scatter them away into the huge hinterlands of India. Whose idea the Monkey Brigade was is unclear: Mrs Gandhi says it was hers, but other people in Allahabad, also former members, seem to feel that the Congress party thought it up and felt that nobody was better suited to lead it than Jawaharlal's only child.

The year 1930 brought more ill health to Kamala, and her

political activities cannot have helped a body already so ravaged by disease. Nevertheless she seems to have been pleased in the sense that she was now on an equal footing with her husband. Prior to this, like Whitman's sea-captain, he could have said, as regards prison and political difficulty: 'I am the man; I suffered; I was there.' Kamala could now tell her husband that she had been through much the same as he had. It would bring them closer to each other, for they had in fact never been all that close. 'I thought of the early years of our marriage,' Jawaharlal wrote after her death, 'when, with all my tremendous *liking* for Kamala* I almost forgot her, and denied her, in so many ways, that comradeship that was her due ... I gave all my energy to the cause and had little left to spare ... ' He adds: 'I had taken from her what she gave me. What had I given to her in exchange for those early years? I had failed evidently and, possibly, she carried the deep impression of those days upon her. With her inordinate pride and sensitiveness she did not want to come to me for help ... she did not say this to me in words and it was only gradually that I read the message of her eyes ... '

The talukdars of Oudh had to pay land tax to the British. This was assessed on the basis of several factors, among the most important of which were the extent and nature of the land they possessed, the extent and nature of the crops sown on their soil, and the rents paid by the tenant farmers. These last the talukdars continually falsified. They would declare a rent of sixty rupees paid by an individual who was actually paying a hundred. These rents, in many cases, were collected by force. By 1930 the talukdars, mostly corrupt and decadent when they first received their land from the British, had become extraordinarily so. Pretty and buxom village women were dragged off by their minions to serve as mistresses to the master: husbands, brothers or fathers who protested were beaten, as indeed they were if they failed to produce the rent demanded by the taluk-dar. Jawaharlal, in 1930, was a great deal more powerful a figure than he had been when, ten years earlier, my friend the I.C.S. officer had watched him consulting his gold chronometer in Lucknow. He, and the other Congress workers in Oudh, went out to the villages and advised the people to refuse to pay rent. It was ironic: he was now attacking the livelihoods of people whom his father and he had

* The italics are mine, since the choice of word seems important.

defended for years, people whose styles of life Motilal had evolved as his own. This style was now changed: the father had become, as so often happens, the child of his son: demoustached, *khadi* clad, shrunken into himself, he did what his son did, except that he would not attempt the extreme measures desired by Jawaharlal. He obviously missed his former life: one of his private secretaries records an occasion when, away from home, a servant offered him a vegetarian meal. Motilal sent it back to the kitchen and asked for some sort of specially cooked meat dish. When it arrived he did not like it. The cook argued with him, which some years earlier would have been an awful mistake. Motilal, however, had been tamed by the years. 'O brother,' he said to the cook, 'don't say all this to me. I was once a real man. Don't be misled by this *khadi* that I wear ... '

He had seen the cities of his own country: he had seen the cities of Europe. He was old, tired, and, perhaps, happy in his son and his grandchildren, even if slightly perplexed by them. He knew that his name would be remembered, which is what most men want. As many people who have retired do, he pottered around doing the unnecessary with extreme enthusiasm. He designed a portable commode which apparently looked like a despatch case, which he carried about with him on visits to the more remote parts of India. His secretary used to install this unusual apparatus in the lavatory of whatever bungalow he stayed in, but to Motilal's annoyance it was constantly removed by helpful servants and placed among his other despatch cases. He also experimented with an Icmic Cooker, which was a kind of solar cooker. While in Central India, in a place where only rainwater was available, he also rigged up a rainwater filter whereby he procured a more or less potable liquid. He no longer really had a home in that Anand Bhavan was so frequently empty, the children away on political work or in prison, the huge house echoing to the voices of his wife and himself and the quiet footfalls of servants.

Of these servants, only two remain in Anand Bhavan, now merely a repository of memories. One is called Becchu, the other, his wife, is called Sonia, and she is blind. On a day when rain, mist and heat took it in turns to scrub one another out of the sky, they were called to the museum offices by the director. Mrs Gandhi had provided me with their names and with a certain amount of their biographical

material. Becchu, she told me, had been one of the household
sweepers, but her grandfather (this was after Jawaharlal had turned
him into a liberal) felt that the boy had potential: he therefore had
him taught to drive a car. But Becchu, unfortunately, did not stay
in the jobs Motilal found him. He is now a skinny old man who has
probably seen eighty monsoons in Allahabad, and Sonia, though she
can no longer see the rain or the mist, cannot be less than ten years
younger than her spouse. 'Previously', said the museum official in
whose small, antiseptic chamber we sat, 'Becchu was beating Sonia
too much. Now he is not beating. Since she is becoming blind, he is
taking care.'

Sonia and Becchu seated themselves: they were dripping and
shivering after coming in from the cold. I told them that Mrs Gandhi
had sent them her best wishes, whereupon, to my horror, Becchu
burst into tears, more profuse and more noisy than the slow rain
that tumbled from the clouds outside. It took a long time to quench
his tears, but since every few minutes they recommenced, the interview became increasingly incoherent. Sonia, who seemed sensible,
tried to interpret the sobs of her husband: Becchu, obviously
annoyed at these attempts to upstage him, occasionally ceased to
cry, but only because he wanted time to shout her down.

He could not remember anything very clearly. He recollected
that the lawns had once suffered an infestation of snakes, and that
Motilal, like some legendary Hindu hero, had wrestled with an
enormous cobra and killed it with his own hands. He recollected
that one of the chauffeurs had also been called Becchu. He recollected the marriage of Indira, though not the details. His opinion
of his employers was that they had been excellent people, though
he could not remember much about any of them as individuals,
except that Motilal used to organise wrestling matches between the
servants, in which Becchu participated. But between the inco-
herences and the sobs a blurred picture emerged: the picture of
what was almost a feudal household, ruled by a patriarch: where
splendour, hedonism and ostentation were all to be found, until
Motilal became a nationalist. At this point I made a serious mistake
by asking him how he felt about Mrs Gandhi's defeat in the elections. His convulsive sobs turned into positive roars of sorrow.
Through this torrent of tears he informed me, like a rather grubby
naiad crying out behind a waterfall, that Mrs Gandhi had promised
him a pension, which had not been paid for some time, and that he

doubted, after her defeat, if it would ever be. I attempted to console him with a fairly substantial tip, for which he stretched out a wizened hand. Sonia, blind or not, had quicker reflexes than he did: she whipped the money away and stuffed it into her blouse. Becchu started to cry once more, and I thought it best to bring this peculiar interview to an end.

Towards the end of 1930 there were two invalids in Anand Bhavan. One was, of course, Kamala: the other was Motilal. He was nearly seventy, and had become grey and frail. At about this time his private secretary asked him for permission to return to his hometown, Benares. 'Yes, my dear fellow,' replied Motilal. 'How can I ask you to stay? *Na woh mai rahi, na woh jam raha, na woh mahfil rahi ...* The wine, the cup, the party: all, all are gone.'

On January 1 1931, as Mrs Gandhi recalls, Kamala, herself in poor health, was arrested for the first time. The previous evening, mother and daughter had been alone in Anand Bhavan, reading *In Memoriam* aloud to each other: a curiously Victorian way to pass the time, but then there was something curiously Victorian about life in Anand Bhavan. Suddenly the telephone chirruped, and an unknown voice told Indira that her mother was to be arrested the next day. 'I was stunned. She asked me to pack, and herself spent the whole night working, talking to the local Congress workers, giving them some papers, giving them instructions.' Next day the police came.

Jawaharlal was himself at this time in prison at a place called Naini. With him was Swarup's husband, Ranjit Pandit. On January 12, Motilal was allowed to visit them. Jawaharlal was shocked by Motilal's physical condition. 'He had now changed for the worse, and his face was even more swollen. He had some little difficulty in speaking, and his mind was not always quite clear. But his old will remained .... It certainly did: partly because of Motilal's insistence, and partly because of the old man's rapid physical deterioration, Ranjit Pandit was released a few days after the visit, and on January 26 Kamala, who had only served 26 days, was released from her Lucknow prison and Jawaharlal was discharged from Naini. Homing pigeons, they sped back to Allahabad.

I said earlier that the Nehrus, from Motilal onward, were para-doxical people, but the political situation at the time was paradoxical in itself. The Nehrus liked the British as individuals: there were also

Englishmen in India as well as in Britain who supported the cause
of Indian independence. Nowhere else in the world but India would
three political prisoners have been unconditionally released because
of the ill health of a relative. Despite the occasional unpleasant
incident, the Indian nationalists had a smoother passage to independence than those of any other country. Even imprisonment was not
all that bad: the Congress leaders were not insulted or tortured:
they grew flowers, they read and wrote, and though they may have
lacked home comforts, their regimen, if austere, was not usually
anything less than bearable. To have been in a British prison
became a matter of pride: had the prisons been modelled on the
Russian ones Kamala had so fancied in 1927, it is probable that the
emotions of a Congressman on arrest would not have included a
sense of pride. Relations between the Indian nationalists and the
British were, as a rule, civilised and correct, almost ludicrously so.
On one of the occasions that Gandhi was arrested, an English
witness, a disciple of the Mahatma, was present. The Inspector
who made the arrest, also English, started out by apologising to
Gandhi. He then dropped his hand, almost caressively, on Gandhi's
shoulder, and it was not for some time that the onlookers realised
that this was the formal token of arrest. After this, Gandhi was
permitted to perform his ablutions and write notes to his disciples
(it was one of his days of silence)* while the Inspector patiently
stood by. This was a far cry from the normal political arrest, the
world of the Gestapo, pistols, whips, and closed vans, that so many
people have suffered, suffer, and will suffer in our century. No
tremendous battles were necessary for the eventual achievement of
Indian independence: it was a process of adaptation and concession
between the nationalist leaders and the British. The bloodiest
massacres of all came immediately *after* independence, and were
wreaked by Indians upon Indians.

Motilal, his family around him, dwindled away in the huge
mansion he had built. From its windows he could see the other
house, acquired thirty years back and now used for Congress
conferences. He spent most of the time in bed, but every morning
and evening he would slowly rise, dress, and seat himself in a chair
to receive friends, relatives, and Congress workers, all of whom
trooped in to say goodbye in case it was their last opportunity.

* Gandhi observed days of silence when he spoke to nobody, as an act of self
discipline.

'There he sat,' wrote Jawaharlal, 'massively and rather expression-lessly, for the swelling on his face prevented much play of expression. But as one old friend came after another, and comrade succeeded comrade, there was a glitter in his eye and recognition of them, and his head bowed a little and his hands joined in salutation. And though he could not speak much, sometimes he would say a few words, and even his old humour did not leave him. There he sat like an old lion mortally wounded and with his physical strength almost gone, but still very leonine and kingly ... Even when a constriction in his throat made it difficult for him to make himself understood, he took to writing on slips of paper what he wanted to say.' One of the last things Motilal said was to Gandhi, who had been released from Yeravada prison in Poona on the same day that Jawaharlal and Kamala were released from their respective confine-ments. Motilal had a deep feeling for the Mahatma. 'I am going soon ... ', said Motilal, 'and I shall not be here to see independence. But I know that you have won it and will have it soon.'

On February 4 he seemed better, and the doctors decided that he could be moved to Lucknow, where additional medical facilities were available. Jawaharlal took him there by car, followed by Gandhi and numbers of other people. Lucknow is about 150 miles from Alla-habad, and though the car went slowly, the trip exhausted Motilal. Early next day he seemed to rise from his stupor: but as the slow sun climbed the sky, he commenced his own decline. On the morning of February 6, Jawaharlal and his mother were by the bedside of the old lion, when, Jawaharlal writes, 'suddenly I noticed his face grew calm and the sense of struggle vanished from it. I thought he had fallen asleep, and I was glad of it. But my mother's perceptions were keener, and she uttered a cry. I turned to her and begged her not to disturb him, as he had fallen asleep. But that sleep was his last long sleep, and from it there was no awakening.'

When Jawaharlal first went to prison, it is said that Motilal used to sleep on the floor of his own bedroom to find out what it was like, as he was under the impression that all political prisoners had to sleep on the floor and wanted to share the hardships of his beloved son. Indeed, the story is told by Jawaharlal himself. There is no doubt that, whatever their differences, father and son were tied by more than blood: by a mutual affection, care and respect for each other. Motilal, in the relationship, probably sacrificed more than his son; he gave up the life he had known for nearly sixty years, and put himself on the other side of the fence from the British, so many of whom he had known as friends, from the talukdars, his former clients, and from Allahabad society. When, eventually, he was imprisoned, he was not forgotten by his friends: from the other side of the political fence, Harcourt Butler of the Allahabad High Court, one of the most famous British lawyers in India, allegedly sent champagne to his cell.

Of the legends wreathed round the family since the time of Motilal, few have included his wife, Sarup Rani. Gandhi, after Motilal's death, said: 'My position is worse than a widow's. By a faithful life, she can appropriate the merits of her husband, I can appropriate nothing. What I have lost through the death of Motilal is a loss forever.' He added, quoting from an English hymn, for no visible reason, 'Rock of ages, cleft for me, let me hide myself in thee.' But the widow Sarup Rani, gentle and forgotten after the upsurge of nationalism brought by Jawaharlal, may well have been the governing strength behind Motilal.

Both her husband and Gandhi forbade her to associate herself with any part of the nationalist movement. She was not supposed to be at Motilal's funeral. Swarup, or Vijayalakshmi Pandit, writes: 'Father's death was a cruel blow – for the long period of his illness she would not admit that the end would be near. How could she imagine that her great and powerful husband who had always emerged victorious from every struggle, was now to be defeated?' The image of the lion seems to have pervaded the imagination of everyone in the family: at the end, Swarup says, 'when the rest of us collapsed, it was she who stood up a lioness worthy of the mate she had lost. She accompanied Gandhi to the Shamshan* – a thing not normally done among us. She was quiet and dry-eyed and as the body of her husband was placed upon the gigantic sandalwood pyre, the erect little figure walked round the pyre three times and after a deep obeisance to her beloved departed, she returned to her place by Gandhiji's side ... '

Sarup Rani's life then became utterly desolate. Jawaharlal, Kamala, and Indira were all away: Vijayalakshmi and Betty were married. Betty's wedding, in 1933, was described by the bride. 'Though she was far from well in that autumn of 1933, Kamala took enormous pains with my trousseau and saw to all the details of the

* The cremation ground.

wedding. The one thing that upset her was that her family had very little money left. Nearly all her jewellery, and mother's too, had been sold; there was not much left for me. But still she gave me part of what little jewellery she still had; and mother gave me a little of hers. It was Kamala more than anyone else who made the wedding a gay and happy occasion.' Kamala, meanwhile, suffered from fainting and a feeling of suffocation. She coughed, delicately, all the time. The doctors advised Jawaharlal that she ought to be moved to the hills, to a sanatorium at a place called Bhowali. While all these matters were being discussed, Indira, who had by this time, at the age of seventeen, been to about nine different schools all over India and Switzerland, had become interested in a young man called Feroze Gandhi.

India has always been peculiar in its ability to assimilate people. The Hindu and Muslim cultures intermixed for years. Ships from Palestine, wrecked on the coasts of Western India, disgorged numbers of Jews, who were accepted by local people, and formed a community known as the B'nai Israel. Buddhism, the main religion in India before the organisation of Hinduism, was still prevalent, though most of its devotees had either moved to the north or across the narrow sea to Ceylon. There were also Jains, a sect so dedicated to the preservation of all life that the more devout wore (and still wear) a sort of gauze veil over their mouths and nostrils, to prevent small, errant insects from entering these orifices and dying. The Sikhs turbaned, bangled, bearded, were a religious sect which basically arose out of a fusion of Hindu and Muslim cultures. They were the opposite of the Jains, ferocious in the extreme, wont to sudden fits of berserk fury, like the Vikings they resemble physically, tall, bearded, and, in their early days, carrying amulets and swords into battle. The earliest inhabitants of the country, tribes now crouched amidst forested hills, were animists and remain so. One of the last religions to enter India was Zoroastrianism, whose devotees were driven from Persia by the Muslims in the eighth century A.D.

The Zoroastrians worshipped fire. While the Hindus cremated their dead, and the Muslims buried theirs, the newcomers from Persia exposed the corpses of their people to the elements. Sun, rain, wind and air were supposed to consume them, perhaps through some primitive idea of maintaining an ecological balance: in any event, what usually consumed the Zoroastrian dead were hawks, vultures and rats. These Persians were shrewd, not always scrupulous, businessmen. Their original language was Farsi, the language of the Persians: Indians on the western coast of India, where most of these migrants settled, pronounce F as PH: hence, when they speak English, the word *father* for example, becomes *phather*: also Farsi became Parsi. The Parsis found an opportunity for financial advancement on the arrival of the British in India. They were more willing to trade with foreigners, and also whiter (one typical physical trait of the Parsi is his pallid, sometimes almost albino skin) than the normal Hindu or Muslim of the western coast. They were the first inhabitants of India to play cricket, perhaps not so much because they liked it as because their playing it ingratiated them with the British, who, lost children under a strange sun, had nobody else to play with. Until about the 1950s the Parsis were probably the wealthiest community in India. The higher echelons owned airlines and industries: many aged and lunatic Parsis (as a race they suffer from inbreeding) had been knighted by the British: the lower echelons maintained what are known as Irani restaurants, especially in Bombay, where they still exist: restaurants which serve very cheap food, very sweet tea, and undrinkable coffee, and which also sell cigarettes either by the packet or one at a time, and sometimes commodities like sugar and canned foods.

Since the British found Persian names as unpronounceable as Hindu or Muslim names, the Parsis, born migrants, adapted themselves. Some named themselves after the professions they pursued. Thus there were Parsis who were called Mistri (carpenter in Hindi), and Parsis who were called, like two recent Indian cricketers, Contractor and Engineer, and even, though admittedly this is a somewhat exceptional case, Parsis who were called Sodawater-bottlewalla. This was not universal among the community, however. Some Parsis made their homes in the western state of Gujarat, and most now speak the Gujarati language, which is in fact their *lingua franca*. These particular Parsis have adopted Gujarati names, such as Gandhi. Feroze was unrelated to the Mahatma, and, given their respective upbringings, could never have been. Nevertheless I have found it a popular fallacy in the West, particularly in America, to think of Indira as the wife or daughter of Mahatma Gandhi, and not to do with Jawaharlal Nehru at all.

By 1931 Kamala was receptive to all sorts of influences. The prescience of death had probably been upon her for some years. In 1928 Jawaharlal had taken her to Benares which he had to visit for some political reason, where she met a person called Swami* Sivananda, by whom she was much impressed: three years later she was in Calcutta for treatment, and from there, visited the Swami in Belur. By this time the Swami was seventy-eight, and too ill to meet her: she was received by another Swami, a disciple of Sivananda's. Kamala 'desired to be initiated into spiritual life'. The disciple, Swami Abhayananda, apparently persuaded Sivananda to perform this ceremony 'which ... a very simple one, lasted half an hour, it consisted of the *guru* giving the disciple a mantra† and other instruction pertaining to spiritual life and secondly in dedicating her life and soul at the feet of the Lord.' Kamala asked that her initiation be kept a secret from the rest of the family. Indira says that at about the same time Kamala became a devotee of Anandamayi Mai, a spiritualist or religious figure, of whom Indira herself is still a follower. But at the time when Kamala was dying, she told Indira that 'it was important to get educated ... to stick to principles ... ' and, really another paradox, an Indian paradox, does education as understood by Indira's father, a socialist Western education, and the education in the mind of her mother, with her reliance upon what might be called 'spiritual figures'—does that mean the same kind of education? If education is supposed to be a continuous process, Indira, shuffled from school to school over the years, cannot have been all that educated when she first met Feroze. In fact, of the family, it was Kamala who first met him.

---

* A Swami is supposed, in India, to be a sort of saint.
† A *mantra* is a Sanskrit incantation.

❧ 5 ❧

Feroze and the Family

AT SOME POINT at the end of the 1920s or the start of the 1930s, Kamala, with a number of other volunteers, was picketing a college in Allahabad. It was a college for young men, a number of whom were seated on the outer wall, laughing at the Congress workers. The day was sultry and unpleasant: after a while Kamala's stamina, faltering anyway, failed her: she collapsed on the pavement in a faint. The laughter on the wall stopped suddenly. One of the young men seated there, in fact the leader, leapt down to help Kamala. He fetched her water, and later took her back to Anand Bhavan. He was a stocky boy with a ruddy complexion, who was often mistaken for an Englishman, but he was actually a Parsi and his name was Feroze Gandhi. After that first day, he was a constant visitor to Anand Bhavan, where he was befriended by Jawaharlal and by Indira. His provenance was very different from that of the Nehrus. He was from the lower middle class, the son of an officer in the merchant navy, and had been born in Bombay in September 1912. His parents lived in a Parsi colony in Khetwadi, a ramshackle part of the city, but when Feroze was a little over two years old, the elder Gandhi sent his wife and children to live with his sister, Mrs Commissariat (another classical example of a Parsi name) in Allahabad. There Feroze grew up. He was a bright boy, skilful with his hands and interested in the world around him, though he was possessed of a somewhat perverse sense of humour which expressed itself not only at the expense of his peers but the expense of his schoolmasters. He placed live frogs and pigeons in their desks and set fireworks off under their chairs. It is remarkable, in view of these activities, that he remained not only unexpelled but popular.

When he first met the Nehrus, he was eighteen or nineteen, an age at which young men tend to be attracted to women older than themselves, and there is no doubt that he was attracted to Kamala, though he may not have himself been aware of this. Indira, in her very early teens, shy and very frail (until she was twenty, she never weighed more than a little over 5 stone), seems to have been treated by him, initially, as a sort of younger sister: but his attitude towards Kamala was romantic in the troubadour sense. He wished to serve her as much as he could without recompense: and towards Jawaharlal he felt awe and reverence. He started to become politically involved, to volunteer for picket duties and to court arrest. This alarmed his family, and his mother went to see Gandhi to ask him to advise Feroze to continue his studies and abandon his political activities.

Gandhi was all for maternal love, but in this case, though benevolent, he was also adamant. 'Sister,' he is supposed to have said, 'come back and tell me any harm comes to your son. If I had seven boys like Feroze working for me, I could win independence in seven days. In the India of the future nobody will ask if he had a B.A. or an M.A.: they will ask how many times your son was imprisoned for his nationalist activities.' This was rather cold comfort for the lady, and some time in 1931 Feroze was sentenced to a year of imprisonment. He was put into Faizabad prison, which at that period was full of nationalist leaders. This, incidentally, was a tactical error on the part of the British. Since the nationalists were normally in the same prison, they were able to talk to one another and determine policies for the future. Separated, they could not have done so. Feroze became something of a leader to the young political prisoners: he initiated protests and fasts, and in fact made himself a thorough nuisance to his gaolers. He emerged, eventually, from prison, to find Kamala much worse in health and Indira nearly a young woman. He himself had by this time passed the age of being attracted to older women, but he remained devoted, almost filially, to Kamala.

Between 1931 and 1935 Jawaharlal was constantly in prison: in fact he spent only six months out of it. During this time Kamala's condition deteriorated so much that she had to be rushed to Bombay, then to Calcutta, for treatment. In 1932, the year after Motilal's death, his widow, hitherto an orthodox and pacific Hindu woman, became active in the nationalist movement. During the course of her activities, while accompanying a procession in Allahabad, she was knocked down and repeatedly struck on the head in a police charge. She was an old woman, and had always been delicate, but luckily she was not badly hurt. Generally speaking, however, the physical condition of the family in the early 1930s was not very good, to say the least. In 1933 came a new development: Feroze proposed to Indira, who refused him. 'I thought I was too young,' she now says. 'And I wanted to continue my political work.' Though still at school, she picketed shops and took part in processions. 'I had lots of proposals. None of them was for an arranged marriage: I couldn't have stood a man who wanted an arranged marriage.'

Jawaharlal was anxious, moreover, that she pursued her studies: he was unsure that Feroze, who had no income as such, was the ideal husband for his daughter: he may also have had a sense of possessiveness about her. She was, at the time of the proposal, at a small school in Poona, not far from Bombay, the metropolis and seaport on the western coast of India. A Mrs Vakil, who ran this establishment, says that Indira 'willingly did her share of household chores and took a hand at keeping the school and the residential part of it clean and tidy. She helped look after the younger children and also took a hand in the school's cultural activities as well as in debating.' In 1933 she matriculated from this school and was sent to university at a place called Santiniketan, 'the abode of peace', which was near Calcutta and some distance away from Feroze. This was, and is, an extraordinary institution.

It was thought up, and founded, by the poet Rabindranath Tagore. Tagore, whose translated works still have a following, was consciously a Poet: he wore, in addition to flowing robes, a long white beard. His brow, like Shelley's, was high, so, like Shelley's, was his voice. Apart from his production of poems, plays, novels, short stories, essays and reviews, he drew and painted, composed music, had a fairly comprehensive knowledge of modern science, and supported the nationalist movement: in fact, he was the twentieth-century Bengali equivalent of a Renaissance man. His poems, much admired in translation by Yeats and even Pound, now seem slushy in English, but in Bengali are still greatly revered by contemporary poets in that language.

Tagore, like a Renaissance man, thought and theorised about every conceivable topic, including education. His concept for education in India was for schools and colleges based on the ancient Indian traditions. Lessons were to be delivered in the open air, near flowing water, under shady trees. Not only would these lessons encompass the normal school curriculae, but the arts, music, and handicrafts: Santiniketan, in his original concept, was to have been a centre for the manufacture of other Renaissance men and women. If it did not quite work out like that, the fault was probably not Tagore's, but lay in the raw material from which he hoped to build.

While Indira was in Santiniketan, Feroze was moping in Allahabad and Jawaharlal was sitting distractedly in prison, Kamala, whose main comfort was probably Feroze, had a severe attack of pleurisy. Her temperature hurtled upward and she found it hard to breathe. Jawaharlal was transferred by the British from the gaol at Dehra Dun, north of Delhi, to the one at Allahabad. On the way there, he was met at a railway station by a British official, who told him that Kamala's condition was critical and that the government was ready to release him on parole. Jawaharlal and the Englishman walked up and down the platform together, discussing this proposal: it was night, and July, the weather hot, cooking-fires smouldering and smoking in the little wayside halt. Jawaharlal said that he would not accept parole: he did not want to make any promises to the government. The officer, obviously born to be a diplomat, replied that if Jawaharlal did not want to make commitments to the British, that was fine: but, considering Kamala's condition, would he make a promise to him personally? Jawaharlal agreed to this, and on his arrival in Allahabad, he was paroled for eleven days, during which Kamala's health improved. It deteriorated once more when he returned to prison. The government offered to release him if he promised not to be politically active: he refused.

The doctors now advised that Kamala should be moved to a sanatorium in the hills at a place known as Bhowali. The arrangements were made. One of her attendant physicians, Dr Atal, an uncle of hers, offered to accompany her there. It was Feroze who, in Jawaharlal's absence, arranged the logistics: Indira, back in Allahabad, who packed. Three servants, including a cook, went on this trip, and Kamala was installed in the sanatorium, where her condition failed to improve. Bhowali was a fair way from Allahabad, and a difficult place to reach, involving numerous train connections and, towards the end of the trip, switches to car transport. Nevertheless Feroze, in the months that followed, travelled to and from Bhowali constantly, to see what he could do to help. It was a long time since he had sat on his college wall and laughed, with his friends, at a sick woman. Though Jawaharlal was still in prison,

Indira came when she could, and letters from the Swamis who had initiated Kamala into 'spiritual life' seemed to comfort her.

In May 1935, Kamala wrote to Abhayananda: 'I have full confidence in your assurance that Lord Krishna* will appear to me, but I wish to see him soon. At times I feel that I myself am Krishna. It has now become a practice with me to offer him whatever I think or do ... I feel the presence of God, only I cannot see and touch him. I do not know when I will be able to place my head at His feet. If only he could appear to me ... ' What the agnostic Jawaharlal thought of all this is not known, but one deeply doubts that he could have approved.

Bhowali did not help Kamala. It was decided by the doctors that as a last hope she could return to Europe for treatment. At about this time, in 1935, Mrs Commissariat, who had shared, in common with the rest of the family, a disapproval of Feroze's political activities, decided to embark on a last attempt at dissuasion. She would pay, she said, for his education in London. This, from her point of view, served a dual purpose. Not only would it complete Feroze's education and increase his earning potential, but it would safely remove him from the theatre of political activity and the danger of prison. She did not realise why Feroze took so readily to this proposal. It was because he had been informed that Kamala and Indira were to leave for Europe in May 1935. He fully intended to be there with them, and this seemed the easiest way. He did not actually accompany them on the journey: Dr Madan Atal, who had attended Kamala through her illness and taken her to Bhowali, did this. Feroze went to the London School of Economics, and from London travelled frequently to Europe to help Kamala, who had been installed at a sanatorium in Badenweiler, and presumably to court Indira, who was at a school in a place called Chezières, which she hated because, she says, 'a horrible woman ran it.' Jawaharlal was still in prison, and Kamala, lonely most of the time, became worse and worse. In September 1935 Jawaharlal was released and instantly flew to Badenweiler. He stayed there through the slush and rime of a hard winter, visiting Kamala for some hours every day. They talked quietly, of the past and sometimes of the future that it was now clearly evident they would not share. He read to her,

---

* The Hindu deity who descended on earth and lived among men, who could crudely be called the Indian equivalent of Christ, except that Krishna seems to have had a happy and far from celibate life.

and energy seemed to flare back into her. But it was a false dawn. She was moved to a sanatorium near Lausanne, and Indira to her old school at Bex, a considerable relief after Chezières. The improvement in Kamala's condition did not continue, and by February she was too ill to sit up in bed or write.

Her doctors told Nehru that it would only be a matter of time before her exhausted system failed completely. He had to stay with her: at the same time he could not detach himself completely from politics. He had to return to India. He was torn between his wife and his country, a terrible period in his life: he also had Indira, shortly to be motherless, to worry about. He decided to return to India, booked his passage, and planned to leave Lausanne on February 28 1936. Kamala said nothing, but seemed distressed at this. She had never wanted to be a trouble to her husband, but she must have known that she would probably die soon, without him. As the 28th approached and she flagged rapidly the doctors advised Nehru to postpone his departure, which he did. The departure that day was made, not by him, but by Kamala.

In the early hours of the morning, Kamala drifted from sleep into the death she had desired. She had been in considerable pain for several days, but she died peacefully. Jawaharlal and Dr Atal were by her bedside: Indira was in the hospital, but in another room. The light husk of the body was reduced, in Lausanne, to ashes which Jawaharlal carried back to India. Before he left, he took Indira to Montreux for a while, to soothe her (and himself) out of their initial sorrow. Then Indira returned to school at Bex. Her loneliness was almost complete: her father had flown away, and her mother, whose ashes had flown with him, had left no physical trace of herself behind. Feroze came when he could, and she had some friends in the school, but she must have had empty days to fill with memories and reflections, being by nature introspective. She had been close to her mother, closer, indeed than to anyone else, with her father so often away. She had watched while her mother was hurt by relatives at home: more recently she had watched Kamala endure her physical calvary. She had been hurt when her mother was hurt: she had suffered when her mother suffered. After Kamala's death, Indira withdrew, with a few exceptions, from close personal relationships: perhaps because she did not want to be badly hurt once more. She had always been shy, but her shyness was to harden into an aloofness and remoteness of manner which often prevented her from showing warmth to others.

In London, Feroze saw a lot of V. K. Krishna Menon, a South Indian lawyer who had lived in England for more than a decade. A gaunt, dark, tallish man with a bony and saturnine face (his enemies described it as satanic) he lived mainly on tea and biscuits. He permitted himself the luxury, at widely spaced intervals, of a grilled tomato or a teashop bun. Though he had a legal practice, most of his time (night and day were all one to him, since he seldom slept) was spent in operating the India League, an organisation of nationalistically minded Indians who lived in Britain and ran a newspaper. He was fond of children, but adults had to bear the unpredictable whiplash of his not infrequent wrath. He was very arrogant, but could be very kind. Along with Nehru he was the most complicated and psychologically fascinating of the Indians involved in the movement for independence.

The importance of Krishna Menon to Indian politics was that he was the only figure of any stature to operate, not out of India, but from the hub and heart of the British Empire, and that he was a permanent fixture in London. He collected around him an aviary of bright young men, but most of these were students who eventually took wing for India: Krishna Menon remained, usually in extreme poverty, sipping at teacups, crunching biscuits, and haranguing every unwary visitor to his office. Feroze was soon involved in Menon's activities. When Indira arrived in England to go up to Oxford, Feroze introduced her to Menon, and very shortly she was involved as well. The death of Kamala was still deeply imprinted on both their minds. The result was obviously that they were thrown together by a common interest. A common interest is often the cause of a hopeless marriage, since opposites usually attract each other, but Feroze and Indira were often seen around together, as the first, least formidable decade of Hitler neared its climax.

An extremely grumpy old lawyer called Mulla, in Allahabad, watched me closely as the rain fell around his thicketed house. He had known Feroze and the Nehrus for what to me seemed like centuries: for him, I suppose, in terms of centuries, like twenty minutes. He was thin, angry like most old people about everyone not old, furious about anyone who did not share his own opinions and generally very opinionated. He was rich, like other lawyers in Allahabad: his hands twitched over his teacup: withered, they reached out for the sweets, sticky and sad, that lay on plates, unmistakably Indian sweets, besides thinly cut English sandwiches: wilted at the corners, they were sad too, and lonely: servants with steady hands showered the teacups with streams of golden liquids, white liquids, and sugar.

'One Dr Sen', he said, as the servant handed out the sandwiches and sweets, 'ran a bookshop in Bloomsbury called the Bibliophile. He was engaged in Indian nationalist activities and had to leave Britain ... I had known the family in Allahabad ... I mean the Nehrus. All the Indian students collected at this bookshop to buy books and hear small anecdotes. Feroze used to come there with Indira. She used to keep very quiet. To bring her out was a problem. He, of course, talked a lot. I knew him very well.'

According to Mr Mulla, Feroze used to share his flat, but was not too desirable a flatmate. 'I used to live,' he said, and spat the address out, 'at 23, Queensgate Gardens in Kensington: Feroze shared my flat. When the bombing started, I shared a room with him at the Strand Palace Hotel. He never paid his share of the rent. He never paid his accounts. Even his thinking was borrowed. I don't think he was at all educated.' He made a small gesture, and his servants plied me with more sweets and sandwiches. Speaking about Feroze's relationship with Mrs Gandhi, he said, 'They did not appear to be engaged. She was always morose in her appearance.'

Certainly, the silence of Indira, and the talkativeness of Feroze, the isolation of the young woman and the desire of the young man to communicate and socialise, were hardly a basis for a shared relationship. Between them, however, the ghost of Kamala hovered: this ghost, with intangible hands, drew them together. It is said that Kamala, a few days before she died, had expressed a wish that Indira should marry Feroze, though to whom she expressed this wish has not been recorded. To her Feroze had become the son she had never borne. It was gratitude and loneliness as much as anything that attracted Indira to Feroze. Her career at Oxford does not appear to have been very colourful: she was studying P.P.E., a dull course unless you are specially interested, which she apparently was not: but the grey stones and wrinkled trees of the University

town appealed to her. She liked to walk, but unlike most under-
graduates, male and female, possessed no bicycle. I suppose that
manoeuvring a bicycle and a sari simultaneously must be nearly
impossible. For she now always wore a sari: it stamped her as
Indian, though her colouring and features did not, and she wanted
people to know she was Indian.

Her London life was possibly of more interest to her. There was
Feroze to squire her around, people like Krishna Menon, and his
cohorts the novelist Iqbal Singh and K. S. Shelvankar (who, years
later, when she was Prime Minister, she appointed Ambassador to
Hanoi), to meet, the Bibliophile and Shafi's, an Indian restaurant,
to visit. She did not live more exotically or much more differently
from other Indian students except for two factors. One was that she
was a woman, and there were very few saris swished around in the
English universities at that time: the other was that she was the
daughter of Jawaharlal Nehru, which opened doors to her. She met
Harold Laski and Fenner Brockway, though she does not remember
what she said to them or they to her. Though she is somewhat
unclear, indeed opaque, about these years, the likelihood is that her
commitment to Indian nationalism was emotional rather than
intellectual, and that these particular interviews were in the nature of
kindly smiles bestowed, through her, upon her father. Nehru was
frequently in the news, as was Gandhi, and for the liberals in
Britain they were, in a sense, folk heroes. Many of these liberals
rather resembled Kipling's M.P., Paget, in that they did not know
what they were talking about, but there were people who were
knowledgeable about India, intelligent, and capable of action, and
these seem to have been the people Indira mostly met. What
impression she made upon Brockway or Laski one does not know,
since they did not write about it, but at about this time the widow
of the German writer Ernst Toller sent a letter to Nehru in which
she told him of meeting his daughter. She informed him, Teutoni-
cally and, to a proud father, redundantly, that Indira was beautiful.
'She is like a little flower,' wrote Frau Toller, 'which bends in the
wind ... but I think she will not break ... '

This is the most interesting comment made about Indira in her
youth. It suggests two things (Frau Toller, having lived with a poet,
was obviously used to analysing complex and difficult personalities),
one, that Indira was quiet, shy, and open to influence: two, that
Frau Toller sensed that the stem of the little flower was made of

highly tensile and resistant materials. It would have to be, for an only child not to have crumpled up completely under the destructive blasts of wind which had deprived her of family life and the companionship of her parents.

Hitler roared in Berlin: Mussolini thundered in Rome: Chamberlain squeaked in London, and the world shook under their combined, if various, noises. The Jews of Europe were already in a state of siege. The British Empire maintained itself sombrely but proudly, until Chamberlain, twirling his magical umbrella around at Munich, sent the world plunging into war. Nehru, no friend of the Fascists since his trip to Spain during the Civil War, and intellectually no friend of theirs anyway, saw the approach of a war that would dwarf all previous wars. He therefore began to wonder what would happen to his daughter in England, which would obviously be the main target for Fascist attack, and whether he should not bring her back to India. Despite the Japanese threat from the east, of which he was aware, he thought India would not be endangered. The Japanese were already bellowing about their plans to liberate Asia: Subhas Bose, a chubby, bespectacled Bengali, voluble and thus typical of his race, was already thinking of some kind of Indian coalition with the Japanese which would drive the British out of India. Nehru, however, regarded the Japanese as part of the Fascist Club, and he wrinkled a delicate nostril at the idea. The Japanese had made no war plans, and he did not trust Fascists. Gandhi whispered to him: Indian independence could not and would not be achieved by violence. India would be safe.

In Oxford the young intellectuals who, in 1933, had voted in the Union that they would not fight, under any circumstances, for their King and Country, were girding themselves for war. The elderly tried gasmasks on, their already gnomish aspect becoming ghoulish, to serve in the Home Guard. On September 3 1939 war was declared. At first it was a phoney war, the Axis did not spin, being busy with the transportation of innocent Jews and the gypsies who had once provided pleasure to children, to camps where most of them would die: the Germans were planning the *blitzkreig* upon London which would force the British to their knees. Before the air attack began, in 1940, Indira, summoned by her father, left by ship for India. Because of the war, she had to sail by way of South Africa. She arrived at Capetown: the local Indian merchants, obsequious not only to the South Africans but to the daughter of Jawaharlal Nehru, of whom, in a vague way, word had been heard by the rich Sindhi* shopkeepers, invited her to speak to an audience of Indians. She spoke: a small figure, made smaller by the large platform she stood on. Jawaharlal would have been astonished by her attitude; Feroze who knew her real character more closely (though they were not yet married) perhaps less astonished, but astonished none the less. She told the rich Indians, to reduce it to a phrase she did not use but which was the main point of her speech, that they were bastards: that while salting away money in South Africa, they not only did not help the nationalist movement in India, but they did not help the beaten African tribes, now abused by British and Boers alike, whom Gandhi had once tried to assist. Then she left. The Sindhi merchants were surprised.

As the first bombs dropped on to London, heard in the Strand Palace by Feroze, where he was presumably glowered at by Mr Mulla from the opposite bed, Indira reached the India she was to hold, in the tradition of the Moguls, courtiered and bowed at, for many years. This time was still far away. She was twenty-three. Her father and she met. Shortly after the bombs started to fall, Feroze left London for Allahabad, where Indira was. Here he continued to reside with his family.

I spoke to an aunt of his, Rhoda Gandhi, who now runs a small hotel in Allahabad. After Feroze's return from London, he stayed with her. She is an elderly, talkative woman whom I interviewed on the balcony of her hotel, facing a garden full of trees. 'Feroze put up a lovely garden, full of roses,' she said, 'when he came home. He was very good at that kind of thing.' Her voice was by no means soft, but she seemed a kind lady, and anxious to convey her impressions of her nephew to me. 'He was not a big eater,' she said to me, and though this information seemed to me irrelevant as regarded the character of Feroze, she continued in the same vein. 'He was', she informed me, 'a very clean and precise eater. He particularly loved to eat eggs.' She paused: rain dripped from the eaves of the

* Not only in South Africa, but in most of the habitable world, there are Indian merchants from, for some reason, the northwestern part of the country, who milk whichever people they serve for whatever money or produce they have, who lend money at exorbitant rates of interest, and who generally do not improve the Indian image anywhere. These people are normally from the areas of Sind, now in Pakistan, Gujarat, and particularly in Rajasthan, from which Indian state ooze the moneylenders and merchants called Marwaris.

hotel. 'Once, after he came back from London,' she said, 'when I was pregnant, he used to make a habit of coming home late at night and waking me up. "Come on," he would say, "get up, make me some eggs." I felt,' said Mrs Rhoda Gandhi concluding this saga, 'like bashing in his head.' Through this dietary story, I began to form an impression of Feroze: she had tears in her eyes: I had not.

What Jawaharlal thought of Feroze at this time is hard to determine. When Feroze was in Europe they corresponded frequently, though despite the affectionate term of address and salutation, the content of the letters was somewhat formal on both sides, and particularly on Jawaharlal's. Feroze, for example, wrote to him from Switzerland, enthusiastically describing a series of photographs which he had taken of Indira. He then sent the photographs to Allahabad. Jawaharlal replied '*If* you have taken these photographs, I must congratulate you.' To a bouncy young man, this sort of answer could not have been more deflatory. Jawaharlal was obviously grateful to Feroze for his caretakership of Kamala, but Feroze's courtiership of Indira did not appeal to Nehru. 'I don't think he liked it at all,' Mrs Rhoda Gandhi told me. She paused, eyed a gluey lizard on the ceiling, and amended her statement. 'At first,' she said.

How long 'at first' was is debatable. Feroze had known Indira since 1931. By the time they were both back from England, they were obviously in continual close contact, for they both lived in Allahabad, and Allahabad was by no means an enormous city. The Congress workers there bumped into one another all the time, and Feroze and Indira were both Congress workers. In pickets, in processions, in rallies they must constantly have encountered each other. Jawaharlal was usually away from the house, and was perhaps not entirely aware (or perhaps interested) in the solidifying of the relationship between his daughter and Feroze. Indira, as she had been and was to be throughout her life, had nobody to talk to, nobody to communicate with, except Feroze himself. They grew to be closer and closer.

In 1941 Feroze was offered a post by the *Times of India*, a newspaper owned by a British concern, and working out of Bombay. He refused this offer on nationalist grounds, but, rather strangely, wrote articles for it and its associate publications under a pen name. At some point in 1941, Indira told her father she wanted to marry

Feroze. Her father started, in the hesitant way that was typically his, to pick over the points, the pros and cons, relevant to the wedding. The pros were Feroze's long connection with the family, his long attachment to Indira, his long dedication to the nationalist cause. The cons were that he was Parsi, not Kashmiri Brahmin, that he came from a completely different background, and that he was poor. Nehru peered at the cons, and decided that, since another member of the family, still alive in Allahabad today, and now Mrs S. K. Khan, the widow of a Muslim police officer, had done it already, there was not an awful lot of harm in Indu, the affectionate name for Indira, marrying a person outside the caste. But he could not overcome the fact that Feroze was poor.

Nehru, throughout his life, relied on people as props. He himself was usually wholly indecisive. He never made any firm decision unless it was backed by others. In his very early years he had the crutch of Motilal to support him. Then it became Gandhi. These were his two great crutches, to take him through to independence, when he started to lean heavily upon people like Maulana Abdul Kalam Azad,* upon his private secretaries, and, as we shall later see, upon Indira. If, in 1941 or 1942, Feroze was not exactly a main crutch, Feroze was one of the many little stilts supporting Nehru's main crutches and when a small element falls from a large frame, the frame itself tends to fall. Indira had demonstrated some stubbornness about her marriage: if Feroze unhooked himself from Nehru's propping mechanism, it was likely that it would slip in the mire of Indian politics. By this time there was an open fight between the Congress and the elegant, precise leader of the Muslim League, Mohammed Ali Jinnah. Jawaharlal said Yes.

Mr Jinnah did not like Indians. Mr Jinnah, quite apparently, did not even like the Muslim Indians, largely smelly, fezzed or turbaned, and talkative, which he was not, apart from a few well chosen words to a chosen few. Nevertheless, he was their representative, and he had broken his party away from the Congress. Nehru and he and the English were talking: Bose was off, having escaped from India to Germany, thence to Japan. When in 1941 the lethargic American personnel in Pearl Harbor discovered that American ships were burning in the bay after an onslaught of midget Nipponese planes,

* A Muslim scholar and political leader allied to the Congress.

Roosevelt, who had wanted for some time to do so, declared war on Germany, Italy and Japan.

Many of the troops in the East were Indian: it is not untrue to say that most of them, the little Gurkhas, happy with their *kukris* in night warfare in the forests of Burma and Thailand, the tall Sikhs, shouting their warcry as they swept down on the foe on open plains, were used as cannon fodder by the British, to be killed before the old English and Scottish regiments came behind, to be destroyed in their turn by tiny yellow people growing like tropical fruit in trees. In Singapore, when that famous fortress fell, with its great guns pointed seaward while the Japanese rode up on bicycles from the mainland, Bose appeared.

The captured Indian troops were either made to become members of Bose's Indian National Army, a Japanese organisation which he had founded to fight the Allies, or were executed in many terrible ways, the worst of which was being flayed alive. Bose died in the end: in an aircrash on Taiwan: an aircrash probably manufactured by the Japanese, who had found his use to them was over, since most of the captured Indians, told to fight the British whose salt they had eaten,* fought badly and got themselves recaptured as rapidly as they could. Nehru, a peaceful person, and Jinnah, a man careful to keep his shirts clean and his suits pressed, meanwhile stayed in India, talked to British Viceroys, themselves in unrumpled uniforms, most of them military men, and the words were unconnected with all the jungle deaths and sweat going on a few hundred miles off, in the terrible thickets and scrubby plains of Burma.

Nehru absented himself awhile, to attend the wedding of his only child. There was a kind of unreality about the Second World War in Asia, as contrasted with the independence movement in India. At one point Gandhi stated that if Japanese or British tanks were to roll down the Indian streets, the entire population should lie down in their way to stop their passage. The difference he never seemed to understand was that the British tanks, confronted with masses of inert but living bodies, would probably have stopped: the Japanese tanks would certainly not have done so. Nehru's concern with words, with a war crucial to the world raging around him, drew to a halt while he wove, on his personal handloom, a pink cotton sari for his daughter to wear at her wedding. There was one more problem, apart from the clothing of Indira: in what way

* See above, p. 23.

should she be married? Feroze was a Parsi, Indira a Hindu: apart from the register office, there was no way, and the register office was anathema to a family which considered itself aristocratic. Eventually it was decided that a ceremony of the same kind as was apparently performed at the time the Vedas, the Sanskrit scriptures, were written, would do: somebody had to design this ceremony: someone did. Tents, or 'shamianas' were erected on the lawns of Anand Bhavan.

On March 26 1942, with hundreds of Allahabad socialites and Congress workers present, a sacred flame was kindled in the main shamiana, a fire hazard probably, but nobody minded: Nehru brought his daughter into this tent, where Feroze and his people sat awaiting her. Nehru then placed her hand in Feroze's, giving his daughter up to her husband, and the couple walked, seven times, around the sacred fire. They then repeated marriage vows, unclasped hands, and rushed off to Kashmir for a honeymoon. They returned to enter into a married life which was much more of a fire hazard than the ceremony which had initiated them into it could have ever been. Nehru now had Feroze, a prop to support him: he also had Indira.

❧ 6 ❧

Prince Consort

BY 1942, THE year of the marriage, the Quit India movement had reached its peak. There seemed little doubt that the British, with most of Asia an ant-heap of Japanese, and jackboots stamping down the streets of nearly every European capital, would not be the rulers of India for very much longer: even if they were not evicted by the Axis powers, they were certain to be so financially crippled by the war as not to be able to afford colonies, which were expensive as well as profitable. The Congress, however, never ceased to remind them of this fact. I remember, from my childhood in Bombay, the QUIT INDIA slogans chalked or painted on every wall, on the red sides of the buses imported from London: I remember, under the barrage balloons that cluttered the city sky in case of Japanese air attack, surges of white-clad demonstrators roaring down the streets, clenched fists rising and falling like the batons of thousands of bandmasters to keep time to the onrush and recession of the shouted admonitions to the British, demanding that they leave. I remember harassed British policemen in khaki shorts trying to make Indian constables who were both somewhat timorous and somewhat in sympathy with the Congress, stand fast when the crowds collected in the roadways ahead, whitecapped waves that thundered on the barricades.

Had the British left India at this time the Japanese would probably have walked in, with dire consequences to people like Gandhi and Nehru. They would certainly have been liquidated, or would simply have disappeared, to provide a clear field for Bose to be set up as a puppet ruler, manipulated by yellow hands clever at imitating other people's artifacts, even including democracy. A man like Nehru must have known this: but the Quit India movement continued. There was a spirit, at the time, which must have been like that prevalent during the French revolution: 'Bliss was it in that dawn

to be alive, And to be young was very heaven'. Wordsworth, with
hindsight, recanted, but none of the Indians concerned in the civil
disobedience movement has ever done so. The dawn dazzled them,
and later the eyes of some of them saw very badly. One of those to
be dazzled was a Gujarati Congressman called Morarji Desai, a
man who physically resembled Cassius and spiritually Calvin. He
was to exert a considerable influence, undesired by her, upon the
future life of Indira.

Morarji Desai was, in 1942, a gaunt, austere man of forty-seven. He
had abandoned his civil service career in Bulsar, a small town on
the west coast, to work for the Congress. A highly ambitious, egocentric personality, with a smile that froze everyone who encountered it, he was already respected by the party leaders because
of his capacity for work, the prison spells he put in, and his adherence
to Gandhi's tenets. Indeed, he went some way beyond Gandhi. Not
only did he not drink or smoke, and tell others not to, not only did
he toil and spin, but he refused to follow modern medical methods.
It was rumoured that his fitness was due to the fact that he consumed
a lengthy draught of his own urine every morning: his kidneys, no
doubt, wryly remarking, every time this breakfast came down to
them, '*Déja vu*'. He was a man without humour, a man who did not
tolerate habits in others which he did not himself approve of. He
was not the kind of man you could laugh with: or indeed at. He
had not travelled: unlike the Nehrus, he disliked the social habits of
the British. He laboured under the impression that liquor and
tobacco had been introduced into India by the British in order to
corrupt the innocent indigenes: they had not: both were mentioned
as being lavishly consumed by not only heroes, but gods, in the
Sanskrit epics composed before Christ was more than a gleam in
the eye of an angel. He was the kind of man creative people dislike:
cold, critical, correct.

Feroze and Indira were, in a way, creative people, in that their
minds were open and they were alive in a true sense. They did not
inhabit a vacuum: they breathed the world, and the world came
alive to them. They lived in a small two-room flat in Tagore Town,
an area in the old part of Allahabad, where his hands tended roses
in the damp earth, and hers collected them and arranged them in
vases. 'It was so sweet,' says a surviving Allahabad aunt, 'to see her
when she came to Anand Bhavan—quite the little housewife, though

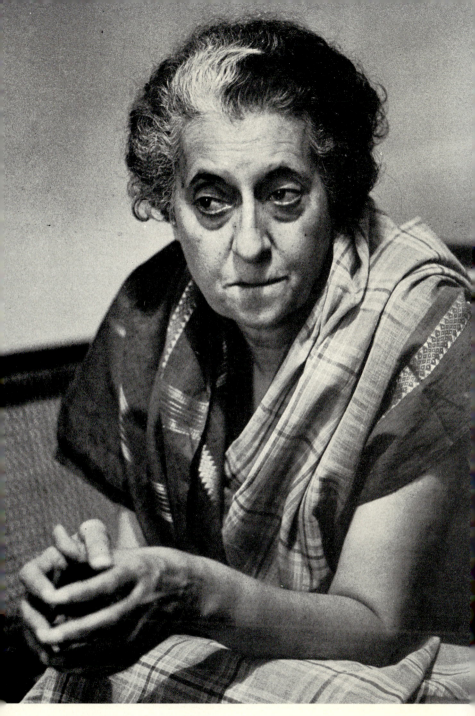

1   Mrs Gandhi after her 1977 defeat

2a Kamala and Jawaharlal Nehru
    with their young daughter

2b Indira before the family
    abandoned Western clothes

3 Anand Bhavan, where Indira spent her childhood

4 (a and b) (*left*) Motilal wearing Western-style clothes.
(*right*) as a nationalist Motilal adopted homespun *khadi*

5 Indira with Mahatma Gandhi

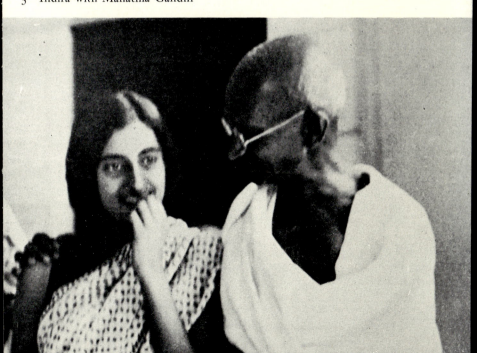

6 Indira and Feroze Gandhi at their wedding in 1942

she'd never been taught how to keep a house—with two bunches of keys pinned to her sari.' Mrs Gandhi, actually, has never learnt to cook, though according to the same aunt, 'Indu once told me, when she was married, "I can cook much better than you." ' A short while after her marriage the ability to cook became irrelevant for her: she was supplied with cooked food, by the British, in prison.

After the marriage Feroze decided not to involve himself in political marches. But Indira did. These marches and rallies were forbidden, but in August 1942 she addressed a rally in Allahabad while Feroze watched from a window above the street. A large number of policemen arrived and a British police sergeant threatened Indira with a revolver. At this Feroze hurtled down to try and protect his wife, the upshot of which was that they were both arrested, tried and imprisoned. Indira had become a member of the club. What apparently surprised people at the time who thought of her as sweet, shy and basically unadventurous, was the boldness with which she defied the order against public meetings and the stoicism with which she faced a British revolver.

Thirty-five years after this incident, Mrs Gandhi, in New Delhi, murmuring partly to her hands and partly to me, said, 'I have always been very quiet, and when I was younger people thought there was no fire in me. But this fire has always been there, only nobody saw it except when it flared. But it has always been there,' and she raised her head and looked at me with one of her more bewildering expressions, the large, hooded and strangely beautiful eyes defiant against denial, anger in them, but also posing a quizzical kind of question. The question would not have been asked by those eyes to many of those people with whom she dealt as Prime Minister: and, with the question unasked, and the eyes presenting their answer, I have never been surprised that so many people were afraid of her, and still are.

Indira used Feroze as a link with the Congress workers underground, passing on money and political literature. Feroze, indeed, did the mole act himself, persuaded his upper lip to produce a moustache, and clad himself in khaki. Because of his pallid skin, ruddy cheeks, the moustache, and his consequently English appearance, he evaded the police who were looking for him. On one occasion he slipped off from Allahabad to Lucknow to escape arrest: when he returned he

4

disembarked at a small wayside halt, feeling that he might be recognised at the station in Allahabad. He then found there was no transport available and eventually hitched a ride in a truck full of British soldiers, who were not only unsuspicious but so solicitous of his welfare that they tried to stop him from getting off the truck in Allahabad. The bloody natives, they said, would chop him to pieces. Feroze allayed their fears and disappeared into the dark, heading for home and Indira.

The Indian nationalists always had newspapers at their command. One of the first of these, entitled the *Independent*, first appeared in Allahabad in 1919. Motilal started it. It was edited by Syed Hussain, with assistance from the British writer, B. G. Horniman. Two days after the first issue appeared, one of those banquets Motilal was so fond of holding took place in Anand Bhavan to celebrate the event. The *Independent* recorded this occasion. Motilal apparently made a speech, in which he said that the purpose of the paper was 'to wage war against autocracy', though he did not say whose, and 'to think aloud for India'. This concept of a newspaper that talked was certainly something new in the history of the press. The *Independent* waxed fulsome on the events which followed Motilal's speech. 'The scene that followed,' it reports, 'was one of great enthusiasm; for the guests jolly rose to their feet and sang, "For They are Good Fellows" ... ' Whether the guests, jolly or not, were able to rise to their feet, the *Independent* reporter certainly rose to the occasion.

Unluckily the newspaper turned out to have nothing which could be called a fixed policy. It ran articles about 'The King Emperor's Activities in Wartime', alongside pieces called, 'Asthma—an Unfailing Cure', and 'Blood Poison—how to cure it'. For those less medically minded, or less interested in British royalty, there were pieces about racing, cricket, army horses, and the cinema. The advertisements often consisted largely of appeals from mesmerists, hypnotists, and astrologers, and some of the last sourly said, 'Beware of new astrologers'. It could scarcely be called a nationalist paper but it was certainly intended to be one. It ran a column called 'Th─ ─── Discourses', aptly named since the successive editors ─per folded in 1923 were nothing if not discursive, but ─ remarks on 'the agony and anger' of the *Independent*, ─ perceive where the agony and anger came in.

─, the *Independent* played a John the Baptist role for

other, more obviously nationalist publications to come. In 1919, the same year but a bit later, Gandhi started a magazine called *Young India* where he wrote on every imaginable faddist topic: prohibition, vegetarianism, the beauties of poverty. He also pilloried one of his sons for bad behaviour. In 1932 Gandhi also started a magazine called *The Harijan*, which was devoted to the uplift of the Indian untouchables or sweepers. Gandhi had renamed them Harijans, children of God. In 1938 Jawaharlal founded a newspaper called the *National Herald* in Lucknow. This was to play an important role in Indira's life.

The importance was in the sense that Feroze had no income apart from the very occasional articles he wrote. How the couple survived in the early years of their marriage is difficult to say, though it is likely that they were financed by their respective relatives. In 1944 Nehru decided that Feroze should be gainfully employed. He created an appointment for him on the editorial staff of his paper and sent the couple off to Lucknow. Considering the finances of the *National Herald*, it is probable that Feroze's employment was not very gainful: nevertheless, he was now an employed person and that was probably what Nehru wanted him to be.

On the other hand, Nehru was not himself a man who could live alone. Without a wife, he needed a daughter to look after him since it was not very proper, in the terms of the culture in which he lived against his will, for him to remarry. He therefore sent for Indira to come to Allahabad, every month. 'Obviously I had to do it,' Mrs Gandhi said to me in 1977, 'because my father was doing more important work than my husband.' She became a sort of housekeeper to Nehru as well as to Feroze.

So frequently a grass widower, it was little wonder that these months formed a winter of discontent for Feroze. It was also little wonder that his discontent turned to a degree of resentment. When, in 1944, Indira produced a son, who was named Rajiv, Feroze may have felt that she would spend more time at home in Lucknow. This did not prove to be the case. She continued to flutter to and fro between her husband and her father, and wherever she was, the child, naturally enough, was with her. This deepened and solidified the inchoate feelings of deprivation already within Feroze. It did not seem to him that Nehru really needed Indira, whereas he himself did, nor could it have seemed fair that having given his daughter away in marriage Nehru should so frequently, if only temporarily,

wish to reclaim her. Feroze had been gregarious always and he
became more so, not that Lucknow society offered many opportunities for a wild life. He solaced himself, like his boyhood idol Krishna
Menon, with a continuous stream of tea, and doubtless pondered
upon the future.

Nobody could conceivably have called Gandhi an extrovert, but he
was by no means a complete introvert. He looked outward at the
world much more than he looked inward at himself. He thought
and wrote incessantly, of course, about his own idiosyncratic and
individual beliefs, but his continual searchings of his own motives
and behaviour were undertaken as a species of spiritual exercise
rather than the expression of a deep interest in himself. It was
probably true to say that he searched himself in public so that other
people could find themselves in him. In this he showed himself to
be, however unique he was as an individual, a recurrent part of the
lengthy stream of Asian spiritual leaders, who investigated themselves and left their findings for disciples to decipher.

Nehru, however, was an introvert in the true sense: he looked into
himself because he found himself puzzling and of interest: if Gandhi
was typical of a certain kind of teacher, Nehru was typical of a
certain kind of poet. In 1936 he wrote and published, under a pen
name, an article about himself, which looked into and criticised
him. The article talked of his vanity, his autocratic behaviour, his
love of crowds, and remarked that he had in him the makings of a
dictator. Certainly he liked to have his own way, the case of Feroze
and Indira being an example, but he was assisted in this by the fact
that most people he knew complied with his wishes. In the years
before Indian independence there were only a handful of people
who dared to, or wanted to, criticise Nehru except Nehru himself.
Nehru was a prototype manufactured in England (though with parts
supplied by India), and had he been English he would be thought of
now as a liberal of the old school. Moreover, in England he would
have expected and accepted criticism. He was thought of in India
as a fiery revolutionary, not only, as was natural, by the British
from whom he wanted national independence, but by the older
Indian leaders, none of whom had heard British liberal opinions
expressed by an Indian before. He was offered little criticism, apart
from his own, and he therefore became slightly apart, a mind and
body enthroned upon his country, like the Moguls, though a greater

man than any of them were. His wilfulness and his sharp temper were therefore allowed full play through most of his life.

Feroze, his worshipper at the start of the relationship, resented these patterns of behaviour more and more. The pleasure Feroze took in his marriage became less and less. For Indira to rush to the side of her father in case of dire need was one thing: the situation that had been created, by his wife as well as by her father, was another. Even the child was rushed away to accompany his mother and grandfather on their trips together. This was a by no means understandable factor in the lives of the Feroze Gandhi family.

Desai was an extraordinary man: also a totally egocentric one. He agreed with much of what Gandhi said, but little with Nehru. A man for all seasons, he believed in Gandhi, but the man he worked under for much of his life, his back bowed under homespun cotton, a bent bridge of service, was Nehru: the woman he worked for, reluctantly and for a short time, was the daughter of Nehru. Indira was to break him, and then he, having rebuilt himself, was to break her. But in 1944 it was hardly conceivable that they would ever be political rivals: Desai was a solid, careful sort of man of whom nothing much was expected: a fossil compared with the stars that flared over the Indian sky, Gandhi, Nehru, Vallabhbhai Patel, Maulana Azad. Indira was, politically, nothing at that time, simply Nehru's daughter and Feroze's wife.

However, her watchful eyes, showing little, were perpetually upon her father as he moved within the Congress framework among people who were not always in agreement with his views, and as he went outside it to do battle with Jinnah, who, riddled with cancer, remained crisp, incisive and resolute in his demands for a Muslim state in the subcontinent. The British commissions that came and went in the last years of the war listened to everyone: they drew their own conclusions, one of which was that the creation of Pakistan was inevitable.

Indira may have been, in a sense, wedded to her father, but Feroze was still her husband. In 1946, the war over, independence on the horizon, and the last British viceroy, Lord Mountbatten, seated in the enormous palace built by Lutyens, now the residence of the President of India, she gave birth to a second son. He was named

Sanjay, and her future troubles were bound up not only with Desai but with him.

I had an extraordinary lunch, in 1975, in the palace where Mountbatten had once presided over the partition of India. The hostess was Mrs Gandhi, and the occasion was in honour of Prince Charles. In the garden of the presidential palace, filled with roses and trees, the guests lined up before lunch while Mrs Gandhi introduced the royal party to them. That is, she introduced Charles, and the Duke and Duchess of Gloucester, but for some reason she omitted to introduce Mountbatten. He wandered along behind the rest, explaining to everyone, 'My name is Mountbatten,' and, waving his hand around the lawns, 'and I had those trees planted.'

I had never previously met Mountbatten, but my father, who died in 1974, had, in Burma during the war, when he accused Mountbatten, then Commander-in-Chief of the Allied forces in Asia, of having used Indian troops as cannon fodder in attacks on the Japanese. There was apparently a rather acrimonious exchange of words, but when Mountbatten later became Viceroy, my father and he became friends. They came, in fact, to know each other fairly well.

I tell the story of this lunch because three people important in Indian politics revealed certain aspects of themselves to me during it. I was seated at a table with the Gloucesters and Y. B. Chavan, now leader of the Congress, amongst others. Since nobody appeared to have anything to say, the Duke started to talk, saying that if he had not been a Duke he would have liked to have been a photographer. He then described the equipment in his possession. There was then another short silence. Mr Chavan, a stout, brown, rather toadlike person, broke it. 'Oah,' he said, 'in my youth in Maharashtra I was famous for my photography. Particularly I was making pictures of weddings and funeral processions.' Another short silence: then the Duke, having already described his own Rolleiflexes and Nikons, said, 'How splendid. What cameras did you use?' Mr Chavan beamed proudly and replied, 'Oah, I was using only the best equipment. I was having one Baby Brownie.' The Duke did not reply. I looked at him: he was shaking all over, though it was hot in Delhi.

After lunch, the Gloucesters shot off. I needed to see Mrs Gandhi, so, as she was saying goodbye to Prince Charles, I hovered around.

The Prince having departed, I asked her for an appointment. 'Yes, yes,' she said. 'Tomorrow. Phone my secretary.' Her normally impassive face displayed some irritation. 'Where,' she asked, 'are the Gloucesters? Weren't you sitting with them?' I said yes, but I thought they had left. 'From which entrance?' inquired Mrs Gandhi. I said from the front (the Prince had left from the side entrance). 'Come with me,' said Mrs Gandhi abruptly. She then sprinted across the lawn towards the front entrance. Though I had become a sort of unofficial equerry at that moment, I could not match her speed. Panting behind her I heard her ask somebody where the Gloucesters were. This person said they had left. Mrs Gandhi turned back to me and she was obviously furious. 'They didn't even say goodbye,' she told me. 'Don't they know that I am the Prime Minister of India?'

The third somewhat revealing incident of the afternoon was that, while trying to catch my breath beside a rosebush, I found myself standing beside Lord Mountbatten, who was peering at the flowers with a rather Emsworthish expression. He glanced round, saw me, and smiled. 'Oh, Frank,' he said, 'nice to see you. I thought you were dead.' My father, who, had he been alive, would have been seventy, might have been pleased by this remark. I must confess that I certainly was not.

Nehru, for all his nationalism, loved the British and things British. Mountbatten may have had Greek blood but like the royal family, and indeed like myself, he was exceptionally British in his ways: the assimilation of foreigners used to be prevalent in England. Even today, in Delhi, there are hundreds of people, especially military personnel, who sprout R.A.F. whiskers, play cricket on Sundays, and, slapping each one painfully on the back, call their friends 'old boy'. Nehru, a sensitive man, did not go to these extremes, but he did not like his colleagues in the Congress, at least not as personal friends, and in Mountbatten and the viceregal family he found the kind of people he did like.

Mountbatten liked Nehru but was not all that keen on Jinnah. Jinnah, indeed, was not the kind of man people did like unless he liked them, and there were very few people to whom he had any personal attachment. He was, in a way, a Muslim Krishna Menon. There were even some physical resemblances: both tallish, very thin, high cheekboned, nervous, fanatic men, acerbic of temper, meticulous (in different ways) in their habits. Nevertheless, Mount-batten had apparently been told by his government that Pakistan had to be created. Whatever his own misgivings, or Nehru's, about this, and the huge factor of Gandhi being against the division of India, his friendship with Nehru led to independence — which involved partition — being expedited.

When Mountbatten decided to pull out in August 1947, the country was totally unprepared for the transition, much less for the partition. Jinnah had wanted a huge tract of the subcontinent, situated mainly in the northwest, to be Pakistan. What was even-tually agreed to between the British, the Congress leaders, and Jinnah (who *was*, basically, the Muslim League), was that a certain tract of land from the borders of Kashmir in the northwest to roughly halfway down the western coast, plus the whole of Eastern Bengal (all of these were areas in which Muslims pre-dominated) would be components of the new country. Jinnah described this arrangement as 'a moth-eaten and truncated Pakistan'. This may have been true: what was even more true was that there were large numbers of Hindus and some Sikhs left in these areas: and large numbers of Muslims left in areas of what was to be India. With the Muslim League shrieking on one side, and the R.S.S., or extremist Hindu leaders, on the other, it was unsurprising that riots broke out all over the land. Enormous numbers of non-Muslims flocked into India from Pakistan: the trains on which they travelled were stopped, the men castrated and killed, the women raped and, their breasts cut off and their genitals gouged out, left to die, the children bayoneted: Hindus and Muslims alike in places such as Calcutta shared the same fate, butchered in the slums, their deaths made a humiliation as well as a finality.

Gandhi went on a fast, his usual answer to any problem, a rather presumptuous answer since it presupposed that his life was essential to the continuation of the country. Nehru raged: Feroze wrote: Indira watched. The quality of her watchfulness was intense and in Delhi she also assisted the refugees, hurt both in body and mind, whatever caste or creed they followed, whatever new nationality they had chosen. Her separation from her husband was, in a sense, becoming more complete. For her father was drawing away into a new India, and in this India he would need her even more.

On August 15 1947, India achieved independence.

The riots continued: the intrigues continued: this was the India of the Emperor Farrukh Siyar, not the India Nehru wanted. The palace plots being laid were against Gandhi, whose fast on behalf of the Muslims was taken as a personal insult by most of the extremist Hindus. They were laid not in palaces but in slum tenements far away from where Nehru and Gandhi then were: but they repeated the refrain, shaken from *shehnais*, broken out of *sitars*, of a much earlier India.

The difference was that it would be difficult to poison Gandhi. His sparse foodstuffs passed through his own hands. Moreover, his death by poison would not be a spectacular event, not an event witnessed by thousands, not an event which would implant, in the minds of the highly credible population, the idea that the Hindu extremists had at last avenged themselves upon their enemy, the friend of the Muslims, Mahatma Gandhi. In the slums of Maharashtra, where the Hindus had most hold, things were planned. Although he was still vowing poverty, Gandhi himself, as paradoxical as the Nehrus, was living in the house of a millionaire, G. D. Birla, in Delhi.

There in the sumptuous garden he held prayer meetings, during which Hindu and Quaker songs were chanted. In January 1948 a bomb went off under his window: but nobody was hurt. On January 30 1948, as he came down to his prayer meeting supported (he was seventy-nine) by his two nieces, a young man named Natharum Godse came out of the crowd, rather inexpertly raised a revolver, and fired three shots into the chest of the most remarkable man India had ever seen. Godse was a wretched boy from the Poona slums, specially trained by the extremist Hindus of the Mahasabha (later the R.S.S.) party, for this task. Gandhi fell. His last words were 'He, Ram, Ram', i.e. the name of God. He died, ironically enough, in the house of a millionaire.

Bernard Shaw said, 'This comes of being too good.' Nehru, climbing the staircase to the gate over Birla House, wept as the gigantic crowd outside wept. Later he said, 'A light has gone out of this world ... ' The absent light apart, he had lost one of the main crutches that propped him up. Years later I met him in New Delhi and he sat, amidst roses, behind his enormous desk of office, playing with a paperknife. He said, 'No, I do not think any of the Mahatma's ideas are applicable today. But, whenever I have to make a decision,

I try and think first of what he would have advised me to do. Of course, I do not always follow that advice ... '

Godse, murderer of the apostle of non-violence, and some of his accomplices in the murder, were hanged in August 1948, going to the gallows with the shout of 'Long Live Mother India', on their lips. India might be independent, but everything was as complicated as ever, if not more so. Through these extraordinary times, Feroze, Indira, and their two sons lived, in a rather extraordinary way.

The first and most crushing blow delivered upon Nehru's exceptionally nervous and sensitive mind was that of the death in 1931 of his father. Seventeen years later came the death of the surrogate, Gandhi. To the amazement of many he turned to a third crutch, Krishna Menon, a man virtually unknown in India and hated by most who knew him. On Krishna Menon he was hugely dependent for years: on the crutch of Menon he eventually tripped. When India reached the status of a Dominion within a Commonwealth jolly, as the *Independent* might have described it, Menon became the Indian High Commissioner in London. From rags to riches was putting it mildly.

Later, Mrs Pandit,* Nehru's elder sister, was fetched to London, having already served at the U.N., Moscow and Washington, an example, as it were, of hierarchic rule, and I happened to be a student there when she was High Commissioner. She invited me to lunch, and I set off by bus to Kensington Palace Gardens where the Indian High Commission was. I was seated on the upper deck, smoking, and reading a book, probably, since it engrossed me, a detective story. In the middle of the trip I became vaguely aware that the bus was full of smoke. I looked around in astonishment, until the conductress came and pointed at my trousers. I had dropped ash on them and they were on fire. I extinguished the fire and considered my circumstances.

Were I now to take a taxi, turn back to Knightsbridge where I lived and change, I should be awfully late. However, if I continued to Mrs Pandit and explained what had happened, she would probably understand. At least, so I thought. I continued my journey. A horrified butler stared at my appalling trousers, but on my production of a invitation card admitted me, dubiously. Mrs Pandit looked at me in utter astonishment, though I do not recall the expressions

* Swarup or Vijayalakshmi.

of the other guests, all fairly distinguished, because I was staring at my hostess, attempting feebly to explain.

She then became very charming, explained to the other guests, who obviously did not believe it, what a splendid writer I was, and told a funny, but very lengthy story, of how she had once nearly set herself on fire in New York by smoking in bed. After lunch I left, scorched but consoled. I was less consoled when my father wrote to me from Bombay, saying he had had a letter from Mrs Pandit in which she described me as having the manners and appearance of a tramp. Looking back at the incident I can understand what Kamala must have felt: it is never pleasant to have a smiler knife you in the back: I can also understand the later attitude of Indira towards her eldest aunt, also Mrs Pandit's attitude towards Indira, who in her opinion had burnt her trousers (or her petticoat, if you like to put it that way) though it may not have been through any fault of her own.

❦ 7 ❧

The Farthest Horizon

THERE ARE CERTAIN distant horizons, some of which can be reached in a lifetime, though the farthest is only reachable at the end. Feroze reached his farthest horizon a few years before his wife reached a skyline which must once have seemed impossibly far. A close friend of hers, Mrs Pupul Jayakar, now an elderly lady with beautiful, quietly burning eyes, who has been a key figure in the preservation of Indian handicrafts and ancient arts, has known Mrs Gandhi since 1931, and she described Feroze's wife to me as she was in the middle of the 1940s at the time of independence.

It was March: Delhi was warming itself up after winter. The dry wind from the north had ceased to be cool. Mrs Jayakar sat in front of the french windows of our drawing room, the garden ablaze with flowers behind her, sipping iced lime cordial. She said, 'Indu was fourteen when I first met her. The impression she had on me was of a particularly withdrawn and — well, how shall I put it? — a grave child. She's changed, but there is still something in her which shrinks from people, a shyness, a sense of inadequacy left in her from the overpowering influence of her aunts, particularly Mrs Pandit. Betty was fond of her in her own way. When Indu was pregnant with Rajiv, I met her in Betty's house in Bombay. She seemed very shy, very delicate, and still very withdrawn.'

Later they spent a holiday together in the hill resort of Mahabaleshwar, not far from Bombay. 'I travelled back with her in a car,' Mrs Jayakar said. 'You know, certain people make impressions on your mind. Either they are remembered as strong people or as weak ones. Indu simply left a vague impression, the impression of an undeveloped personality. It was only after 1946 that she started to have a proper relationship with her father. This was after her aunt left on her first mission to the U.N. Indu was no longer overpowered by Mrs Pandit. She started to come out of her shell: in fact, she blossomed. She started to read: she started to meet minds on equal terms.'

One mind she does not seem to have met in this way is that of Feroze. I think it true to say that while Feroze had a sort of inbuilt shrewdness and brightness, Mrs Gandhi possessed intelligence and determination, and his were completely different qualities from hers. Her intelligence may not have manifested itself much before 1946, though her determination had, but, however shy and withdrawn she may have appeared, however vague an impression she left on those who then met her, this intelligence was clearly present in her. 'Yes,' said Mrs Jayakar, finishing her soft drink, 'there are so many sides to her which were never allowed to grow: so many springs inside her which were never allowed to flow, because of her peculiar circumstances.' She fell silent, thinking back.

Mountbatten and the British troops had left: on the ridges and mountains around the valley of Kashmir Indian and Pakistani troops, not to mention guerrilla tribesmen from the wild territory north of the Khyber Pass, were fighting a bloody and inconclusive war. 'There will not,' the tribesmen boasted, 'be a rupee or a virgin left in India when we have finished.' Fortunately for those who valued both commodities, the tribesmen were driven back by the Indians. Nehru, preaching neutrality and peace to the rest of the world, could not find it at home. Neither, in a sense, could Feroze, nor could he be said at this stage in his life to have had a home. Nehru now lived in Delhi, in a spacious house at 4, Teenmurti Road, not far from the large red sandstone building which housed Parliament.

His days were a whirlwind of appointments, cabinet meetings and paperwork. There was so much to be done, the country was in chaos, and he had to do most of the work. Gandhi had gone, and Vallabhbhai Patel, his greatest help at the time, was busy pacifying, browbeating and coaxing the Indian princes to become part of a united India. The British, while holding more or less absolute sway over the country, had allowed several native princes to remain in power under the cold eyes of civil servants. The civil servants were there to ensure that the princes paid tax and did not torture and rape too many people, as was their wont. However, the princes were left free to do so many undesirable things, to spend money on whatever they wanted (Jit of Kapurthala maintained a mansion in the South of France where at parties the fountains spouted champagne) and to behave, under a degree of restraint, as they behaved before the British came. It was evident that to unite the remnants of India after partition the princes would have to surrender their small thrones to the new state. Patel's thankless task was to make them do so. He succeeded, though in Hyderabad, where the elderly and eccentric Nizam opted to throw in his lot with Pakistan, Indian forces entered in what was tactfully termed a police action, and took over.

Patel was probably the best administrator modern India has produced, and his enforced involvement with the princes threw an immense load upon Nehru. For years he had to solve every minor problem in India, for anyone with some petty complaint usually had to go up to the Prime Minister to seek redress. This meant that Nehru worked something like eighteen hours a day. The huge house had to be run and the only person available to run it, with Mrs Pandit abroad and Betty now married to a journalist in Bombay, was Indira. She moved into the house with Feroze and the two boys, and looked after it.

Families in India are accustomed to living together. Three or four generations may simultaneously inhabit the same house. The idea is basically to ensure family solidarity, also partly for the sake of economy. Mrs Gandhi today lives with her two sons, their wives and her grandchildren. Sanjay's wife Maneka once informed me that this was a very sensible mode of existence in that while the members of the family had separate quarters and led separate lives, not interfering with one another, they shared the household expenses, so that life was cheaper than if they all lived apart. This may be so, though it is not the kind of life I myself would gladly accept. Nevertheless it is a part of Indian tradition. From the point of view of Feroze, however, the fact that the head of the house was also the Prime Minister, and that he himself was virtually nobody, must have been irksome in the extreme. 'In 1948,' Mrs Jayakar remembered over lunch, 'my husband and I came to live in Delhi. We often used to ask Indu and Feroze to dinner. Feroze seldom came. When he did, he used to take me out on to the balcony and launch into a tirade about his family life.' A naturally gregarious person, he may at this time have felt a lonely man.

The result of all this seems to have been to instil in him a desire for flight, also a desire to fight: to fight the kind of life he felt he was forced to lead. Nehru had little time for him now: the days of their long talks and a sense of kinship were over. Even more bitter for Feroze, Indira had little time for him. He decided to try and become a member of parliament, and stood as the Congress candidate, from a small and remote township called Rae Bareilly, not very far from Lucknow. This was in 1952, the year after India became a republic. Feroze won his seat.

One of the perks of being a member of the Indian Parliament is that you receive a small house in Delhi from the government. Having been allotted his house, Feroze moved into it and started to cultivate roses. He also, in Parliament, cultivated the habits of a wasp: he stung ferociously and once or twice his stings found their lodgement in Nehru.

In fact Indira had been with Feroze in Rae Bareilly. She had helped his campaign. So, in a sense, had Nehru, who came to the constituency a few times to make speeches backing him. Nevertheless, even at this time the slight, but definite animus that existed between the two men showed itself. Nehru snapped at Feroze. Why did Feroze drag his wife all over the countryside, exhausting her? Indira said she felt fine, which slightly tempered the storm. Feroze apparently said nothing at all.

To say that the relationship between Indira and Feroze ceased when he moved into a separate house would not be exactly true. They seem to have preserved reasonably amicable feelings towards each other, and the children were a natural bond between them. Their elder son, Rajiv, came to my flat in Delhi one day, and I asked him about his memories of his father. 'He used to visit us a lot,' said Rajiv, a stocky, quiet, amiable young man who works as a pilot for Indian Airlines, the internal service of the country. 'We were very fond of him. He was very good with his hands: he used to make fretwork toys for us.' Indira spent a lot of time with the children, but Nehru, naturally, could not. The boys, however, seem to have had a proper relationship with their parents, even if their parents lived apart. Nehru created a kind of private zoo in the grounds of the house, which included tiger cubs, though whether this was for the benefit of the boys or, since he loved animals, for his personal pleasure, is a debatable point. Nevertheless, he seems to have loved his grandsons.

Gossip is rife in India. It spreads not only from the lipsticked

mouths of society ladies, but from the less attractive lips of politicians. In Delhi taxi drivers tell you everything that is, or that they
think is, happening. Everybody thinks he knows something about
someone, and nobody is less than anxious to inform you of it,
however much you tell them you do not want to hear. Gossip about
Mrs Gandhi has always been prevalent, and much of it has had to
do with her sex life after she and Feroze embarked upon their
curious separation. Now I personally, and many other people,
think her an attractive woman, but I very much doubt that she herself thinks so. Only attractive women who are physically conscious
of themselves have affairs. 'It's stupid,' Mrs Jayakar told me. 'In a
house always full of guests, servants, and children, how can anyone
have affairs? It wasn't like that at all. After the difficulty with
Feroze, she turned more and more towards religion.' Mrs Jayakar
did not mean organised religion, but Mrs Gandhi's consultations
with Anandamayi Mai, whom Kamala met first, and more recently
with a holy man known as the Brahmachari, who is not without
worldly goods, since amongst other things he possesses an aeroplane. The gossips are bores: I believe Mrs Jayakar. The relationship between Feroze and his wife may not have been exactly that,
at least after 1952, of a normal couple, but remarks made to me
in the course of past interviews cause me to believe that until Feroze
died, Mrs Gandhi had loved him.

In 1970, shortly before an election, an American magazine asked
me to write a profile of her. I thought the best way to do this was
by interviewing, not only her, but her political enemies, of whom
Morarji Desai was already one. I sought and obtained an interview
with him which I shall never forget, though I must admit that I
would like to.

When I met him Mr Desai was spinning yarn, looking gloomy
and, in a way, distinguished, in his *khadi* clothes and cap, and
presumably after his breakfast of urine. He asked me what I wanted
to write about him. Slightly embarrassed, I said all I wanted from
him were his views on Mrs Gandhi. 'Ah,' said Mr Desai. 'I never
speak ill of anyone.' I inquired if he wanted to say anything nice
about the lady. 'No,' he said sombrely. Feeling, therefore, that my
interview was at an end, I made to go. 'Do not take notes,' he said,
'but Mrs Gandhi is worse than Hitler or Stalin.' I asked how he
thought she had achieved this apotheosis. 'Do not ask me,' he

replied. 'Ask Tarkeshwari Sinha.' He then launched into a long discourse, the gist of which, in so far as it was relevant to Mrs Gandhi, I did not catch, and concluded by telling me that since he knew and loved my father (who once, when Mr Desai was Chief Minister of Bombay had attacked him in the press and was taken to court by Mr Desai) he would like to assist me, firstly by teaching me how to spin cloth, and secondly by expounding his philosophy of life to me for three or four hours. From these suggestions I fled.

However, I took up his initial idea that I should talk to Tarkeshwari Sinha. This lady, who throughout her political career has made a habit of switching parties as the wind shifts, was at this time known as 'the glamour girl of politics'. Considering the appearance of most Indian women politicians, this was not a terribly difficult title to achieve. She is a lady who, in Indian parlance, is 'well built', i.e. somewhat buxom.

I went to see her with my wife, who takes notes for me. My wife, telling the driver what to do, lagged behind me. Some years before I had written a book about India called *Gone Away*.* Waiting for my wife to arrive I said to Mrs Sinha, 'I don't know if you understood me on the telephone but I am a writer and I wanted to ask you about—' She said, 'Ah yes. Of course I am knowing you are writer. I am reading your *Gone with the Wind* fifteen times. Also I am seeing the film.' Before I was forced to disabuse her of the idea that I was Margaret Mitchell, my wife arrived, luckily, and we began to talk about Mrs Gandhi.

Mrs Sinha agreed with Mr Desai that Mrs Gandhi was worse than Hitler and Stalin. She also said Mrs Gandhi had never liked her, the reason being that Mrs Gandhi had once found her talking to Feroze in an empty office. 'Because,' she said, 'I am beautiful, isn't it?' Whether or not Mrs Sinha is beautiful, I think this story, if true, highly significant in terms of the relationship between Mrs Gandhi and Feroze.

'Feroze was an oaf,' a former Indian Chief of Protocol told me. 'All he wanted to do was flail out, to hit people and hurt them. Nothing he did was in any way constructive.' Certainly in Parliament Feroze flailed out a lot, but in psychological terms this was surely the expression of some kind of deep personal frustration, and I cannot see that this frustration was his fault.

* Heinemann/Little Brown, 1960.

Nobody can live within an ambience which he is incapable of controlling. Feroze could obviously not live within the ambience of Nehru's enormous house, of which his wife had become the *châtelaine*. It was obviously also difficult for him to live outside it, without his wife and sons. He exposed various scandals in Parliament, one of which, in 1958, led to the dismissal of the Finance Minister: if he did nothing constructive, there seems to have been little constructive for him, outside the Cabinet and resentful of Nehru, to do: though the exposure of governmental misdeeds does not seem to me a purely destructive act. By 1958, however, he had mild heart trouble.

His temperament had become increasingly explosive. At one point an Eastern European dignitary came to India on a state visit. Indira set up a party for him on the lawns of the house. This included a dance performance, and people were allotted seats around the dance area, the seating being arranged by Mrs Gandhi. One section was for the press, another for M.P.s, and so on. Feroze was seated in the press section. A friend of mine, Mrs Tara Ali Baig, was helping Mrs Gandhi with the arrangements. Feroze, in a terrible temper, came up to her. 'I'm in the press seats. I'm an M.P. Why am I not seated with the other M.P.s?' Mrs Baig replied that she had nothing to do with the seating arrangements: Indu had fixed those. 'Why don't you ask her?' she suggested. Feroze's eyes looked across the lawn to where his wife, cool in her sari, was in conversation with the visiting firemen. According to Mrs Baig, he inquired, 'Why should I ask that woman for anything?'

This does not prove or disprove anything about the relationship between Indira and Feroze, except that Feroze had become more and more capable of expressing his anger and his frustration. He was not a boy any more, not the boy who had sat by Kamala in Switzerland or who had walked into a Bloomsbury bookshop with her daughter. Where he went now Indira did not necessarily go: but where Nehru went, she went. In this way she encountered statesmen in the corridors of world politics: people famous in the arts: the people doomed to be dedicated to humanity. She was not yet one of them, and her role was that of a sort of backseat driver to her father, who, as he aged, showed more and more signs of the famous Nehru temper. On one occasion he decided to make a state visit to Indonesia in the flagship of the Indian Navy, I.N.S. *Delhi*, accompanied by Indira, the children, and a protective convoy.

Rashid Ali Baig was at that time the Indian Ambassador to Indonesia. His wife Tara, mentioned above, told me of two extraordinary incidents that she witnessed during the visit. The first was on the arrival of the convoy at Jakarta. Nehru, Indira, and the two small boys trim in sailor suits marked I.N.S. *Delhi*, stood on a dais, surrounded by thousands of cheering Javanese. Nehru had to make a speech, but the crowd seemed more interested in the children. As they cheered, Indira raised one of the boys in her arms so that he could look out over the applauding multitude. The applause at this redoubled, for Javanese are fond of children, with the result that Nehru could not be heard. Angrily he turned on Indira and ordered her and the boys to leave the dais. 'What did she do?' I asked Mrs Baig. 'She did what he told her,' she answered. The second incident took place later in the trip. At a reception Mrs Gandhi was talking to some women, coming out of her shell, when her father passed by and overheard her. 'Don't talk nonsense,' he snapped. 'What did she do?' I asked Mrs Baig once more. 'She stopped talking,' said Mrs Baig. Rashid, her husband, added, 'In those days, she was like a small mouse, that is with her father. Nehru seemed then to adopt a very peremptory tone to her, and the answer was always this very meek, soft, "Yes, Papu". My wife, who has always been a very independent woman, was horrified.' I only want to add that Rashid and Tara had been friends of my father before I was born, that during a violent childhood attack of asthma, Rashid obtained medicine that probably saved my life, and that they told me all this in a disinterested way, as friends should do.

What Indira did at her father's house was multipurpose. She told the actual housekeeper, Mrs Vimla Sindhi, what the menus for each meal should be, and she also organised entertainment programmes for guests. These were very often dance programmes, and to one of these W. H. Auden, then as large, grumpy, and wrinkled as an elephant, and as gentle as this maligned animal, came. He was a sort of hero in Nehru's mind because of his leftist poetry of the 1930s. Mrs Gandhi obviously felt that, as an artist, Auden would like to watch an Indian dance, and a performance was arranged. I knew Wystan when he was Professor of Poetry at Oxford, and later in New York, and I know that he would not have suffered anything,

least of all a dance performance in some foreign idiom, unless he had
had a number of drinks before. Mrs Gandhi did not know this. In
the Prime Minister's house liquor was not served. This was largely
on the advice of the dead saint, Gandhi, who felt it was the ruination
of the masses. So all Auden received was the healthful squeezes that
come out of certain fruit. In a letter written to Nicolas Nabokov
subsequently, he complained about the absence of alcohol and the
presence of dancers and said that, in the middle of the performance,
he decided to leave, presumably since in his hotel there was a closet-
ful of gin and vermouth. He said he was shown out by Indira, 'the
Prime's daughter', who, he added, seemed 'grumpy'. I admired
Wystan but I can understand Mrs Gandhi's point of view. Nevertheless, it must have been through this sort of incident that she gained
experience of dealing with people.

In addition to the oppressive influence of her aunts, I think
Indira had to bear her father's oppressive influence too. What the
Baigs say about the visit to Indonesia seems to indicate that she was
quiet, subservient, without much of a role to play, but she obviously
watched, and she obviously reflected. It is exactly what an only, and
lonely, child does: but most of these children, by twenty or thirty,
know what their future life will be. With Indira this was not the
case: from her childhood until the death of her father she was in
some senses enclosed by her family. Nevertheless her watchfulness,
her travel with her father, her experience of statesmen and of
countries achieved through her father, seem to have carried her to
the first point in her extraordinary career: a point where she was the
only person who could control his temper. There is a famous story
concerning an occasion when Nehru entered his office, seated himself at his desk, and looked around for a top secret file. It was not
there. He shouted for his secretaries, who came, looked, and could
not find it. The wrath of Nehru increased. The terrified secretaries
phoned Indira, who drifted in, glanced round the office and said to
Nehru in dulcet tones, 'Papu, you are *sitting* on that file.'

Meanwhile Feroze continued with his own life. When he was not in
Parliament he received a constant stream of visitors and petitioners
in his own small house, where he fed them with tea and advice. His
roses flourished, but his own body did not: his heart continued to
trouble him. He threw himself into his work, and managed frugally

on the small salary he received as an M.P. In 1959, with the boys
already adolescent and Indira forty-two, an event took place which
may have surprised Feroze. It surprised everyone else.

Mrs Gandhi's public activity had hitherto been fairly limited.
She was frequently in the public eye, but this was only because she
was the daughter of Nehru. She did, however, sit on several committees, mainly to do with child welfare and education. Her image was
that of a very feminine woman whose main interests were in the
household. This image was magnified by her rather shy and nervous
behaviour. A member of one of these committees was Durgabai
Deshmukh, the wife of a Finance Minister, C. D. Deshmukh.
Mrs Deshmukh was a lady of excellent intentions but somewhat
formidable manner, and Indira was terrified of her. Whenever
Indira had to tell Mrs Deshmukh some unpalatable news, she did
not go in person, but sent her secretary. Her entire reputation was
one of shyness, of withdrawal, a sort of frightened fawn.

The Congress party has a leader, but also a President. The
leader's duties are purely political, while the President is in charge
of party affairs and administration. In 1959 Nehru made it known
that he would like his daughter to become Congress President. The
party members were amazed, but Nehru's word was holy writ in
those days and Mrs Gandhi was duly elected.

Why Nehru made his decision is difficult to say. His daughter had
no political experience as such, and she went into power over the
heads of several senior Congressmen. There was a certain amount of
internecine strife within the party and possibly he wanted Mrs
Gandhi to act as a buffer between opposed factions. Though she
lacked experience she had political knowledge. She knew the
members of the party as well as anybody, their minds and their
strengths and weaknesses. She had travelled around the country
with her father: she knew the Indian scene. In some senses she was
an excellent choice, which surprised many people but didn't offend
many.

The following year, 1960, Indira was on a trip to the south. It was
September, and still hot and dusty in the capital. One morning
Feroze complained of a pain in the chest. The doctor advised him to
rest but he insisted that he must attend Parliament. On September 7
he phoned his doctor for an appointment, drove to the hospital and
collapsed with a massive heart attack. Indira was immediately
informed and she sped back from the south. On the morning of

September 8 Feroze died in hospital, clasping the hand of his wife.
He was only forty-eight years old.

There was discontent in the country and Nehru was not quite as
popular as he had been. There was some nervousness in the country,
too: not only about a shortage of food, but over the activities of the
Chinese on the northern borders. In 1959 Chinese forces entered
India briefly, then withdrew claiming that tracts of Indian territory
in the north belonged to China. The Defence Minister was now
Krishna Menon. Indian troops on the borders complained of
shortages of arms and ammunition. There was a rumour that Menon,
because of his Communist sympathies, had deliberately withheld
hardware from the forces. Nehru defended Menon: the chiefs of the
army, the navy and the airforce resigned in protest. Nehru persuaded
them to return, but it was not a happy situation. Nehru was probably
less happy than anyone else. For years he had believed that India
and China were allies and brothers: indeed the people had believed
it and a popular slogan, *Hindi-Chini Bhai Bhai* (India and China
are brothers), had been coined. Now this slogan rang a bit false.
Nehru had always believed the two huge nations, standing shoulder
to shoulder, could bring peace and prosperity to Asia. His trust had
suffered a setback, but he clung to his old faith in China, though
warned by several of his advisers that this was a mistake. It was to
prove the biggest mistake in a career which had hitherto contained
few.

The death of Feroze had a peculiar effect on Indira. Strange though
her married life had been in its later stages, his was the second
important death in her existence. Kamala's death had made her more
withdrawn. Feroze's, though it made her no less withdrawn, caused
her to move with increased momentum into the political scene. She
adopted his constituency, Rae Bareilly, as her own. There is a
memorial to him there in a college named after him, which he
founded, since there was no college in Rae Bareilly before.

   The other memorials to him are those most people leave, his
children, and also sundry roads named after him. But he did not
play an important enough role in India to be widely remembered.
There are university students today who think of him as the
Mahatma's son and of Indira as his sister. Actually, their relationship, in a way, much resembled that of siblings.

In 1962 the biggest single catastrophe in Nehru's life occurred: the Chinese attacked India. They poured their troops into the northeast, and the Indian troops, confronted by vastly superior numbers and firepower, retreated southward. The Chinese could probably have swept down the whole country. For no clearly perceptible reason, having come within a short distance of Shillong, the capital of Assam, and the first real town on their way, they turned round and went home. Some observers think that they wanted to avoid foreign troops coming to help India and precipitating a second Vietnam. They would obviously have thought of this, however, before they invaded. The reason was probably twofold: they wanted to show the Indians that their northern neighbours were no longer feeling fraternal, and they wanted to humiliate the Indians, to show them that China was their military master. Assuming these to be their reasons both their sudden onslaught and equally sudden withdrawal are understandable, and their campaign can be said to have been a complete success.

India was saved, but the effect of the invasion on Nehru was as bad as it would have been had the country been overrun. The Chinese had this time totally betrayed him: they had waged an actual war against India. The fact that they had withdrawn proved nothing. Nehru had considered Chou En-lai a friend. It was not only a nation which had betrayed him: it had been a personal betrayal. It was not only the heartbreak but the fact that he had been made to look a fool by a supposed friend. All his Asian policies of the past fifteen years, broadly based on the assumption that China was friendly, had been based on a false assumption. For the first time in his life Nehru came under widespread critical fire from press and public. There were those who said that he was too old, that he should resign. The spectacle of her father virtually unaided, left in the lurch by those who had earlier looked to him as the unquestioned leader, hardened Mrs Gandhi and filled her with a distrust of disciples. The events of 1962 shattered Nehru's spirit, and it could never be entirely repaired. Mrs Gandhi made efforts to hearten him, to cheer him, but they were only partly successful. She tried to persuade him to shift some of his burdens and responsibilities to his Cabinet colleagues but if much in him had been killed, the ancient stubbornness remained. He worked himself as hard as ever: he scarcely slept. At the time the Chinese came he was seventy-three but physically and mentally as fit as he had ever been.

He aged incredibly during the months that followed. My father used to recall his last encounter with Nehru, which took place in the corridor outside the Prime Minister's Office in Parliament House. My father was on his way to see someone else when he saw Nehru coming very slowly towards him. 'Hullo, Frank,' said Nehru. 'How are you?' 'What's more important, sir,' said my father, 'is how *you* are.' 'As well as can be expected,' the Prime Minister said in a very tired voice, and continued on his way. I asked my father how he had looked. 'He seemed,' he replied after reflection, 'to have become smaller.'

He was tired, incredibly tired; even he felt he could not take any more. The inward fire that had lit the whole of his life was dying in the same way as his exhausted body. He was felled by a heart attack: he announced his wish to retire. It was partly his daughter who decided him to do so; now, at the end, she had become the last of all his human crutches. But the party would not leave him alone and in peace, they begged him to stay and he stayed. He still worked incredible hours: it was the last flicker of a dying system.

The reason that the party would not permit him to retire was simply because there was no automatic successor to the leadership. Nehru, producer and director in the theatre that was India, had never rehearsed anyone for the part. There were of course, several who wanted to be auditioned for it: Desai, now Deputy Prime Minister and even more ambitious than before: Kamaraj, a corpulent southerner who was said to know only two words of English, Yes and No, and to employ the latter much more frequently: Lal Bahadur Shastri, 'the little sparrow', who was considered much too mild for leadership: indeed, every Tom, Dick and Hari in the senior echelons of the Congress was at one time or the other mentioned as a possibility by those who professed to be in the know.

Mrs Gandhi's name was faintly murmured by a few, but only by a very few. Her only claim to leadership, most people remarked, was hereditary, and India had been an electoral democracy for some years. Anyway, they added chauvinistically, how could a woman lead a cabinet full of men? A very usual title for articles written (incessantly) by political commentators, was 'After Nehru, Who?' There were innumerable supposititious replies to this plaintive query, but no solution. The lobbying that went on inside the Congress party seemed rather insensitive in that by pleading with him to remain, the party leaders had certainly shortened his life, and he was not yet dead. Like vulpine relatives whispering outside the bedroom of a sick uncle, the Congress leaders plotted as to who was to obtain the immense legacy unmentioned in the will. In this rather squalid political situation, Nehru went wearily on.

Perhaps he had happy memories: his English years, the good days with Gandhi, the long friendships with remarkable men and women, beautiful animals, high mountains, swift rivers. But there were also the dark memories: so many deaths, so much sacrifice. He probably with his murderous work schedule, had no time to remember, or was perpetually too tired. The reality in which he found himself was not the one he had visualised in his early nationalist days. India was not a place of happy, healthy people striding towards prosperity: the general good was not foremost in the minds of the politicians of a free nation, as he had imagined it would be. All that idealism, all that fighting, had only produced this. Sick men turn over their memories carefully, like tattered old books: Nehru was a sick man, but he had no time.

One evening in 1964 Jawaharlal Nehru said to his daughter, 'I have finished my work.' Slowly he went up to bed. Outside his bedroom window crickets chirped, and occasional dogs barked far away. The blue-black night sky had dropped over the capital: the moon was up and the sharp stars out. Nehru went to bed and fell asleep. At some time that night, as he slept, and the last lights went out in Delhi, the inward flame that had warmed him all those years flickered. The next day he died.

On his bedside table was a slip of paper on which he had written lines from a poem by Robert Frost. 'For I have promises to keep', the lines went, 'and miles to go before I sleep'. The journey was shorter than Nehru expected and the promises remained to be kept by his only child.

PART TWO

The Ascent

✣ 8 ✣

A First Encounter

I FIRST MET Mrs Gandhi in December 1968 in highly inauspicious circumstances. At that time I had not visited the country of my birth for nine years: London was my home. Though I knew very little about India, when a Fleet Street editor wanted something about it without the trouble and expense of sending a correspondent there, or when a television producer needed someone to pontificate about the woes of the subcontinent, they asked me. Young and impecunious, I could hardly decline these offers, and wrote and talked on every topic remotely connected with the country, from Jawaharlal Nehru to *tandoori* chicken. In 1967 an editor asked me to write about Mrs Gandhi on the occasion of her fiftieth birthday. She had become, a few months before this, in 1966, the second woman in history to be Prime Minister of an entire country. Now I did know that she was Nehru's daughter, but that was about all I knew of her, for I was not in those days much interested in politics, especially not in the politics of a country seven thousand miles of sea, desert, and mountains away from the British Isles. Nevertheless I accepted the assignment and read the office file on her. It consisted largely of critical articles: indeed, very critical articles. I concluded that she was a monster. As I said, I was less responsible then than I am, I hope, now, and I did a reasonably skilful piece which poked fun at her doings, though I did not know exactly what they were.

But when in 1968 I arrived in India, with the intention of writing a book (it never materialised) on the country, I realised it was necessary for me to interview the lady. I was staying with my father in Delhi, and, since he could arrange most things, I asked him to arrange this. He was uncharacteristically nervous about it. 'You see,' he said in his usual indistinct murmur, 'when you published that stupid article, parts of it were quoted here. Somebody asked her what she thought about it, and all she would say is that you were a very immature young man. I don't know if ... but she's a mature person.' Using the phrase by which we affectionately called each other, he said, 'You stupid old fool, I'll try. But what do you want to ask her?' Having no knowledge of Indian politics, I could not say.

Despite all these difficulties, the interview was fixed. I saw her in her office. She was tiny behind an enormous desk, the white streak already in her hair seeming to be carved through the black of it. Her hooded eyes seldom looked at me, but over me at a photograph of her father that hung on the wall opposite her. She answered my questions more or less monosyllabically. She never smiled. Indeed, she appeared to become very tired of the whole interview about sixty seconds after it began. In these somewhat galling circumstances, I laboured on: the only time I got any real response was when I inquired if her father had had a tremendous influence on her in terms of the policies she adopted (what these policies were, in fact, I did not know). She looked at me for the first and only time during this ill-fated interview, frightening me with her eyes, and said, 'Does everyone who interviews me have to ask the same question?' I hastily switched to something else, and she returned to murmured monosyllables, occasionally looking rather pointedly at her watch. I hung on doggedly until an aide entered and whispered something to her. A look of some relief came to her face and she nodded to the aide, who said, 'Madamji has another appointment.' I rose, wanly folded my hands to her in farewell, and trailed out in the wake of the aide.

One reason for my disappointment at this meeting was that during the course of it I found myself liking her. It is very difficult to say why one starts to like anybody. The sexual relationship between casual lovers, or husband and wife, seems to me usually to be a fusion, magnetic almost, of opposite poles: love, liking may come into it, but the actual liking of a person with whom you are not physically involved is different. You normally start to like somebody because you see resemblances between yourself and the other person. I had suddenly perceived, in the lady, that she and I resembled each other in a way: both with an inbred shyness born out of tumultuous childhoods: both with a certain dislike of too much talk and loquacious people: both, at our different ages, with a total tiredness of, and a total interest in, this burning and turning world. What upset me after the interview was not the fact that I had liked her and she had not liked me: she had given no real indication of dislike: it was the fact that I had liked her and I had been of no interest to her: she had done what was expected of her and then shelved me in her memory: the whole thing was over.

Though I saw resemblances between us even then, I did not and, of course, do not, ever expect to be seated behind a huge desk running a huge country. What I became interested in was how she came to be seated behind such a desk, how she came to run such a country.

All history is a corridor of mirrors, in which adventitious images are recorded for posterity to accept or not to. All these images are to some extent distorted, not so much because of flaws in the mirrors as because of the enormous misconceptions that exist between person and person and between person and event. It is notably more difficult to write on somebody who is alive than on somebody who is dead. The dead are pinned down like butterflies under the lids of many cases, and in each case the specimen may be labelled and described. The researcher simply has to sift through the crumbled, lifeless squares of paper, select those which form some kind of pattern relevant to his own preconceptions, and there he is, his views in his head and the source material to support them at his elbow. When the people a writer is concerned with are alive, there is no question of neatly labelled, perpetually skewered specimens: groping through a giant haystack, he occasionally, and sometimes rather painfully, pricks his questing finger on a needle. His hand may be septic in the end: but out of these myriad tiny pinpricks his book will be made.

My hand was already a bit sore when I called on Mrs Gandhi one afternoon in 1977 to clarify a couple of points. Outside the house in the roadway loitered a number of men trying so desperately to look normal that they were obviously from the Central Bureau of Intelligence. At the gate was a sort of redbrick pillbox from which Mrs Gandhi's own people checked prospective visitors. They knew me and waved me by. There is a short horseshoe drive in front of the house, surrounded by lawns dotted with flowerbeds and trees. The grass had started to brown and the flowers to wilt, for it was March, and the heat had begun to crawl into the city. On the tired turf stood tents furnished with chairs, where Mrs Gandhi meets her supporters. There were not many around today: it was hot, bees murmured stickily above the flowers, and such supporters as there were slept in the shadows of the tents, waiting for Mrs Gandhi to come forth in the cool of the evening. It was a good time for me to have come: the tents and lawns are usually full of raucous Congress workers.

The house itself has only one storey and rambles away to more lawns at the back, where a variety of tropical birds imitate the more discordant sounds of the Congress workers. There is a balcony in front, off which Mrs Gandhi's reception room opens, as well as a corridor that leads into the main body of the house. Here not only Mrs Gandhi but her two sons and their families live. A huge bamboo screen shields the front of the house from the dusty road, for 12, Willingdon Crescent had now become a milestone on the tripper route: tourist buses drew up outside, and inquisitive eyes and cameras peered around for the small, famous figure in its pastel sari, once ruler of the very dust churned up by these buses.

One of the Irish wolfhounds (there are five in the house, each the size of a large donkey) shambled out of the corridor and sniffed at me with the bored air of a sensualist in smells who finds nothing to detain his interest. Simultaneously Mrs Gandhi popped her head out of the door of the reception room, smiled, and said, 'Come in.' I followed her in. I had some flowers in my hand: she loves flowers, or rather, as she once said to me, she loves arranging flowers rather than the flowers themselves, a remark I think perhaps psychologically significant. She did not say anything as I handed them to her: it had now become a ritual between us, so that I did not need to say anything either. However, her right eyelid flickered in rapid succession several times, a facial mannerism that may mean irritation or pleasure, and she hurried off with the flowers to put them in water. The whole atmosphere surrounding my arrival was familiar to me now, the ritual like the formal steps of a dance. The reception room is small but comfortable with a sofa and several armchairs, and now came the final step of the dance: Mrs Gandhi entered and seated herself in the armchair to the right of the sofa, and I seated myself on the sofa to her left. This is our normal spatial relationship in this particular room: perhaps Robert Ardrey would understand. As usual, Mrs Gandhi started off by saying nothing whatever.

Presently I inquired about her entry into politics. Why, I asked,

7 Feroze, holding his elder son Rajiv. Indira and Jawaharlal look on

8 Indira with her father after India became independent in 1947
9 Rajiv and Sanjay with their mother, on the way to visit Indonesia

10 Nehru and his sister Mrs Pandit arrive at 10 Downing Street

11 Mrs Gandhi and her sons, Rajiv (*left*) and Sanjay (*right*)

12   Indira accompanies her father on a visit to President John F. Kennedy and his wife Jacqueline, at the White House

13   In 1966 Mrs Gandhi, now Prime Minister of India, breaks a journey between Washington and Moscow to talk to Premier Harold Wilson

had her father proposed to the Congress in 1959 that she should be President? Was this indicative of a desire that she should succeed him? The faulty mirrors of history: Mrs Gandhi stared at me, then said, 'I was *bullied* into the Congress Presidency, you know. I didn't want it at all.' But, I inquired, had her father not taken her wishes into account? 'He was against it too,' she said. Everyone I had spoken to or read had conveyed an exactly opposite impression. She had not felt qualified for the post she said: she had felt shy, and she had wanted to look after her family. Her father had not wanted to seem to be pushing his only child into power. 'Pandit Pant,'* she said, 'bullied me into becoming President.' When I asked her why, she shrugged. Pant, a wise old walrus of a politician, must have seen her as a choice that would offend nobody, a harmless and manipulable young woman who would provide the senior party-men with a hot line to Nehru himself. Curiously enough it had been Pant who in 1946, when he was Chief Minister of Uttar Pradesh, then known as the United Provinces, who had urged Indira to stand for election to the state legislature. Indira was then twenty-nine, and pregnant with Sanjay, and she had told the Pandit that her children needed her more than the U.P. state assembly. The reasons Pant had for pressing her into the political scene then were quite possibly still valid in 1959: unless one takes it that from 1946 onward he divined within her, like some dowser, hazel twig in hand, rewarding springs which, if only tapped, would fertilise the Indian soil.

Certainly if Pant had expected her to be a tame and malleable President, he, and other Congress leaders, were in for a considerable surprise. 'As a child,' she once said to me, 'I used to dream that I was Joan of Arc.' Her surviving aunts in Allahabad recall watching her deploy her dolls in martial array to fight imaginary battles in which the enemies were always British. She had told me of the fire which had always burnt in her but which nobody saw (or felt) for years. Now, while the elders who had appointed her President threw up their hands in astonishment as much as in dismay, she started to infuse young blood into the higher echelons of the party, and, though Congress Presidents are not really supposed to be active in a political sense, she was closely involved in two important political events.

Kerala is a beautiful, rivery state on the southwestern coast of India. The rivers and seas are alive with fish, coconuts filled with a

* A veteran Congress leader, now dead.

5

sweetish, faintly acrid water and a pulpy white meat hang like anthropoid skulls from the palm trees, and there are delicate and various fruit. The literacy rate is the highest of any state in India. Kerala should have been rich, but one factor militated against its affluence. Because of the nature of the terrain, the available employment was mainly manual, on land or water. There was thus an immense amount of unemployment. The combined factors of a potentially rich area, a high literacy rate and colossal unemployment, led naturally to the election of a Communist government, the first constitutionally elected Communist government in history. Nehru, in a weird way, seemed rather proud of this: he felt that this could be the precursor of other democratically elected Communist governments all over the world. When the Kerala government adopted rather extreme policies, especially towards the Nayyar Hindus and the Catholics, Nehru let sleeping wolves lie. Indira had other views. Whether they were prompted by ideological opposition to the Kerala Communist policies, or by chagrin at the Congress defeat in the state, she appears to have started to lobby within her own party. The Congress threw in its lot with the Nayyars and the Catholics. The result was disorder in Kerala. At the Congress national committee in Delhi in 1959 Indira so pressurised Nehru and Pant that the Kerala government was dismissed. Because of the situation of lawlessness in the state, rule was imposed from the centre for some months before new elections were held. The Congress won these as head of a coalition where it had some strange bedfellows, including the Muslim League whose policies had some years earlier led to the partition of India.

The second important event of Indira's time as Congress President concerned the brawl over Bombay. Though Bombay, a huge, teeming, filthy city, hardly seems a place anyone would want to brawl over, it is the most important commercial city in India. Therefore, if the bulk of the population are dullards, they are dullards drawn from all over India by the rumour of rupees to be had. The largest elements in the city come from the neighbouring states of Maharashtra and Gujarat: those from the former speak Marathi, those from the latter Gujarati, which is a completely different language. In 1959 these two groups formed one state called Bombay but each wished, on linguistic grounds, to split from it, and each wanted the city of Bombay. Riots broke out; black flags of protest flapped slowly in the stale sea-wind of the metropolis:

Nehru, whose entire policy was against the creation of linguistic states and the consequent destruction of the unified India of which he had always dreamed—unified in language as well as everything else—stood fast. Indira, more practical, saw the risk of Congress losing the state at the next elections, and beyond that the risk of more bloodshed. Y. B. Chavan,* then the Chief Minister of the bilingual state, went with her to see Nehru. After a lengthy argument Nehru capitulated. Maharashtra and Gujarat became separate states and though Bombay is actually the capital of Maharashtra, Gujarati businessmen have equal access to whatever benefits the city affords and the settlement has proved both amicable and successful.

The initial dust of summer floated in through the open door, and for the first time in months the wind that rustled the curtains was warm. Mrs Gandhi, with an irritable click of the tongue, closed the door and turned on the fan. Looking at her abstractedly, I had a strange sense that I was not in the room at all, but an observer peering down a telescope from some chilly star. To see an ordinary woman suddenly do something extraordinary: move across the room say, with the beauty of a ballerina, and, completely unconscious of that completed movement, sit down once more and talk of her servant problems, takes me aback. It took me aback far more to see an extraordinary woman suddenly doing something ordinary: pulling doors shut, drawing curtains to, flicking at switches to find the right one, then returning to her chair, the drawing of the sari across her shoulders like the reassumption of some mantle worn by right. Observing from my star, I reflected that the woman who had shut the door was the one most people had seen and known until 1959. In 1959 she had suddenly, and against all expectations, proved that, firstly she had ideas of her own, secondly that her father had come to respect them, and thirdly that she had acquired, certainly in the cases of Kerala and Bombay, the drive to see her ideas carried out. Furthermore, I believe that 1959 was the first year in which she herself definitely realised that she *did* have ideas of her own. Miss Betty Friedan, an American writer, said that 'an un-identified source' told her 'that in the early days Nehru would bully Indira in an absolutely shocking way ... shatter her self-confidence' and turn her 'into a mass of nerves'.†

* See p. 86.
† See p. 99.

This account may or may not be true, but by 1959 Indira had developed confidence and not only the respect of her father but influence over him. Also, she had tasted power.

I glissaded down from my star and looked at her. Somebody had fetched her a file. She had put on her spectacles and was frowning at it. She scribbled a note in the margin and turned back to me. I said, 'You really came into politics in 1959, didn't you, in an active sense?' One of her more enigmatic expressions came to her face then, as usual, was followed by a smile. 'If you like to think so,' she said. I pushed my question: she played with the hem of her sari in silence. I have noticed, though I cannot analyse the reason, that while she usually answers complex and difficult questions fluently, perfectly innocuous queries seem to drive her back into unplumbable depths of silence. Perhaps it is that a complex question is obviously a complex question, but that she is afraid that an uncomplex question may be a complex one wrapped up in wool. Finally I said, 'OK, ma'am, we'll *assume* that the first active part you played in the politics of independent India was in 1959.' At this she laughed, and said, 'All right, *you* assume that.' I said, 'And you liked it.' She replied, 'I was needed.' Said in another way, it would have been a highly pretentious remark: but there was a kind of dual sadness in her voice, as though firstly she was glad that someone *had* needed her, so that she could be of use, and secondly as though the need for her that had started then had since pulled at her whole life hard enough to hurt. 'But,' I said, 'you refused to stand for a second term as Congress President in 1960. Weren't you needed then?' She looked a little irritated. 'My husband was ill,' she said. 'We were closest in his last years. My father was old, and my sons were young.' 'But between 1960 and 1965, you weren't much concerned in politics, were you?' 'Yes, I was.' It was a sudden irritable flash. 'I was in politics all the time. Let's be clear about it. I didn't hold any cabinet post or anything like that, but I was on the Congress Working Committees and on other committees. I watched it all ... I watched them all.' I said, 'In 1962, when the Chinese attacked India and your father was heavily criticised, and abandoned by his supporters, did you develop a distrust of people which you have still?' She thought about this for a moment, right elbow on knee, right thumb pressed against her underlip. At this moment Sonia, the wife of her elder son Rajiv, entered with the flowers I had brought. Mrs Gandhi turned her attention from me to them. 'Put the pink ones in the vase here,' she said. 'I think we should break up the colours ... and the red ones in the dining room. And the rest in my bedroom. Don't arrange them, I'll come and do that later.' Sonia smiled at me and went out with her dripping and fragrant burden, a wolfhound who looked as though its ancestor might have persecuted the Baskervilles at her heels. Mrs Gandhi turned to me again. 'Well,' she said, 'if you have heard that I've distrusted people since 1962, that isn't true at all. In fact, I don't distrust people, rather the opposite. I often think that my chief fault in life has been my trustfulness.'

The whirlpool that preceded and followed Nehru's death was not like most whirlpools. A whirlpool is normally symmetrical, but this one was not. Choking for survival in its blind eddies, the Congress leaders clutched at random twigs rather than at one another. It was certainly no time for trustfulness. To some extent the figure twirled around most rapidly in the muddy water, his white cap bobbing above the broil, was that of Morarji Desai, whom luck had left. The difficulty with Desai was that Nehru did not like him. Nehru was not by any means a bibulous man, and contented himself with a very occasional sip of sherry: but he was a tolerant man, and Desai's fixed, manic insistence on prohibition annoyed him: not the desire for prohibition, but the obsessive insistence upon it. 'We were repelled by his fads,' said Mrs Gandhi, and if by this (she was too delicate to say so) she meant Desai's consumption of his own urine, Nehru, a fastidious man, must certainly have been repelled. To add to Nehru's personal reservations about Desai, he was the source of considerable embarrassment to the government of India. Desai had at some time discovered that vaccine is obtained from cows. He therefore steadfastly refused, when he had to travel abroad, to be either inoculated or vaccinated, even if required to by the laws of the host country. This entailed a lot of exhausting explanations which were received by the concerned officials abroad with either ire or amusement: which galled the Indians more would be difficult to say.

There were moreover certain less comic aspects to Desai. He was supposed to number a horde of rich industrialists and businessmen in the ranks of his friends, and his son was involved in a fraud case which was hushed up. But Desai, after Pant died in 1961, was the senior minister. Nehru, however, deprived him of the Home

Affairs portfolio, normally a very powerful position, and left him discontented and more than ever in the mood of Cassius, with the minor honour of being second in rank in the Cabinet. Two years later the monosyllabic South Indian, Kamaraj, tired of Congress corruption in Madras, expressed the desire to resign from his post as Chief Minister and work for the poor. The idea caught on, with the public more than with the politicians, and the result was that under the Kamaraj Plan a number of state chief ministers and central ministers resigned. Desai, Gandhian or not, in a very uncharitable mood, was among them. Nehru then started to allocate more responsibility to little Shastri. He did not orally name him as his heir, but his actions seemed to. It does not follow that he was clearing a way through the forests of the Congress hierarchy for his daughter: when, after his first illness in early 1964, it was suggested to him by senior Congress officials that Indira should be made Foreign Minister, he turned down the idea. The Congress party was, however, full of ancient and sapless trees and fallen branches, and it was to these that Nehru, physically weak as he now was, applied his axe.

Nehru died on May 27 1964. Desai thought he saw an opportunity to stake his claims to the Prime Ministership which he had always coveted. He was to be disappointed. Some time before Nehru's death, Kamaraj, a powerful if not charismatic man, with two other chief ministers from South India, N. Sanjiva Reddy of Andhra and S. Nijalingappa of Mysore, and two powerful party bosses, S. K. Patil of Bombay in the west and Atulya Ghosh of West Bengal in the east, had formed a group, known to the Indian press as 'The Syndicate'. None of them could possibly have become Nehru's successor, but theirs was the attitude of kingmakers: they wanted to have someone who, ostensibly at the helm of affairs, could be made to steer in the direction they desired: someone mild, pliable, and without too much willpower. Desai was exactly the kind of man they did not want, while Shastri appeared to be. The Syndicate had influence inside the party, there was menace in the silence of Kamaraj under which Congressmen uncertain of their future swayed: Shashtri was so mild a man that he was liked but not feared, but with the Syndicate behind him he was far more powerful than Desai, who was disliked not only because of the abrasive nature of his personality but (a very Indian reason) because he was out of favour. When the new Prime Minister was announced a month after Nehru died,* he was, as everyone had expected, Shastri. The Syndicate rubbed its collective hands: and immediately received a shock.

Nehru was not always sound in his choice of associates. If, as Mrs Gandhi says, her chief fault in life has been trustfulness, it is an inherited quality. Nehru was not himself a conniver, and he therefore could not understand that certain other people were. His association with Krishna Menon was a disaster. Nevertheless, once he had associated himself with a person he maintained his loyalty to them when they most needed it. The natural consequence was that he was ringed around by sycophants and timeservers whose loyalty deserted them when he most needed it. Nehru was an intuitive person, and the possession of intuition is like the possession of a lethal device. It may blow up in your hands, or it may save you when you most need salvation. In the case of Lal Bahadur Shastri, Nehru's intuition worked.

The Syndicate looked on Shastri as a sort of lilliputian Pygmalion, material ready for the mould. The general idea of him, indeed, was embodied in his nickname, 'The little sparrow', a tiny, nervous, fluttery creature. Moreover, for a humble little man from a poor family to step into the shoes of 'the rapt one with the godlike forehead, the heaven-ey'd creature', seemed an impossibility. Shastri's task was made no easier when Nehru's sisters both wrote him discourteous letters virtually ordering him not to live in Teen Murti, the official residence of the Prime Minister, since it had been hallowed by the presence of their brother. Whatever Shastri's respect for Nehru, his feelings for the rest of the family must have been mixed. Nevertheless when after his election as Prime Minister he spoke to Mrs Gandhi, he told her that he wished she could have succeeded her father, though this was probably some elaborate form of Indian courtesy. He also made her the Minister of Information and Broadcasting, with the fourth rank in the cabinet. As regarded his occupation of Teen Murti: the letters of Mrs Pandit and Mrs Hutheesing, seen in context, looked rather foolish: for Shastri, a simple man, had no intention of living in Teen Murti, where he would have felt out of place. He remained austerely in his own small house. His wife cooked for him. This led to Teen Murti being turned into a Nehru Museum, and the elaborate culinary service

* He was chosen by a consensus within the party.

which the External Affairs Ministry (strange to say) had created for the former Prime Minister being dismantled. In these small details Shastri proved to have a mind of his own.

But this was also true of the larger issues, both at home and abroad. His manner was as mild as ever, but he had his own policies and he held to them. Though his attitude towards Indira remained outwardly paternal, he obviously had some inward reservations, since a few months after he came to power she made some rather unfilial observations about him, accusing him, at a party conference, of abandoning her father's policies. Certainly in the first year or so of his Prime Ministership he came under heavy criticism, and speculations were made as to his successor. Desai came forward once more, obviously eager to claim what he considered his right. He was considered the most likely contender now, but Shastri was still there, and the name of Indira Gandhi was adrift on the wind.

On my visit to Mrs Gandhi, as the day started to cool down and the voices of Congress supporters shrilled over the lawns outside, I suggested that we might open the door and let some air in. She smiled her sudden, charming, slightly mischievous smile. 'If we open the door,' she said, 'we'll certainly let some air in, but we'll also let a lot of noise in, and possibly we'll let some people in, and all of them will want to talk.' We left the door shut. Mrs Gandhi became serious once more. 'I didn't want to become Prime Minister,' she said. 'I never wanted to be Prime Minister.' She was thinking back to 1965.

Some political commentators have had remarks to make about such statements. After her father's death in 1964 Mrs Gandhi announced that she wished to 'drop everything and go to London for a few months to live with her sons', who were then studying there. She also declared that on her return from England she would like to retire to a cottage in the hills: no doubt the idealised wooden cottage, surrounded by trees, within earshot of a stream and far from everyone else, which she had once described to me, wistfully and with a small smile. However, when Shastri offered her a post in his Cabinet, within days of her saying all this, she accepted. I asked her why. 'They couldn't make a stable government,' she said, 'without a Nehru in it. That's why I accepted.' Shastri's version was different. He said he invited her into the Cabinet as a tribute to Nehru's memory. 'You had no administrative experience,' I said to Mrs

Gandhi. 'Surely you were a bit diffident at taking up a Cabinet post?' The noise outside increased and she frowned, but she was in a relaxed mood and eventually she answered. 'Well,' she said, 'I had enough experience to be an administrator. At least, I had as much as most of the other people in the Cabinet.' She adjusted, with light fingers, a pink rose awry in its vase, positioning it precisely.

Until 1965 Mrs Gandhi had remained a rather colourless figure to the Indian public. People were aware that she had been Congress President, not in itself a very thrilling position to occupy, and anyway that had been some years back, and that she was now some sort of central minister. The charisma of her father seemed to have bypassed her, though some observant pressmen noticed that when she addressed crowds she carried conviction, and they listened to her, more than they did to most ministers. The trouble was that the topics on which she had to talk were not particularly interesting or important: but they helped her to develop her technique with crowds.

Then, in the south, a crisis arose, on a subject Indira had seen cause trouble before in Bombay, in 1959: language. The problem had its roots in events that had taken place some centuries before Christ. When the Aryans had entered India and found in the plains a thriving and sophisticated civilisation, and a population of small, dark people, they fought them. Eventually the original inhabitants, the Dravidians, fled south. Northern India was occupied by the fairskinned Aryans, southern India by the dark Dravidians, and the area between by an intermixture of the two races. Today India has fourteen separate languages and a number of dialects. The language of the north is Hindi, a derivative of the Sanskrit spoken by the Aryans, and bastardised versions of Hindi are spoken as far south as Bombay. In the deep south, however, the guttural, hawking sounds of Dravidian languages are heard, and Hindi is hardly known at all. There are also other languages, like Bengali and its derivatives, and Assamese in the east. The only common language of the country is English: wherever you travel in India there is always someone who can speak, or at least understand, a minimum of English. English was therefore the official language in India until the time drew near when, according to the Constitution, it would be replaced by Hindi.

The southerners naturally were enraged by this. They saw in it a northern attempt at a conquest of the south, especially since there is a certain amount of contempt in the north about 'the black monkeys' of the south. Violence broke out in Madras: trains were derailed and burnt: northerners killed. Shastri, himself a northerner, pleaded with the southerners, but his origins prevented them from believing his assurances. In the midst of all this chaos, Mrs Gandhi flew to Madras. She was a northerner too, and a minister of the government which was trying to force Hindi upon the south. But nobody touched her. She went around, unafraid: she talked to the people: she talked to the leaders. All she said was what Shastri had already said, but there was a difference. The Madrassis had not believed Shastri: but they believed her. The charisma had manifested itself, after so many years, for the first time.

The next incident which displayed this new development in the character of Indira Gandhi took place at the other end of India: in fact, in Kashmir, from which her ancestors had come. In August 1965 she flew to Srinagar for a rest. It was not to be much of a rest, since in the hours before her arrival several thousand Pakistani troops, disguised as swaggering, filthy Pathan tribesmen, had crossed the border. When Indira's plane landed they were within a few miles of the airport. She was advised to turn back to Delhi, but she would not. She insisted on being driven to the military control room which had hastily been set up. The opinion of the military commanders there was that the invaders were only a small guerrilla force. Indira disagreed. The Pakistanis, she argued, would not let off squibs which could explode in their own faces. Since they had come at all, they must have come in force. Whereupon she more or less took over command: she demanded to be driven through the city, though the senior officers warned her it was unsafe: she was in constant touch with Shastri in Delhi. The Kashmiri Muslims, bombarded with broadcasts from the Pakistani radio and in sympathy with their co-religionists, could have formed a dangerous fifth column. Indira set up citizens' committees to keep up the morale of the people. She returned to Delhi from her unrestful rest perhaps happier than if, as planned, she had ridden amidst slopes vivid with flowers, walked, laughing, in the rockstrewn valleys, or lain in her tent, listening to the nearby streams chiming like small bells. On this trip the charisma had manifested itself once more, but also a quality of initiative and authority, a quality of leadership, which nobody, perhaps not even she, had ever dreamt that she possessed.

Because he was so diminutive, Shastri was beloved by cartoonists wherever he went, but I myself think a photograph I saw in an English newspaper funnier than all the cartoons. It depicted the introduction of Shastri to De Gaulle. Shastri's tiny whitecapped head came up to the carefully regulated swell of De Gaulle's corsetted paunch, so that it appeared that he had his face buried in De Gaulle's uniform belt. Shastri's right arm was raised vertically as if in a Nazi salute. The General, an expression of bloodhound depression on a face anyway not usually wreathed in radiant smiles, had his own arm at a very odd angle, as though it were in a sling, and was clutching Shastri's hand. I remember, in fact, that I cut this picture out and glued it to my study wall. It attracted more attention than my Francis Bacon painting.

Shastri was, however, not a comic character. He was intensely serious, and intensely anxious to succeed and to be remembered as a leader of his people. In order to succeed, in order to be remembered, he obviously had to stay in power. He already had Desai to contend with: the Syndicate, finding Shastri less malleable than they had expected, were slowly starting to turn away from him: Kamaraj was turning towards Mrs Gandhi. Feeling that he had been mistaken in the pliability of Shastri's personality, Kamaraj felt that a woman would be an ideal tool for the Syndicate, especially Nehru's daughter. He had watched her, gentle, sedate, obedient to her father, properly courteous to her elders: her parentage would capture the public imagination, and once she was properly in power the Syndicate could switch professions: from queenmakers to puppet masters. Like so many other politicians of the time, Kamaraj completely misunderstood Mrs Gandhi. Shastri did not.

He praised her successes in Madras and Kashmir, but though he consulted a number of his ministers, he never, or hardly ever, consulted her, which tended to isolate her in the eyes of the Congress rank and file, to whom this information percolated, or, in a typically Indian way, was allowed to percolate. When, after a mild heart attack, Shastri found himself unable to attend the Commonwealth Prime Ministers' Conference in London, he sent two ministers to represent him. One was Krishnamachari, the Finance Minister, an experienced talker and a veteran politician. The other was Indira. Krishnamachari did the talking: since he was hardly a glamorous

figure, Indira was supposed to supply the deficiency, but so far as
actual representation of her country went, she stayed in the shadows.
In this way, while Indira was seen to be part of the Cabinet, she was
seen as a very minor part of it. If Shastri wanted to nullify her as
a possible opponent, he played his cards well. His own position
continued to be shaky but, as in the case of Churchill, it took a war
to turn him into a national hero and to bring out the best in him at
the end of his life.

Four weeks after Indira had telephoned Shastri from an embattled
Srinagar, warning him that this purported random attack on
Kashmir by wild tribesmen was much more than it seemed and that
it could very well turn into a real war, her prophecy came true.
Delhi was blacked out as Pakistani planes droned like metal bees
over the borders: Pakistani troops and tanks attacked from the west.
Shastri stood firm, called his commanders, and the Indian forces
closed in on the Pakistani frontiers, the bombers rumbling and the
fighters caterwauling above the khaki men, some of whom were
Muslims themselves, comfortably working their way forward and
with seraphic slowness pushing the Pakistanis back. As the tanks and
artillery cleared the way for the human professionals behind them,
Shastri kept himself and the people cool, and when foreign powers
protested to India he showed a shrewdness and a toughness which
Nehru may have seen in him, but which few other people ever had.
He let his troops push a little way into Pakistan and, the war won,
stopped it from escalation. It was an honourable victory.

Shastri flew to neutral territory to conclude the peace treaty with
Ayub Khan of Pakistan. The territory was Russian, and considering
the Russian vested interest in the subcontinent perhaps not all that
neutral, but Tashkent, the place of signature, is a pleasant city, and
Shastri must have been happy as his pen scratched down his
signature, obituary to the short aborted war. It was January:
Tashkent was crisp and cold: Delhi would be too, when he returned.
In his own capital he would be hailed as a hero: he had won a war
and produced a peace. His political position had become stable.
The threats from Desai, the Syndicate, and even, more remotely,
Mrs Gandhi, were over. The little Prime Minister looked down at
the treaty. The flags would be flying at Delhi when he came home,
and the crowds cheering. It was peace rather than war that he had
won. I have finished my work, he may have said to himself, as he

shook hands and nodded at the tall men around him, and went to
bed.

When he came back to Delhi a little later, the flags were at half-
mast, and the crowds weeping.*

---

* Shastri died in the night after the peace treaty had been signed. He had
suffered from mild heart trouble for some time and the likelihood was that he
had suddenly suffered from a massive attack which killed him, an attack brought
on by the strain of the preceding day. Years after his death, however, his widow
issued a statement in which she alleged that he had been poisoned. By whom
and for what reason she did not make clear, but she affirmed that there were
discrepancies in the accounts of several of those present when he died. These
cannot now be checked and Mrs Shastri's statement seems a little eccentric.
Nevertheless, a curious if minute coterie has formed which believes that
Shastri was murdered, not by the Russians, who had no reason to kill him, nor
by the Pakistanis, who had come to terms with him, but at the instigation of his
Indian political opponents. I append this footnote partly as a curiosity, and partly
to show that there is still a racial memory in India today of a time when the
stealthy annihilation by poison of a political enemy was more or less a common-
place and that this kind of racial memory may solidify, even in rational minds,
into an obsessional belief. The occasional child sacrifices still made in rural
areas are an extreme example of this. These are acts of propitiation that probably
date back to prehistory.

✥ 9 ✥

A Tangled Web

WHEN THE JANUARY wind that sweeps down on Delhi from the high snows had dispersed the last embers on Shastri's funeral pyre, the expressions of sorrow etched upon the not very appealing features of the Congressmen standing prayerfully around were scraped away as by the same wind, and replaced by human, greedy, anxious, inquisitive looks. Eyes looked into eyes, searching for secrets: eyes veiled themselves, sealing their secrets away. Mouths started to speak as the whiteclad mourners walked back to their serried cars, and the unprivileged crowds who, beyond the police barricades, had also been spectators and mourners at the cremation, milled noisily homeward. The Congressmen and the crowds talked on the same topic: who would succeed Shastri? The Congressmen also discussed who would rise into the Cabinet and who would be tumbled back from it on to the wooden benches reserved for ordinary members of parliament.

Gulzarilal Nanda, who had acted as Prime Minister during the period between Nehru's death and Shastri's election, now once more stood in until the appointment of a new Prime Minister. But he had little political support and it was thought highly unlikely that he would be asked to continue his duties. Desai, hungry as a hawk, waited to pounce from the sky. But he did not have the Syndicate behind him. The five shareholders in the Syndicate in their separate states each held solid packages of votes, but were unsure to whom they should give them. Outside the Syndicate another candidate was Y. B. Chavan, but he came from Maharashtra, and though he had a considerable amount of support in his own large state, he was virtually unknown through the rest of the country. The Syndicate, towards which Desai had been bitterly scornful, realised that he must be defeated. It was not so much that the Syndicate and Desai were very different in their policies, but they were similar in their mutual dislike. The comment of Desai on this was, 'Shri Kamaraj had got prejudiced against me in 1964 and his prejudice continued.' The Syndicate, meanwhile, were determined not to repeat the miscalculation they had made with Shastri. They had imagined him, in 1964, to be safely enmeshed in their net: but Shastri had slipped through and, like a minnow eluding five voracious pikes, found his way to clear shallows where they could not reach him. Indira seemed to them a different proposition. 'They had put up Smt Indira Gandhi only in order to defeat me,' Morarji wrote. 'They probably thought that nobody except Smt Indira Gandhi could contest against me successfully. They opposed me because they felt that I was a man with a very strong mind and would not allow myself to be controlled by anyone ... '

Indian politics remained as unprincipled as they had been in Mogul times. 'Shri Jagjivan Ram initially supported me, but Shri Kamaraj won him over by promising him a ministership in the new Cabinet. Shri Jagjivan Ram met me and told me that I did not have the support of the majority and that he would go with the majority ... ' He adds, 'Indiraji had publicly said that Shri Kamaraj was her leader and also the President of the Congress and that she would do whatever he asked ... If Indiraji had stood on her own and these friends had not supported her with onesided propaganda, she would not have got 25 votes.' In the light of all these remarks, it is rather surprising that Desai, perhaps taking a step or two aside off the Gandhian path of truth he aspires to follow, stated: 'It was not my ambition to be the Prime Minister.' The only reason he stood for the appointment, he added, was because 'I did not consider Indiraji suitable for this office and considered it my duty to oppose her in the election.' He did, and collected 169 votes: Mrs Gandhi, the slight, shy young woman who had lived in the stooped shadow of her father for so many years, obtained twice as many, and she was swept into the seat her father had once occupied, the third Prime Minister of independent India, the second woman Prime Minister in the world. It is strange that the massed crowds outside Parliament House who heard the results should not only have shouted, *'Indira ki jai!'* or 'Long live Indira', but *'Jawaharlal ki jai!'*, that is, 'Long live Jawaharlal!' The Hindu theory of reincarnation, of rebirth, may have been echoed in this: the slight woman in the sari, acknowledging the surf-like thunder of the crowds with bowed head and folded hands, from balconies and cars and amidst

the scented winter flowers that dappled her lawns, may have been
transformed by the imaginations of many into the beautiful, erect
young man, a red rose in his buttonhole, who years before had
looked into the eyes of British troops and had not been afraid.

Indira now had to look her own immense problems in the eye, and
not be afraid: a difficult task. She had, first of all, to form a Cabinet.
The formation of a Cabinet, especially in India, is like the selection
of a cricket or football team, only of course a thousand times more
delicate and important a business. It has to be a united whole, not
a random collection of talented individuals. Jagjivan Ram was one
of the people Indira definitely did not want in her Cabinet. But
Kamaraj had dangled a carrot in front of him, causing the Harijan
leader to follow his natural dietetic instincts. The ingestion of the
carrot, it seemed to Kamaraj, constituted a commitment between
Jagjivan Ram and himself. He therefore urged Mrs Gandhi to find
Jagjivan Ram some kind of corner in the Cabinet, and the lady
consented. Kamaraj and the Syndicate were satisfied: their new
Prime Minister would do what they said. Desai said bitterly, 'I was
not invited to join the Cabinet,' and then, petulantly, 'but even if I
had been I would not have accepted.' He then withdrew into his
tent and sulked. When the followers who, magi-like, were still
trailing the parabola of his star towards a then inconceivable rebirth,
came to visit him, he told them at length of his spiritual virtues and
how he had acquired them. Mrs Gandhi, as usual, stayed silent, and
occupied herself with the task of acclimatisation to the affairs of
state. She had watched her father at work, of course, 'but that
wasn't really all that much help,' she said to me one day, gravely
examining the carpet, of which one of the wolfhounds appeared to
have made use. 'You can learn a little from other people, but most
things you have to learn to do yourself. And learning, well, it has its
own different aspects. Take politics: it's mostly mechanical work
but the most important part is mental work. You have to learn the
mechanical part, then you have to shape your mind to meet the
problems it will have to face. Even making decisions: you must learn
how to make a decision, to look at the situation from every angle
before you decide. Then,' her voice, always soft, became virtually
inaudible, 'there are other ways of learning, which haven't anything
to do with motivating yourself or being motivated. When you learn,
you sort of change, you are changed. For example, knowing

Mahatma Gandhi, I changed. You could not meet Mahatmaji
without being changed in some way. He may not have lectured you
about the world, but your attitude to the world changed somehow.
You had learnt something new about the world.' Concluding this,
for her, lengthy speech, she gave a girlish, nervous laugh.

At the beginning of her lonely road of leadership she had a lot to
learn. She formed her Cabinet in January 1966, only a few days
after Shastri's death, and she formed it quickly and precisely. She
dismissed a couple of the older and less effective ministers, but then
had to accept Jagjivan Ram. She removed Nanda from the powerful
Home portfolio and made him, though he still ranked first in the
Cabinet after the Prime Minister, Minister without portfolio.
Nanda, furious, went to Kamaraj and also to Dr Radhakrishnan,
then the President of India. Once more Indira had to back down:
Nanda stayed on as Home Minister. The quickly but carefully
planned Cabinet lay scattered about her office floor, and she, a
Cabinet maker without any tools, had to let the pieces lie around her
for the meantime.

The attitude of the Syndicate towards the Prime Minister at this
time seems to have been that of forbidding uncles towards a way-
ward child, an attitude which became forgiving when the child
capitulated. Indira, however, had become, both through the
circumstances of her life and her own inwardness, a tough and
resilient woman, though the Syndicate was not yet aware of this.
Moreover, she had a burning sense of family pride. Her conversation
today (she may not be aware of this) is full of references to 'we',
meaning the Nehrus, the pronoun 'our', also pertaining to the
Nehrus, and direct references to 'our family'. Whatever Pandit Kaul
may have done at the court of Farrukh Siyar, the members of the
family whom she had personally known, her grandfather and her
father, had never bent a knee to anyone or anything. Meanwhile, she
waited for a time when nobody would dare forbid her anything and
she would be the one with the power to forgive. Desai, though he
had declared his intention never to accept a portfolio in her Cabinet,
became the Chairman of an Administrative Reforms Commission
in the month of her appointment as Prime Minister, and then
approached Indira to demand that all members of the Commission
should be allotted the rank of Cabinet Minister. Desai's only purpose
in requesting ministerial status for the members of the Commission,
he explained to her, 'was to know what places the members would

get when they attended Government parties or dinners'. If the
Prime Minister was surprised, she had learnt enough by now not to
show it. I picture in my mind the flicker of Mrs Gandhi's right
eyelid as she pointed out that it was not essential that the members
of the Commission should attend such functions.

Desai, in pursuance of his duties as Chairman of the Commission,
was then supposed to visit Australia and New Zealand. In both
countries he became embroiled with the health authorities, due to
his refusal to be inoculated or vaccinated, but after some diplomatic
kerfuffle the matter was settled. In his autobiography Desai says
that Sir Robert Menzies, the Australian Prime Minister, told him
he was the first person ever to be admitted to Australia with all
health requirements waived.

Desai's descriptions of Australia and New Zealand can hardly be
called imaginative. 'I went round the Port of Sydney which is a very
large one ... The people are very fond of boating ... I also found
that the city of Sydney was very beautifully situated and built.' Of
New Zealand he remarks profoundly, 'There are neither extremely
rich people in New Zealand nor any poor people. All have proper
houses and there are no slums.' This reveals an ignorance of the
world remarkable in somebody chosen to represent his country
overseas.

Travel may broaden the vision of some people, but it narrows the
vision of others: and though it is as necessary and natural for people
to change over a lifetime as it is for the weather to change over a
year, Desai is one of the handful of people I have met who seems
never to have undergone any obvious change in thought or in
temperament. From his autobiography, he would appear to have
remained in the same hermetic cell from his boyhood to the present
day, carrying it like a carapace when he moves.

Mrs Gandhi, a woman whose life has been the exact opposite of
Desai's, had learnt quickly in the early days of her rule. She owed
something to the Syndicate but she was not willing to play at
puppets. She now proceeded to assert herself. In Parliament her
shyness was still with her, and she was sometimes hesitant and
unconfident when confronted by sharp questions from the opposition: but away from the clamorous floor, quiet and small behind her
desk, she made her decisions. The Punjab, a large state which is the
home of the tall, martial Sikhs, turbaned, bearded men whose holy

city, Amritsar, is not far from the Pakistani border, had been clamouring for a linguistic state, a state whose language would be Punjabi. Nehru, always opposed to the concept of linguistic states, had vetoed this idea: so had Shastri. Violence erupted within the state: so close to the border, it was open to Pakistani propaganda which would possibly lead to some kind of civil war. Indira saw this, and with the militant Akali Dal, the extreme party of the Sikh separationists, becoming increasingly restive, she agreed that her government would demarcate the linguistic state demanded by the Sikhs, though this state would not, as the Akalis demanded, become autonomous, but would remain part of the Indian Union. She took this step very shortly after she assumed office, and it landed her in a minefield. The public felt that a new and inexperienced Prime Minister had been terrified into acceptance of the Sikh demands: two panels, one headed by Kamaraj and the other by Nanda, were more than dubious about her decision. As it turned out everything went off perfectly.

But in June 1966 came another crisis, and a worse one. She devalued the rupee. Indian exports had for some time been heavily subsidised from government funds: devaluation was inevitable, but instead of taking small, wary steps towards it that would not awake the somnolent lion of the public to sudden fury, Indira characteristically decided to settle the matter once for all. She announced a 57 per cent reduction in the international value of Indian currency. She had not discussed it with Kamaraj beforehand, and Kamaraj felt himself, in a sense, her creditor: he denounced her decision. As it happened, the rains which had failed in 1965 made a repeat performance in 1966. There was drought, the crops failed, and with them the bulk of the exports. Devaluation was denounced all over the country. The Syndicate was now angry, very angry, and in November their anger turned into utter fury. The root cause was a uniquely Indian one: cows.

India at the last count had a human population of some 600 million people. This is exceeded by its bovine population. If the human population is not exactly healthy, the bovine standard of health is unspeakable. Most Indian cattle are underfed, diseased, and often ownerless: scavengers and wanderers, yielders neither of meat nor milk. They gnaw away pastureland vital for healthy cows: they ruin crops: in the cities they are an impediment to traffic when alive, and even more so when they drop dead. Occasionally these cattle infect healthy cattle, or, by copulating with them, ruin the stock. The only useful purpose they could conceivably serve is if they were to be slaughtered, in which case their hides could be cured at the tanneries, glue made out of their hooves, bonemeal from their skeletons, and, according to one WHO expert, canned pet food out of whatever flesh they have retained since their undernourished calfhood. Some of these items could be exported, and considering the number of such cattle around, they could be exported in plentiful quantities.

Unfortunately, the cow in India is holy. No orthodox Hindu will eat beef, let alone kill a cow, in whatever physical condition it may be, not even if it might prefer death to the kind of life it has to lead. Cows are slaughtered and eaten by Muslims: in fact, the extremist Hindu parties have, in the past, used this to incite communal hatred. In any event, there has always been a movement amongst fanatic Hindus to abolish cow-slaughter altogether. In November 1966 this movement gathered pace. Its onward rush was assisted by the *sadhus* who wander the country, naked or clad in animal skins, some with tridents and conches which they blow from time to time. Their main occupations are obtaining food from the villages through which they pass, and seducing credulous women who wish to be impregnated by a holy man. Rather curiously, these *sadhus* belong to a registered Trade Union.

Nanda, the Home Minister, had implicit faith in such people as well as in astrologers. He did little to stop the agitation of the *sadhus*, but since the government did not intend to ban cow-slaughter, he could not yield to their demands. When the Shankaracharya of Puri, the head of the great temple in eastern India, declared that he would fast until he died unless cow-slaughter was abolished, the situation really did become explosive. A great wave of naked and partially arrayed *sadhus*, thousands of them, armed with tridents and staffs, swept down on Parliament House on the cool morning of November 8 1966. Screaming and waving banners and makeshift weapons, with beards and long matted hair, their gaunt bodies smeared with ash and ochre, their bloodshot eyes (most *sadhus* use opium) burning, they must have made the cordon of policemen who sealed the entrances to Parliament House feel like the British handful who faced the Zulu *impis* at Rorke's Drift. Fighting started: several *sadhus* were killed and a large number injured. The rest scattered, and a semblance of normality returned to the huge red sandstone edifice. Dusk came down peacefully, hanging cobwebs of mist in the trees.

The fanatic movement had been effectively broken that day, but Mrs Gandhi summoned Nanda. It had been in his power, she said, to prevent all these events, but because of his involvement with these supposedly holy men he had done nothing, except to cause chaos. She told him that he was dismissed, or, more politely, asked him to resign. Kamaraj had saved Nanda once before, but this time Indira was adamant.

The Syndicate and Indira had now more or less parted company. There were many in the country who saw her first year as Prime Minister as a disaster. Already, within the Congress party, those who listened carefully could hear the long slow creaks and deep internal rumbles of a huge iceberg breaking up. Some thought it was about time: the Congress had turned into a frozen mass static in a tossed and shaken sea, its own moribund bulk pushing it deeper into death. It was time for some new current to shift it southward into warm waters, so that the dead ice collected over the years could melt and fall away. For all the criticisms of Indira, there were some who thought of her as the new wave, the current of salvation. 'She is the only man', it was said at this time, 'in a cabinet of old women.'

Mrs Gandhi had not spent the whole of her initial year of leadership at home. Shortly after she came to power she flew to America to meet President Johnson. I have met Johnson, and I would hardly have thought him the kind of person who would have appealed to Mrs Gandhi. He was a big, hard, icy man, as I saw him: however, that may have been because I was a foreign correspondent. With Mrs Gandhi he seems to have been big, gentle and warm: he called her 'a good and gracious friend', and, in the same speech, lauded Nehru and said that Americans liked to think 'he belonged to us too'. What Nehru would have said to this is difficult to imagine. On a visit to New York some years previously, he had been the guest of honour at a lunch in Wall Street, where several of the richest men in America were present. 'Just think, Mr Prime Minister,' said his host as course followed course, 'at this very moment you are lunching with men worth 40 billion dollars.' It was apparently difficult for his aides to persuade Nehru not to throw down his napkin and walk out. I mentioned this story to Mrs Gandhi once, and asked if she had been there and if the story were apocryphal or true. She laughed a little but did not answer directly. 'Well,' she said, 'you see, the Americans irritated my father. But that was because of his British upbringing.' I could imagine that to someone brought up at Harrow and Cambridge at the time that Nehru was there, Americans, so eager to be friendly, so anxious to talk about their families and their financial affairs, might have seemed beyond the pale. But Johnson and Mrs Gandhi seemed to become friends: Johnson assured her of 'everlasting friendship and understanding' and said that he would recommend to the American Congress that India should be aided and tided over her food crisis. He also said he would recommend that the United States should finance an educational foundation for work in India. To Chester Bowles, then Ambassador in India, Johnson said that during his private discussions with Mrs Gandhi he had been 'particularly impressed by the political astuteness she displayed', a noteworthy remark which few in India at that time would have made. Mrs Gandhi, in turn, seemed briefly to ally herself with the United States.

Indeed, on the way home from Washington she made a stopover in Moscow, where she talked to Kosygin. 'How can you expect the Americans to pull out of Vietnam until they can find a way to save face?' she asked. Kosygin replied, 'And how many Asian lives will be lost while the Americans are thinking up a way to save face?' There could be no answer.

1966 was not Indira's lucky year. Her apparent triumph in America, the promises of aid she had brought back, delighted the people: but then things started to go wrong. The educational foundation the Americans had promised, for various administrative and political reasons, simply faded away. Then, in July 1966, she made a state visit to the U.S.S.R., where a joint communiqué was issued at the end of her stay. This called for an end to U.S. bombing in Vietnam and contained a reference to imperialistic powers. 'These ungrateful Indians!' Johnson snapped, and the promised food supplies began to arrive not in bulk, as originally scheduled, but in dribs and drabs which did not materially assist the food crisis. Painfully the country fought its way onward. It fought every possible disadvantage any country could have: an economic crisis, food shortage, a whirlwind upward spiral of population, political corruption, immense inequalities of opportunity, unemployment, too few schools and hospitals, too few teachers and doctors, a brain drain, in fact everything. Its one advantage was a young Prime

Minister who was already learning, like her father before her, that what a country like India wanted was not so much a Prime Minister as a symbol, a leader, a *Shekinah* to lead them through the night, a pillar of fire.

The speculations abroad that followed Mrs Gandhi's initial election were, surprisingly, not so much as to whether she could make a success of it as whether or not the Indian electorate would accept a woman as its leader. Images of Muslim women draped from head to foot in black robes so that no man could see them, of Hindu widows hurling themselves (or being hurled) into the blazing pyres of their husbands, a wife walking five submissive paces behind her spouse, polygamy, and maidservants beaten like the carpets *they* were supposed to beat, filled the minds of the readers and writers of the more sensational Western newspapers. All these things have certainly been seen in India in the past, and some of them can still be seen today, but the position of women in India is not confined to this sort of thing. For example, a young man who meets a girl of his own age will address her as '*behnji*', or 'respected sister': a man of any age, meeting an old lady, will call her '*mataji*', respected mother. The '-ji' suffix, meaning respected, is applied equally to men and women, except that a woman may call a total stranger '*bete*' or son. Thus, in a sense she addresses him as an equal, since she omits the suffix. A number of societies in India are matriarchal, notably in the south, and also in the extreme north, where polyandry is practised. Moreover women, whisperers behind the wall, combine in most orthodox Hindu families to manipulate the men. In orthodox families they may, perhaps fortunately for the aesthetic sensibilities of the chance visitor, remain invisible, or appear with their saris veiling their faces, but their presence permeates the house. Humanity reflects itself in what it worships: in the Hindu pantheon, for example, the great Shiva is often conned into consent by his consort Parvati.

Quite apart from all this, the Indian people have accepted queens as rulers in the past. These queens usually came to the throne when their husbands had died, their sons were too young to rule, and no courtier could be trusted as a surrogate leader. Diddarani in the tenth century, and Kotarani in the fourteenth* were both accepted as rulers, and no man in Kashmir, from which they both, oddly

* Both Kashmiri queens (see Chapter 1).

enough, came, thought it a humiliation to accept their edicts or to
pay them the scandalous taxes they demanded. There were other
queens in India, two of whom at least became folk heroines:
Kitturani Chanamma in the south, who had a kind of private war
with the British, killed the local Collector, Thackeray, and was
captured and sent to prison, where she died shortly before the
Mutiny of 1857: and the Rani of Jhansi in Central India, who not
only played an important political part in the Mutiny proper, but
led her armies into war against the redcoats and was killed on the
battlefield.

Indian films, which, bad though some of them are, and perhaps
because they are so bad, influence the masses in their attitudes more
than any government documentary, have portrayed these women as
heroines: they also usually show other women, particularly mothers,
widows, abandoned or misunderstood wives, and social workers in
a sympathetic light (though the last category usually conclude their
careers by dancing round trees singing duets with some noble,
enamoured young doctors). All this, combined with a rooted tradition
of respect for mothers, sisters, etc., though not necessarily for wives,
makes it comparatively easy for the Indian male to accept that he
can be ruled at the highest level by a woman, though it is probable
that many are also ruled by women at home.

In this sense, the acceptance of Mrs Gandhi by the Indian male
public was uncomplicated. She was a woman, but the sort of woman
the legends spoke about: the daughter of the contemporary equivalent of an emperor (little though Nehru would have relished this
appellation, that is what the peasantry who form 84 per cent of
the Indian population considered him to be): she was a widow,
the mother of sons, and she was powerful, like the mother of a
household to which a young man returned. There was something
irrefrangible about her: as Toller's widow had written to Nehru
years back, she was like a little flower, who might bend in the wind
but would not break. It was the first time in her life that this quality
had really manifested itself. She was firmly rooted.

Nehru loved to address people, but he hated talking to sophisticated audiences. What he had always liked was to enter villages, to
tell grimy, intent peasants with hard hands and sad eyes what India
could be like, what he and they could make of it. He never tired,
and if at the end of the day the red rose in his buttonhole had wilted,
he himself had not. The happiness these meetings with the peasants

brought him perhaps justified him to himself: the years of Harrow,
Cambridge, the shelter of Anand Bhavan, had kept him from these
people: now he was free to drift his dream into their tired minds,
and he did. Mrs Gandhi did the same. She went to the peasants
and they listened to her, the reincarnation of her father: and she
had more effect on the women than Jawaharlal had had. The women
may often have been downtrodden by their men, but they, not the
men, ran the house: the husbands who had been in the fields and
had not heard Indira came back to the evening meal of unleavened
bread and lentils, and their wives told them what Indira had said.
She was gathering up around her the innumerable masses of her
country, and they were with her and for her. It was a pity that the
future was not decided in the dusty or rainsoaked fields, between
Indira and the peasants: it was a pity that though her crusade was
in the countryside, the final battle for the holy city Nehru had
dreamt of and she, more concretely, had visualised, had to be fought
out against ambitious politicians in the city of Delhi. But she had
established in the minds of the peasants that there was one country
and one central power, knowledge that they needed and wanted.
In later years, driving around the country, friendly villagers who
offered me food, milk, shelter, and asked me the usual Indian
questions about the number of children I had, how many were sons,
where I lived, how much I earned, would, on discovering that I
came from Delhi, always ask the same question, seriously and with
tremendous anxiety: 'Have you ever seen her? Yes? When did you
see her? How is the health of our Empress?'

Whatever the popular support for Indira was, the situation in Delhi
had become impossibly convoluted. The elections were due in
February 1967. The Syndicate had not set its face implacably against
her, but it was none the less a face that did not smile. However,
Kamaraj, Desai and the rest milled restlessly around in an attempt
to campaign. It was more or less accepted that the Congress would
win, for the rather naïve reason that it had always won in the past,
but the coalition of the opposition parties would obviously be a
factor that would have to be taken into account, and the Syndicate
and Desai felt that the turbulence of Mrs Gandhi's first year of
power would militate against the Congress. The lady herself,
however, had been thinking about this. The other Congress leaders
might campaign, but the Syndicate men had little power outside

their home states, and Desai, to the public, represented the interests
of rich industrialists. It was Mrs Gandhi whom the people wanted to
see and, in a sense, it was a turning point in the elections when she
arrived at Bhubaneshwar, the capital of the eastern state of Orissa, to
address a large crowd there. The speech and the applause had
started when suddenly somebody hurled a large stone at Mrs
Gandhi. It hit her in the face, inflicting a deep cut that bled pro-
fusely. She waved aside a rush of helpers, and mopping the blood
from her face with her sari but otherwise apparently unmoved,
continued her speech. This courageous action turned into a sort of
legend, and though the Congress won by a much reduced majority
Mrs Gandhi became Prime Minister for the second time: this time
not through an accident of history but by the will of the people.
This led to another extraordinary development.

According to Desai, she telephoned him shortly after she had been
elected Congress leader and, when they met, asked him to co-
operate with her and to become a member of her Cabinet. For one
who had not only declared Mrs Gandhi an unsuitable Prime Minister
but said that he would not accept office under her even if it was
offered to him, Desai's response was rather odd. He demanded
that he be made Deputy Prime Minister and Home Minister (the
latter being the second most powerful Cabinet post after that of
Prime Minister). Mrs Gandhi agreed in principle to the Deputy
Prime Ministership but pointed out that Chavan was the incumbent
in the Home Ministry. Later in the day Desai was asked by reporters
if he had said that Mrs Gandhi was not fit to be Prime Minister and
Chavan unfit to be Home Minister. He concluded that this story had
been spread by Mrs Gandhi, though what purpose this could have
served her is difficult to see, and that night he taxed her with the
matter: ' ... she persisted in her denial and said that she had not
said anything in the matter. It has been my experience that she
generally gets out of a difficult position by such denials ... ' Anyway
Desai eventually became Deputy Prime Minister and Finance
Minister.

The changes in Indira were now cloudily emergent. It must be
remembered that despite her storm-tossed childhood and her
difficulties with her aunts, despite the deaths that had bitten into her
life, she had never known personal enmity as such. She had seen the
effect of political enmity on her father: now she felt it upon herself,

and it must have been a strange and new sensation. The attacks, often personal, made upon her in the Lok Sabha, or Parliament, by people she hardly knew, left her pale and shaken at first. The least dignified of all emotions is anger, loss of control, and it is undignified not only in the person who is angry but also for the recipient. The rage of the opposition in the Lok Sabha was not only uncontrolled but irrational, and Mrs Gandhi at first could not handle it at all. Strangely, it was Desai, as Deputy Prime Minister, who helped her to find her feet. He was himself a very old hand at parliamentary techniques. He knew that it is better to deflate a critic than to attack him; he knew how to deflect a question that came too close to the bone. Mrs Gandhi may well have learnt from him how to conceal a velvet hand behind an apparently iron glove.

Desai himself, one gathers, still did not approve of Mrs Gandhi, and still thought her an unsuitable person for the role in which she had been cast. Nevertheless Chavan's unconcealed hostility towards him (Chavan must obviously have been aware of Desai's abortive attempt to throw him out of the Home Ministry) forced Desai closer to Mrs Gandhi. The next important political event in India brought them closer still, a curious confluence, as when the brown ripples of the Ganges merge with the blue ripples of the Yamuna outside Allahabad. This confluence came about because of the election of the new President of India. The President is a purely constitutional head with no executive authority, his main duties being to sit around at parades, to welcome foreign notables and to distribute national awards. Mrs Gandhi felt that like the incumbent President, Radhakrishnan, an ancient man, and nearly blind, the new President should be entirely outside politics. Normally speaking, since the President was not supposed to have political affiliations, the Congress and the opposition would have decided on a name. But the Congress lead in Parliament was a small one, and the opposition demanded to be allowed to select their own candidate. There was prolonged bickering about this, and eventually Mrs Gandhi put down a small, firm foot. The Vice President, Dr Zakir Hussain, she said, would be the next President. Desai agreed with this, and manipulated Hussain into the Presidency. Zakir Hussain was an eminent scholar and had, like the Mogul Emperors, a passion for roses, which he cultivated extensively and knowledgeably. He was a respected man, and politically an excellent choice: Radhakrishnan, from the south, had been a satisfactory President for an important geographical part of the country: Zakir Hussain, a Muslim, would be a satisfactory President for an important religious sector of the country. He was a harmless man, afloat upon manuscripts and roses, and was not likely, as Radhakrishnan had, to poke his nose into affairs of state which did not concern him. Mrs Gandhi was pleased that Desai had helped her in the establishment of the new President. They worked: they talked: but on neither side was there what could accurately be called trust. The relationship between them could have been called an armed truce. Already the rifles were being cocked.

The trouble was that neither Mrs Gandhi nor Desai had ever really liked each other. Mrs Gandhi may not be exactly a tolerant person, in the sense that she does not suffer fools gladly, but she does not attempt to proselytise those with whom she comes in contact. Desai is an intolerant man in that he sees anyone who disagrees with him as a sort of moral leper and, as I mentioned earlier, he has even tried to convert as unlikely a person as me to his political and spiritual beliefs. Mrs Gandhi is observant and very sensitive to situations. Desai is not. For the brief early period after the 1967 elections, when they worked together, each provided protection for the other. Desai held off the opposition orators who made Mrs Gandhi so nervous, and his support and organisation helped her to make Zakir Hussain President. Mrs Gandhi kept the Syndicate off Desai's back, and consulted him fairly often. Each was a shield to the other, but each shield was tempered from a different metal, and it was inevitable that when they clashed sparks would fly. Obviously this clash would not be delayed for long, for apart from their temperamental differences, Mrs Gandhi had liberal, or what Desai called leftist tendencies bred into her blood and bone, and Desai was as rigid in his rightist attitude as he was towards his religion.

Still, before the inevitable rift, Indira shielded Desai from the undying enmity of two ambitious men, Chavan and Jagjivan Ram, a man who, if that is possible, is less pleasing to look at than Chavan. (Once, I recall, having watched her seated in the government front bench at Parliament between the two, I wrote that she resembled a gazelle seated between two gorillas.) The ironic twist to this mutual protection was that Mrs Gandhi used Desai to keep Jagjivan and Chavan from aspiring too high. She was learning politics the hard way, and fast. But now the first hints of friction came. Mrs Gandhi had some sympathy towards those states that had voted the Congress out and new leftist governments in. Several of the new state ministers had been students with her in England. This was probably another black mark against them in Desai's book, and he believed that the minimal aid stipulated by the Constitution should be provided by the centre to these states, which, like West Bengal, were mainly poor and deprived and desperately needed aid from the centre. The initial friction between Mrs Gandhi and Desai started on this issue, but it was followed by a number of differences on other issues, each one minute in itself but adding steadily up to a point when the two were in more or less open disagreement. The Syndicate, while it could no longer affect Mrs Gandhi's policies, could still harass her to some extent, could still remind her that they had helped put her where she was. Kamaraj watched the rift between Indira and Desai with a pleased and beady eye. Basically it was an unavoidable quarrel: not so much because they were politically different, but because as people they were so far apart. Mrs Gandhi, who has a flexible mind, probably understood Desai, but that inflexible Calvinist certainly did not understand her. Years later, on a quiet Sunday afternoon, I asked her what her opinion was of Desai. Had it changed over the years? She was vehement, for her, she compressed her lips and said in a whisper more penetrating than a scream. 'I have always felt the same about Mr Desai. He hates people. You can see it in his face. We,' by which she meant the Nehrus, 'are not like that. No,' she repeated. 'We are not like that.'

The Lonely Listener

THERE ARE A number of festivals in India which take place every year, and the two most widely publicised by the Indian Tourism Development Corporation are Deepavali or Divali, the festival of lights which celebrates the Hindu New Year and takes place in November, and Holi, the festival of spring, which occurs in March. The tourist promoters send innocent tourists to visit over-publicised monuments at Agra, Jaipur and Udaipur, all conveniently close to Delhi, but neglect to send these tourists to such places as the caves and temples of Aihole, Badami, and Pattadakal in the south, largely because there are no five-star hotels available near these places. They do, however, recommend that tourists 'partake', as an official brochure puts it, of the pleasures of the festivals of Divali and Holi. Divali, which celebrates the first icy exhalations of air from the mountains, heralding the new year, is certainly rather beautiful: tiny lamps are floated down the rivers by orthodox Hindu women, wicks fluttering and flaming in leaf boats, like fallen stars, on the slow surface of the water: fireworks trailing like meteors across the night sky. These fireworks are also used on the more solid surface of the earth: children whirl sparklers in the dark, Catherine wheels and rockets are whizzed away to burn themselves out above every town and village. The noise accompanying this festival is indescribable, and since many of these incendiary devices are home-made, the foreign tourist who partakes of these pleasures is likely to lose a finger or eye.

Holi is also rather violent, though less physically dangerous. It seems to me rather misplaced seasonally, as spring festivals go, for it takes place at the precise moment when the sharp, pleasant coolness of the winter air is replaced, with no intervention of nippled pink buds on the branches, or a slow float of the sun across dead and clouded skies, by a sudden cloudlessness and the arrival of the burning, dusty, ravenous heat of the Indian summer. It is celebrated by people daubing each other with coloured powder, or squirting coloured water at the chance passer by, or bursting balloons filled with pigmented fluids on the heads of strangers, particularly women. The predominant colours used are green and red: green may be a symbol of spring, though in most parts of India every green leaf and grass-blade turns brown at this time of year: but the predominance of red leads me to believe that Holi was originally a fertility festival, the red being representative of hymeneal or menstrual blood. Winter and darkness have always been times when people make love: the baby boom nine months after the black-out of New York City some years back seems to prove that the conditions modern man finds most appropriate for sexual activity are the same in which the cavemen let population thrive. Hence, the winter and the time when husbands, wives, and lovers most frequently tousle their bedsheets being over, comes this hurling of red powders and liquids, particularly at young women, married or not.

Jawaharlal Nehru liked to 'play Holi', as Indians say, that is to daub others and himself be daubed with lurid colours. Holi is today mainly a festival for children, its probable provenance forgotten, and Nehru, when with children, liked to turn himself into a child. I had no idea what Mrs Gandhi's views on Holi were, but being summoned to see her during the festival in March 1978, I put on some very old and tattered clothes, of which I have a large supply in my wardrobe, and set forth for Willingdon Crescent. The garden was full of people whose clothes and faces were bespattered with various colours, so that each one looked as though he had been used as a canvas by Jackson Pollock. They were shouting, dancing, beating wild tattoos on drums, and singing. As I hesitated on the balcony of the house, noticing with dismay the advance towards me of revellers with handfuls of coloured powders and pastes and squirters full of undesirable liquids (surely the use of these squirters is in itself a phallic symbol), the door of the reception room opened and Mrs Gandhi's neat head peered out. 'Come in here,' she hissed, 'quickly.' I did. She was immaculate in one of her usual patterned pastel cotton saris: not a speck of paint showed on it or her. She did, however, wear one of her more irascible expressions. We assumed our habitual seats. Outside, the drums thumped. 'Happy Holi, ma'am,' I said. She said furiously, 'I can't hear a word you say.' I repeated my remarks in a sort of roar. She nodded, not very enthusiastically, but did not reply. At this point a secretary, who looked like a mixture of Grock done up before a performance and Joseph in his multicoloured coat, entered, and said that a delegation of peasants had arrived and awaited her on the balcony. A kind of groan came from Mrs Gandhi, then her face became impassive. She said, 'I'll come now,' the secretary opened the door and she went out. The drums thundered more enthusiastically than ever, and there were yells of '*Indira Gandhi ki jai*', and '*Indira Gandhi zindabad*', that is to say 'Victory to Indira Gandhi' and 'Long live Indira Gandhi', and of '*Indira Gandhi, desh ki neta*', which means 'Indira Gandhi, leader of the country'. Mrs Gandhi looked even more harassed than before, until she saw the delegation of villagers on the balcony.

They were obviously poor people, dressed in their best, which was now stained with pastes and powders. They carried garlands of marigolds, and each had a piece of paper in one hand, containing coloured powder. The hands in which these papers were cupped were hard and calloused, the faces, both male and female, had seen much privation and much weather. Their eyes looked up at Mrs Gandhi, wide and somehow hopeful, like the eyes of children. I was standing beside, but a little behind her, so as not to be in the way: my eyes went from the faces of the villagers to Mrs Gandhi's face. It was harassed, tired, still, as always, with dark circles under the eyes: but when, for the first time, she turned her head irritably away from the dancing, drumming Congress workers and looked at the villagers, her entire face unfroze. I cannot describe the look that came to it. It was not exactly a look of sympathy, or one of compassion. It was a look of *knowing*, a look of understanding what these people were all about, and then, slowly, came that remarkable smile, which can charm birds of any known species out of the trees, and her hands folded and rose in welcome. She spoke to them in Hindi, which I did not follow, and accepted their garlands. Then they said something to her in Hindi. I couldn't understand this either, but it appeared to me that they were all asking her (there were about twenty of them), if they could play Holi with her, that is, smear her with the pastes and powders they had brought. She replied, still smiling. 'She is saying,' the secretary explained, resting a hand covered with yellow paste on my shoulder, 'that she is very grateful, but she would prefer it if they selected one representative who may put colour on her.' After some debate, a woman was selected, came up to Mrs Gandhi, and very reverently, with a bowed head, touched a forefinger smeared with red powder to Mrs Gandhi's face. At this point a deluge of Congress workers invaded the balcony, shouting and flinging coloured water about. I decided to retire into the reception room and returned to my usual corner on the sofa. There was a great deal of noise and confusion outside: suddenly, above it, rose the small clear voice of Mrs Gandhi, not loud, but very explicit. Silence fell. She came back into the room, and though as immaculate as ever, she dusted herself furiously, then sat down. She wiped the little smudge of red powder carefully off her forehead, carefully as though not to repudiate an offering she appreciated but had not wanted.

When she had resettled herself, she cocked her head a little, not pleased: the drums on the lawn had redoubled in intensity, and the crowds, excited by their glimpse of her, were shouting more raucously than before. 'You'll have to talk very loudly,' Mrs Gandhi said, and then, perhaps sardonically referring to my normal mode of speech, 'if you can.' I yelled my head off: to my amazement, though she replied in her normal voice, which is soft but very clear, I could hear her. To start off informally, I said, 'Don't you like Holi, ma'am?' She said, 'No. I don't like it now. I did when I was a child, and when the boys were children, and I play Holi with my grand-children. But no, I don't like it.' It seemed to me, in her, natural. Nehru was an introvert, but he loved Holi, a return to a childhood that had basically been happy. Mrs Gandhi is also an introvert, but she obviously has no desire at all to return to her childhood for as much as a moment. Moreover, she is obviously one of those people (I am another) who dislike the close physical proximity of other people unless they are known and loved. She appears to dislike being touched by strangers: the Indian *namaskar* of welcome and farewell, made with folded hands at some distance from the person at whom it is directed, must in this sense be something of a godsend to her, in that she does not have to wring a chance visitor's paw, like a Western politician, with a warmth whose core is arctic. She has said of herself that she is 'a very private person': nobody who knows her, even a little, needs to be told this.

She added typically, an afterthought to what she had previously said, 'Of course, when my husband was alive, we played Holi with the children. I don't know if my father was always there. He wasn't

6

keen on my marriage, you know, and after that Feroze and he never got on very well.' One can see from a certain alertness in her eyes and hands when a topic interests her: she started to say something about Feroze, then she stopped, before I could catch what she was trying to convey.

But there had been something in the downward sweep of her eyes towards her hands, as she spoke, that had intrigued me. I decided to ask her a question to which I had always imagined I knew the answer. It was a question which required to be asked in quieter circumstances, but the drums had now acquired cymbals as intermittent assistants, and somebody had started to wail a hymn on the balcony. The door and walls between the reception room and the balcony are not what one would call solid. I shouted at the top of my voice: 'Ma'am, I think you'd agree there have been four important deaths in your life, your grandfather's in 1931, your mother's in 1936, your husband's in 1960, and your father's in 1964. Which affected you most?' She looked at me very shrewdly and sharply: perhaps nobody had ever asked her this particular question before. Finally she said, 'Well, you know, they all affected me in different ways. My grandfather died when I was a child, and my mother when I was very young.' Then she stopped. 'Yes,' I said, 'but, ma'am, what I asked was which death affected you most,' and answering myself with what I believed to be the truth, I said, 'Perhaps your father's?' The flutter of her right eyelid was her only reply for a while, but I waited: she was obviously thinking, looking into herself and into the past and the dead who had collected in that past. Then she said, 'My father first fell ill in 1961. I remember when I was with him at the Congress conference in Bhubaneshwar in 1964. He had changed, it was a visible change. He had lost all interest. He was a very disappointed man.' She stopped once more, lips pursed.

She had still not answered me. I said, 'So his death affected you more than any other?' She looked at me for a long while from a long way off. Then she said, 'I didn't say that. The most important death in my life was my husband's. I could see my grandfather dying, though I was a child, I could see my mother dying, and my father dying, but my husband's death was so sudden. My whole mental and physical life changed suddenly, my bodily functions changed. Obviously, when my father died I was very sad, but it was not at all the same kind of thing.' Then she entered into that particular type of silence that indicates that she does not intend to be drawn out any further on the topic under discussion. After a while her face softened a little and she said, 'Whatever happened between us, Feroze never made a fuss.'

A great deal about Mrs Gandhi can be explained by the account of herself she has given. She had no childhood as such: her childhood was a sort of votive sacrifice made by her family at the altar of nationalism. Her earliest memories, as she had told me, were of burning foreign clothes as a political act, and of witnessing the death under a hail of British bullets of an Indian nationalist. Her gawky adolescence was given to her dying mother, her young womanhood first to nationalism, then to nationalism and Feroze, then to the children as well. Finally she had given seventeen years of her life to her father. During this period, she had for the first time taken something away from a person, she had taken herself and the children away from Feroze. She may feel guilt about this. Their relationship was certainly a very odd one, but even when they lived separately, they frequently met: Feroze visited her and the boys, at the Prime Minister's house, though presumably he arranged these visits as far as possible at times when he was unlikely to bump into the Prime Minister. Feroze seems to have tried to be a father even when mainly separated from his sons. The irony and the pity of the whole affair lies in the fact that Mrs Gandhi herself says that they were so much closer in the months before Feroze died (he was unwell, but his death, as she says, was unexpected and frighteningly sudden). In these months they spent 'a perfect holiday' together in Kashmir, and when he died his hand clasped the hand of his wife. Giving had been the whole of Indira's life: but giving herself to Nehru had meant taking herself from Feroze. Thereafter she gave the whole of herself to her country. For a private person, it must be horribly painful to lead a public life.

One day in 1969 I was travelling in an airconditioned Mercedes across the sterile desert country of Rajasthan, a state west of Delhi. The word 'Rajasthan' means in Hindi, 'The Place of Princes' and the state is full of them, rich, poor, and in between, but all of them supposedly of royal blood. I was to lunch with one such prince and I was looking forward to sitting down for a while. It was July, the hottest month of the year, and no rain had fallen in the particular area I was traversing for two years, which was why I had come there, to look into reports of famine and migration on an enormous scale.

Heat-haze shone and danced like oil-slick on the endless road. Every so often, this road would be blocked by great dunes of tawny sand swept across it by the occasional burning wind. The driver and I then had to stop and dig the sand away before we could proceed. Moreover the tarmac of the road was so hot that about twice an hour friction with it caused a tyre to burst. Our trip was therefore slow as well as hellishly uncomfortable, but at last we arrived at a ramshackle whitewashed palace whose front door had fallen off. I did not have anything to knock on, therefore, neither was there a bell to press, so I went in. I found myself in a huge, shabby salon unfurnished but for a dusty chandelier and, on the floor, a colossal block of ice. A carpet was spread over the ice, and upon the carpet lay one of the fattest men I had ever seen, completely and grotesquely naked, being fanned by a small boy. This, I surmised, must be the prince.

He was. He invited me to share his arctic couch but gloomily informed me that there was no food or drink in the palace. He could, however, he said, despatch his servant to the village well to fetch some water, and we could then chip bits off his frozen bed, chill the water with them, and drink it. I had a better idea. I had brought provisions for a long trip: crates of tinned food and beer, a few bottles of Scotch. I suggested that the servant should take some of this out of the car and that we should then lunch off it. This was done: we departed: the afternoon part of the trip was, if possible, worse than the morning, until eventually we arrived at a dark bungalow in the middle of the desert. There was no water, for a bath or anything else. I told the driver to open the boot and break out a few bottles of beer and tins of corned beef. 'Sahib,' said the driver, 'there isn't any.' 'You're bonkers,' I said, 'the boot is full of it.' 'The boot *was* full of it,' replied the driver sadly, 'but His Highness took it all.' For the remainder of the trip, made through an area like the Sahara, we lived off chapatis* and whatever water we could find. On the way back, a stone lighter than I had been at the start, I decided to call on the peccant prince. He was once more naked, and once more lying on a block of ice, presumably a new one. He looked a little guilty, as well he might. A naked man, especially one of such gargantuan proportions, is at a disadvantage when it comes to making excuses for wholly inexcusable conduct. The prince confessed to his sins, apologised for the fact that he had consumed the

* Unleavened wheat bread.

entire contents of my crates, and blamed it all on Mrs Gandhi. 'In the old days,' he assured me, 'I would have fed you with peacocks and you would have had champagne wine to drink. But that woman, she has taken away my money. All I have left is my title. Soon she will take that away too.'

The romantic India still visualised by more naïve tourists centres around princes and tigers. There are now no princes and very few tigers, though in 1969 there were more princes than tigers. The princes, who hunted for pleasure rather than for food, were sleeker and normally in better health than the tigers. Sardar Patel and his lieutenant V. P. Menon had, in 1947, persuaded the princes to swear fealty to the Indian government. The revenue extorted from the peasantry by the rulers was stopped by the government: taxes became fixed and fair. The princes were induced to abandon some of their more nefarious activities, and in compensation were allotted privy purses by the government. These were allotted according to the amount of land the ruler held and the revenue he drew from it. Thus, while some, like the Maharajah of Mysore (so fat a man that, legend has it, a cry would arise from the courtiers when he arrived at state functions: 'Three chairs for His Heaviness'), remained immensely rich, others, whose states consisted of little more than a few scruffy acres, were brought by their privy purses incomes equivalent to those of labourers. Nevertheless there were an awful lot of princes, hence an awful lot of privy purses, and it all mounted up. Mrs Gandhi looked at this situation and did not like it. There were only a very few princes who actually did anything. Dr Karan Singh, the Maharajah of Kashmir, a tall, handsome, scholarly man, was a politician and a liberal, a supporter of Mrs Gandhi, and he wrote poetry as well as rather solemn books on religion and culture. The Nawab of Pataudi played cricket well, captained the Indian team, and at one point stood for election into Parliament. Though the Nawab was a national hero as a cricketer it perhaps demonstrates the innate common sense of the Indian peasantry that he lost his deposit. Other princes played polo: some had interesting little collections of stamps and coins: most, under the floorboards or in padlocked rooms, had considerable amounts of family treasure. The princes cost a lot to keep, and it was difficult to argue that they earned their keep: they did not. They were not too pleased with life themselves, for with foreign exchange restrictions their simple pleasures, such as annual trips abroad and the purchase of pedigree dogs and racehorses, were severely curtailed.

Not only were most of these princes parasites, but they were frustrated parasites. True, they had their privy purses, but most princes looked upon these as trifles in comparison to what they thought they needed. Some had their treasures, gems, gold and ivory, but under the law they could not use these as a source of funds since they were mostly undeclared assets. If they were suddenly disclosed the assets were liable to confiscation and their owners likely to be punished.

The princes, with the exception of a few like Karan Singh, were no towers of intellect. They had never been taught to think: indeed most of them had not been taught anything whatever. They had never entirely grasped the idea that a republic was a reality. The Maharajah who, rather like Caligula with his horse, threw enormous wedding parties whenever one of his dogs was put to stud, simply could not comprehend why he was now forbidden to do so.

There were certain other little luxuries of which they had been deprived. In Rajasthan, for example, the richer princes brewed a kind of liqueur known as *asha*. The Rajputs were a warrior race, and long ago, before they rode out in a sort of *kamikaze* squad against besieging Muslims, who were bound to slaughter them all, the nobles, while their wives and children prepared to burn themselves alive rather than fall into enemy hands, would drink a cup of *asha*, don saffron robes the colour of *asha* and, in Rajasthan, the colour of mourning, and gallop out of their fortresses, swinging their swords in the sunlight, to die. I may add that, having myself drunk *asha* a hundred years old in the palace of a prince, I would imagine that a cupful of it would be enough to prepare a man to do anything, even to die, without feeling too upset about it. It is probably the most potent spirit I have tasted in my life, and there used to be numerous varieties of it, like different brands of Scotch. Basically it is a sweetish but pungent drink, a kind of mead, tasting mainly of saffron. It was distilled, in the old days, in enormous vats. The vats would be distinctively flavoured, each with a different sort of herb or flower, but the most prized kind of *asha* was that flavoured with flesh. Into the vats, the brewers would throw the carcasses (doubtless plucked beforehand) of peafowl, chickens, pheasants, and, a particular favourite, partridges. The *asha* was left to mature for several years, during which the carcasses deliquesced and eventually became part of the drink. Another such drink was *gulab*, made of fermented roses: it involved the butchery of thousands of roses to produce a bottle of this liqueur.

Now the making of such cordials was a royal prerogative: peasants could neither afford to make them nor, according to the princes, would they ever be able to appreciate their delicacy of flavour. Under the new government, however, the princes had to have licences for the manufacture of liquor, which, since it was for their private consumption, were difficult to obtain, and some enterprising local breweries started to produce and bottle cheap commercial *asha*. This was mainly for tourists, but it was within the price range of the richer peasants, and they bought and drank it. This was a humiliation for the princes: that commoners could swallow the elixir once reserved for royalty, however different in kind the royal and the commercially produced varieties were, was somehow unthinkable, largely because the thinking of the royal families had not shifted very much over the last few centuries of Indian history.

The princes, therefore, were disaffected, frustrated, humiliated, very angry and in search of redress. In the 1940s, Gayatri Devi, the Maharani of Jaipur, where the maternal ancestors of Mrs Gandhi had lived so long, had been called by Cecil Beaton one of the most beautiful women in the world. Though now a somewhat faded rose, she retained a structural beauty in her face, she was elegant, and though she may not have had much to do with the peasantry in the past, she decided that she was popular enough with them (this was probably true) to be voted into Parliament by them. She allied herself with the Swatantra Party, a new mushroom party which was basically for the upper middle class and the rich: a party which was for an increase in the privy purses and a decrease in a socialist approach towards the offspring of kings. The Maharani, a woman not devoid of intelligence, attempted to do her thing in a democratic way: at least she campaigned, she asked the people for their allegiance. It is doubtful whether the peasants realised that to vote for Gayatri Devi was to vote for a new feudalism: that she had nothing specifically to offer them and that the Parliamentary platform she sought was not one from which she would make demands for the poor but for the rich, for those, like herself, who came of royal blood.

The peasants may not have realised this: Mrs Gandhi did. Her hooded kestrel eyes blinked briefly at Gayatri Devi, and then moved, luminous and swift, from prince to prince. She did not approve of princes, she found the privy purses an unnecessary drain on the government exchequer, and now she saw that the princes could be a disruptive element in the country. Some of the younger and sillier of them were talking, already, of a kind of coalition of princes which would collect the people they had once ruled and whom they supposed still to be loyal to them, and fight the government, by which they meant Mrs Gandhi. During this period, 1968–9, I met a number of such princes, and though they were unconscious of how foolish they sounded, they were serious about what they said.

Mrs Gandhi already had trouble with the Naxalite terrorists, followers of Mao, and mainly students, who were educating each other in the villages of West Bengal and Andhra Pradesh, and the dying octopus which is the city of Calcutta, whose writhing tentacles daily raise the bodies of thousands of paupers to its mouth. The Naxalites were educating one another in the art of beheading policemen and the science of chopping a village landowner into pieces and writing manifestos on any convenient wall with his blood. The Naxalites spelt real trouble: any trouble with dissident princes would be relatively minor, but a nuisance. Mrs Gandhi prepared to swoop for the kill. She would stop the privy purses of the princes; she would take away their titles. If they wanted money they would have to work for it. They would no longer be able to use their titles like earned badges of honour. From her point of view she was not only morally correct in putting an end to a colossal waste of government money, but she was obviating any possibility of foolish action by the younger princes: if they wanted to fight, they would have to do so in Parliament.

The issue had first been raised at a Congress Working Committee meeting in May 1967. At this time Desai had said that it would be unethical to break the agreement on privy purses, that the existing agreement between the princes and the government could be revised, and 'if we do not succeed in these efforts, we can take legal measures to give effect to our intentions … ' This is more or less what Mrs Gandhi was saying at the time, though by 1969 her views had hardened on this issue decisively.

At this 1967 conference, a more important change than the abolition of privy purses had been proposed: that banks and insurance companies should be nationalised. Most of these institutions had been founded by rich businessmen, and the result was that they loaned money most readily to other rich businessmen. People involved in small-scale industries, however much initiative or ability they might display, however good their references, found it immensely difficult to obtain loans, and a peasant attempting to borrow money from a bank would have been more profitably employed trying to borrow his airfare to Britain from Mr Enoch Powell.

These were the rationalisations for the proposals about the banks which, as Finance Minister, Desai was called upon to answer. He pointed out that the government had deliberately asked commercial banks in the past not to lend money to peasants.* This was apparently a policy designed to facilitate the formation of more rural co-operative banks and to encourage those which already existed. But, said Desai, it was possible that what he called 'social control' could be exerted through the Reserve Bank, the Indian equivalent of the Bank of England, upon the commercial banks, to widen the scope of their loans. 'Social control,' he said, would be far more effective than nationalisation. 'We can also formulate a credit policy for banks and ask them to implement it. We can then think of taking over those banks which do not implement our policy ... While it is thought of nationalising five or six major banks only, we can control *all* the banks through social control and can cover also foreign bank-through this method.' What is interesting about the pronounces ments both about the privy purses and bank nationalisation is that Desai appeared not only to be sitting on the fence but on both sides of it at once. He suggested that a new arrangement between the princes and the government should be negotiated, then appeared to say that should these negotiations fail, the princes could be brought to heel by force of law. As regards the banks, he proposed a mild policy of 'social control', suggested that the government should formulate a credit policy for the banks, then added that if the banks would not accept this, the government would take them over anyway.

At this time, in 1967, he had warily to test every political step he made: not only had he to maintain his stance as Mrs Gandhi's lieutenant, from which Chavan, Jagjivan and the Syndicate were all trying to shift him, but he was now uneasily aware that the lady had other advisers, and that she was by no means a prisoner of her own situation, as he may once have thought. Indeed the number of

* Quotations in this paragraph are from Desai's autobiography, *The Story of my Life*, Macmillan, India, 1974, vol. II, ch. 36.

people she consulted was wide and various, and his discovery of
this propensity of hers must have surprised him as much, when he
discovered it, as it did me when I did. Mrs Gandhi, in the comparatively peaceful years before she entered the political arena in 1959,
had a small circle of close friends, including Pupul Jayakar, to whom
she talked largely about her personal affairs and the work of the
child welfare committee and so forth, in which she was involved,
but she does not appear to have consulted any considerable number
of people about her committee work. Why, after she assumed the
leadership of the nation, she began to collect around her a squawking
aviary of advisers, to few of whom she appears to have listened,
remains a mystery to me. In 1967, for example, when the issues of
the privy purses and bank nationalisation were initially brought to
public attention — though the issue of bank nationalisation had been
vaguely mentioned every so often since 1948 — she had around her
what her critics called 'a kitchen cabinet', who met her at home when
she had the time. These included some people who were already
distinguished, and some who were later to become notorious, and
were nearly all politicians. Fakhruddin Ali Ahmed was to become
the President of India: Nandini Satpathi, a young leftist politician
from Orissa, served in Mrs Gandhi's Cabinet: later, after she had
been appointed Chief Minister of her home state, Nandini Satpathi
was faced with several charges of alleged corruption. There were
others, some senior Congressmen, some young politicians, whose
careers were to fluctuate wildly over the years to come, to whom
Mrs Gandhi in 1967 was a magnet to which they homed like chips
of iron, but to which they seldom adhered. Either they lost the iron
in themselves and fell away from her, or her magnetic power failed
for some of them. But those who departed were always replaced:
I have never known Mrs Gandhi to be without many advisers.

For a woman who appears to me one of the loneliest people in the
world, this seems weird: some say that Mrs Gandhi, having sifted
through reams of varying advice from different people, collects and
collates it, comes to a conclusion, and acts on it. This may be so,
though I have noticed that her advisers, after she has made a decision
and has implemented it, have often complained to me that she never
listens to a word they say. This to some extent supports a theory I
have, totally unproven but based on my own psychological experience, as regards her need for advisers. A lonely person, left alone
with work to think of, finds it very difficult to concentrate on it — at

least this is true for me. Instead, such a person comes face to face with himself, and the confrontation can be painful. However, if he is surrounded by people, all of whom are earnestly discussing topics which are of no particular interest to him, he is not exactly alone; and if he has a reputation for silence he surprises nobody if he does not say very much, but appears to listen, while in reality he is thinking about work and other matters important to him: and he does not think about himself, conscious from a small distance of the presence of others. Obviously neither I nor anyone else has seen Mrs Gandhi by herself, but I have often seen other people talk to her, and watched her while I talk to her and observed the way in which she listens. Until something said interests her, a chance shot flying into her thoughts, she is politely attentive yet completely remote. She usually appears relaxed but there is a frail tense quality in the poised body, like a bird about to fly: to fly back into the eyrie of her own mind. Her advisers over the years—her 'kitchen cabinet'—have changed with such frequency that she is often accused of treachery and disloyalty towards her supporters. I would think, completely without frivolity, that from time to time Mrs Gandhi feels the need to have around her new voices not to listen to.

Another reason for Indira to collect people around her was her insecurity. As a Prime Minister she led a party with a minimal Parliamentary majority, faced by a coalition of rightists and leftists. Mass rallies of protest are a popular political pastime in India and are usually efficiently organised. Party workers visit the small towns and villages outside Delhi, say, and pay a tiny fee for a collection of people to attend the rally. Trucks are despatched to these villages on zero day, the villagers are crowded into them, issued with flags and banners of protest, which they usually cannot read, and are taken into the city. They may not know what they are supposed to demonstrate against, but the general atmosphere of tension, the yells of the party cheerleaders, and the flags and banners that flap in the wind before their serried ranks, above them and behind them, plus the fact that they have been paid some princely sum like U.S. 50 cents for their very presence, rouse them from their normal torpidity. They shout what the cheerleaders shout, wave their banners like Crusaders, and advance upon their target, Parliament House or whatever it may be, down roads lined with policemen bearing bamboo riot shields and *lathis*, long, heavy sticks which, when expertly swung, can be very painful to the person they are swung at. Harmless though these demonstrations basically are, they can be incited and excited into violence, and, in a marching, yelling, flag-waving mass, they are a terrifying spectacle. One day in Delhi in 1969, when I was making a couple of films on India for B.B.C. television, my crew and I went to cover one such rally, the target of which was the home of Mrs Gandhi. The road that led to her residence was completely cordoned off by armed policemen. The demonstrators, members of Jan Sangh, an extreme Hindu party (their leader, Atal Behari Vajpayee, was later the Foreign Minister of India under the Janata government), therefore set up a platform in front of the police cordon, from which various speakers were to harangue the crowd. Our crew set up, ready to film, beside this platform. We heard the demonstrators long before we saw them: a kind of ragged but rhythmic roaring, faint at first, increased in volume until birds, shaken out of trees by the uproar, blundered wildly overhead, filling the sky with wings, and the demonstrators appeared, mostly men, white-clad, their banners flapping, shouting catch-phrases or simply, blindly, mouths open like mutes, shrieking incoherently as they advanced towards us, their faces snarling and masked in dust. 'Sweet—fucking—Christ,' said my cameraman with deep emotion, as he stood by his tripod, with the rest of us, uncertain, around him, while total pandemonium supervened. The howls of the Hindus, mingled with the shrieks of the terrified birds overhead, filled the air, by now heavy with scuffed dust and the rancid odour of innumerable bodies. The demonstrators made attempts to break the police cordon and rush down the road to Mrs Gandhi's residence, and were driven back by the rising and falling *lathis* of the police. The speechmakers screamed wildly into the microphones, but though they could not be heard above the noise their obvious hysteria infected the crowds even more. By the time it was all over the crew and I were drenched with sweat and covered from head to foot with dust. Back in the hotel, air-conditioner purring, feet up, icy beers in our hands, we talked about the morning. 'Christ, what a mob of yobbos,' somebody said. 'Does this sort of thing happen often, then?' Our Indian assistant nodded, smiling happily. 'To Mrs Gandhi,' he said, 'often, often. These days, very often. She is a *most* unpopular lady.' 'If I were a bird who was Prime Minister,' said the sound man, who was understandably irritable after being deafened through his earphones all morning, 'and that kind of mob came to call on me often, I'd bloody well resign and buy a cottage in the country.'

Mrs Gandhi may have had, at the back of her mind, the idea of eventually buying a cottage in the country. In fact she has often told me so, but the last thing in her mind was a wish to resign. Years later I told her I had watched this rally. 'There were quite a lot at that time,' she said. 'I don't remember.' I said, 'Facing crowds, hostile crowds, knowing there may be grenades in somebody's pocket, or a gun, or even a knife, doesn't that bother you? Aren't you afraid of the process of dying, or of death itself?' She gave me the standard answer to that particular question: 'Of course not. I don't think about it.' Most politicians, however, put considerable emphasis, in a tone of simple sincerity, behind such statements. The very fact that the question clearly did not interest Mrs Gandhi, the slight impatience in her voice as she brushed it aside, convinced me that she really was sincere. 'But you must think of death and the afterlife,' I said. 'You see Anandamayi Mai and Swami Brahmachari, don't you, who are supposed to be spiritual people?' She said, 'Yes, I do. Anandamayi Mai is a very old friend of my mother's. She influenced my mother tremendously. But I go to see her because she's an old friend. Swami Brahmachari is my yoga teacher. I have started to practise *yoga* like my father. He teaches me the *asanas*.' I persisted despite her evident irritation. 'And what do you think,' I inquired, 'about the possibility of an afterlife?' She said, 'I don't think about an afterlife. I have too little time in this one.'

It was true, in 1969, that she had little time. Her popularity, which had fluctuated since she became the national leader, was at a low ebb. Not only did she have enemies in front of her, the angry and vociferous opposition, but enemies behind her, silent and full of cold fury: the Syndicate and Desai, and the rightist elements in the Congress. Desai at this point must have felt confident that he would replace Mrs Gandhi. She was determined that she would not be replaced, that she would break the Syndicate, and that unlike her mother she would not allow herself to be broken.

❦ 11 ❧

The Anguish of Arrival

IF YOU WRITE about someone, you need to keep the person concerned under your eye, and you need to have kept them there for some time. I was fortunate to be in India, which I made a base for my Asian operations during most of the time between 1968 and 1970, the time when Mrs Gandhi finally slipped the coils of the old Congressmen. Motilal's legendary wrestling with cobras cannot have equalled, in uniqueness, the feats she performed in these years, shaking off Desai, the Syndicate, and other people who thought they had the right to pressurise her, largely because they were older than she was and farther to the right than she was. 'Right of what?' Mrs Gandhi once asked. 'Left of what?' and I see what she meant. Mrs Gandhi, so far as I have ever been able to observe, has no ideology as such. She is a totally practical person and her lack of application to an ideological line is due to this. When she perceives a solution to a problem, she adopts it. Her father was the same, it seems to me, in the opposite way, because he dreamt. He took, really, no ideological line: he looked for solutions implicit within the possibilities of solution. It needs many pliant faceless men to make an ideology work. The Syndicate and Desai loved the red tape of ideology and bureaucracy: Mrs Gandhi trapped them in it, because it is practical, when bothered by creatures of any kind, to use a trap where the bait is attractive. They took the bait and then she had them where she wanted them.

This took some time for her to accomplish. In early 1969 the pillars of the Syndicate, and other potential Brutuses within the Congress, stout and happy fellows like Jagjivan Ram (once, when Mrs Gandhi vaguely thought of kicking him upstairs by making him President of the country, she was advised not to, since he would hardly provide an example to the people, allegedly not having paid his taxes for ten years), Cassiuses like Desai whose son was charged with alleged fraud and defalcation, to which charges the father devoted a whole chapter of denial in his autobiography, walruses like Chavan, willing to flop about as heavily through political hoops as anyone desired, even if a wet fish was all that was thrown to him in the end: these people surrounded her, cutting her off, like a temple deity, from the outside world. It must have been with the emotions of numerous Frankensteins that they watched what they took to be a monster stir and come to life. Slowly her image of temple deity, stone once, became bone, flesh, skin, voice, hands, and a self, and, rising from inanimate life, offered itself to the Indian people: widows, untouchables, peasants, illiterates, children: the entirely poor, the entirely defenceless. The pillars of the Syndicate were in her way, so she pulled them down, though, more cleverly than Samson, she slipped from under the tumbling temple whose foundations she had destroyed. Looking back at what she had left behind her, old and terrified politicians who trembled with the debris of their beliefs around, she must have been aware of a sense of arrival.

The issue of bank nationalisation, in the early part of 1969, was still unclear. 'Social control' of the banks, as prescribed by Desai, continued to be in force. This had been decided upon as far back as May 1967, but it was a much criticised policy, and most criticised by a gaggle of rather elderly young politicians who had collected around Mrs Gandhi, and were known as 'The Young Turks'. They wanted instant bank nationalisation. A grave, gentle man, P. N. Haksar, then Mrs Gandhi's Private Secretary and the best adviser she has ever had, kept the Young Turks from exercising too positive an influence over her. Nevertheless, her mind was on bank national-isation and on outfoxing her political enemies both inside the Congress, a house divided against itself, and outside. The latter was probably uppermost.

Though the Congress is avowedly socialist, it had floated for many years on money donated by capitalists: annexation of the banks would clearly alienate these benefactors. 'Social control' was a kind of middle course: the privately owned banks were advised to make loans to peasants by government committees set up by Desai: these committees also checked tax evasion, a traditional habit with most very rich people, notably industrialists and film stars. The commit-tees were firm, but they adopted an attitude of sweet reason towards the banks which infuriated the Young Turks with their all or nothing policy. Chavan, who also supported bank nationalisation, drew closer to Mrs Gandhi: Desai drifted farther and farther away, flotsam tumbled in spindrift seas. Mrs Gandhi had at first advocated a 'fair trial for social control': by 1969 she clearly felt that it had had its trial and her own verdict was that it had failed. There were now two clear divisions in the Congress: the Syndicate and the other older leaders, and the younger, liberal politicians around Indira, who formed what was called the Indicate.

In May of that year the President, Dr Zakir Hussain, died of a heart attack, and the Vice President, V. V. Giri, a labour leader from the south and rather more pliable in Mrs Gandhi's delicate hands than his predecessor, took over as temporary President. There were lengthy obituaries, black borders on the newspapers, a state funeral: that done with, the question of who was to succeed Zakir Hussain arose. Mrs Gandhi had discussions with a number of people, and it became apparent that her candidate for office was Giri. Giri was, like several other senior Congressmen, a stout, talkative man, who had been an excellent labour leader but could scarcely be called an intellectual. The three previous Presidents, Rajendra Prasad, a veteran Congressman, a shrewd man and dignified, Dr S. Radhakrishnan, a scholar and author, and Dr Zakir Hussain, also a scholar, in the old delicate Persian tradition rather than in the South Indian tradition manifested by his predecessor, were all men of presence and prescience: however admirable his achievements, Giri could not be said to resemble any of the previous three. Moreover, he had a (literally) small difficulty in his wife, who though tiny had an exceptionally dominant personality. It must be remembered that many South Indian societies are matriarchies, and when Giri as Vice President had travelled abroad, or indeed anywhere, on official duties, his wife, who had not seen much of the world, but wished to, accompanied him. So had the rest of his family, all at government expense. Desai remembers that one of the first remarks he made to Mrs Gandhi when she astounded him by expressing her desire for Giri as President was that 'Shri Giri had attracted a great deal of criticism on account of his fondness for travelling with his family'. Mrs Gandhi brushed this aside, apparently, as an amiable aberration.

She said to me once, when I asked her about her brilliant ability to manoeuvre politically: 'I don't manoeuvre. If you try to manoeuvre when you are dealing with people, you fail.' I think Mrs Gandhi usually says what she believes to be true – otherwise she either becomes evasive or holds her peace—but if what she did in 1969 was not a brilliant manoeuvre, in the sense of a series of rapid thrusts and forays in and out of the ranks of her opponents: the probing for weakness, the intuitive sense of where to attack, the wheeling away and the flanking movements by which the enemy fell or were scattered—I no longer believe any observation of anything or anyone I have ever made can be true. Mrs Gandhi wanted Giri for President, I thought then and think now, for a specific purpose. Desai may not have entirely seen this, but apart from his other ideas about Giri, he may have smelt something in the air. Mrs Gandhi airily suggested Jagjivan Ram, and then Rajagopalachari, the old Madrassi politician and writer who had been Governor General of India after 1947, as other candidates, but in the main she brought the otherwise unmemorable name of Giri up frequently enough to annoy Desai, who, with the other elders of the Congress, had decided that N. Sanjiva Reddy, a politician of rightist views, who hailed from South India, would be the best President available. Mrs Gandhi did not appear to approve. However, the President of India is voted into power by a consensus in the Upper and Lower Houses of Parliament, and different candidates have to be nominated by different parties. The government candidate, for example, had to be nominated by the Congress Parliamentary Board. This was mostly run by the older Congressmen, and the Congress President, S. Nijalingappa, another southerner, was for Sanjiva Reddy.

On July 12 the Congress Parliamentary Committee met at Bangalore to decide on the party candidate for President. At this meeting Mrs Gandhi re-proposed the name of Jagjivan Ram, supported by Fakhruddin Ali Ahmed, one of the old 'kitchen cabinet', and by Jagjivan himself. Desai, Chavan, and two Syndicate members, the old black bear Kamaraj, who still had claws and teeth and whose hug could crush the unwary, and S. K. Patil of Bombay, who would have been happiest in Tammany Hall, supported Reddy. So did Nijalingappa. That meant that Reddy had been nominated as the Congress candidate by a 5-3 margin. Thereupon Mrs Gandhi said that Reddy would be a poor candidate and his nomination would lead to 'serious repercussions'. What these were she did not elucidate. However, it was agreed that Nijalingappa and she should meet the next day and come to some mutually agreeable settlement, which the rest would accept. Next day they met, while the others rumbled miserably to one another. It would have been easier for a herd of bulls to catch a butterfly. Mrs Gandhi fluttered back to Delhi, the whole problem still in the air. A goaded Nijalingappa, on the evening of this ill-fated day, declared Sanjiva Reddy to be the Congress candidate.

Mrs Gandhi, as is her wont, then made some quick and efficient strikes. On her return from Bangalore to Delhi, with Desai still, quite literally, up in the air, on his way back on the flight after hers, she told certain people that she would drop Desai from the Cabinet. Desai says in his autobiography that it was on July 14 that he learnt of this. Then, 'when I was in my office in the Finance Ministry on July 16 1969, a special letter from the Prime Minister was handed over to me at about 12.30 p.m. Soon after, at about 1.30 p.m., an announcement was officially made that the Prime Minister had taken over charge of the Finance Ministry. This made it clear that the Prime Minister did not want to discuss the matter with me at all and that her decision had already been implemented ... She had stated in her letter that I should continue as Deputy Prime Minister and that she would discuss with me later on what work should be entrusted to me ... This was an amazing proposal, and a very clever move ... ' Mrs Gandhi, in other words, had made it possible for Desai to resign from the Cabinet: she knew he would: she also brought right in on her side, if he did so, since she had offered him an option: his refusal of the option would leave him some dignity, a commodity very important to him.

She then telephoned Desai at 8 p.m. that night, asking him to come and see her. He replied, according to his biography, that he could not 'because it was late' and would come next day. Next day she asked him to continue in the Cabinet. Desai, according to his own account, then delivered one of his famous moral lectures, ending, 'Even when I have differed with you in some matter, I have never been guilty of impropriety or discourtesy. What I have felt is that you have behaved towards me in a manner in which none would have even with a clerk.' Mrs Gandhi, who likes people to come to the point, 'accepted that the method was wrong'. Desai said, in what he obviously feels was a magnanimous manner, 'If you now feel you acted wrongly, you can retrace your steps.' This, Mrs Gandhi murmured, was difficult to do. Desai went away: wrote her a letter: did not, according to him, receive a reply: and on July 19 expressed his woes to the Congress Parliamentary Party. The members present stared at the frail source of all this apparent disorder, as men might who have suddenly heard a nightingale roar: Mrs Gandhi remained small and impassive. 'The Prime Minister accepted my resignation at 3 or 4 p.m. by a letter she wrote to me. I sent my reply to her immediately.' The same night, Giri, for the first time, demonstrated how useful he could be to her. As acting President, he was empowered to issue ordinances that would bypass the two houses of Parliament and pass into law. He issued his first such ordinance: by it the government took control of fourteen leading banks with assets of $66·6 million. From that day onward, Mrs Gandhi, the woman, the unpopular one, the shy one, the awkward one, was beseiged, every day, by the poor: those who had never expected that any banks would lend money to them, those who had fatalistically accepted that like bullocks they would wait, heads down to the dusty wind, acceptors, always, never makers of demands: and this woman, their Prime Minister, had unyoked them, released them into fresh pastures. The small-scale industrialists, the peasants with or without land, these profited and they knew it: '*garibi hatao*,' said Mrs Gandhi, drive poverty away, and the poor of the land answered and applauded. They brought her flowers, sprawled yellow marigolds and small taut tuberoses, and sweets, and sometimes when they saw her they wept, though it was only from happiness. '*Garibi hatao*,' they echoed: unluckily the implication was, *you* do it: *you* drive poverty away.

It was still not over. The Congress, at least the ancients within the Congress, had nominated Sanjiva Reddy, and he remained the party nominee. But Mrs Gandhi, from whose mind the candidature of Jagjivan Ram appeared to have slipped, was now behind Giri once more. Giri stood as an independent. This was a terrific risk, but I have always found Mrs Gandhi likes taking risks (she also likes people who are willing to take them) because, with a lean lead in Parliament and a section of her own party separated from her by the Syndicate and Desai, the chances of her candidate becoming President were small. She took the risk and, exactly a month after she had nationalised the banks, Mrs Gandhi saw Giri elected the fourth President of India.

One of the reasons for this was that Indian politicians have always been motivated by a passionate desire to be with those who seem powerful. Bank nationalisation had brought Mrs Gandhi so much popularity with the masses that there was no question of holding back to consider: those who were not with her were against her, and few were willing to be against her. Nevertheless, Desai, like Achilles, was still sulking in his tent or rather in his large and well appointed house on Dupleix Road in Delhi. Around him were his remaining supporters, begging him, like the supporters of Achilles, to come out and fight. One of these supporters was Nijalingappa, still the Congress President, and on November 12 1969, he announced the expulsion of Mrs Gandhi from the Congress Party. She had been prepared for this, of course: nobody had expected her not to be.

She announced that the real, the original, the fighting Congress, was no longer in the hands of the old men. In fact, in so far as any section of the party was left in their hands, it was not the Congress. She had redesigned the Congress and re-formed the ranks, and the real party was the one she ran. Since Desai, the leader of a broken remnant, disagreed violently with her over this point, two separate Congresses came into existence: Desai's party, which included the Syndicate members, was called Congress (O) or the Old Congress: Mrs Gandhi's was called Congress (R) or the Ruling Congress. Mrs Gandhi had with her Chavan and Jagjivan Ram, Chavan important for votes in his home state, Maharashtra, of which he had once been Chief Minister before he entered the larger and more testing political arena of Delhi: Jagjivan Ram because the Harijan vote was supposed to come with him. Two lieutenants less dependable on for loyalty would have been hard to come by anywhere, but they were the best available in India, at least to Mrs Gandhi, and all the other timeservers and opportunists came with her, so that eventually her Congress held 228 seats in the Lok Sabha, and she allied herself to the leftist parties, including the orthodox Communist Party of India, i.e. the Russian orientated one, thus holding fast against the Congress (O) who had only 65 seats in the Lok Sabha, and allied itself to the fervently Hindu rightist party, the Jan Sangh, and the rich men's party, the Swatantra, to whom Gayatri Devi of Jaipur belonged. Mrs Gandhi, at this point, must have had fingertips of steel to stay where she was, and obviously she wanted to be free of sycophants and friends who were forced upon her. She wanted to have a clear field: Joan of Arc, dreamt of as a symbol in her childhood, stood before her as a symbol, though not yet Joan at the stake, but the Maid of Orleans, pale face uplifted to the stars, on her doomed way into battle.

Nevertheless, advised by Haksar, and listening but not listening, as is her habit, to the advice of many other people, she did not ride out for a while, though attacked as a dictator, a megalomaniac, and, rather interestingly, as a woman. In September 1970, she came back suddenly to the matter of the privy purses. She brought into the turbulent Lok Sabha a bill which abolished all princely privileges. This did not only include the privy purses but other perks. Princes did not have to pay customs duty on their imports: it was not demanded of them that they possessed driving licences (many other drivers, not to mention pedestrians, had reason to regret this), they could not be taken to court for any offence and they were entitled to a salute of cannon (the most important princes were 64-gun men).

The privy purses, as I mentioned in the last chapter, had interesting variations: of the 278 princes in India in 1969 the largest privy purse went to the largest prince, the Maharajah of Mysore, 'His Heaviness', who received a yearly $350,000: incidentally, all privy purses were tax-free. The smallest privy purse went to the Talukdar of Katodia, and Katodia is a state so minuscule that I cannot locate it on any map: the Talukdar received $25 a year, and whether or not it was tax-free cannot have mattered very much to him, though one wonders how many cannon he was entitled to as his royal salute, poor fellow. The Lok Sabha passed Mrs Gandhi's bill, 339 to 154. It had now to be heard in the Rajya Sabha, the upper house, the equivalent of the House of Lords. There, 224 members voted, 149 for the bill, 75 against. But, for Mrs Gandhi, it was an irritating, minimal defeat. For a bill to be passed by the upper house in India, two thirds of the members present have to vote for it. Two thirds of 224, unfortunately for Mrs Gandhi, came to 149⅓. The bill was defeated, therefore, by a ghostly third of a person. Mrs Gandhi, who can be very patient or very impatient as the circumstances demand or her mood dictates, called the Cabinet into session that night. Next day Giri, always ready to oblige, issued another Presidential ordinance whereby the princes were stripped not only of their rights but their titles. Another uproar followed this. The followers of Desai compared her to Hitler, Stalin, and other of the less desirable characters of history — something to which she was to become accustomed in the future, though in 1969 it shook her a little. The princes wanted to take their case to the Supreme Court of India, to finance an alliance of rightist parties, to hurl Mrs Gandhi from the white horse the peasants imagined her to ride, into the muddiest available ditch. But the peasants themselves flocked back to her house, sometimes coming from villages miles away, to thank her, as they had done after the nationalisation of the banks. There was no longer, now, any question of the peasants being oppressed by the princes: but Mrs Gandhi had proved to the peasants that the princes were no more than men, and that a woman, if she so wished, could control them, provided the people were behind her. This was an important lesson for the people: *garibi hatao*, yes: if a woman could take riches away from the rich, perhaps she could drive poverty away from the poor.

What is astonishing about the events of 1969 is surely not the reaction of the poor, or that of the rich, but the reaction of the intelligentsia. The nationalisation of the banks took away money from the rich, and it was at least possible, for the first time, for the poor to obtain loans. The action against the princes ended dynasties of parasites and proved something to the people. It also added $6 million from the privy purses to the national exchequer. Whatever finagling Mrs Gandhi had to do to bring Giri into the Presidency and make him her instrument, the ends she achieved were highly desirable. As for the means, they may not have been democratic in the way that democracy is understood by the West, but it seems to me—and years later when I asked Mrs Gandhi about this, I found my answer more in her face than in her words,—that the democratic principle theoretically begun in Greece has never really worked, in its pure form, anywhere. It has continually to be adapted and re-adapted, even within a single country over a period of time: for a country whose people are totally unused to western democratic patterns, the style of Mrs Gandhi is applicable and understandable. Mrs Gandhi understands, in her blood and bones, how to run such a country: she knows that loyalties are undependable and that your closest contact will sell out at the drop of a ministership from the opposition: she knows that eventually you are by yourself, and that without an angrily close hand and eye on your ministers and advisers—as it was with the Kashmir rulers centuries back, and with the Moguls—and without the ability to fight faster and more intelligently than your opponent, and also, if needs must and you have the opportunity, less fairly—you will fall, and the elephants will trample you in the dust, and you will be forgotten.

But the intellectuals, those who disapproved of her, did so either because, having been educated in or from the West, they thought that the ethics of the L.S.E. or even the C.I.A., demanded something different from her: if they thought Simonov and the rest the most wonderful of Marxist writers (which of them has escaped whipping?) they asked for something else: a kind of mixture of committees ideally run by either Harold Laski or Hoover (J. Edgar) or by the young children of rich parents who had turned into Naxalites. She could never satisfy them, but like some rulers of India before her, she did what she could for the poor; and even they, in the end, were not content.

But that time had not yet come. As 1970 spun back like tickertape on a machine into a recorded past I talked to many people, because I wondered what she would do, what she could do, and if she would or could do it. Nandini Satpathi, at that time deputy Minister attached to the Prime Minister and Minister of State, later to be Chief Minister of Orissa, and now under charges of alleged corruption (having a couple of years back abandoned Mrs Gandhi, once her friend, and crossed the floor to Desai), a pretty and flowerlike person in those days, said to me: 'You ask me if she is an effective leader. She herself looks at it like this: there was the period, before independence, when we needed someone like Gandhi. With independence, Nehru became the leader. He was necessary to the nation: he started to build it up from zero. Then he died. Mrs Gandhi, in turn, feels the world is changing fast. We can't afford a leader who doesn't keep pace with all this. Once, she told me a sort of parable. Suppose your parents send you on a trip. They know there's a forest ahead and they teach you how to cross it. You come to the middle of the forest and there is a river across the way. Your parents foresaw the forest but they never foresaw the river. Unless, of your own accord, you learn how to swim there and then, you will have to turn back or die.'

At the time she said this to me, the Opposition were clamouring for a mid-term election. This Mrs Gandhi, despite her tiny hold on power, always steadfastly refused. The Opposition, accordingly, became accustomed to the idea that no election would take place until the one scheduled for 1972, and tailored its plans to fit. On December 15 1970 the Supreme Court, which for days had been in conclave over the privy purse problem, declared the government abolition order was null and void, and restored full privileges to the princes. Mrs Gandhi stayed passive until December 27, then struck.

In a characteristically unexpected way she called on President Giri
to dissolve Parliament, which he did: whereupon she announced that
there would be a mid-term election in March 1971. The Opposition,
caught with its pants down, emitted a howl of protest at this sudden
exposure of its bareness to the elements. Then it began to make
hasty preparations for the election into which it was so soon, for it
too soon, to be plunged. Possibly her childhood and adolescence,
her young womanhood, had taught her about the forest: perhaps her
father had bequeathed her a mental map, such as those shown in
children's books, or at least very good children's books such as you
cannot buy any more, with drawings as then captioned 'Heere Bee
Fruite' or more frightening in terms of the picture, 'Heere Bee
Tygeres' and now even if the river ('Heere' presumably 'maie bee
Crocodyles') bisected the forest the child Indu would not be afraid:
at the age of 52 she had learnt to swim, by herself, because not only
would she never turn back but she was not willing, yet, to die.

The political scene in the last months of 1969 was turbulent in the
extreme. I visited the Lok Sabha before Mrs Gandhi closed it, on
the first day of its winter session. Streams of cars and people were
flowing down the endless arrowlike avenues towards the red sandstone bulk of Parliament House. Inside, the galleries that held the
spectators, full to capacity, formed a huge circle high above the
politicians. It gave one the sensation of looking down into a bearpit,
which the Lok Sabha not infrequently resembles. At the moment I
arrived the House was, for once, silent and attentive. At the head of
the government front bench Mrs Gandhi was speaking. She addressed herself to the microphone in the clear and careful tones of a
child at elocution class. What she was saying was not particularly
brilliant. She was, in fact, reading a message to the Egyptian
government on the death of President Nasser. But her careful,
inexpressive voice, and even her manner, had a curiously authentic
touch. It was the touch of invested authority. She finished reading
her message and slipped quietly down into her seat. The leaders of
the main opposition parties now started, one by one, to rise if not to
shine. Each expressed his not excessively informed views on Nasser
and deplored the Egyptian leader's death. Some were largely inaudible, some, because of the quality of their English, incomprehen-
sible. While they spoke, Mrs Gandhi appeared, understandably, to
lose all interest in the proceedings. She bent her dapper head over

a sequence of yellow files, flicking over the leaves with small delicate hands. From time to time the right hand made a note on the file, but the intent head seldom lifted. Facing her from the Opposition front bench, arms folded, Desai eyed her cynically. The condolences ended. Mrs Gandhi rose without ostentation and vanished down a side aisle, followed by a train of peons carrying files. Question time started. Within minutes the bearpit quality of the House was fully in evidence. The male members leapt about, waved their arms, and yelled simultaneously. The female members shrilled like fishwives. It was as though with the disappearance of Mrs Gandhi some kind of control had been lifted. The Speaker, Dhillon, a turbaned, bearded Sikh, clattered an ineffectual bell for order. In a far corner of the chamber, amidst the yells and the sound of the bell, a few members from remote rural areas, heads pillowed peacefully on their arms, slept the sleep of the innocent and uninformed.

Shortly before the elections I went to see Mrs Gandhi in her office in the Secretariat, not far from Parliament. It was an official visit, made on behalf of an American newspaper, and her secretary had warned me beforehand that she did not want to be asked questions about current affairs. When he showed me into her office she was seated at her desk, her delicate hand busy over more yellow files, the hooded eyes behind the spectacles intensely alive.

She put down her pen, looked up, took her spectacles off, and smiled very prettily. I thanked her for agreeing to see me when she was so busy. 'Oh, well,' she said, and awarded me another of those smiles, 'if it weren't you it would be someone else.' I had tried to plan my interview so that, without reference to current events on the political scene, I could draw her out on the state of the country. I started by asking her about the internal disturbances of India, particularly about the guerrilla activities of the Naxalites in Calcutta and the countryside around. 'It's a law and order question,' she said, 'and as yet it is confined to definite areas, like West Bengal and Andhra. The whole thing started as a movement for land reform, and it will exist in the rural areas of those states as long as the land reforms there aren't completed. But in Calcutta itself the Naxalites are young intellectuals who are involved because of the problems peculiar to large cities. As long as there's unemployment for graduates and other young people, there'll be this trouble.' I had recently been in Calcutta myself, writing about the Naxalites, and

I referred to the brutal nature of their methods. She looked at me thoughtfully. 'It's what happens when people don't know what they want. That's not exclusive to young people in India, it applies all over the world. The Naxalites want to destroy first of all, but they don't know what to build afterwards. I'm not against destroying existing systems, but only if you know what you are going to put in their place.' As she talked her eyes kept straying, as they always did in that particular office, to the portrait of Nehru opposite her desk, studying it in an abstracted, expressionless way. 'Do you think,' I asked, trying to bring her back to me, 'you meet such opposition because you're a woman?' She looked a little annoyed. 'It's an excuse which appeals to the reactionary forces. It's like the people who attacked Kennedy because he was a Catholic.' Suddenly she switched topics and started to answer a query that had not been made. 'We have to move faster,' she said. 'We can't afford not to, and certain people oppose this. But if we don't move faster, people aren't prepared to wait for us. They'll try to take the solution into their own hands, to resolve matters in their own way. The people of this country today are more and more conscious of what they need and want. You'd be surprised at the number of people – women included – who vote now, and who never did before.' Her eyes went back to the portrait opposite her. 'Even my father met a lot of hostile criticism at the end of his life. The criticism he faced was often because he insisted on a rational, scientific approach. This is difficult to achieve. For example, we know nowadays what causes a solar eclipse. But Hindus still have a ritual bath when it happens, even if they know why it happens. What we need now is the opposite of that – a truly rational approach.' I asked her if she thought that the whole of so large and traditionalised a country could all be made to adopt a rational approach. She shrugged: she did not answer for a moment. Then she said tiredly, 'There's so much to be done. We have to have a phased economic programme that will decentralise the monopolies. The monopolies did help start up industries in this country but now we need to give a chance to small industrialists. We have to pursue an agricultural revolution and raise the living standards of the people. It's a tremendous challenge,' and now her eyes suddenly shone. 'Many old standards simply don't apply any more,' she said, 'and we have to realise this. In the Bhagavad Gita, it was said that the larger the family the better. Now it's exactly the opposite. The family planning programme has become absolutely vital to us. Its success depends on the imagination of the officers who carry it out.' In the light of events which took place much later, this was a very significant statement. 'The reactionary forces,' said Mrs Gandhi (she was at this time much addicted to the term) 'say we're opposed to religion, but we're not. We stand for the rational approach, the approach my father stood for.'

She stopped, nodded at the press officer who had been taking notes of the conversation, and smiled at us. The interview was over. As we rose (my wife was with me), she made the *namaskar*, her greying handsome head bent over neatly folded hands. With a delicate, almost noiseless, very feminine sigh, she turned back to the stacked files on her desk.

Desai told me she 'is not truthful. She is after power for herself. She is deceitful and ruthless.' Mrs Satpathi said, 'There's been a tremendous change in her since I first met her in 1958. Even when I didn't see her I always had a sort of admiration for her. I don't think it was for anything in particular, but I felt she was the sort of person who could achieve something ... the change has been in the personality itself: she's become more decisive and courageous, clearer in her ideas. She's clear about her plans, and also she has become quite bold. She's simply wonderful to work with,' added Mrs Satpathi, dimpling, and qualified this statement by saying, 'She loses her temper quickly, of course, like her father, but she has tremendous consideration for her colleagues.' Chavan, who received me in an extraordinary drawing room with furniture upholstered in yellow satin and purple and red Persian carpets on the floor (he looked, himself, like my idea of Nero Wolfe,* with two differences, the colour of his skin and the fact that he was so anxious to please) said, 'She was very close to events,' speaking of the Congress split. 'She was not prepared to compromise on specific issues. The moment of split came when resolution was passed to expel her. But it is very difficult, isn't it, to think of splitting a party which was—oah—more than one century in age. She told me to try and be patching things up. Even she was helping me to draft unity resolution ... she did not cause the split.' He pouted a bit, like Nero Wolfe, when I asked him about the elections. 'The reactionaries,' (a word I had started to tire of) he said, 'will put up

* Rex Stout's fat fictional detective.

a fight. The elections will be a very complex battle ... But bank nationalisation has been a step forward.' I pointed out that it was not only the new economic policies but the dispute as to who should be President that had precipitated the split. Chavan, who had for some minutes past, worn a shiny smile, now let it slip and fall heavily on to a Persian carpet. 'As for that,' he said, 'I was myself campaigning for Reddy as President. But,' he added glumly, 'I am rather not to be discussing this particular matter,' and shortly after this ushered me out.

It is curious that of this ill-mixed trio, only one has proved consistent in his opinions, and that a decade later, it is only Desai who says, in his flat, limited way, what he said to me in 1969. The other two have been classically Indian in their patterns of broken promises and betrayal. They took what they could from Mrs Gandhi, but they did not stand by her when trouble came. I think perhaps she expected such a fluidity of faith in Chavan, but not from Mrs Satpathi, who in 1969 was one of her friends. She became used to betrayal but she has developed an extraordinary capacity not to show hurt at it. For someone hurt from childhood onward there are two things to be expected: one is that he or she will be driven mad, the other that each new hurt is absorbed into one burning but hidden wound, hidden for the sake of one's own sanity. It seems to me that Mrs Gandhi was hard and positive enough in her mind to take the wound and keep it as a souvenir, as people keep bullets extracted from them during the war, pieces of shrapnel, appendixes floating in bottles of spirit. Who has ever guessed at her courage, I do not know—Nehru, perhaps, towards the end of his life: I do not know whether her own children and their wives see it in her: perhaps Feroze did, and perhaps that is why his was the most important death in her life.

In 1971 I departed for Hong Kong to edit a magazine there. This was in February, and I left from Bombay with my wife on the first day of the Indian elections. Meanwhile my article had appeared in New York, an article in which I said that it would be a personal tragedy for me if Mrs Gandhi lost the elections, for she was the only person capable of running the country. There is a sort of agency in Washington for publicity of government of India material, and this agency telexed copies of my article to India, where it was used, presumably without Mrs Gandhi's knowledge, since she is delicate in these matters, to compare me, saying it would be a personal tragedy were she to lose, to certain statements of my father's, with whom, because I loved him, I frequently disagreed, who said it would be a personal tragedy for him if she won. As the voters all over the country flocked to ramshackle booths, to slip their ballots into the box which showed the emblem of a cow feeding a calf, the Congress emblem, we arrived at our first stop between Bombay and Hong Kong, Delhi, where my father, pulling one of his numerous strings, appeared in the transit lounge to say goodbye. During the course of a rapid conversation I told him that I had never authorised any comparisons in the press about what he thought and I said about Mrs Gandhi's prospective victory or defeat. He said, 'Oh, that! It isn't a very important business, but, believe me, she will lose.' In Hong Kong, reading one of the English newspapers a couple of days later in the Hyatt Hotel, I saw that she had won. Indeed, it was not only a landslide, but a sort of avalanche, which swept her back into power. Out of the 525 seats in Parliament, 350 went to Congress (R). Desai's Congress fought 238 seats and won only 16, and its right wing allies collapsed with it. Mrs Gandhi was not only back, but she could now choose her Cabinet and her advisers (always, with her, separate entities) without recourse to the Syndicate or any of the ragtag parties whose dubious support had enabled her to stay in power after the Congress split. She had shattered a bushel of eggs, but she had created her omelette. She was no longer indebted to anyone: like her father, she had won on her own merits, and on the faith of the people. The verse by Robert Frost, found by her father's deathbed, said 'I have promises to keep'. She intended to keep them.

PART THREE

The Pinnacle

❧ 12 ❧

Crusade to the East

SOON AFTER WE got to Hong Kong I sent Mrs Gandhi a letter of congratulation on her election victory. She replied very promptly, and though I have lost her letter I recollect that in the final paragraph, telling me how busy she was, she said that most of her time was taken up by worrying about the chaotic situation in Bangladesh, which worsened by the day. She couldn't imagine, she added, what the outcome would be. The letter had a tone of annoyance in it, as though a schoolmistress had suddenly found a member of her class awkward. It was March when I received this missive: in Hong Kong the weather was still mild, still weeks away from summer and the cyclones. Six months before, I had been in Bangladesh, East Pakistan then, on the heels of a cyclone that had killed 300,000 people, and after my trip had written a book* that predicted a worse one to come, this time a political cyclone. It had come, the predictable result of a historical process, and, amidst the cobweb of rivers, swamps and waterways that formed Bangladesh, it raged on still, man-made and only to be stopped by men. The eastern half of Bengal had always been an unlucky country, but in the year after November 1970 its fluctuating fortunes reached their nadir.

When Pakistan was formed in 1947, some 31,000 square miles of territory in the western part of the subcontinent were allotted to it. These were predominantly Muslim areas. A thousand miles away, across the breadth of India, the eastern part of Bengal went to Pakistan. This was also a predominantly Muslim area, but in a different way. Eastern Bengal had once been a ricebowl, its muslins and spices shipped to Rome and China, and known to the traders of the Renaissance period. The attraction of wealth is universal, especially when that wealth belongs to a frail and unwarlike people, and in the thirteenth century the Turki hordes from the north

* *The Tempest Within*, Vikas Books, Delhi, 1971.

swirled down into Bengal and occupied it. The province was under Muslim rule for the next 500 years. The Hindu caste system in Bengal had fossilised, even more than in other parts of India, by the time the Muslims came. The lower caste Hindus, denied any upward mobility in society, sought an opportunity for equality and embraced Islam, which preaches universal brotherhood, at least among Muslims.

The West Pakistanis were, in the main, descendants of the invaders who centuries back had swept down from the high northern passes. They were tall men with quite pale skins, who spoke Urdu, a Persianised form of Hindi. The East Pakistanis were converts from Hinduism, moreover from the lower Hindu castes. They were mainly short, stocky men, with dark, faintly Mongol features, and they spoke Bengali. They wore a kind of sarong, a garment suited to the unvaryingly hot, sticky climate: the West Pakistanis vested themselves in loose shirts and trousers, the materials of which varied with the weather, which was hot and dry in the summer and cool and dry in winter. If the West Pakistanis, physically and culturally, seemed akin to the inhabitants of the Near East, the East Pakistanis seemed akin to the people of Southeast Asia. There were virtually two different races in Pakistan, with nothing in common except Islam. Even this did not keep the two together.

The West Pakistanis, when they came to East Pakistan, did so in the manner of a colonial race visiting an outpost of Empire. The weather and the people irritated them: they cursed the first and exploited the second. Colonel Mohammed Ahmed, who was attached to the staff of the first GOC of the Eastern Wing (this happened to be General Ayub Khan) wrote: 'Most of the senior officers had come from West Pakistan ... feeling too unhappy to be discreet. They would complain in extremely bitter terms, even in the presence of East Pakistanis, whom they blamed for all the misery and inconvenience. A thousand mile gulf already existed geographically between the people of the two provinces. The temerity and impudence of the West Pakistanis was widening it emotionally much further ... '

Leaders arose in the east, a series of fiery suns: among them were Manland Bhashani, an ancient weathercock of a politician, who in 1970 encouraged the Naxalites of the province to fight the West Pakistani apparat as the Naxalites across the Indian border did the

Calcutta police, and Sheikh Mujibur Rehman, who was an intellectual and a liberal, if either term means much these days, and, most of all, was consistent in his politics. His Awami party was a buffer to the extremists led by Bhashani. What Mujib asked West Pakistan for, in 1969, was only reasonable, taking into account the fact that of an estimated population of 125 million for the whole of Pakistan at the time, 70 million lived in the eastern portion, crammed into a land area five times less than that in the west. Mujib asked the military dictators of the country to establish a federal parliamentary democracy, with the representatives of the people chosen by direct election and full adult franchise. The representation in the federal legislature was to be on the basis of population. 'The principle of parity in each wing,' he said, ' ... is based on the false premise that representatives ... are likely to vote on a regional basis ... East Pakistan has always subordinated its regional interest to the overriding national interest.' He pointed out that East Pakistan had consented that the capital and all the defence headquarters should be in the western sector. This meant that the bulk of expenditure on defence and civil administration, 70 per cent of the Central Budget, was incurred in West Pakistan. If the West Pakistanis refused the demand for representation on a regional basis, Mujib said, the East Pakistanis would be compelled to demand that the capital and defence headquarters be shifted to the East. He produced, in the course of the same speech, statistics to demonstrate the disparity between east and west. 'In 1960,' he said, ' ... the real per capita income disparity between East and West was 60 per cent ... it has been steadily increasing.' In 1959–60, in fact, the per capita income in the East was Rs 278, in the West Rs 366. By 1966–7, the per capita income in the East was Rs 313, in the West Rs 463.

The capacity for power production in the West, Mujib added, was '5–6 times higher than in East Pakistan, the number of hospital beds in 1966 in West Pakistan was estimated to be 26,000, while the number in East Pakistan was estimated to be 6,900 during 1961–6. Only 18 polytechnic institutes were established in East Pakistan against 48 in West Pakistan ... More than 80 per cent of all foreign aid has been utilised in West Pakistan in addition to the transfer of East Pakistan's foreign exchange earnings to West Pakistan. This made it possible for West Pakistan over twenty years to import Rs 3109 crores* worth of goods against total export

* A crore is the Indian word for 10 million rupees.

earnings of Rs 1337 crores ... during the same period East Pakistan imported Rs 1210 crores of goods against total export earnings of Rs 1650 crores.'

He made a number of reasonable proposals to amend this situation. The military dictator of Pakistan, General Yahya Khan, a plump, and, as usual with dictators, preposterous man, could not follow what the East Pakistani leader said. Nevertheless, he caught one point out of many. 'Elections, old boy,' he probably said to his advisers, 'we'll have 'em.' The synthetic Sandhurst voice resounded over a synthetic country, more than half the population needing a fair deal, and its echoes rebounded to the East. 'We'll have elections, don't you worry. We'll have 'em.' Some months later, after the East had exploded, Mr Henry Kissinger sat by Yahya as he drank in his capital. Hundreds of thousands were by this time dead in Bangladesh, the corrupted rivers and the too deeply fertilised land steamed and stank, and Yahya's troops were all over the country. 'Do you really think, old boy,' Yahya is alleged to have said to Kissinger, 'that I am a dictator?' Kissinger's reply is not quoted in this perhaps apocryphal story.

Yahya remembered about the elections. He declared that he would hold real, independent, democratic elections all over Pakistan. Rehman and Bhashani were by this time, in late 1970, both combined in demanding autonomy for the eastern province, but theirs was a house divided: Rehman wanted to trade with India and establish a friendly relationship, Bhashani did not: he hated Hindus, but liked the Chinese. Yahya may have thought, in so far as he was capable of so complex an operation, that the vote would be split between them in the East. In the West, Z. A. Bhutto, a violent opponent of India and a friend, like Bhashani, of the Chinese, had the Pakistan People's Party, which would probably win most of the seats. With a fragmented vote, the military could probably declare the final results inconclusive, and stay on top. Yahya was eventually dethroned by the forces of nature, by the cyclone that stamped up out of the sea over the offshore islands and inland villages of East Pakistan on November 12 1970.

East Pakistan had, for centuries, been cyclone country. Geography as well as history has been unkind to the area. The Bay of Bengal is shaped like a funnel, at the apex of which the country squats amidst its swamps. The disturbances of air that take place in the

Indian Ocean, particularly between May and October, when the rise and shift northward of hot air from the equator occurs, tend to be forced into the mouth of the funnel. As the landwalls on either side close in, these disturbances (caused by an initial low pressure area, the eye of the cyclone being created in easterly seas and sucking in the air around so that it forms a circle of fighting winds around the eye) are squeezed together into a narrower and narrower compass, until eventually they explode at the apex of the funnel, on the offshore islands and the southward coasts of East Bengal. This happened so often that the Pakistani government must have been well aware of it as a problem. Nevertheless the West Pakistanis, who had the money, put up no organised flood control system or warning system around the coasts of what purported to be their own country, and disaster resulted. On November 9 1970, the American satellite ESSA, floating high overhead, focused on the huge dark spiral of an enormous cyclone as it lumbered leisurely over the sea, building itself up as it came, towards the coast of East Pakistan. ESSA flashed warnings to the radar centre of East Pakistan, situated at a place called Cox's Bazaar. Indian cyclone experts were meanwhile trying to keep track of the advancing fury, afraid that it could veer, unpredictable as a missile out of control, southwest to Madras or northwest to Calcutta. It did not do so. Heavy and inevitable, it moved up the Bay of Bengal and appeared on the radar screens of Cox's Bazaar. Radio Pakistan immediately started to broadcast warnings to the areas likely to be hit.

The broad rivers of East Pakistan, once so essential to trade, pour into the Bay of Bengal. The Ganges and the Brahmaputra had deposited colossal quantities of silt in the coastal sea, and this had massed up into islands. The silt soil was highly arable and the islands were therefore densely populated. Few of them, however, rose more than twenty feet above the sea. On the mainland shore that faced them were other low-lying, riparian districts, also densely populated. The cyclone would first hit the islands, then the coastal districts. Radio Pakistan said so. What it failed to say was that the cyclone coming was an immense one, and that the areas in question were in terrible danger. The people had suffered cyclones before: unwarned of this one's size, they were not too deeply perturbed. Moreover, even had they been warned that they should flee, where were they to flee to? There was no flood control system.

The islanders could only hope to reach the mainland coast, which would be hit anyway. The coastal areas in many parts had no road or rail communication with the interior. An evacuation of the coast would have to take place along the rivers and waterways, and to be caught on moving water in the midst of a cyclone of whatever size was obvious madness.

The people of the islands and coastal areas stayed where they were. On the night of November 12 most of them were asleep, under coarse blankets, in thatched straw huts: it was high tide, with a rough, broken sea and rain falling. Over the sounds of rain and sea came a distant roar, swelling slowly to titanic dimensions, drowning all other sound. Then an immense and deafening wall of water towered above the waves. Some of its survivors have said it was fifty feet high. It thundered down on the offshore islands. Houses, people, animals, trees, vanished under it. As the wave roared on coastward, a blinding, driving, killing wind followed it over the wrecked islands.

Wave and wind now exploded on the mainland shore. They rushed onward, unchecked and uncheckable, cutting a swathe fifty miles across in which all villages and living creatures were ploughed irresistibly under. At last the onrush halted, and then came the new terror. The titanic mass of water that had broken on the East Pakistan coast was in fact a wave. All waves, once they have broken on land, recede into the sea, and this one proceeded to do so. It swept back seaward the way it had come. The survivors of the villages in its forward path now found themselves enveloped in choking, muddy water as it returned. Thousands of people, together with dead cattle, the debris of houses and boats, and up-rooted trees, were swept helplessly out into the open sea.

Communications between the coastal areas and the centre were limited at the best of times. The cyclone destroyed what there was of them in a comprehensive and concise manner. It was two days before Dacca discovered the extent of the disaster on the coast. The sea and the rivers were choked and contaminated by corpses: other corpses decomposed softly on the land. The Pakistani Army was despatched to the coast to bury the bodies and try and prevent epidemics. The British and the Americans flew in troops to help with the relief work, and helicopters and launches to implement this assistance. Food, medicines, clothes and money were flown in from other countries. The U.N. characteristically sent in teams of experts and observers, though what they were supposed to be expert on, or what, except for putrefying bodies, they were to observe, remained unclear.

Pakistan accepted aid from everyone, but they had reservations about India. Mrs Gandhi offered the condolences of the country and a crore of rupees, the second of which offers was delightedly taken up. She also offered supplies. These were accepted too, on condition that the Indian convoys stopped at the border and handed their loads over to local officials. Other countries which had offered supplies sent their own men into East Pakistan to ensure proper distribution: a wise precaution, since it was said that most of the Indian supplies handed over to Pakistani border officials wound up being sold on the black market. The Pakistanis had twenty-odd helicopters available for relief lifts. The U.S.A. rather meanly, lent them no more than half a dozen more. Mrs Gandhi offered fifty, complete with crews, but the Pakistanis refused to accept them, saying that the presence of so many Indian Air Force personnel constituted a security hazard.

Thai Airlines deposited me in Dacca a couple of days after the cyclone. The gigantic and crowded bulk of the Intercontinental Hotel sheltered me. The night of my arrival, a Pakistani reporter (admittedly, this was in the bar, and at a late hour) told me that the cyclone had killed a million people. 'That,' he said with an air of pride, 'makes our cyclone', his air was positively proprietary, 'the worst natural disaster in history. When the Yangtse Kiang flooded in the nineteenth century, 900,000 Chinese were killed, but we have beaten that: Pakistan,' he announced, with a triumphant upsweep of his arm, 'now holds the world record.' He was, of course, a West Pakistani.

Yahya Khan flew over from the western sector. He was full of the correct responses to the situation, that is, up to a point. Beyond that point he betrayed himself. When asked why the government had not attempted to provide a flood control system in the east he remarked, 'We are in the hands of Allah. Who can stop a cyclone? The Pope came in his wake, and blessed the dead and dying: after which, proceeding to Manila, he was nearly assassinated by a mad surrealist painter. The whole situation in Asia at that time, as 1970 died to be resurrected in the newer madnesses of another year, was more or less surrealist. The day after my arrival in Dacca I came down after breakfast to the information desk in the lobby, where a slightly built student was handing out the press releases for the morning. As I collected mine, the student, looking hard at me, asked me my name. When I told him, he seemed delighted. 'Ah,' he said, 'the poet! How strange that we should meet here. I am myself a poet, not good, sir, not good, but at least I know this. My friends are poets too. *All*, all my friends. They will be so pleased to meet you, sir,' and he whisked me off in a rickety bicycle rickshaw to meet his friends. They were all University students, they all wrote verse, and they all hated the West Pakistanis. 'Look out of this window,' one said as we ate sticky sweets in his minute apartment, 'and you will see small, black, poor people. Not like the tall, fair, handsome West Pakistanis, sir, heh? After the cyclone, and our dead in the cyclone, it is finished in the East. Our country will have B.C. and A.C. yes, sir, but these will be "Before Cyclone" and "After Cyclone". Never we will trust the West Pakistanis after this. The elections are to come: you will be seeing that Sheikh Saheb will be winning.' I suggested to them that the amalgamation of East Pakistan with the West Bengal province of India might be a possible alternative to its present association with the western half of Pakistan, and they (young, thin, intelligent, soon to die) stared at me in horror. 'Oh, no, sir,' one said. 'You are British national, therefore we can tell you this: we hate the West Pakistanis, but the Hindus we hate more.'

They gathered me up, as a group: took me round Dacca: interpreted during my interviews: showed me their city in a way that allowed me to see it as no other correspondent did. They even came with me to the airfield to fix up trips for me to the flood areas. I travelled over the yellow sprawl of rivers and swamps by amphibion, helicopter, and riverboat, and whenever I came back from one trip the young poets were ready to launch me upon another. The most peculiar of all my trips was one by a river steamer from Pataukhali, where sharks, come in from the sea, and huge crocodiles, fought over the swollen corpses in the water, and the shore was being excavated like an archaeological site to provide a home for the dead. Cholera was rampant, and people were fleeing towards Dacca. The river steamer, which was equipped to carry 200 people, therefore carried a thousand. There was one lavatory to service the whole ship on a voyage that took thirty-six hours. There was also one cabin, minuscule, which I shared with a stout and affable West Pakistani doctor. I had no bedding or food: he was equipped for this kind of travel and shared his bedding, food and boiled water with me. He showed me photographs of his wife and their four children. On the first night of the trip, as we chugged upriver, past a flooded landscape upon whose lid of mud and water corpses lay, the doctor, a braver man than I, decided to use the lavatory. He had previously locked the cabin door to prevent the incursion of poorer passengers. He now unlocked and opened it: outside a young woman, with a beautiful but totally ravaged face, was lying on the floor moaning, clutching a shrivelled infant to a shrivelled breast. The doctor bent over, looked at her, then kicked her hard and uttered what seemed to be a command. Painfully she pulled herself up, and clutching the child still, staggered away. 'She is suffering from cholera,' the doctor beamed. 'It was not healthful that she should lie outside our door.' Very tired, and not quite comprehending what had happened, I suggested that he could perhaps help her medically. He looked at me in astonishment. '*Help* her?' he said. 'Help *her*? My dear friend, these East Pakistanis live like dogs, and they die like dogs as well.'

My last day in Dacca was the day of the long-promised election. My young poets took me out to breakfast, and then escorted me round the city. There were long, but orderly queues outside the polling booths, not only short, saronged men with slant eyes and caprine beards, but women swaddled in their *burkhas*, with children in their arms. I had watched Mujibur as he swept through Dacca in a triumphal motorcade, a few days earlier; balloons had been released above his car, where he sat with gleaming eyes behind his spectacles, twitching lips, raised hand, recently released from prison and now back with his people: music had brayed in every alley: men had danced on the pavements. There was no doubt that his Awami League would win, and, as my aeroplane took me past Mount Everest on the way back to Delhi, I wondered how massive his victory would be and what would be its consequences.

I read about the victory in Delhi. Of 153 seats contested in East Pakistan, the Awamis had won 151. Nine seats in the flood area were still to be finally decided, but they were pledged to Mujib. With seven nominated seats for women, Mujib took 167 seats out of 313 over the whole of Pakistan. Of the 138 seats in the western sector, Bhutto's party won 82: less than half the number captured by the Awamis. Mujib had the mandate: it was for him to frame

a new constitution, for him to float Pakistan once more. This was
not at all what Yahya Khan had had in mind. He delayed: he post-
poned: then he acted. On March 6 1971 he declared that the
National Assembly would open on March 25. Meanwhile Bengali
troops were moved from East Pakistan and replaced by West
Pakistanis. Strikes started in Dacca, the university students (amongst
them, I imagine, my poet friends) clamoured for a declaration of
East Pakistani autonomy. General Tikka Khan, whose exploits on
the northern borders of the western sector had earned him the
cognomen of 'The Butcher of Baluchistan', took over as Martial
Law Administrator in Dacca. 'Sort them out,' Yahya said, and
left him to do so.

On the night of March 25 Tikka Khan unleashed his troops.
The first targets were the intellectuals, by which the West Pakistanis
meant the students and professors of Dacca University. They were
shot, their bodies pitched into a trench, there to putrefy as the
bodies of villagers had done on the coast when the November
cyclone was over. Some people, however, attempted resistance. This
enraged the troops from the West: they fanned out from Dacca
over the countryside, killed, raped, looted and burned: performed
in fact all the usual ceremonies of war: and refugees started to flood
westward into India. I have never heard from the young poets
who befriended me in Dacca, though they had an address to write
to, so I presume that their bodies huddled and sprawled with
those of other intellectuals in the pit so eagerly photographed and
so graphically described by reporters from all over the world. Mujib
was arrested, but not before he had proclaimed the foundation of
the Republic of Bangladesh on March 26.

Mrs Gandhi, meanwhile, was studying the situation. It was no
time for merely academic research. America was openly for Yahya,
and China for Bhutto: in other words, two big guns were lifted
in defence of West Pakistan, and, with these behind them, the
Pakistanis started to protest about the Indian attitude. They particularly protested against the acceptance by India of the refugees,
who by the middle of 1971 could be counted not by the thousand
but by the million. Camps housed them, and they were clothed
and fed: but not all who came to India from Bangladesh were
refugees. The Bengali army units left in the east had turned themselves into guerrilla fighters: so had a number of young civilians of

mixed political sympathies but an unmixed loyalty to their people. These guerrillas, under the umbrella of the Mukti Bahini,* slashed at the Pakistanis out of the swamps and forests, and, when hard pressed, as from time to time they were, retired to safety across the Indian border. Other guerrillas, for a while, stayed across the border, where the Indian Border Security Forces trained and equipped them to return and fight. All this could be construed as interference by India in the political affairs of another nation. Bangladesh was not yet a recognised entity in world politics: indeed, it was not recognised as a separate country even by India. The grumbling guns of the U.S. and China sounded backstage, as Yahya and Bhutto kept the audience out front entertained. Mrs Gandhi reflected: then, delicate as a deer or a chess player, she moved: on August 9 1971, India signed a twenty-year treaty of peace, co-opera-tion and friendship with the U.S.S.R. Moreover, each country agreed to come to the military defence of the other in case of need. The bear was now on the scene, watching while eagle and dragon flapped their wings overhead: a rather dubious eagle, since most liberal opinion in the U.S. was in firm opposition to the support by Nixon and Kissinger of Yahya Khan.

Mrs Gandhi timed this move to perfection. She had shown how she could manoeuvre on the national scene: now, on an international issue, with India and Pakistan on an obvious collision course, she had provided herself with the comfortingly large buffer of the bear. Bhutto remarked that war between the two countries was unlikely: but nobody seemed to share his opinion, and the U.S. not only cut off its arms supply to India but escalated its support of Pakistan. Meanwhile the Muslim soldiers of the west continued to kill, rape and torture the Muslim civilians of the east, and those who could continued to flee to India. At the end there were ten million refu-gees in India, and their upkeep cost the government U.S. $3 million per day. It was a situation not to be borne, especially by a very poor country.

Some commentators are on record as having said that the Bangla-desh situation was prodded into continuous flame by the C.I.A. The Nixon administration disapproved of the leftist slant which they felt Mrs Gandhi manifested in her policies. For an army to commit such atrocities as the Pakistanis did in Bangladesh over so long a

* An organisation partially Communist and mainly financed and helped by the Indians.

period of time, these commentators said, there must be a force
pushing it onward: even Macbeth, in the end, tired of bloodshed.
According to them, the idea was to topple Mrs Gandhi by forcing
a deluge of refugees upon India, out of which no ark could take it,
and by forcing India into a war situation against a militarily equipped
nation with powerful allies. This seems to me an unlikely theory,
but it is possible.

Mrs Gandhi had raised, during her election campaign earlier in
1971, the slogan '*Garibi hatao*', or 'Drive poverty away'. But
government aid to peasants and bank assistance to the poor which
she had envisaged during this campaign had been made impossible,
or nearly so, by the onrush of refugees from the east. Popular
feeling, moreover, was very hostile to Pakistan. The atrocities across
the border, the pitiful condition of the refugees, were a real and
continual reminder that a neighbour is not necessarily a friend.
Skyjackers, earlier that year, had forced an Indian passenger plane
to land in Lahore, where it had been burnt. The insult to India
had not yet been wiped out. The Pakistanis seemed to be allowed
to do whatever they wanted, and the Indians as a nation resented
this bitterly.

On October 4, Mrs Gandhi flew out of India. She visited Russia
and the western capitals, and she acted as a spokesman for Bangladesh. What was happening there, she said, could not be allowed to
continue. A whole nation was being systematically exterminated. It
was genocide and it must be stopped. The implication was that
though India wanted peace, she was prepared for war. In view of all
the events that followed her trip, it was perfectly timed. She had
explained the stance of her country and the tragedy of Bangladesh
to the leaders of the world. She had furnished them with a background against which to interpret her subsequent actions. Now
she could turn her full attention to the matter immediately at hand.

'Bangladesh?' she said to me, seven years later. 'Oh, yes. We got
involved, first of all, for purely humanitarian reasons. The refugees,
all that ... We couldn't stand by and see a whole population
liquidated. But also,' she added, the slight quizzical touch of a
smile on her lips, 'I was certain the revolution would succeed.' She
did not, in those days, make any move unless she had a degree of
certainty as to its outcome: Joan of Arc, perhaps, but not Quixote.
She had every reason, in fact, to suppose that the revolution would
be a success.

The Bengalis have always been looked upon by most other Indians and by foreigners, such as Kipling, as talkers rather than doers. There is some justification in this, for they do talk, interminably: but they also have deep political involvements and the ability to dedicate themselves to a cause. The Naxalite movement, one that demanded physical action rather than dialogue, started up, after all, in Bengal. The Moguls and the British had been mindful of the fact that the Bengalis were hard to handle: the Pakistanis were not. They had based their tactics in the east upon the assumption that the Bengalis would crumple under pressure, but they had been proved wrong. At the time of the initial attack there were about 70,000 armed Bengali personnel in East Pakistan, not only soldiers but home guards and members of other paramilitary organisations. The bulk of these, especially those who were home guards, remained loyal to Pakistan, but a number of them broke away. The police force, which numbered about 45,000, some armed, also decided to fight for independence. These forces coalesced with students and peasants and formed the guerrilla army, the Mukti Fauj. Since most senior army and police officers had been arrested by the Pakistanis, the leaders of this army were usually very young men, some of whom, like 'Tiger' Siddiqui, whose forces were active in the Tangail area, in Mymensingh and around Dacca, became legendary figures. Politically the guerrillas were a mixed bunch, but their motivation was patriotic rather than political, certainly at first.

Flitters in the forest, saboteurs as well as soldiers, the guerrillas had the people behind them, and they were equipped and trained by the Indian border forces. This meant that they were in no danger of betrayal and that they were not unskilled at their work. They harried the Pakistanis every day, but theirs was basically a nuisance value: unaided, they could not hope to push the invaders back into the sea. After April 1971 the activities of the Mukti Fauj slowed down somewhat, and a new guerrilla force, the Mukti Bahini, emerged. This was not purely a land force: they had gunboats and sloops and operated in the rivers and waterways as well as on the open sea. Their gunboats intercepted foreign merchant vessels bringing supplies to the Pakistanis, which implies that the guerrillas had an efficient information service, while blown bridges and shattered railway lines testified to the activity of their land forces. Still, with the Mukti Bahini as with the Mukti Fauj, victory over

the sophisticated military machine from the west was virtually inconceivable. The Pakistanis, whenever the guerrillas struck at their
forces, took their grievances out on the helpless peasantry with
such feral ferocity that it seemed possible that the entire civilian
populace would soon disappear. This inspired the peasants to an
increased hatred of their masters, but slaughter and rape did not
help the battle for freedom. Women of all ages, children and widows,
pregnant after rape, were to be found all over the country as well
as in the Indian refugee camps. Their plight was a peculiarly in-
soluble one: the obdurately obscurantist sexual mores of the
subcontinent ensured that nobody would marry the unmarried vic-
tims: the married ones were more than likely to be divorced by
their husbands. The Pakistanis had brought birth as well as death
to Bangladesh: but birth as unwanted by the people as death.
The activities of the Mukti Bahini were thus, in a way, counter-
productive, especially since they were embroiled, unassisted, against
hopeless odds: every guerrilla success was followed by a Pakistani
reprisal. Resistance would soon falter without outside help: the
real value of the Mukti Bahini was that they formed a paramilitary
complex throughout the country, which would be of immense help
in terms of guidance and intelligence operations to any army that
might come from outside. By November 1971 it was clear whose
army that would be.

The military commander in what the West Pakistanis still called
East Pakistan was General Amir Abdullah Khan Niazi. He sent
forces out to pursue the Mukti Bahini whenever they took shelter
beyond the Indian frontier. In the third week of October 1971, he
declared to a crowd at a place called Saidpur that 'the war would
be fought on Indian territory'. Through November, villages on the
Indian side of the border were shelled by the West Pakistan artillery.
Reconaissance flights were made over Indian territory, in the east
and the west, by Pakistani Air Force planes. On November 25
Yahya Khan stated that 'in ten days ... I may not be here in
Rawalpindi (then the capital of Pakistan) ... but off fighting a war ....
Mrs Gandhi told the officers of the eastern frontier that their troops
were empowered to chase Pakistani forces back across the border,
indeed into Bangladesh, 'but only in self defence'.*

    The Chinese, Bhutto's friends, were at this time too involved in

* *The Times of India*, November 27 1971.

fighting the Russians on the Ussuri River over a frontier dispute to 'intervene'. They had, moreover, recently become members of the United Nations, and did not want to fight in a war that was not theirs. Bhutto led a delegation to Peking in November: what discussions the delegation had were not publicised, but they were obviously unsatisfactory to Pakistan. Pingpong diplomacy, the greatest weapon Richard Nixon ever possessed, was no longer used by the American President: the pingpong champions are mainly oriental, winning by subtlety rather than strength, and subtlety was a quality Nixon did not have: Kissinger did, but by this time he had let his intellect drift in the interests of the White House. The State Department started to wag the flag at Mrs Gandhi. She did what she had to do: which was simply that she remained entirely unafraid.

A Prime Minister committed to war is special. He or she has to have a belief in what happens when soldiers, not necessarily intelligent people, are released by one country upon another. The Prime Minister of India wanted an excuse to fight: basically, her people were fighting already. She had her excuse when the Pakistani Air Force decided to make an air strike upon India, to show the Indians that they could do so, and they also had the idea that they would make this air strike in the manner of the Israelis fighting the Egyptians in 1967. They dive-bombed nine Indian airbases on the western frontier in early December: because of their entire silliness, they did so when there were no Indian Air Force planes on the runways. The Indians therefore went into attack.

They attacked on the western front, blasted what remained of the Pakistani Air Force out of the sky, and drove the armies back in the northern and eastern sectors. Then they turned their attention to Bangladesh: the general idea was to get there quickly. On December 4 1971 the Indians, following the Pakistani airstrikes, declared war upon Pakistan. On December 6 they recognised Bangladesh as a country. By this time the Indians were deep into Bangladesh: they had been preparing for this for a long while. The eastern command sector had been mainly for mountain warfare: but Mrs Gandhi had been reorganising it for river warfare, essential in the swamps of East Bengal. There was no doubt whatever that India had been readying itself for war, slowly but thoroughly, since the initial invasion, under quiet orders from a quiet woman.

Meanwhile Nixon, on December 6, as India recognised Bangladesh, asked the Seventh Fleet to enter the Indian Ocean. The idea was that in case of outright war the Seventh Fleet would scoop American citizens up from Bangladesh and, keeping them happy with Coke, bring them safely home. The Seventh Fleet not being a travel agency, but a fighting fleet, there was some doubt in India as to the final purpose of this mission. But the Indian troops were racing into Bangladesh as the Seventh Fleet snaked over the long sea. The Mukti Bahini welcomed them: so did the peasants: the big, turbaned Sikhs and the squat Gurkhas were garlanded in every village. The Indian Air Force bombed ahead: the Indian Navy were shepherds of the sea. It was typical of the pattern of warfare in the subcontinent that the first of the Indian commanders to reach Dacca had been with the Military Commander, General Niazi, at Sandhurst. The old boy network was still functional. The Indian commander sent his A.D.C. under a white flag, into Dacca: the A.D.C. took a note to Niazi: it said: 'My dear Abdullah, I am here. The game is up. I suggest you give yourself up to me and I'll look after you.' Eventually Niazi agreed.

The remainder of the Indian troops entered Dacca. At what had once been the racecourse, the instrument of Pakistani surrender was signed. It now remained to bring Mujib back to his own country and reinstall him as the leader of his people. Mujib, under close arrest for months in West Pakistan, was utterly bewildered by what had happened. He had expected death, not this astonishing release. Blinking through thick spectacles, wrapped in a very long and dirty overcoat, he was flown from West Pakistan to London, from London to New Delhi. At Palam Airport Mrs Gandhi stood, small and spry, to welcome him: a guard of honour awaited his salute. He flapped a hand in vague acknowledgment, and crowds thundered beyond the security perimeters. For him, returned from the dead, it was a tremendous moment: but for Mrs Gandhi, it must have been a climactic moment. She had performed the impossible. She had brought the leader of Bangladesh back as though from the dead. By this act she stood or she fell: it was ironic that, with the act so acclaimed, she fell, in a way, because of it: and more than ironic that the great leader, brought safely home, should have been killed by his own people three years later; and that Bangladesh should now be far more friendly with Pakistan than it is with India.

I prophesied this in my 1971 book:* but nobody would listen.

Mrs Gandhi had done it. She had achieved the status of a myth. She was Joan without the inconvenience of prison, fire and cross. Some of these awaited her; she may even have known that they awaited her, and she may have been delighted by the idea of martyrdom, to which she had aspired since her childhood. I do not know, since at this time I was a wanderer around Southeast Asia for my magazine: curiously enough, I was in Vietnam when the Bangladesh war ended. In a small bar purred over by air conditioners I talked to another correspondent, an American who had come to Saigon fresh, if one can call it that, from Dacca. 'They'll never get her out now,' he said. 'She's become a folk heroine.' I reminded him that Indians, like other people, have short memories. 'The Dacca people,' he said, 'put flowers on the Indian trucks.' Mrs Gandhi, I thought to myself, was not a truck, and cut flowers have very short lives.

Her performance in 1971 had been brilliant, her decisions perfectly timed, as they had been when she came to power in 1966, as they had been when she smote and split the rock of the Congress Party in 1969. She could now do anything she wanted to without asking advice from anyone: yet she still asked for advice. She made the downfall of the princes law. The *Garibi Hatao* movement recommenced. The trouble was that so much money had been expended on the refugees from Bangladesh that there was little left to rehabilitate the Indian poor: and people began to complain. Why, they wanted to know, had she spent so much money on foreigners? Why had she so minimal a sum to expend on the poor of India? The whole Indian breakdown of trust in an individual started once more, the centuries of mistrust reversed their heavy wheels. In 1973 I was back in India: my father, whose political predictions were more often than not true, said, 'She's on her way out. One day she'll do something very silly or dramatic, and her whole power structure will collapse. It's collapsing already.'

She, when I met her that year, was calm as usual, but a little petulant. She did not seem to want to talk about Bangladesh. Indeed, she didn't seem to want to talk about anything. Except that she asked me for my opinions on the work of Graham Greene, most of whose heroes are, in one way or another, martyrs.

* *The Tempest Within.*

❧ 13 ❧

The Coming of Chaos

HER OVERWHELMING ELECTION victory, her triumph in Bangladesh, should have made 1971 a tremendous year for Mrs Gandhi. On the surface it was: the shattering flash of her success blinded political commentators to the consequences of certain events, which would later cause serious problems for her. Of these, the most noteworthy was the one that followed her election to Parliament from her constituency, Rae Bareilly. Her principal opponent was a Socialist, Raj Narain, a shaggy, bearded man considered by many people to be a buffoon, but like most eccentric exhibitionists, able to commit himself unswervingly to a course of action, however unimaginable to others the viability of this course might be. Narain, after his defeat, charged Mrs Gandhi with fourteen breaches of the election law, brought his case to court, and demanded that her victory be declared null and void. Few people at the time took his action seriously. It seemed a gesture made from the gallows: but its repercussions were to be considerable. The events in Bangladesh wiped the case from public memory, and also temporarily obscured the existence of other controversies that had built up slowly, like cyclones, since 1970. The first and most important of these had arisen around Mrs Gandhi's younger son.

In 1969 Sanjay Gandhi was twenty-three years old. As a child his favourite toys had been model cars, and machines still fascinated him as a young adult. He did not read much apart from magazines and books about mechanics, which affected his education somewhat: he had been anything but a model student. He had been taken out of Doon School, a fashionable education factory in northern India, early, to be tutored at home. Mrs Gandhi, observing that his was not an academic nature and that he had a passion for cars, sent him to England to be trained at the Rolls-Royce factory at Crewe. He did not complete his course. However, in November 1969 he was one of a number of applicants for a government licence to manufacture a small, cheap car. This was to be built without foreign aid of any kind and made readily available to the masses. In 1970 Sanjay became the only one of the applicants to be granted the licence. He declared that he would produce 50,000 cars a year and the Maruti car factory was started. But the granting of the licence to Sanjay, whose qualifications seemed mainly to rest in his heredity, was immediately and bitterly criticised, in Parliament as well as in the press. Mrs Gandhi was charged with nepotism.

Moreover, shortly before the Maruti licence was issued, she was accused of attempting to suppress the freedom of the press. The Ministry of Information and Broadcasting drafted a scheme to diffuse the ownership of newspapers with a large circulation. Ninety-five per cent of the shares in each such newspaper, it was proposed, should be allocated to the staff. Five per cent would remain with existing shareholders, but no shareholder would have more than half a vote per share in management and policy decisions. The other half of the votes, 50 per cent of the total, would be invested in a person appointed by the government. This scheme very naturally created a considerable amount of brouhaha: if it was carried through, it would mean that the government was to all intents and purposes in control of the chief newspapers. Did Mrs Gandhi, some leading editors asked, want to become a dictator?

1971 brought up a further stormcloud. On May 24, the chief cashier of the State Bank of India in Delhi, V. P. Malhotra, was telephoned by a person who identified herself as the Prime Minister. This disembodied voice ordered him to take Rs 6 million out of the bank, carry it to a stated spot in the city, and hand it over to a man he would meet there. This man would identify himself by saying that he was 'the Bangladeshi clerk'. Malhotra did all this, and then repaired to the residence of the Prime Minister to report the completion of his mission. Haksar, the Principal Secretary, utterly horrified, said that Mrs Gandhi had never made such a call, and advised Malhotra to pay a rapid visit to the police. 'The Bangladeshi clerk' was traced the same day, for he had made no attempt to cover his trail, and the money was recovered. 'The Bangladeshi clerk' turned out to be Rustum Sohrab Nagarwalla, a Parsi officer from the Research and Analysis Wing (R.A.W.), an intelligence organisation founded by Mrs Gandhi and described by the Communist leader Jyotirmoy Bosu as fascist in its methods. Nagarwalla, the

police said, had told them after his arrest that he had imitated Mrs
Gandhi's voice on the telephone, and that he wanted the money to
support the freedom movement in Bangladesh. The tape on which
this confession was allegedly recorded was never produced in
court, in spite of which Nagarwalla was sentenced to four years in
prison. He made an abortive attempt to tell his story to the editor of
a Bombay paper of dubious reputation, and also asked for a retrial,
for, as he said, his case had been dealt with by three different magis-
trates in three days, and had been conducted and concluded at a
speed hitherto unheard of in the courts of India. Nagarwalla died in
prison in 1972. Mrs Gandhi's opponents accused her by implication
of having arranged for his death to stop him from involving her in
the matter. The whole business was described in Sherlock Holmes
style by one such person as 'a murky plot'.

The Nagarwalla affair was murky, certainly, but it is difficult to
see any connected plot in it. The State Bank of India had no account
either for the government or the Prime Minister. For a bank officer
to hand over cash to the equivalent of, at that time, U.S. $100,000
to an unidentified stranger on the strength of a telephone call,
seems curious in itself: nor could Malhotra have been so habituated
to speak to Mrs Gandhi as to instantly recognise her voice on the
phone. For Nagarwalla to have kept the money and his own person
in Delhi, and not have either decamped with it or dumped it somewhere also seems rather weird. The behaviour of the principals in the
case was aberrant. There was nothing to connect Mrs Gandhi with
it except wishful thinking on the part of her enemies: but the idea of
an empress who employed poisoners was endemic in the racial
memory of India. Mrs Gandhi, her accusers admitted, might not
have wanted the money for herself: but perhaps she wanted it to
subsidise her younger son, hence the curious events of May 24.

All kinds of rumours were adrift on the wind about Sanjay and
his mother, and a mysterious hold he was supposed to have over her
to bend her to his will. These had been intensified by Mrs Gandhi's
reticence during the uproar over the Maruti licence. Not only had
she not said enough, but she had seemed uninterested by the uproar:
she had pursed her lips and turned her patrician head away. This
apparent contempt for her critics had naturally maddened them
still further: it was taken as gospel in many circles that Mrs Gandhi
had deliberately intervened to procure the licence for her son.
Licences were not issued by her own office, but a word dropped by

her would have its echo anywhere in the government. Personal intervention is not really her style, but this was a peculiarly special case. Of her two sons, Rajiv, the elder, is a quiet, serious young man, whose main interest in life apart from his Italian wife Sonia and their children, is flying planes. Rajiv, however, had no desire to *make* planes: he is a pilot with Indian Airlines, and perfectly happy. Sanjay, on the other hand, could not be said to have had a particularly tranquil career: Mrs Gandhi worried about him: she wanted him to work. People knew this, they knew that the Prime Minister would be pleased if her son started to work. Whether she dropped a word to the relevant officials or not, they were aware of the situation, which was enough for Maruti to receive a licence. This was hardly an ethically laudable course of events, but the desire to please your prince, even if he has expressed no wishes thereto, persists in India more than in most other countries, the heritage of thousands of years. Once Sanjay had applied for his licence, he was virtually certain of obtaining it. The Opposition pressed for an inquiry, and mentioned Sanjay's youth, inexperience, and lack of qualifications. Mrs Gandhi shrugged. She did not, she pointed out, personally issue licences: that was done by committees. Her other main argument was that it was unfair to demand that a young man, because he was the son of a Prime Minister, should be forbidden from taking up work in which he was interested. She interposed herself between her son and his hunters: in doing so, she made a serious tactical mistake, and exposed her flank to the harrying teeth of her enemies.

The attacks upon her in the press increased in intensity. Mrs Gandhi has a fixed distrust of Indian media (when it is not under her control) which manifested itself recently when I asked her what she thought of its effect on the masses. 'The press is all manipulated,' she said, angry and blinking furiously, 'it's all motivated and led by different influences from outside, and by the capitalists. It had always been like that in India.' Given these beliefs, the scheme her Ministry had drawn up to enforce increased governmental control on the press was psychologically true to her. But it was not psychologically true to the temper of the nation at the time: those who had started to see a potential dictator in her, a Stalin in a sari, had their opinions reinforced. She had made her first mistakes: but all of them were temporarily swept away when Bangladesh exploded.

In early 1972 the Congress was on the crest of a wave that swept its opponents before it. The elections for the State Assemblies were held, and the party rolled home nearly everywhere. Her advisers urged Mrs Gandhi to surge onward, and sweep poverty away as she had promised. But after the failure of the 1972 monsoon ruined the crops all over the country, the prices of everything soared upward: there was a shortage of most commodities, not only of foodstuffs but of industrial products, for heavy power cuts adversely affected all mills and factories. Faced with shortages and unemployment, the students of nine Universities reacted with such violence that some of these institutions were forced to close down temporarily. Drought struck, followed by famine. The food stocks and economy of the country had been so depleted by the war and the influx of refugees that Mrs Gandhi had nothing left to fall back on. The wave on which she had hoped to ride had subsided, and her advisers stood around nervously.

For the Opposition was out once more. It was a motley assembly of political interests, but the disparate parties were unified in protest not only against the physical, but the spiritual collapse of the country. Charges of Congress corruption were more frequent: angry fingers were pointed at the borders of Haryana, where 300 acres of land had been requisitioned, and from which 1,500 peasants had allegedly been evicted, to provide the Maruti car factory with a site. The nationwide lack of cement and building materials had not prevented the factory from being put up at high speed. Sanjay had been financed by certain industrialists who, the Opposition said, might thus establish a hold over the Prime Minister. A cabinet sub-committee examined Bansilal, the Chief Minister, on the subject of the Maruti factory, but they exonerated him from any misuse of authority. The Union Minister for Railways, L. N. Mishra, was accused of exploiting the Kosi Dam scheme in Bihar, a drought area, for alleged financial defalcations that had apparently brought him a substantial fortune. The urban coffee houses where young intellectuals had traditionally met and talked since Mogul times buzzed with resentment: Bangladesh had been forgotten by a disaffected nation; only the present was harsh and real.

P. N. Haksar, by far the most able of the Prime Minister's advisers, had been opposed to the Maruti scheme. He was dropped from the post of Principal Secretary early in 1973, and things immediately became worse. In April that year it was announced the rice and wheat crops would be taken over by the government for

mass distribution: a plan that failed because it was hastily conceived
and shoddily implemented. As the food situation became anarchic,
a small armed rebellion broke out in Uttar Pradesh, where Mrs
Gandhi had her constituency. The Provincial Armed Constabulary
captured several armouries and refused to surrender. President's rule
was enforced, and the revolt was put down by the army. It was the
first instance of rebellion by an official armed force in the history
of independent India, and it did not look likely to be the last. Mrs
Gandhi had now started to lose support within her own party:
Mohan Dharia and Chandra Sekhar, two of the Young Turks who
had fought for her in 1969, veered away from her: circumstances
were forcing her into a smaller and smaller circle of whispers to
which she listened, suddenly unquiet.

In 1959, I happened to be in Delhi, where the main topic of conversation was, as always in those days, who would succeed Nehru.
Some people mentioned the name of Jayaprakash Narayan: 'he's not
in politics now,' they said, 'but these days that could be an advantage'. Narayan was at this time fifty-seven years old: he had been
born in Bihar, the son of a revenue officer in the canal department,
and had not seen a city until, at twelve, he was sent to school in the
provincial capital, Patna. He proved an assiduous student and
eventually won a scholarship to Patna College, but when Nehru
and Azad visited the city in 1921, appealing to students for help in
the fight for freedom, he abandoned his books and prepared to
answer the appeal. His family did not think this a good idea at all:
eventually he was prevailed upon to pursue further studies in
America. Equipped with intelligence, hope, and U.S. $600, he
sailed west, and spent seven years in various American colleges. He
eked out his minuscule capital by working in mines, factories and
hotels: for a while he even set up as a shoeshine boy. In 1930 he
returned to India, met Nehru, and became a member of the
Congress: he went to prison several times. On one such occasion he
escaped, fled to the Nepalese border, where he marshalled a small
guerrilla force, and then wandered about, disguised, over various
parts of India, spreading the word. He was recaptured and put back
behind bars: his release came only in 1946, when most of the other
Congress leaders had been free for some time. He disagreed with
Nehru's policies, and helped found a socialist party: but then he
became interested in the work of Acharya Vinoba Bhave, an elderly

Gandhian, who was trying to implement land reform in a new way, through what was called the *Bhoodan* movement. Bhave and his disciples travelled around the country on foot, asking rich farmers for land which was then distributed to poor farmers. The drawback to all this was that the rich farmers normally handed over with saintly smiles whatever uncultivable land they had: admirable though the movement was in theory, it simply did not take human nature into account. In 1959, however, Jayaprakash was still following Bhave round the country.

His seemed to have been a more physically active life than most Congress leaders had aspired to: moreover, he seemed to command widespread respect. I asked my father if he thought Narayan would succeed Nehru. 'He's a very nice man,' said my father, 'a very *good* man: but I'm sure that he won't succeed Nehru.' I asked why not. 'He's in Delhi now,' said my father. 'He's going to speak at someone's house this afternoon, as a matter of fact. If you want to know why he won't succeed Nehru, go and listen to him.' I did.

The meeting took place on the terrace of a private house. The audience sat on the floor. Narayan stood. He had a kind, lined, rather beautiful face, with eyes that did not wrinkle under the afternoon sun. When he started to speak, I understood what my father had meant. He spoke very slowly and softly, with lengthy pauses for reflection, and the shift and flux of his speech from topic to unconnected topic made it difficult to follow exactly what he was talking about. He seemed, as my father had said, a very nice man, a very good man, but I agreed with my father that modern Prime Ministers were not built as he was.

J.P., as Narayan was popularly called,* parted ways with Bhave. He then retired from politics and settled down in Patna with his wife, who had been fourteen at the time of their marriage. He said that he had retired from public life, but this was not wholly true.

Madhya Pradesh, in Central India, is an area of dry ravines, barbed bush and small rocky hills: good terrain for guerrillas, and provably so, since for centuries gangs of *dacoits*, or bandits who operated on a guerrilla principle, had made it their home base. These *dacoits* were by no means of the Robin Hood type: they terrorised the villagers and wayfarers, and were far from averse to rape and murder. It was a hard life, not only for the villagers but the

* He died in 1979.

dacoits, ceaselessly on the run from the police. Madho Singh, one of their leaders, suddenly asked J.P. to intercede for them with the government. If the government promised not to enforce death sentences on them and treated them humanely, he said, the *dacoits* would surrender their arms and themselves, not to the government but to J.P. himself. J.P. negotiated with the government, obtained promises from it, went to Madhya Pradesh, and, accompanied by police officers, received the surrender of 400 *dacoits* complete with arms and ammunition. The episode naturally caused an immense amount of publicity. J.P. started, slowly, to move back into politics. He had been opposed to the policies of Mrs Gandhi's father: in 1953, when Nehru suggested that J.P.'s socialist party should co-operate with the government, the reply from J.P. was that such an alliance would mean nothing if it merely strengthened Nehru's hand to carry out his present policies. Now he opposed himself to Mrs Gandhi. In 1973 he wrote to various M.P.s with a programme designed to protect individual rights and democratic institutions. He founded a body called Citizens for Democracy, wrote an open letter to young Indians urging them to start a Youth for Democracy movement, and became a kind of patriarch of dissent.

The Gujaratis are a placid, vegetarian race, much interested in money, and averse to physical violence. But the food shortages and price rises now endemic to the nation had severely affected the state, which was under Congress rule. The most vehement protests came from colleges in Ahmedabad, the state capital, and Morvi. Students the world over are keenly concerned with their stomachs. They shouted, they waved banners, they made lengthy speeches. The police came out to restrain the demonstrators, but this not only created public sympathy for the students, but led to a mass movement all over the state, which demanded that the Gujarat government should resign. The movement was on a very large scale and the police were not equipped to deal with it: so paramilitary forces such as the Border Security Force were moved in. In the first three months of 1974 nearly a hundred people were killed in the state, and in the middle of March the state government resigned. Gujarat, like Uttar Pradesh, went under presidential rule. However, student unrest had spread widely all over the country. No sooner had Gujarat settled uneasily down then Bihar flared up. This was J.P.'s home state, an unfortunate place which seems to have floods when it does not have drought, and where consequently there are recurrent famines.

There had been a smallpox epidemic in the state in the early weeks of 1974, which had exacerbated public opinion, since it was felt that the government had not taken proper steps to control it. The Ahmedabad students provided an example for the Patna students. In the prevalent mood of bad temper and resentment, 30,000 Patna students (and other people) demonstrated outside the State Assembly, protesting against the Education Minister's failure to reply to a memorandum on educational reform presented to him three weeks previously. The police set up barricades, since the mood of the students was by no means Gandhian. The barricades were rushed: the students who crossed them were beaten up and dragged by the hair into police vans. Stones were hurled at the police, who, wearing gas-masks assumed the appearance of gargoyles. Gas scattered the students; a *lathi* charge dispersed them. Their dispersal had a backlash: within a very short while private houses and two newspaper offices were on fire. This was on March 18: in the three days that followed, restaurants, hotels and department stores were looted and burnt. The Border Security force and the Central Reserve Police (C.R.P.) were deployed to deal with the situation, as they had been in Gujarat. Anarchy spread out from Patna over the smaller towns of the state, though the villages were quiet. The brutality of the government reprisals was much commented on by the opposition.

It is difficult to see what the opposition expected the government to do. They could not stop mob violence with words: if anybody could have done so, it was J.P., who now began to say that the government should differentiate between organised and planned violence, such as the burning of newspaper offices, 'and', as an apologist of his wrote,* 'small violence, such as brickbatting or setting fire to stray vehicles in anger or retaliation ... ', implying as it were, that there should be a delicate psychological differentiation between one arsonist and another. Then J.P. started to lead processions. The first of these was supposed to demonstrate non-violence and the members of the procession went out with cloths bound around their mouths, some with hands tied behind their backs. As they passed the Patna prison, inmates recently incarcerated waved

* S. K. Ghose, *The Crusade and End of Indira Raj*, Intellectual Book Corner, Patna, India, 1977.

and shouted to them: these inmates had been put inside for violent acts, but the silent procession made pacifist martyrs of them all. On June 5, having led several other much less silent processions, J.P. said, in a speech, 'Friends, this is revolution, a total revolution. This is not a movement merely for the breaking of the Assembly. We have to go far, very far ... ' For one acclaimed by many, including himself, for his pacifism, these were fighting words. The aged sage behaved as though he were still fighting the British, attempting to cast down a foreign crown by disturbing the government with the nearest means that came to hand. What he does not appear to have understood is that he was now fighting an Indian government, the government of the country by Indians which he had himself worked to bring about, with the same methods and the same lack of sympathy he had deployed when embroiled with the British. He was fighting not for his country but for his own political preferences; for the situation in India, though dramatic, was not as disastrous as he and the opposition (who, having no figure of any stature within their ranks, except the cold, idiosyncratic, and unpopular Desai, had fastened on the ancient hero for a symbol) wanted to lead people to believe. J.P.'s remark that the dissolution of the State Assembly was not the main aim of a total revolution, that the revolutionaries had 'to go far, very far' — by implication, to dissolve the Central Government — was, at the time that he made this statement, a kind of idiocy, since he proposed nothing to replace it. Granted the disparate nature of the opposition parties' interests, what he was actually proposing as an alternative to Mrs Gandhi was anarchy. He was an intelligent man: what brought him to make this proposal is highly problematical, and I suppose will remain so for some time, until history probes and proves.

At the beginning of 1974 I was posted to the U.N. Fund for Population Activities (UNFPA), in New York. I had come back from a tour round the Third World, had written a book about population,* and was editing a volume of essays by different people in different disciplines, not exactly about population, but about their view of the human condition as it was now and as it would be. I had invited my father to contribute an essay: he was beyond doubt the best Indian editor of his time. I saw him in London in May 1974 when he was already very ill: 'I'll finish the essay,' he said, groping

* *A Matter of People*, André Deutsch, and Praeger, 1974.

at me with his intelligent eyes. 'Whom are you asking besides me?'
I gave him my list, which included Mrs Gandhi. 'Oh,' he said,
grunting a bit, since at that time it was painful for him to speak very
much. 'Yes. She was like a convent girl when I met her, but she's
like her father now. Yes, she would be very good. I disapprove of
her, but, for India now, she's the only one who could ... Anyway,
she'll be too busy to write.' He added, 'I used to attack her all the
time. But do you remember what I once told you about J.P.? He
will never succeed in anything he does, because he's suggestible.
Indira isn't, and if she ever writes this essay, she will say something
truthful. At least, I hope so.' I went back to New York, and shortly
after this my father died. Mrs Gandhi sent me her condolences.

Hers was the last essay to arrive, and it came to me in the form of
a protracted telex through the Embassy in Washington, as the book
was about to go to press. I was furious at the inconvenient timing,
but I recalled her smile, and was greatly mollified by a letter she
subsequently sent me. It simply said she was sorry for the delay,
she had been very busy, and that she had written it on her knee
while bumping up and down between her house and Parliament in
her small car. (This small car was not the Maruti, which indeed
few people had been lucky enough so far to set eyes on. One reporter
who had done so wrote graphically about this experience. 'I could
not believe it stood before me,' he said. 'Perhaps it was evanescent
and a dream? But no! I kicked it, and it was solid.')

Mrs Gandhi had once told me, as had her father ten years
previously, that had she not been a politician she would have liked
to be a writer. Perhaps she could have been. The essay she wrote
for me was slight, but it had form and no pretensions. The prose
was terse and clear. She recalled Motilal's house, the splendid
dinners and the conversations, and then went on to say that things
had changed and nobody could live like that now. She outlined the
way she thought people should live, which included a deeper
contact with nature, but the essay was realistic in that it admitted
that most people in India could not live in the way she envisaged. A
significant note was that, rather like the Queen at Christmas, she referred to the inhabitants of India as 'my people' and wished them well.

Her attitude towards writers, and indeed towards artists of any
kind, has always been somewhat reverential, though this may be
because she has never known any of them very well. Once, around
this time, she visited London. Pupul Jayakar was there, and

presumably with the intention of broadening Mrs Gandhi's cultural
horizons, she invited the Prime Minister to one of the poetry
readings at the Albert Hall. Amongst the poets were Allen Ginsberg,
a friend of Pupul's, Gregory Corso and Lawrence Ferlinghetti. As
they volleyed and thundered, Pupul recollects, Mrs Gandhi sat,
hands folded in her lap, leaning forward, with wide eyes that
became wider at the scatological bits. She had probably never heard
such language anywhere before, let alone at the Albert Hall.
Presently Ginsberg saw Pupul. He waved, and invited her and
Mrs Gandhi to sit on the platform with the poets. Mrs Gandhi was
utterly thrilled. 'She was like a little girl, being taken to the circus
for the first time,' Pupul said. It was late when the reading ended,
and there were no taxis. They therefore had to walk back to the
Indian High Commissioner's house where they were both staying.
They were hungry: they found a small café open: a very grubby one,
Pupul remembers: ate sandwiches there and finally returned home
well after midnight. Pupul twinkled at me as she told this story:
'Mrs Gandhi loved every minute of it.'

But there was little time left for these cultural activities. J.P. was
hard at work among the untrodden ways of Bihar, and the number
of his disciples multiplied day by day.

There were continual demonstrations in Patna. The houses of State
Ministers were picketed in order to stop them going to their offices.
J.P. called for all colleges in Bihar to be closed down for a year so
that the students could participate in his 'total revolution'. Anyone
who not only wanted the students to have a year's holiday, but
ardently advocated it, was bound to be popular on the campus: J.P.
certainly was. What was somewhat alarming was that he seemed not
to think about the consequences of his exhortations. The Indian
public is highly inflammable: the scarifying conditions of society,
the climate, and a curious national love of commotion and confusion,
manifested at festivals as well as at riots, are conducive to this: and
a flame successfully kindled among hundreds of millions of people
would be impossible to put out: a shift of wind could turn it back
upon those who had caused it and destroy them. The anarchic
nature of J.P.'s statements—despite the fact that he incessantly
talked of peaceful methods his followers did not always employ
them—was best demonstrated by the fact that they led nowhere but
to chaos. He demanded that the Congress Ministry in Bihar should

resign, but he did not say who should replace it. The Congress apart, there was no stable party in the country, except for the racist Jan Sangh, most powerful in the north. For J.P. to associate himself with them would be extremely discreditable. Nevertheless, he provided what the opposition needed, a unifying symbol, a respectable figurehead, and if he did not exactly associate himself with them, they certainly associated themselves with him, the Jan Sangh not excluded. There he was then, the figurehead, but he repeatedly declared that he did not want power, so a change in government would result in a cabinet with no single leader wholly acceptable to all the opposition parties. J.P. may have been above all these mundane worries, but, if so, it indicated that his previous retirement from politics was one of the wisest decisions he had ever made. He said that the government used repressive methods in Bihar: but unless he was completely apolitical, he could hardly have expected it to stand by and watch while the entire administration of the state was reduced to chaos.

On November 1 1974 J.P. went to Delhi and had discussions with Mrs Gandhi. His chief demand was that the Bihar State Assembly should be dissolved, a demand to which the Prime Minister would not yield. He had earlier announced that if the Assembly was not dissolved he would call, on November 4, a *gherao** of the state Parliament. He did this: outside help was enlisted, and people who were not Biharis began to stream towards Patna. Predictably, the government took a firm stand. Something like 60,000 B.S.F. and C.R.P. men, armed and ready, were brought into the city, but on November 4 the *gherao* began. The crowd rallied at a park in the centre of the city: the police were present, and the chief of police declared that this was an unlawful assembly and everybody in the park was under arrest. This included J.P. Rather surprisingly, nothing seems to have been done to implement the arrest. The crowd followed J.P. out of the park towards the state Parliament. On the way they were subjected to tear gas and then charged by C.R.P. men with *lathis*. J.P. was hurt. When he recovered sufficiently to speak, he declared a Patna *bundh*† on November 5, the following

---

* A *gherao* is a supposedly peaceful blockade of people in their homes or offices, preventing them from moving out, carried out by a large number of people.

† A *bundh* is a politically organised closure of all shops and offices, whose owners and employees are put under pressure from the *bundh* organisers.

day, and a Bihar *bundh* on the day after that. These were comparatively peaceful days, but November as a whole was a storm of
speeches and demonstrations. Mrs Gandhi suggested, mildly for
her, that J.P. should stop causing chaos and fight things out at the
elections in a democratic manner. In a speech in Patna J.P. agreed
to this: he took 120 minutes to say Yes. During the course of this
lengthy peroration, he quoted a Hindi poet, Dinkar, who wrote,
'*Do rah samayka rath ka gharghar nad suno/Singhasan khali karo
Janata aathi hai.*' ('Listen as time's chariot rumbles this message/
Get off the throne, the people [Janata] are coming ... ') It was,
unwittingly, a quotation of some historical significance.

In November 1974 I was posted to Delhi to help the Indian
government produce software for the new satellite television scheme,
which was to beam programmes to 2,400 villages scattered over
several states. I had not worked in India for some years and was
rather bewildered to find that though I was officially on loan from
UNFPA to the Indian government, the Minister concerned had not
been informed of the fact. To establish my professional existence,
therefore, I had to call on Mrs Gandhi. She seemed even more
abstracted than usual, not unnaturally considering what was going
on in Bihar, but friendly, and once or twice allowed that sunburst
of a smile to take place.

Delhi was full of rumours as usual, all of them about the imminent
fall of the government. It had become fashionable to express one's
commitment to J.P. and his movement: even more fashionable to
say how much one hated Mrs Gandhi: how dictatorial she had
become: the old comparisons with Hitler and Stalin had returned,
though the people who made them, had they been ruled by Hitler
or Stalin, would probably not have survived the next week.

Meanwhile my wife, Leela, found us a flat, which meant we
acquired servants. One of these was a sweeper who lived nearby in a
colony largely populated by Harijans. They had formed a co-operative
society, pooled their small savings, and leased some land near the
Yamuna river where they were trying to cultivate crops. Trying is the
correct word, since they were continually harassed by a rich man who
wanted to build on this land. The Harijans had complained to
everyone they could think of, with little success. Leela went into
their case and found their grievances were legitimate. However, we
now had a problem: to whom were we to complain?

A friend introduced me to Jag Parvesh Chandra, then the Deputy Chairman of the Delhi Metropolitan Council, a seasoned Congressman. Leela presented him with an enormous file which she had prepared on the case. He eyed it quizzically, but read it. Finally he said, 'This is a very complicated matter. You should take it to Mrs Gandhi.' I said Mrs Gandhi was surely busy with more important matters. 'Yes,' said Jag Parvesh, 'but for her this will be an important matter. She's like her father, interested in the problems of poor people.' Leela, with some trepidation, wrote Mrs Gandhi a report on the whole affair and delivered it to her office. I told her not to expect too much.

The land, incidentally, had been leased from the Railway Ministry, and a few days later Leela was summoned by the Railway Minister who told her Mrs Gandhi had demanded action. Jag Parvesh also took her to see the Lieutenant Governor of Delhi, who said the same. With the help of all these people the Harijans were allotted new land, where they would be safe from the harassment of the moneylender.

Some weeks after this I went to see Mrs Gandhi about something quite different. When the business part of the interview was over, she blinked at me over her spectacles and smiled irresistibly. She inquired, 'How are Leela's Harijans?' I told her what had happened. She nodded and smiled once more. 'Good for them.' she said, and after a pause, 'Good for Leela too.' Then, in a dismissive movement, she bent her neat head over her files once more.

Jag Parvesh became a friend of ours. He was a tremendous admirer of Mrs Gandhi, a little awed by her perhaps. But she had his complete confidence. 'I told you so,' he said when the Harijan business was settled. 'She is always helpful when something interests her.' He told me a story of what had happened in the Delhi colleges as the student trouble built up in Gujarat and Bihar. 'Subramaniam, the Finance Minister,' he told us, 'called me. He said there was trouble in Jawaharlal Nehru University. The students in the hostels had been paying Rs 120 per month as canteen bills. They complained about that, but now, because of food prices, the bill was to rise to Rs 135. Subramaniam, after what had happened in Ahmedabad, was very apprehensive. He asked me to solve the problem. Now, I had been organising fair price shops for the people. I arranged that my shops should supply Jawaharlal Nehru University. I went to the

14   The Soviet Prime Minister, Alexei Kosygin, with Mrs Gandhi
    in Moscow

15   With President Tito (*left*) and President Nasser (*right*)

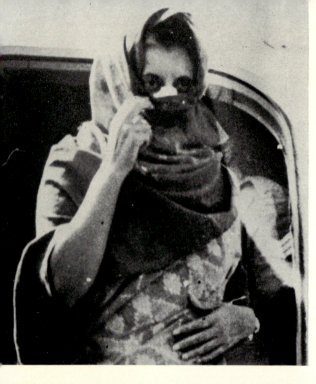

16 (*Left*) Mrs Gandhi
returns from
electioneering in
Orissa State in 1967.
A stone thrown at her
split her lip and
broke her nose

17 (*Below*) Y. B. Chavan
(*left*) with Mrs Gandhi
and Morarji Desai (*right*)

18 (*Right*) Emperor
Haile Selassie in New
Delhi for a State visit

19 (*Below right*) With
Pierre Trudeau, the
Canadian Prime
Minister

20 (*Above*) Lunch in New
Delhi with Prince Charles
and Lord Mountbatten

21 (*Right*) Admiring the King
of Tonga's medals

University and talked to the boys and girls. Each hostel appointed its own food committee, and I went twice a week to meet these children. If they had any complaint, I told them, they should tell me at once, and it would be solved next day. But they must complain at once, I said, not leave things till too late. My initial idea was to start supplying all the hostels at once. I told Mrs Gandhi about this. She was very enthusiastic but she said, "Try one hostel first. See what happens. Then start supplying all of them. There is no point diving in at the deep end." It was excellent advice. Thereafter she kept asking if I had been successful. I reported to her every week, and she always gave me good advice. The monthly canteen bill came down to Rs 97 per person. Without her it would have been very difficult.' Jag Parvesh smiled. 'She was really interested in those children.'

In January 1975, before Leela met the Railway Minister, his predecessor was killed by a bomb at a place called Samastipur, not far from Patna. This was L. N. Mishra, who came from Bihar and who had been charged with corruption. Mrs Gandhi, it was prompt- ly said, had had him killed to get J.P. into trouble. This was in fact implied by J.P., who should have known better. A friend of mine in Delhi, who did not like Mrs Gandhi, swore that he had evidence as to the truth of this. 'Perhaps not evidence in a documentary sense,' he said, 'but real evidence that, to her, all human life is unimportant.'

A Time to Change

BEFORE I WAS posted to India, UNFPA had sent me to a far less likely place, Spokane, East Washington, to attend a seminar about population. With another speaker, I was to talk about population in the Third World and then hold a workshop on the subject. Hotly though Mrs Gandhi had once declared to me that there were not three worlds, only one, I accepted my brief.

The audience for the workshop contained a number of blacks in *dashikis*, with Afro hairstyles, who kept accusing me of Fascism, because, they said, blacks were hated in India. I said, feebly, that I had lived most of my life in Britain: 'They're hated there too, *Fascist*,' chorused the blacks. There was also a large team of Russians from the Embassy in Washington, and an equally large team of State Department people, all watching one another intently while each group made derogatory remarks about the actions of the other country in Asia.

One of the State Department men, black, not in a *dashiki* but a harmoniously tailored suit, said, 'What's your gut feeling about the Indian bomb?' The Russians shouted, 'Good. Very good, yes?' The contingent in *dashikis* shouted, 'They're going to drop it on black people, yeah?'

Being involved in what I was doing at Spokane, I had not read the newspapers or watched television for some days. I was therefore totally unaware that the Indians had exploded a nuclear device in Rajasthan: curiously enough, near the place where my peccant princeling, years before, had stolen all my supplies: Pokharan. This, however, emerged as the State Department man started flourishing cuttings at me. I said, 'Well, they won't use it for war. Whom have they got to fight?' The blacks shouted, '*Us*, Fascist.' The Russians said, 'China, yes? no?'

After the workshop was over, by no means too soon for me, the

State Department people lingered on. 'Man, oh man,' said the black official, 'you handled that real well in there, but you can tell us now: is *she* going to use it on Pakistan?' I said I honestly had no idea: I did not think Mrs Gandhi wanted more wars: the last one had been bad enough. Outside the classroom (the State Department buzzing behind me) the Russians surrounded me. 'Chinese very aggressive, is not so?' inquired a huge lady. '*She* will use on them, no?'

It struck me that the only consistent factor in these two conversations was not the question of whether India would use a nuclear bomb, but whether Indira would.

Even after Spokane, I was pestered by people in New York who asked me why India should want a nuclear bomb. I did not see why any country should not. To become a member of a club with an exclusive membership may prove how horrible you are, but it also, in a sense, proves how powerful you are. You can blackball: you can vote. The Indian experiments in nuclear physics had gone on for years: at Trombay, on the west coast, there is an institute for nuclear research, which, when I last saw it, specialised in blowing flowers and fruits up to hideous sizes and colours. It was an open secret that India was trying to develop a bomb: there must have been other trials before the final declaratory blast at my fat prince's doorstep. Everyone in India protested indignantly that the nuclear experiments had been made for peaceful purposes. The device exploded was small: though to deny that it could be used lethally was equivalent to saying that given a fruit knife you cannot cut a throat. Mrs Gandhi, more nervous than ever of her immediate neighbours to the north after her treaty with the Russians over Bangladesh, had hurried it all up, and it had happened. Moreover, there *are* peaceful purposes to which nuclear energy can be yoked, and what is not to be denied is that under this urging, arguing, untiring, fiery force contained within a silent woman, India had come a long step towards becoming a technocratic nation. Under Mrs Gandhi, India had started to build its own machinery, make its own medicines, have its own starvation internally solved. Also to manufacture its own cars: of which the Maruti was visibly not one.

A sudden ferocity appeared in her, as J.P. went on rambling, in words and on foot, through Bihar. The opposition parties included a man called George Fernandes, an Indian Christian, like Raj Narain something of a buffoon, but a bitter buffoon, and a labour leader. He started a railway strike all over India, though this was not entirely connected with J.P. The result was the paralysis of a system: the railways, originally built by the British, rumble over the length and breadth of the country, delivering food, information and relatives to the inhabitants of remote rural areas. A railway station in India is also in some senses a cultural centre, where, packed on the platforms, the population hawks, spits, belches, farts, sneezes, eats, drinks and most of all, talks, as it awaits the slow, clanking metal centipede, smeared with paint of a faecal colour, which will eventually, in dust, metallic odours, steam and thunder, arrive. All kinds of people share the experience of the platform and, subsequently, the hot, womblike compartment. The railway strike therefore affected the people, who like trains; it also affected the entire economy of the country. Mrs Gandhi, a practical woman, lashed back at the strikers with as much force as she could summon. There was a dual programme of mass dismissals and mass arrests without warrants under the DIR* and MISA† ordinances: On May 28 1974, the three-week-old strike became another victim of the high incidence of infant mortality in India: but it was estimated to have cost the country Rs 500 crores, ‡ in twenty days. It is hard to see that action against the strikers could have been anything but harsh, given the circumstances and the enormous loss to the nation. Mrs Gandhi, however, was accused by the opposition of undue harshness, all part of the character being built up for her, not least of all by the national press.

To understand the Indian press it is necessary to be aware of the nature of its proprietors. As in most other countries, the important newspapers have for some time been owned by large business combines, mostly family concerns run by a patriarch: but in India this patriarch is often hardly literate, and even less aware of the world as it affects anyone else but him, than his British and American counterparts. My father used to tell a story about the proprietor of a mass circulation Indian paper he edited in the 1940s: this man, having acquired the paper, wanted to possess other symbols of contemporary life: he decided to start an airline. While my father

* Defence of India Rule.
† Maintenance of Internal Security Act.
‡ A crore is Rs 10 million. Five hundred crores are roughly £33,000,000.

was in his house the proprietor received an overseas call. 'What?' he inquired of his caller. 'Yes, yes. *Very* good. Please be so good as to buy twenty.' He hung up and turned to my father. 'I have decided to buy twenty Dakotas,' he said. Then he hesitated. 'I am told they are necessary for an airline. But, Moraes, kindly tell me, *what* is a Dakota?'

This kind of proprietor remained in charge of most Indian newspapers in the 1970s. There was normally a competent senior staff and a multifarious sprawl of mainly incompetent subordinates. The editors ran the paper most of the time, but the proprietor came in sometimes, asking for praise of or attacks upon the government, according to how his other businesses were being affected by its decisions. This was one use he had for his newspaper: the other was for it to lose money, thus easing the amount of tax he had to pay. Few newspapers, therefore, had what could be called consistent policies. They were also short of space and money: reporters complained that they were not allowed to take taxis, with the result that they usually arrived late for every story. The photographers of a paper near the Delhi Zoo were sent over to it on foot whenever a filler picture was needed: in consequence it carried, almost daily, a kind of pictorial births, deaths and marriages column on wild life in captivity. In these circumstances the staff was seldom happy, and it was hardly surprising.

This rather stagnant scene created a dreary uniformity in the newspapers, enlivened only by the forays of some editors against the government. These excursions were sometimes motivated by proprietors opposed to the government policy of nationalisation: there were also times when harassed proprietors begged the editor to conciliate the government hoping that in return their tax returns would be studied with a certain degree of lenience. The editors often complained of the absence of dialogue between the government and the press: of Mrs Gandhi's aloofness, her lack of desire to explain herself. In return Mrs Gandhi said that the press, like the Bihar movement, was motivated and led by capitalists and by her ubiquitous 'outside influences', which remained nameless.

'Looking back on those days immediately before the emergency,' Mrs Gandhi said to me one unbearably hot afternoon, a glare and dazzle of heat refracted from the garden beyond her windows, 'what strikes me is the extent to which I was kept from meeting people.' She was in an unusually loquacious and positive mood, and smiled often. 'My secretariat,' she said, 'from top to bottom was full of people who kept visitors away from me. Not only that, but when I wanted to meet people, editors, people from the press, my staff would say it wasn't—what was their usual phrase?—"necessary". This kept me away from a lot of people I would have liked to meet. At one time I actually mentioned to my advisers that I felt that one or two of my staff were from the Jan Sangh: they seemed to make it their main business to keep me away from people. Later,' she added sombrely, 'it turned out that I had been right.' She gave an abrupt little shrug. 'But by then it was too late.'

The breach between the press and Mrs Gandhi widened down the last months of 1974, and little of her publicity was favourable. By contrast, the newspapers reviewed the activities of J.P. and the opposition with attention and sympathy. When by-elections were held in some states, certain opposition parties formed a loose alliance under the umbrella name of the Janata Front, and the Congress candidates toppled to defeat before it. Several newspapers speculated that if elections were to be held Mrs Gandhi's government would fall. J.P. never ceased to repeat this. He moved around the country making speeches to large and receptive crowds. He expressed in his own slow, hesitant way what the masses were feeling, or had been made to feel, by his previous speeches and by the remoteness of Mrs Gandhi. He urged the people, not always wisely, to action. At the Boat Club in Delhi he addressed a number of government employees, to whom he said that the President, the Prime Minister and the cabinet were only transitory people, appointed for a term, afterwards forgettable, whereas gazetted officers were a permanent fixture in the administration. Such officers should not carry out illegal or immoral orders. 'Use your rights,' he said, 'and do your duty without fear.' He said much the same in statements directed at the armed forces and the police. What he obviously meant was 'Don't do your duty'. Such vehement trumpet blasts would have been eminently praiseworthy at certain times in the history of the world: the fact that J.P. was allowed to make music so freely proved that this was not one such time. J.P. had been detained or attacked on several occasions by students who presumably supported Mrs Gandhi. He stated that the police stood by and made no attempt to protect him, alleged that they had been ordered not to protect him, and declared that these incidents were all part

of a plot to murder him. Since J.P. had emerged from all these
episodes unscathed, apart from the knock on the head he once took
in Patna, Mrs Gandhi was obviously not a very good hand at
choosing assassins. But a hagiolatory cloud had formed around J.P.
In this atmosphere of hysteria, the mistakes of Mrs Gandhi,
magnified by rumour and the press, stood, defined in scarlet, as her
sins. 'Render unto Caesar,' she might have said, right eyelid
twitching furiously, to the government officers, the policemen, and
the members of the armed forces to whom such generous and
gratuitous advice had been offered by J.P., 'the things which are
Caesar's.' As it was, she made references to 'outside influences' and
'the forces of reaction' being at the back of J.P. and his followers.
She had already said this about the press, and her remarks might
have been more effective had they been more precise. The opposition derided these inchoate allegations: Mrs Gandhi, they said, was
trying to raise the spectre of 'outside influences' on J.P. in order to
divert public attention from her own increasingly unstable position.
But this obsession with 'outside influences' in India has been
constant in Mrs Gandhi for many years: indeed she has been
mentioning these mysterious influences to me ever since we first
met in 1968, and she has mentioned them even when her power was
unshakeable and she had nothing to fear from anyone. I have known
her to appear to believe agents of foreign powers might be trying to
infiltrate her own staff, a not unreasonable fear, given the evidence
of the existence of spies in high places in other countries from time
to time. But if she had any proof of these 'outside influences' I
would have thought she would have produced it before now. Without
evidence, these dire mutterings sound a little imaginative: but there
is no question, I believe, of her deliberately trying to cloud issues
with these accusations. She herself clearly believes them to be true
—which of course they may be.

March, for Mrs Gandhi, was the cruellest month in 1975. On the
first day Mohan Dharia, once a Young Turk and a fervent supporter
of the Prime Minister, made a speech in Ahmedabad, in which he
pleaded that talks between Mrs Gandhi and the opposition leaders
should take place without delay. He also condemned the brutality
with which young demonstrators had been treated by the police,
and made an angry comment on the Communist Party of India.
Dharia was the Union Minister for Works and Housing. The same

day Mrs Gandhi wrote him a letter in tones of fire and ice, saying that it was not proper for him to continue in the Council of Ministers, since he did not conform to the thinking of the Congress Party. Dharia declared that he had written several letters to the Prime Minister, trying to explain his views, and had also sought to see her but had not been granted an appointment. Had she told him of her feelings, he said, he would have resigned of his own accord. What immediately followed the departure of Dharia was a huge increase in his popularity, not only on the opposition benches, to which he crossed, but in the Congress (R) itself. Other members of her own party experienced her anger and fell away from her: these applications of the axe may have lopped dead wood away but they also created a huge new stockpile of kindling by which her opponents could warm themselves. Before this, the quick, ruthless moves she had always made to break someone she distrusted had worked: now every flexing of her political muscles, every manifestation of her strength, seemed to add to her weakness, and she had still not taken positive action despite all the chaos. Many people said she had cracked at last, she was finished, the opposition had only to wait for the kill. Whenever I saw her at this period, she seemed tensely tranquil, pale, detached: gambling, like St Joan, on the lack of motivation of her enemies: I had the strong and positive feeling that it was she, not the opposition, who was waiting for the kill.

Five days after Dharia's speech at Ahmedabad, on March 6 1975, J.P. led a procession through Delhi. It was five miles long, an endless trail of dust and banners and faces, stopped traffic and shouts, and what it demanded was an end to emergency: this referred to the emergency declared by the President at the outbreak of the war with Pakistan in 1971. The emergency had never been lifted, though there was really no reason for it to continue. The opposition was of the opinion that Mrs Gandhi would use it as an excuse for postponing the elections scheduled for March 1976, to keep herself in power. J.P. announced that he would lead similar demonstrations in every state capital for the following month.

In Ahmedabad on the same day, Desai led yet another procession, this time to the residence of the Governor of Gujarat. He handed the Governor a petition which demanded that elections be held to reconstitute the State Assembly, which had been dissolved after the trouble of March 1974. If no elections were held, he announced,

he would starve himself to death. This was by no means an uncommon threat in the context of Indian politics and had been one of
Gandhi's favourite ploys. Given the fact that most doctors today
hold that a few days without solid food are beneficial rather than
harmful, that no Indian politician I have ever heard of *has* actually
starved himself to death, and that the dietary habits of Desai are
bizarre, few people would have expected a martyrdom: but in the
situation as it stood, Mrs Gandhi could not take chances. She
surrendered in the sense that she announced elections in the state for
early June 1975. She continued to wait.

Slowly the year ebbed into June. It is the worst month in the year
in northern India, when dust and heat become really unbearable,
and tempers shorten rapidly. Air-conditioners purr in bedrooms,
ceiling fans click and deluge those seated beneath with incinerated
air, and the drift of dust from the desert westward destroys clothes
and, not infrequently, eyes. Many people, unable to afford air-
conditioners, coolers or fans, sleep in the open, preferably on the
roofs of their houses if they have houses, or indeed if the houses
have roofs. Many die of heatstroke. The season is made for a
withdrawal from the world into cool water and shadow, but it was
not at all like that in 1975. June of that year, in India, was turmoil
under the crimson sun.

Shortly before the end of May J.P. had announced that he was
setting up *Janata Sarkars* certainly in Bihar and possibly throughout
northern India. A *Janata Sarkar* means a people's government, the
function of these particular organisations of J.P.'s being at a village
level: each village would have its own *Janata Sarkar*, its functions
often overlapping those of government officials. These *Janata
Sarkars* were committed to the idea of 'total revolution', an idea
still not entirely clarified by J.P. Mrs Gandhi, meanwhile, was
campaigning in Gujarat, the state elections a few days away. Stones
were thrown at her, the peasants abused her: J.P. and the opposition
deplored this, though they had created the conditions which would
produce such actions. At Rajkot, a town in Gujarat, Mrs Gandhi said
in a speech that she would welcome into her party any politicians
who had faith in its policies. This seemed a harmless enough statement, but J.P., on June 1, said at Ahmedabad that he was pained
at such sentiments from the daughter of Nehru: did she plan on a
party of defectors and traitors? Such a party could never achieve

democratic rule. This is an interesting remark in the light of the composition of the Janata party proper when it was officially formed two years later.

J.P. continued to wander around the country, saying at one place that Mrs Gandhi was a defector herself, from the original Congress party: at another that she was guilty of corruption on an immense scale, having taken money to back her election campaigns from industrialists, promising them favours in return. Public attention was now ricocheting back and forth, between J.P.'s utterances and the inquiry which was to take place at the High Court in Allahabad. Raj Narain, who had accused Mrs Gandhi of fourteen violations of the election law during her 1971 campaign, had been pushing his case for a long while. 'Raj Narain', as one writer says,* 'was known to have specialised in filing election petitions after defeats in elections ... the petition in question had gone on for about three and a half years ... ' and nobody at first took the case as much more than another of Narain's aberrations. However, the Indian press had become deeply interested in this affair, and it was now being closely covered. Also, to the surprise of most people, it looked as though Narain could conceivably win.

Meanwhile, the Gujarat elections were slowly yielding their results. On June 12 the last figures came in. They showed that in a State Assembly of 182 seats, Congress (R) had won only 12. The Janata Front came into power in the state. It was on the same day that the Allahabad High Court came ponderously to its final decision in the election case.

Mrs Gandhi had spent seven and a half hours in the witness box before her return to Delhi. The charges brought against her were technicalities and she does not seem to have been worried about the eventual verdict until her own lengthy appearance in court: then, she says, she felt a certain uneasiness about the way the decision would go. The decision was curious. Justice J. L. Sinha dismissed twelve of the fourteen charges in Narain's petition, but he found Mrs Gandhi culpable of two, under the existing law of corrupt practice. She was guilty, he said, of utilising the services of Yashpal Kapoor, who had once been her private secretary and was, at the time of the 1971 elections, an officer on special duty in her secretariat. Kapoor was a government officer. Mrs Gandhi had first posted herself as the

* C. S. Pandit, *End of An Era*, Vikas Books, Delhi, 1977.

Congress (R) candidate for the Rae Bareilly seat on January 2 1971. According to the indictment, Kapoor had worked as her agent in Rae Bareilly since January 7, unlawfully, because of his status as a government employee. Kapoor had, in fact, submitted his resignation from government service on January 13 1971, but it had not actually been accepted by the President of India until January 25. For eighteen days, therefore, the court said, from January 7 to January 25, Mrs Gandhi had unlawfully availed herself of Kapoor's services. The second culpable count was that she had used government transport and the assistance of government officers posted in Rae Bareilly such as the District Magistrate, the Superintendent of police, the Public Works Department Executive Engineer and the Hydroelectric Engineer, to guard and illuminate the platforms from which she spoke and to convey her from place to place. Nehru had often done the same kind of thing during his election campaigns, but nobody had queried it.

In any event, said Justice Sinha, and warned the public present in the court not to create noisy scenes after he had delivered his verdict, he had no alternative but to find the Prime Minister guilty on these two charges, and to debar her, as the existing law prescribed, from election to any House of Parliament or any State legislature for the next six years. Her election from Rae Bareilly in 1971 was declared null and void. A stay order of twenty days was granted so that the Congress Parliamentary Party could find a new Prime Minister and the country would not be left entirely leaderless.

There was pandemonium in the court after this, and a rush of reporters towards telephones. The official order was signed by Justice Sinha. A seal was affixed by a court official. Sentence had been passed, and supposedly the case was closed.

Mrs Gandhi heard the news in Delhi, and remained, at least outwardly, unmoved. Her Ministers heard it, and her old power prevailed: in a matter of minutes her entire cabinet was at her house, pledging their undivided loyalty. In the case of some people such as Chavan and Jagjivan Ram, this loyalty may have been caused by terror: they did not know what the lady would do, but, knowing her, they thought she would do something, fight back, turn and rend her enemies, and they wanted to keep their options open.

As a matter of fact, Mrs Gandhi appears, for once, to have been willing at first to bow before the blast: it was the opinion of most of her advisers that there was no way out. Some thought otherwise, however, and Mrs Gandhi listened to them, for deep within herself she did not want to leave. When dealing with so infinitely, and infuriatingly, complex a personality as hers, it seems to me crude to say, as some critics have said, that she simply wanted to hold on to power. Her desire to remain came from far deeper roots than that.

In 1978 I tried to probe her about this desire: as can happen when she wants it to, what she said in answer was far more opaque than her silence. Then I had a stroke of luck. I had fixed an appointment with her on what her secretary had assured me would be an unbusy morning. When I arrived, very punctually, there were about twenty people seated on the balcony of her house, waiting to talk to her: on the lawn outside there were fifty other people awaiting the privilege of her brief presence among them. She came out of her reception room at the far end of the balcony, surveyed the crowd, and presently saw me. Her right eyelid fluttered embarrassedly. She took a large black umbrella from a secretary, and, holding it above her head to shield herself from the sun, trotted rapidly across the lawn, smiled at the fifty people who awaited her presence, said a few words, patted a few children on the head, and trotted back. Fifty down: twenty to go. Studiously avoiding my eye, she said to the other twenty on the balcony, 'I can give you one minute each,' and went back into the reception room. She gave them five minutes each: consequently it was some two hours after the original time of my appointment that she beckoned me into the reception room. She hates wasted time, her own or that of others: it seemed to me that it was with some consciousness of my wasted time that she immediately started to talk, far more freely than usual.

'You know,' she said, before I could say anything, 'I didn't want to be Prime Minister. Once, before 1975, I wanted to resign, but people wouldn't let me, because there was a financial crisis and I was the only one who could handle it. After my judgment in 1975' (she always refers to the event with a curiously proprietary air as 'my judgment') 'what could I have done except stay? You know the state the country was in. What would have happened if there had been nobody to lead it? I was the only person who could, you know. It was my duty to the country to stay, though I didn't want to.'

I think she did want to, but not for the reasons most people debit her with. I think she wanted to stay to continue a martyrdom.

After the High Court order, Mrs Gandhi appealed to the Supreme
Court. There were huge rallies in the Indian cities, protesting against
the Allahabad verdict, and pressing her to stay in power: these, said
the cynics, were organised by her party on the old Indian political
precept of a rupee a cheer. Since she showed no sign of movement,
the opposition started further agitation. J.P. declared a march on
Delhi, to be made by people from all over the country, the purpose
of which was to force her from her throne. Among those who
promised to march were the Nihang Sikhs, a particularly warlike
branch of the martial people. The Nihang habitually carry their
weapons with them: staves, swords and spears. The walls of
Mrs Gandhi's residence in Delhi were low, and there was a limit
to the number of security precautions that could be taken.
The danger of uncontrolled, violent crowds was real, as the
murder of Mujibur Rehman in Dacca, with his family, was to
show.

'Of course,' said Mrs Gandhi to me, after explaining why she had
to stay in power in 1975, 'I wasn't afraid. I am not afraid of dying
or of death. I never have been. But I get a sort of feeling about
things. Nine days before Mujib was killed, I saw him in Delhi. I
knew the political situation in Bangladesh, of course, but beyond
that I had this feeling. I told him not to go back to Bangladesh
immediately, something very bad for him and for Bangladesh would
happen if he did. He laughed and said, "My people are like my
children. Nobody will lift a finger against me." But I had this
feeling … '

On the night of June 25 1975, as a dusty heat-wind swept un-
collected rubbish off the pavements and streets, the daily newspapers
were being put to bed when the lights failed and the presses stopped.
Leela and I were at home when a friend from a newspaper phoned
us to report this. The service systems in Delhi, indeed in India —
telephones, power, water supply — are notoriously unreliable. 'It'll
come on again in a few minutes,' I said dismissively. My friend said,
'But it's never happened before. Something very peculiar is going
on.' I said, 'Don't be a damned fool,' and hung up. About half an
hour later another friend from another newspaper called me to
apprise me of this phenomenal power cut. 'Something very peculiar
is going on,' he said. 'Don't be a damned fool,' I said and hung up.
We were in bed when, half an hour later, somebody else rang up to
tell me that no paper in the city could function. After I hung up I

said to my sleepy wife, 'I think that something very peculiar is
going on.' Something very peculiar was.

That night, most of the opposition leaders, including J.P. and
Morarji Desai, were picked up by the police and taken away to
prison. A few newspapermen were also arrested as well as activists
and workers of the opposition parties. The next day, June 26, newspapers were not available, but the radio said that a state of internal
emergency in the country had been declared by the President.
There was already a state of external emergency, since the declaration made at the start of the war with Pakistan in 1971 had never been
rescinded, despite the protests of J.P. and the opposition, and Mrs
Gandhi, once more displaying her sense of how and when to hit
whom hardest, had made J.P. and the opposition invisible. Nevertheless, India ambled on as usual: nothing much changed.

'As regards the arrests after we declared emergency,' Mrs Gandhi
said, glaring past me at a Congressman who had tried to come in to
the reception room, 'there was a list of the main opposition leaders,
which I approved. The rest of the arrests were left to the discretion
of state governments and the police: the idea was to arrest anyone
who was likely to exert a troublesome influence in the country or
the area. We had spent so much time fighting all the chaos that we
had had no time to work for the country. If we could find time to
breathe, we could find time to work. Emergency was necessary.'

The initial operations of the 1975 emergency resembled the initial
operations of any political coup,* though this was a coup made the
wrong way round, by a government against its opposition rather than
by an opposition against its government. The opponents of those in
power disappeared and were not heard from for some time: that
they were heard from at all, not quietly butchered in a ditch or cellar,
as they might have been in some other countries, says something for
the nature of the 1975 emergency. Had Mrs Gandhi made her move
earlier, knowing the country was in an obvious state of disruption
due to the tactics of J.P. and the opposition, she would probably
have been much less criticised than she was when she eventually
made it under the shadow of her own deposition from power. This
does not mean that the emergency was not to be criticised. The
mass arrests, often made at the whim of a government official or a

---

* Mrs Gandhi, I think, would like to call it a revolution, but the masses were
certainly not involved in the emergency.

policeman, were deplorable to say the least: the treatment of prisoners often abominable. But petty officials had to interpret their orders often far away from the restraining control of more senior and more experienced officials in administrative centres. Obviously in a country the size of India the problems of ensuring that individual policemen and local civil servants display at all times standards of behaviour that would be expected by a civilised government, are immense. Inevitably Mrs Gandhi was blamed for all the excesses, and as the head of government she accepted this.

The strength of any coup lies in its initial power of shock, stunning the people into obedience. At this point its strength is static: it has asserted itself and it *is*. When the people start to recover from the initial shock, however, the machinery within the governing power had to become mobile, that is to say it has to begin to act and move outward. It then exposes itself to the people and their criticism. The more suppressed this criticism is, the more it packs itself into the public mind, so that when it does come out it comes in the form of an explosion. The imposition of heavy censorship on newspapers and the film industry after the declaration of this emergency forced the public to keep its criticism to itself. The radio and television had anyway always been under government control. There was no outlet for the people.

Nevertheless, three beneficial results came from the imposition of emergency. The first was that the Indian population as a whole became very aware that it inhabited a governed country, a fact it had recently needed to know. The second was that it became aware that the government of the country was by and large for the people, for under M.I.S.A. a large number of smugglers and tax defalcators were imprisoned, and a rigorous control of commodity prices enforced, so that the cost of living went down. Third, property and life became much safer, for the penalties for crime increased and murder, armed robbery, theft and rape, which had become very common in the country while the police were dealing with political agitation against a background of high prices, low wages, and unemployment, decreased in incidence. But the mobile phase of the emergency also had its drawbacks.

One was the production by the government of pictures and drawings of Mrs Gandhi, all somewhat unflattering, to be displayed in shops and offices: and a slogan-factory pumped out words, supposedly her sayings, to be printed and displayed, not only under these pictures but on walls, on buses, on the backs of taxis and cycle rickshaws. The first slogan I saw was on a huge hoarding outside a Delhi hotel. The picture showed a snake-charmer piping a cobra out of its nest. The wording said, 'THE GOVERNMENT IS FIGHTING CORRUPTION! OPPOSE IT!' One day when I went to look again at this wonderful advertisement I found, to my disappointment, that the second sentence had been obliterated with purple paint.

My friend, Jag Parvesh, had a memorable encounter with Mrs Gandhi shortly after the emergency was declared. He, with several other Congressmen, went to her house to confirm that they supported her. She uttered a few short sentences on the necessity and purpose of the emergency, then turned to one of the Congressmen. 'Do you know,' she inquired, 'the famous American proverb?' The Congressman shook his head. ' "When the great eagle flies under the stars" ' Mrs Gandhi quoted, ' "the small birds hide". Don't forget it.' A moment later, turning back to the Congressman, she said, 'What was that proverb?' Dazed by such proximity with his idol, the Congressman said, 'Madam, "when the great evil fries under the stars, the small birds hide." ' Mrs Gandhi stared at him for a long moment: then she started to laugh, more at herself than at him. Hitler would not have done that.

At this time, too, the painter, M. F. Husain, did a triptych in oils, which he presented to Mrs Gandhi. These paintings, which are by no means Husain's best work, represent her as Durga or Kali, the goddess of death and also of renewal, riding bloodily across India. I have not seen them hung in Mrs Gandhi's house, but they are probably about somewhere. Sanjay's wife, Maneka, once described them to me as 'the most awful paintings I've seen in my life'. She is not, of course, an art critic, but a sensible young woman, which is probably better. I may add that when Husain paints well, he paints very well indeed.

The point I want to make by recording these minor incidents is that as soon as Mrs Gandhi arrived at the pinnacle of power that only queens had stood upon in the Indian past, she was instantly surrounded, as they had been, by courtiers, by gifted artists, and naturally enough, by people with an eye to the main chance. Mrs Gandhi is hard enough in the head to resist most flattery, but the kind of flattery she received after the declaration of emergency was enough to blur anyone's eye. It was prompted in the main by awe and fear, emotions common enough to Indians who had encountered their rulers in the past, going back beyond the Moguls, but emotions that Nehru had striven to erase from the minds of his people when they met him.

The declaration of emergency, therefore, not only exposed Mrs Gandhi to a political backlash, but to a kind of moral quandary. With everyone fawning upon her it had become more difficult, even to her sharp, scornful intellect, to separate those she could trust from those she could not. A successful revolution, which she seems to have thought the emergency was, is brought about by a concerted effort of strong and truthful minds: she had none or few around her.

⚘ 15 ⚘

When Sanjay Came

THE NEWSPAPERS STARTED to print once more under heavy censorship a few days after the emergency was declared. Some of them, like *The Motherland*, a Jan Sangh* orientated publication, was not allowed to restart at all. A handful of newspapermen had been arrested, and the rest submitted without any show of resistance. Not only were the editorials dead but the news, never wildly exciting at the best of times, was now heavily devoted to reporting the activities of the Prime Minister, and quoting her speeches and comments. An announcement displayed on front pages all over the country, said that Sanjay Gandhi had been asked to reorganise the Youth Congress, the youth branch of the party composed mainly of volunteers. This announcement brought forth excessive plaudits from the press. The national editors had been forced to submit to censorship, but nobody had asked them to drop on all fours in front of the government. Nevertheless, the editors, urged on by proprietors with bad consciences who wished to placate Mrs Gandhi, had assumed this traditionally Indian posture of respectful subservience, and they remained in it, not looking particularly dignified, until the emergency was over, when many were praised by foreign press associations for their courage and independence in the face of dictatorship, and their incessant battle for the freedom of the press.

The inordinate publicity which Sanjay's entry into what could very loosely be called politics (for the Youth Congress is not strictly speaking a political entity but an organisation of young volunteers who help the seniors of the party by working in the field, distributing pamphlets, and cheering at rallies) had no tremendous news value except in so far as Sanjay was Mrs Gandhi's son. Considering that prior to this there had been considerable protest about the Maruti

* See p. 156.

cars he was supposed to produce, it was perhaps unwise of her to expose him to publicity, even as having been offered a minor function in the party at this time. What exactly he was supposed to do was left rather vague, but he issued a four-point programme, possibly to explain his own function to himself. Two of these points were that people should have planned families, something that had been amoebic in government statements since 1949: and that slums should be cleared and the people in these slums rehoused.

These were admirable ideas: but it is widely conceded that Sanjay's implementation of them was an extremely powerful element in the eventual fall of his mother. He had no experience of this kind of thing, and going ahead without experience he was to make himself the target, not only of the entire Indian press, but also of certain sections of the foreign press: in any event the villain of the piece. His initial ascent was too high for him, but it was not fair that he should have had to fall so far, for he was launched by forces beyond his own control, not least by the Indian press during the emergency. They provided him with no ballast for his ride up, and overweighted him as he came down.

The amount of publicity which Sanjay received was not only fantastic, but out of all proportion to what he did, whether, during the emergency, it was favourable publicity, or, after the Congress fall in 1977, unfavourable in the extreme. The latter kind of publicity sprang from the former: newspapermen who had played him up for the nineteen months of emergency, for no reason except that they wished to appear subservient to his mother, so inflated the role he played that it became excellent story material for them after the emergency to prick the balloon they had themselves created. Sanjay seems to have blundered onward into a disaster which someone who thought further ahead than the immediate moment could probably have foreseen and avoided.

'You see,' Mrs Gandhi said to me, 'he isn't a thinker. He's a doer. I mean, cent per cent a doer. When he wants something done, he gets it done.' It was more than a year since the 1977 election but the furniture in the room where she meets people was the same, except that the green upholstery of the sofa had been so frayed by the behinds of so many politicians in the intervening period. Her slippers dropped neatly to the floor in front of her armchair, her small feet tucked themselves up on it. A Peter Pan-like child blew a flute from a painting on the wall: Nehru showed his profile in a shadowed alcove: a huge Irish wolfhound shambled in, sniffed about, went away. She said, 'He's very austere in his habits, you know. He doesn't drink, he doesn't smoke. He wears very simple clothes, he eats very simply. Now they say he was very interested in girls: until he married Maneka I was very worried about the fact that he did not seem to be interested in girls.'

Apart from these maternal views, I wanted to know why Sanjay had come into politics after the emergency had been declared. 'He didn't come into politics,' Mrs Gandhi said, a little annoyed with my lack of knowledge. 'He isn't interested in politics. In fact, I think he disapproves of politics. But when I was in difficulties at Allahabad, he was one of the few people who stood by me. He told me that he wanted to do something to help me, to help the party and the country. If somebody who has shown he is loyal says that he wants to do something to help, can you turn him away?' Never having been in this situation, I shook my head. Since he said he wanted to help,' Mrs Gandhi said, 'I asked Barooah,* after emergency, what he could do. Barooah said there was somebody needed to run the Youth Congress. Sanjay said he would do it. As you know, he did.'

In 1970, Mrs Gandhi had told me that family planning was now the most important of all the government programmes. She herself, as regards the multitudes of her country, had not really said much about it, except that in 1968 she addressed a meeting of women in North India about the necessity for it. This was curious against a background of attempts at population control which had started on a governmental basis as early as 1949. The difficulty had always been, for government spokesmen, that the idea of family planning was alien to Indians, especially in the rural areas. This is common through most peasant societies, those societies spoken of as the Third World. The reason is obvious: if a couple works in their own fields, sowing, fertilising, ploughing and harvesting the plants they need for survival, they must plough the harvest even harder in their own bed, to provide themselves with free labour whose main incentive is survival. Moreover, according to Indian tradition, the children are supposed to look after the parents, but a daughter, married to someone sprung of other stock, cannot invite her parents to come

* D. K. Barooah, then Congress President.

and inhabit her husband's house, fortunately for the husband, whereas a son can and is in duty bound to invite his parents to come and stay with him, unfortunately for his wife. Therefore, if a couple had daughters to start with, they would persevere in having children until a son was produced: mindful, in their own way, of the high rate of infant mortality in India, they would probably persevere until they had two sons: hence the unacceptability of family planning to rural couples of whatever religion: and the rural people were basically Hindus, Muslims, and Sikhs. Of the people basically urban, a large number were Christians, and the bulk of these Roman Catholics who would not accept the idea of planned families, at least not by humanly understandable methods of control. It was thus anything but easy for a political party to urge family planning upon people, since it would instantly lose popularity and votes.

The government of India, in the 1950s, launched a reasonably large campaign of what might be called persuasion to induce people to limit their families to two or three children since, due to the fall in the death rate through improved medicinal methods, the population growth rate had shown an alarming increase. The government used propaganda posters, and the family planning symbol of an inverted red triangle appeared in the most unlikely places all over India. 'If the villagers are devout Hindus of a certain type,' Pupul Jayakar told me once, 'they would recognise the inverted red triangle as a symbol of fertility, which it is according to the Tantric cult.'* Certainly the red triangle did not work very well: by the early 1970s the Indian population was estimated at around 550 million, which meant every seventh person alive in the world had been born in India, though in the absence of proper census figures, since the statistics in remote villages are not reliable, the population figure may have been more. In any event, the estimated increase in population every year came to between 12–13 million, which meant that a number roughly equivalent to the entire population of the continent of Australia was being added, every year, to the population of the country of India. So far the Indian officials had relied on the condom, manufactured in India, the loop, and the pill to try and keep the population level down. None of these was a terminal method, and largely owing to the anger of the husband at a loop being inserted

* The Tantric cult is one of the many branches of Hinduism and lays considerable emphasis on the importance of spiritual activities being related to sex.

into his wife, since it might lead her into infidelity without risk of
discovery, the annoyance of the husband at the ultimum of pleasure
in his not particularly pleasurable life being interrupted by the
condom, and the inability of the wife to count, thus rendering the
pill useless, family planning in the villages which comprise most of
India was not a success.

Then came the idea of sterilisation, both male and female.
Incentives in cash were offered to those who agreed to be sterilised.
Some enlightened companies came forward to say that those of their
employees who took a week off to be sterilised would not only be
paid for the week, but be offered a company incentive equal to, and
sometimes exceeding, the government incentives. This programme
was fairly successful in the urban areas, where there were no extra
hands necessary for land cultivation, and where accommodation
was limited, but it was not a success in the villages for the same
reason as had applied to every other method of contraception.

Broadly speaking, the political hesitancy which had prevented
the government from pushing family planning to any real extent
disappeared with the declaration of emergency. Some time in 1975,
shortly before the emergency, I saw Mrs Gandhi in my capacity as
a UNFPA observer, to ask her about the comparative failure of the
extant programme. I also asked her about complaints from the
sterilisation camps that operations were performed in such haste
that the patient frequently became infected, and that incentives
were being misapplied in that they were not only offered to the
prospective patient but to the man who urged him to be sterilised.
These motivators, therefore, hauled in as many people as they could,
a number which allegedly included very young people as yet
unmarried and very old people unlikely to be blessed with offspring.
Mrs Gandhi, having pondered upon this question (the interview
was in her office and she was being formal) replied, 'Of course, the
success of the whole programme depends on the ability and dedication of the officers in each area.'

One of the other salient points of Sanjay's four-pronged programme
was the beautification of Delhi by the planting of trees and the
destruction of slums. There are in Delhi a large number of people
who are poor, but do not starve, who live in slum areas which have
sprouted up near their work. The Harijans about whom Leela had
written to Mrs Gandhi lived in one such slum area. Their colony

was on the banks of the Yamuna river, in small, patchily white-washed mud edifices. There was a tap for water, but no sanitation, though the banks and the waters of the river provided a communal latrine. The people kept goats and pigs, so the sanitary facilities were to some degree shared between the animals and their owners. They were not healthy conditions to live in, but a continual exposure to deadly bacteria had to some extent hardened the population, and they were not by Indian standards badly off, though they suffered from various endemic diseases transferred to their children. These were among the sort of slums that the government, after the emergency, scheduled for demolition and their inhabitants for resettlement.

At the time of the Kauls from Kashmir, the first Nehrus in the early eighteenth century, what is now called Old Delhi was the city proper: around it there was arid scrub and expanses of dust and rock where the ruins of the earlier Delhis were populated by rats, hyenas, owls, bats, and a very few, very poor people. When New Delhi was built by the British, the population of the old and the new cities were still sited within areas clearly defined by the scrubland around. But after 1947, with the flood of Hindu and Sikh refugees spilling over the new border with Pakistan, the face of Delhi became much more complex and more crowded. Some of the refugees from the city of Lahore, which had become part of Pakistan, and from other parts of the sprawling and populous Punjab, brought money with them: some fled penniless from the clubs and knives of the newly Pakistani Muslims, but had lands, money, or relatives across the border: but the bulk came without resources or support, having lost their relatives and assets in the holocaust of August. To these the government of India offered compensation assessed in relation to the losses they had suffered due to the partition. The refugees were homeless and they needed homes: they began, with their own money or with the assistance of official compensation, to build, and houses sprawled over what had been scrubland, small white uniformly ugly houses, surrounded still by dusty shrubs and trees. Roads were built, services, all rather shaky, installed: now the twin cities sprawl out across the plain over a total area of 134 square miles. What this meant in 1975 was that there was no open space available near the city in which to put the resettled slum dwellers. They had to be moved to areas far from their work, where they were offered small plots of land, free of charge, on which to build.

The point was that the government was not offering these people materials with which to build, or assistance whereby they could procure materials or labour. Neither had the government as yet provided any service facilities to any of these areas: the resettled population had to live in hastily constructed and very temporary hovels, their kerosene lamps and smudge fires flickering uneasily amidst the fields, often without an immediately accessible supply of water. The people and their chattels were taken in government lorries to their new homes, dumped there, and left. They had therefore, if they wished to continue in their former employment, to arise in the small hours to catch buses or to bicycle to their work: and return at night in the same way. This meant that in some cases they could only spend around six hours a day at home, in which time they had to cook, eat, and sleep. The resettlement areas being a long way from anywhere, there was no question of the people being able to find other employment within a workable radius of their homes. The energy wasted in travel by bicycle to and from the city devoured their efficiency. The money spent on bus fares ate away at the heart of their incomes, which were not increased by their employers in a way commensurate with their new expenses. Most of the resettled people had no desire whatever to go where they were sent: however, go they had to, as their houses shattered under crowbars behind them, sending up clouds of dust like signals of distress.

The largest slum area in Old Delhi was around the gigantic old mosque, the Jama Masjid, its geometry of red sandstone bulking over the little houses and alleys beneath, a landmark for centuries. Several generations of Nehrus had seen the Jama Masjid and its environs: had watched the environs of the mosque turn from more or less open spaces dotted with poorhouses and hospitals in the Mogul times, to a clutter of shops and hovels when, after the Mutiny, the British closed the former fleamarket down. The clutter still spread around at the foot of the mosque, dirty, noisy and picturesque to tourists, to the inhabitants a way of life. The little stalls where *kebab* makers crouched over their ovens, the areas where meat, fish, and live birds were sold, still existed, and people still came from all over the city to buy cooked food and supplies there. It was a very fashionable habit, for New Delhi socialites, to send their servants into the area to purchase *kebabs* of meat and fish for the guests at a cocktail party. One of the great gates of the old city, the Turkman

Gate, brooded over the congeries of shops and houses: once, from the Turkman Gate, there had been a clear view of the mosque, now obscured by the clamorous constructions between. Sanjay is alleged to have said to some of the Youth Congress workers, on having had a look at the place: 'I want the day to come when I can see the Jama Masjid from the Turkman Gate.'

The curiousness of the emergency lay not so much in any terror felt by the people for the government, as in the readiness of the people to oblige and please those who ruled them. It was traditional to India, in a way, as much as the actions of the emergency were: an arranged marriage of the rulers and the ruled, where the ruled promised to honour and obey the rulers, and do their best eventually to love the rulers as well: a relationship between a male and active power and a female and passive principle. The Kamasutra describes how the male partner in a sexual act must pinch, bite, and beat the female in several different ways as the act progresses: for this is what is expected of him: the female partner, lying back and taking it, though perhaps not entirely enjoying it, must respond to each type of pinch, bite, or slap with the twitter or coo of a different species of bird, for this is what is expected of her.

Therefore, when Sanjay made certain types of pronouncement during the course of the emergency, only a very few people said anything: most emitted the correct birdnotes. The slum dwellers complained when their hovels were destroyed, but never to the government. They complained to one another, and apologised to irritated employers when they were late for work. Meanwhile, what was certainly true was that government employees turned up on time, took fewer teabreaks, and attended more to their work. Indian bureaucracy—which was after all created by the British—has always been far too top-heavy: six men have always been employed to perform a function one man could have done, the least of the six passing a directive upward until it reaches the first, who passes it on to the person who can take action. One man in this chain who has gone off for tea, or taken the day off, can delay the directive which, when he returns to duty, will be swamped by other files, for weeks or months. This, however, ceased to happen in the days of the emergency. The fall in food prices and the lower incidence of crime were noted by the people as well. The arrests were not noted because few except the most important ones were reported. What did cause a stir was what started to happen in north India, and most visibly in Delhi, as a result of the actions and directives of Sanjay.

Rukhsana Sultana, or Rukhsana Begam, is a youngish woman with the general appearance of an Indian filmstar. That is to say, she appears to be a prisoner within a personality she has assumed. The chainlike clank of her ornaments, many and various, the whiplike hiss of her silks when she moves, and the enormous, round-lensed, pink spectacles through which the world observes her, as through two spyholes into the cell of herself, are more than conducive to this image. She is actually the niece of an Indian filmstar, Begum Para, known in the 1950s for the size of her bust rather than for the size of her roles. Begum Para's elder sister married a Hindu, so Rukhsana originally had a Hindu name which she turned into a Muslim one to fulfil the requirements of a legacy. Her life in Delhi, before she decided to prove herself as a social worker, is said to have been slightly colourful: a more unlikely person for Sanjay to choose as an assistant in his mission to improve the lot of the masses is difficult to imagine.

Even after the emergency, when Sanjay was in trouble, she seems to have been loyal to him, and defended him to various hostile interviewers. However, the women of Sanjay's family do not seem to have a high opinion of her. 'She is,' said Mrs Gandhi once, in slight irritation rather than in anger, 'a very scatterbrained sort of person.' Maneka said, 'Well, she probably went around and talked a lot of rubbish. But she was very earnest, and Sanjay needed volunteers.' This may have been so, but why he decided to take on an outsider, instead of turning to the existing volunteers of the Youth Congress, seems to me a question difficult to answer.

Rukhsana Sultana was put in charge of the most difficult area in Delhi, around the Jama Masjid, and there, amidst the slums, she floated in her silks, pink spectacles and pearls, from July to December 1975. During this time she was apparently mostly engaged in collecting complaints from local inhabitants about water-taps and sanitary facilities, or the lack of them, and sending these to the Municipal Corporation, which does not seem to have done much about them. In December 1975, however, when the programme for sterilisation really started to be pushed, she was told by Sanjay to push it in Old Delhi. The population around the Jama Masjid was mostly Muslim: since Rukhsana was at least partly Muslim, Sanjay may have imagined it would be a case of like calling to like: but the unanswering sea of Muslims around the gigantic old mosque receded rapidly as the pink toes of Rukhsana Sultana, painted to match her spectacles perhaps, intruded into their progenitive lives. A large number of the Muslim women around the mosque still go around, as their ancestors did when the Kauls first came to Delhi, in shroudlike black costumes known as *burkhas*, which cover them from head to foot. The only area left exposed by the *burkha* is the face, and this exposure is compensated for by a veil, attached to the *burkha*, which covers the face. The sight of Rukhsana Sultana, painted and scented, her face shielded only by her pink spectacles, pearls round her neck, her sari of silk and the *choli* or blouse under it cut, by the standards of the area, indecently low, must have shocked the orthodox Muslims, both men and women. She herself does not seem to have thought of these very poor people as particularly human. She is alleged to have told an interviewer that the stench and filth of the slums so sickened her that she had to douse herself with her favourite scent before she could bear to enter them. Certainly, on one occasion, my wife Leela met her near the mosque, and, having herself dressed in her simplest clothes, expressed some surprise at Rukhsana's attire in this ambience of poor and orthodox Muslims. 'My jewellery,' the social worker said, 'is part of my personality. Why should I discard my real personality?' She also developed a habit, when trying to browbeat these women into accepting sterilisation, of telling them that they should break free from the fetters of orthodoxy and tell their husbands that they were male chauvinists. This was heresy to most of the women and it was made worse when Rukhsana Sultana, to encourage them towards emancipation, flicked up their veils and made them show their faces to an audience that included men. This was equivalent to a Western social worker telling women that they must be emancipated and then, in front of an audience which included men, pulling their skirts up to show how they *could* be emancipated.

It was therefore little wonder that as she swished about the crowded alleys of Old Delhi she was always accompanied by an armed police escort: her credibility with the people she was trying to reach, never very high to start with, was reduced by this to nothing. She was a relatively unimportant figure in herself, but her activities may have contributed considerably to a kind of minor insurrection in Old Delhi in June 1976, around the Turkman Gate: though by

that time the demolition of many shops and houses in front of the
Jama Masjid had exacerbated the temper of the people still further.
Gas, batons, and bullets dispersed a protest rally of Muslims:
several were killed.

The episode could be said to have been the end of the beginning
of the emergency.

More gunfire was heard at Muzaffarnagar, a small, bedraggled
industrial town in Uttar Pradesh, where the dun plains start to
straggle up into the hills. This was a pure protest against sterilisation: a number of workers started a protest rally and were answered
by a storm of bullets: more died here. The implementation of
family planning, Mrs Gandhi had said, depended on the ability and
dedication of the officers in the areas concerned. There were not
only officers concerned, under the emergency, but all kinds of
people, such as schoolmasters and policemen, who were supposed
to bring the national birthrate under some kind of control. These
reluctant proselytisers were told that if they did not bring in a certain number of volunteers for sterilisation every month, their salaries
for that month would be suspended. The family planning programme became not only a programme of incentives but of disincentives: for government servants were also told that if they had
three children, they would either have to be sterilised or lose all
chance of promotion and perks. This was an idea modelled on that
of the programme that has been very successful in Singapore.

Dr Karan Singh, the former ruler of Kashmir, is a scholarly man
who writes poetry in English and in his own language, Dogra (the
rulers of Kashmir since the last century have not been Kashmiris
but Dogras from south of the Banihal Pass, who were put on the
throne by the British). When I first met him in 1968, he was the
Minister of Tourism under Mrs Gandhi. In 1974, when I was posted
to India by UNFPA, I went to see him on official business, since he
had recently become the Minister of Health and Family Planning.
He said, 'I used to be called Mr Tourism. I dynamised tourism in
India. Now I'm going to do the same with family planning. Unfortunately I don't know much about it yet.' I commiserated with
him. 'Any new thoughts you have about our programme,' he said,
'come and tell me about them.' Next time we met, some months
later, he appeared particularly interested in the scheme of incentives
and disincentives which had been introduced in Singapore.

It so happened that shortly after this I was sent by UNFPA to Singapore to write a brochure on the progress of the family planning programme there. When I had come back and written the brochure, I showed it to Karan Singh. He was delighted. 'So,' he said, 'this is how they do it in Singapore. And they're very successful, aren't they?' I said, yes, they were, and then some dim instinct fluttered in my mind. 'You're not planning to try this here?' I said. 'Singapore is only 228 square miles, and most of the people there are already fairly highly motivated.' Karan Singh, studying my text intently, failed to answer me.

I am not trying to say that my report influenced the government of India in constructing its family planning programme, simply that there was a certain obsession about the Singapore success in the minds of many officials concerned, including Mrs Gandhi's. In a conversation I had with her about family planning before the emergency, she talked a lot about the island which Lee Kuan Yew had moulded into a miniature Britain, and about applying a system of incentives and disincentives in India. I attempted, mildly, as I did later with Karan Singh, to dissuade her from the idea that what had worked in Singapore could work in India. Nevertheless, in a very crude way, the Singapore system of motivation and implementation *was* applied in India, and it was doomed to disaster.

Disincentives in Singapore were not a very serious threat to the life of a person, especially if that person already knew a considerable amount about birth control. Most people did, since a motivator need only take a bicycle to reach any part of the island, and since the hospitals, and even the register offices, had family planning courses for newly married couples. Also, since the television and the radio, the possession of which horrible inventions were status symbols, loudly proclaimed family planning, family planning had become a status symbol. This was not the case in India.

A government officer in India, unimaginably ill-paid by most other standards, if his monthly salary was suspended, if his chances of promotion were stopped, simply because he did not deliver a certain number of people to a certain hospital to be operated upon for a reason he did not fully understand, would panic: even more if he himself was asked to undergo this operation. The panic spread: the penis is probably more of a symbol of pride in India than anywhere else, if only because the penis is the only banner a poor man has to raise in assertion of the fact that he is himself. One day our doctor sent a fruit-seller to us. He was a very young man, unmarried, and he used to pedal around parts of Delhi on a bicycle to dispose of his wares. To do this he required a licence from the police. His licence expired shortly after the emergency was declared: the policeman concerned refused to issue another unless the boy had himself sterilised. We could do nothing about the fruit-seller, and I do not know what happened to him: but I was sure that the police officer was as terrified about the possible loss of his salary for the month as the fruit-seller was about the loss of his sexual potency. If terror spread, therefore, it was not due to an organised campaign by the government designed to cow the people: it was simply because terror was bound to spread in a largely illiterate and ignorant population, due to the utter disorganisation of those government bodies who should at this time have filled the minds of the people with truthful information and some idea of the benefits resulting from sterilisation, particularly for women. The government may have brought the clerks to their work on time since emergency: but since they had no idea what they were supposed to be efficient about, the red tape which Mrs Gandhi had hoped to destroy during the emergency only wound itself more tightly round the throat of the country.

There was no chain of command, as there had been during British times: that was the pity and the heart of the matter. The emergency, as such, considering the state of the country in the year before it was declared, might have been the only way to settle the mess and prepare for new elections. The emergency as it was carried out merely introduced further chaos. Mrs Gandhi appeared to me at the time to feel she had a British chain of command under her (I am not talking of the British of today, but of the days of the Raj, when people were dedicated to their work), but she was terribly mistaken. She handed down orders to people unable to carry these orders out. From her came Sanjay: from him the frightening and pitiful Rukhsana: from Rukhsana the police who accompanied her around the Muslim slums in Delhi: from a totally unconcerted and spontaneous movement to stabilise the country, which nobody had prepared for, came the resultant backlash. There was no organisation behind Mrs Gandhi when she declared the emergency, rather a totality of disorganisation: which was probably not her fault, but that of the country she was trying to safeguard: the disloyalty, the lack of faith, the private vendettas carried out by government officers, the hushing up of anything which would put the government in a bad position: the frowning upon herself and her family: these were not really her fault. These were the fault of the nature of India, and the nature of Indians, forced upon them by centuries of autocratic rule, which is what the people most appreciate and understand.

Early in the months of the emergency, Sanjay began whistle-stop tours around the states. Maneka went with him. 'It was so odd,' she told me once (a slight, freckled young woman, committed to blouses and trousers rather than saris) 'we went to some place by airplane and the local Congress workers picked us up. They put us in a car and took us to where we were staying. It was about two minutes drive away: we could have walked. When I got out of the car, the workers said to us, "You must rest: that long drive by car must have been very tiring." We laughed: they said, "You have to rest." So we did.'

This was at lunch in our house in Delhi. Sanjay was sitting down the table at Leela's right, Maneka on my right: all very correct, very European. 'You see,' said Maneka, 'I'm the daughter of an army officer, I wasn't used to this sort of thing. I came to accept it, but I always thought it was very funny. Sanjay took it in his stride.' The grandson of one Prime Minister of India, the son of another, Sanjay smiled at me across the table. He is a sturdily built young man, with a rather pallid complexion, features which though handsome are not exactly positive, apart from his quick, gelid eyes that glint at one through rimless glasses. 'Yes,' Sanjay said. 'It was terrible.'

They may have liked the tumultuous receptions they received, Chief Ministers coming to the airport to meet the son of the Prime Minister, garlanded arches raised in the path of their car, because any perfectly ordinary young couple, much though they later deny the fact, would be rather flattered by this kind of thing. Sanjay would make brief, brusque speeches in the villages of the area: then they would fly away. Enormous publicity was attached to each of these visits: the press and television fell over one another to hear and see Sanjay. It was this coverage that later attracted much criticism. According to the then Minister of Information and Broadcasting, V. C. Shukla, who replaced Inder Gujral, Mrs Gandhi asked him three times to ask the government media to cut down on the publicity afforded her son. He did: the newspapers did not.

Later, the correspondents who had written adulatory articles about Sanjay's various trips wrote in a different manner, complaining about his rudeness to Chief Ministers who were much older than he was, and about his rudeness to the press.

There is no doubt that Sanjay is not a young man distinguished by his manners. Even when he is friendly there is that slight aloofness in him that appears to have run in the family since his grandfather, but without the curious redeeming family charm: he is very difficult to talk to, or perhaps not exactly to talk to but to communicate with. He also seems to choose the people he *will* talk to very carefully: an admirable trait, it seems to me, but not one much appreciated in India, where everyone talks to everyone about their most intimate problems, often on first meeting. 'Sanjay,' his wife once told me, 'has been under criticism since 1969, when he first tried to launch Maruti. He's used to criticism.' He seems, however, to invite it by his silences, which punctuate quick bursts of words driven home by a forward thrust of that bespectacled and publicised head.

This head was much wanted after the emergency was over, and in some senses a price was laid upon it. Mrs Gandhi said to me, 'You see, he was young.' That, I told her, was the very reason why I was asking her why he had assumed such authority. 'He didn't,' she said, fell sombrely silent, knotted her hands in her lap, then abruptly said, 'It's not true he became unpopular with the people. Let me give you an instance. Last year, after the elections were over, Maneka,' and suddenly the smile came, the smile that reminds one that she is a woman with children and grandchildren, 'had just got her driving licence. She had to go to Willingdon Hospital, and while she was parking she brushed another car. Well,' said Mrs Gandhi judiciously, defending her family, 'not much damage was caused, just a few scratches on the paint. But Maneka decided that she should wait until the owner came back. If she went away, people would say she ran off because she was Sanjay's wife. So she waited, and the owner eventually came.'

'He was an old man,' said Mrs Gandhi. 'And you know what old people are like, very boring. Old people continually lecture young people on their bad behaviour, their lack of proper responsibility, and so on.' I reflected that a short while before I had sent her flowers for her sixtieth birthday, and then, as often before, looked at her smile and forgot this. 'Anyway,' Mrs Gandhi informed me,

22 Sheikh Mujibur Rehman, President of Bangladesh, meets Mrs Gandhi in Calcutta

23 Jagjivan Ram (*centre*) Mrs Nandini Satpathi (*right*) and H. N. Bahuguna (*left*) announce the formation of their breakaway party, 'Congress for Democracy', in February 1977

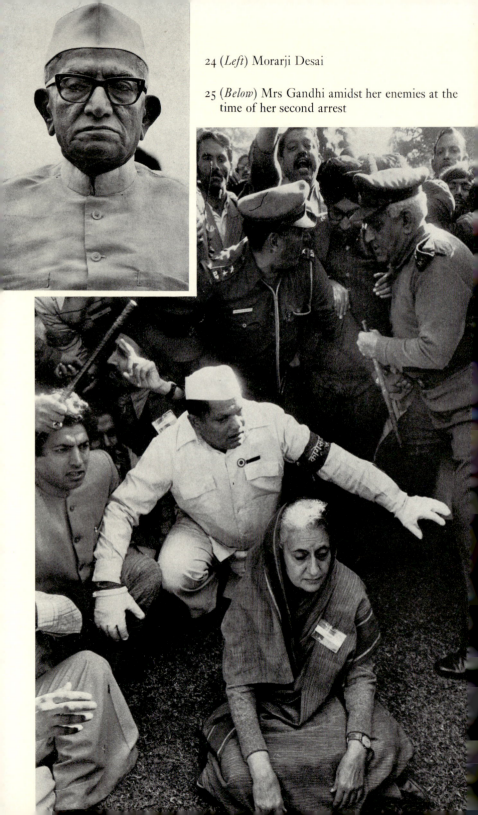

24 (*Left*) Morarji Desai

25 (*Below*) Mrs Gandhi amidst her enemies at the time of her second arrest

26 Sanjay Gandhi on his way to appear at the Reddy Commission inquiring into his activities during the emergency

27 With several cases pending against her Mrs Gandhi enters the Tees Hazari courts, surrounded by her supporters

28 Mrs Gandhi welcoming followers on the lawn at Willingdon
    Crescent

29 Prime Minister again. In January 1980 Mrs Gandhi triumphed
    at the General Election

'he gave Maneka this lecture and she said she had waited for him to come back and offered to pay for the damage. She wrote down her name and address, for him to send the bill to. When he saw the address, he said, "Are you the wife of Sanjay Gandhi? Then I won't charge you anything." '

Upon seeing me unmoved by this narration, she twitched her right eyelid and said, 'When I was campaigning at Azamgarh recently, my election agent told me a story. He said, outside his office there was a group of women. One was weeping. The agent heard the words *beta* and *ladka*, (son and boy) and he thought something had happened to the woman's son. So he went out and asked her if he could help her if anything had happened to her son. The woman said, "It is not my son I am weeping for but Mrs Gandhi's son." Sanjay had just been sent to prison, you know.' She added, 'I told this story in my speeches during the campaign.' I said, 'I'm not asking you about his popularity with the people, ma'am. He seems to have become very unpopular with your own ministers and the press.' She cocked her head sideways, and fiddled with her sari, and said, 'I said he was young. It follows that he's very direct. If he doesn't like what somebody's doing, he says so very bluntly. I don't do that. If I think someone is doing something wrong, I always try and cushion the blow. I tell him what I think in a very roundabout way.'

9

PART FOUR

The Descent

❧ 16 ❧

Things Fall Apart

THOSE IMPRISONED UNDER the emergency were by no means all politicians. They included students, labour leaders, and smugglers. The arrest of the smugglers was a very popular move: these were men who had for some years brought illegal shipments of gold and luxury goods from the Gulf states, had been involved in a number of rackets and had amassed enormous fortunes. Their activities were known, but for want of proof and police corruption they had not been touched until the emergency, when they were arrested and imprisoned. These arrests met with national approval, because they were widely publicised: the arrests of students and labour leaders were not.

Meanwhile, the senior politicians were fairly comfortably lodged, by prison standards. However, they now seemed, in their minds, to associate Mrs Gandhi with the Borgias rather than with the Nehrus. Desai, who spent his time writing his memoirs, had been imprisoned, if that is the word, in a circuit house in Haryana, the kind of bungalow which is normally used to house government officers on tour. He announced that he refused to eat any cooked food except that provided by his family. J.P., in the Haryana capital, Chandigarh, became very ill, suffering from ailments of the kidney and liver. In November 1975 his younger brother wrote to Mrs Gandhi, describing J.P.'s condition, which he said was so desperate that he was unlikely to survive the year. He asked Mrs Gandhi to consider whether his brother's death in prison would be in the best interests of the government. Mrs Gandhi released J.P., who was taken first to the All India Medical Institute in Delhi and then to the Jaslok Hospital in Bombay for treatment. It was alleged that before his arrest he had been perfectly fit and had walked for miles in demonstrations and processions, while now he could not walk at all. His astonishing physical deterioration, they said, must surely be due to something done to him in prison. Such allegations harked back to Mogul times, when important political prisoners had been killed by slow poison. The fact was that J.P. was in poor health anyway: he had had an operation on his prostate in 1974, and he was seventy-three years old. He was treated, in the hospitals where he was sent, the best of their kind in India, for months on end, and though in considerable pain he did not die. Nevertheless it was rumoured that Mrs Gandhi's most celebrated prisoner was reserved for more subtle punishment, which surely, was a rather unfair story: if the lady had been trying to have J.P. killed, she would hardly have sent him to hospital. Logic, however, has never been an outstanding feature of Indian political criticism.

George Fernandes, the labour leader who had brought about the disastrous railway strike, went underground. On December 22 1975 the police arrested and imprisoned his youngest brother, Michael, also a labour leader. Michael filed a petition for *habeas corpus* in February 1976. On May 1 the police arrived at the house of Mrs Alice Fernandes, the mother of three sons, and took away the second son, Lawrence. They said that they wanted to question him about the *habeas corpus* petition. On May 22 Mrs Fernandes wrote to the President of India, sending copies of her letter to the Prime Minister, to other central ministers, and to the state ministers of Kerala, where the arrest of Lawrence took place. In this letter she alleged that the police, once they had her son at the station, questioned him as to the petition for a short while, and then started to ask him for the whereabouts of his brother George. They thereupon, said Mrs Fernandes, kicked Lawrence repeatedly, and beat him with clubs in so violent a manner that five of these implements broke. After threatening to kill him they put him in solitary confinement, tortured him every so often, starved him for three days, and refused him cigarettes. On May 21 Mrs Fernandes saw her son in prison. 'His left side is without use, as if crippled, and both his left leg and hand are still swollen. He is in a mentally and physically wrecked condition, and is unable to talk freely without faltering. He is terribly nervous and mortally afraid of the police, of anyone in khaki uniform, of the approaching sound of anyone walking with shoes on, or of any other person, all of whom he fears to be interrogators and tormentors.' Mrs Fernandes urged that her son 'should be transferred to a good hospital and specialist medical and physical care be given to him ... so that he may regain his mental and physical health and become a human being.'

In 1976 Leela and I were in Bangalore, where we met a famous Kannada film producer Pattabhiraman Reddy, a man of great presence, in his middle years, and his daughter. He had recently produced a very distinguished film, *Samskara*, from a novel by V. K. Anantha Murthy. Reddy's wife Snehalata, a well-known Kannada actress, had appeared in this film and been much praised by the critics. Snehalata was an ardent socialist: she had been a friend of the late Ram Manohar Lohia, who had once led the Indian Socialist Party, and George Fernandes was a close friend of hers. When Fernandes went underground, it is possible that she may have acted as a courier for him once or twice, though her daughter and husband did not say this, and there was no proof that she ever did so. In any event, she was arrested and imprisoned in Bangalore. Her family, when they visited the prison, were horrified by her condition. She had been put in a cell with prostitutes and female criminals, and her bed was on the floor by an open and much used latrine. Snehalata Reddy was an asthmatic, and under prison conditions her health declined rapidly. Her daughter and husband made frequent desperate trips to Delhi to try and see Mrs Gandhi and persuade her to either improve Snehalata's conditions in prison or to release her. No specific charge had been made against her: like so many others, she was there under M.I.S.A.: but apparently the government would do nothing to help. Reddy himself, a stoic, said little about his feelings, but his daughter was naturally very distressed and emotionally upset: to see her mother, active, talented and intelligent, brought to this state must have seemed to her inconceivable, the fabric of nightmare. Snehalata Reddy survived in prison until the end of the emergency: then she came home, wraithlike, the shell of her former self. She knew she was dying, but at least she had the final happiness of dying with her family around her, which she did a week after her release. I had never met her but I was saddened by this unnecessary and wasteful death.

Other women were imprisoned under similar circumstances and survived: the former queens of Gwalior and Jaipur, both Jan Sangh supporters, were put into Tihar prison in Delhi, one of the worst in the country, where they shared cells with prostitutes and criminals. They were physically tougher than Snehalata, and became leaders of the other prisoners, almost matriarchs, sharing with their cellmates the food and vitamin pills sent to them from outside.

Amnesty at one point said that 140,000 people were prisoners
during the emergency, and they mostly suffered considerable hardship: some died. The deaths took place and the arrests were made
under Mrs Gandhi's mandate: but it is impossible to impute every
individual arrest to her personally. There must have been thousands
of cases of undeserved imprisonment and maltreatment of prisoners
that were never brought to her notice: but I wanted to know what
she had done in the cases of Lawrence Fernandes and Snehalata
Reddy, when direct appeals had been made to her.

So I asked her, and she answered me without hesitation. 'In the
case of Lawrence Fernandes,' she said, 'I ordered an inquiry to be
made.' She said this crisply, with the air of one who knows her facts.
'The main complaint was about his damaged leg. He was examined
by five very senior doctors and one young doctor. The senior
doctors said the leg was slightly swollen but there was nothing
wrong with it. They were all quite unanimous about it. The junior
one thought there was some damage, very slight damage and
unfortunately this doctor went and put a plaster on it, which made
it worse. People say that Mr Fernandes becomes very nervous when
he sees uniformed men or passes a police station. They also say that
when he appears in court to describe his imprisonment he walks with
a stick, but that in normal life he doesn't use a stick and seems
perfectly all right. I really don't know. I really couldn't say. But in
that case there was certainly an inquiry.'

She said all this rather brusquely, without seeming to think it
very important, but then her voice slowed a little. 'In the case of
Mrs Reddy, there was nothing I could do. She was said to be a
Naxalite. Under those circumstances, she had to be held. There
was nothing I could do.' Her voice held a slight tinge of some
emotion I couldn't define. She seemed to be thinking. I said,
'Madam, I never met Mrs Reddy, but I met her family. They
didn't seem to me like any Naxalites I have met, and I don't see
how she could have been a Naxalite.' She said, 'Humph,' looked
away from me, and by a slight stiffening of the shoulders indicated
that I could expect no more elaborate comments from her.

Though the law and order situation on all fronts was under control
(curiously enough one of the few cases of burglary during the
emergency took place in the home of Usha Bhagat, Mrs Gandhi's
social secretary, who was attacked and tied up) the unrest in the

country could be felt in the air: not a spoken unrest, but a kind of unrest of the popular mind. It was difficult to identify or pinpoint, but it was starting to take shape. Straws in the wind: nothing to take hold of: but something was coming to birth: suspicions and resentments had started to form into a definite and powerful emotion. Though the central cabinet had not been told beforehand of the declaration of emergency, and no Minister had been consulted by Mrs Gandhi, none of the cabinet had made any protest at being thus slighted, nor did any member of it resign or manifest the smallest flicker of discontent. Once the emergency was an established fact every Minister appeared to support Mrs Gandhi, and though much later many of them insisted that they had consistently opposed her, the opposition seems to have been in thought rather than in word or deed. The reasons for this unanimous withdrawal into silence on the part of the cabinet were never satisfactorily clarified. This leaves the way open for speculations to be made. Firstly the Ministers, most of whom were people deeply attached to their creature comforts, may have been a little apprehensive that they would follow men of more austere habits, like J.P. and Desai, into prison. Secondly, Mrs Gandhi appeared in 1975 to have brought about the rout of her enemies and to be in complete control of the situation. For a professional Indian politician in her cabinet to have tried to break away would have seemed, at that time, political death. Nobody was brave enough to face it.

Maneka Gandhi once tried to explain to me why Sanjay was not overfond of politicians: 'I mean, he's been meeting them all his life,' she said. 'He's known most of these fellows since he was a child. Mrs Gandhi had such a limited choice.'

The fact is that Mrs Gandhi, since 1977, has often made scathing remarks to me about some of the members of her emergency cabinet. When I asked her about them she flashed her eyes at me, compressed her lips, and presently said, 'I don't think I want to say anything about them, because I don't know *what* I might say.' Y. B. Chavan, Jagjivan Ram and Karan Singh, three of her chief lieutenants during, the emergency, did not, however, escape the whiplash of her tongue when she *did* say something. It might be said that she had developed harsh views on the trio because all three had abandoned her and publicly attacked her, but I did not feel this. Her opinions may have intensified in rancour since their desertion, but I formed the impression that they were opinions she had formulated a long while ago.

She seemed, always, aloof from her Ministers, an aloofness which culminated in her neglecting to consult any of them before she declared the emergency. This, most of all, indicated a certain distrust of her Ministers on her part, as well as a certain slight contempt. The Ministers were obviously aware of her attitude, and their behaviour after she declared the emergency was that of a pack of hounds trained to stay at heel. Now and then the gleam of a tooth might be seen, but it was quickly hidden by the subservient droop of a lip. It was a picture from the Indian past: cowed courtiers, capable of treachery, around a powerful queen. The queens of ancient India, however, had a network of officers and spies, more or less reliable, to keep them informed of the state of the court and the country beyond: Mrs Gandhi had not. She had to rely mainly on her own perceptions and this was mainly her own fault. She had created by her own actions a situation in which her access to reliable information was minimal.

Her Ministers and advisers were, understandably, given the circumstances and their own precarious positions, a little apprehensive about telling her what they felt she did not want to hear. The consternation caused by the mass sterilisation programme was not properly reported to her, or at least not in such a way that she understood the volume of unrest it had caused. The nervousness of the intellectuals and students about the arrests and detentions was a factor she seemed unaware of. The country-wide disquiet over the protracted nature of the emergency was something not communicated to her. Her own secretariat, as she told me, made no effort to put her in touch with those people whom she wanted to meet. She had, herself, severed her other lines of communication.

The press, heavily censored, did not record the minuscule seismic quivers of discontent that had started to manifest themselves all over India, while the television and radio, both the appendages of the government, mainly reported Mrs Gandhi's own speeches and activities. She did not listen to the B.B.C., where she might have heard what observers thought of the mood of the country, because, as she once told me, 'the B.B.C. had always been hostile to me.' The correspondents of foreign newspapers who filed stories critical of the emergency situation were liable to be deported, and some were. She had increased her own loneliness in that her actions seemed to have isolated her from events. Before the emergency, involvement with events and people, movement, action had fed and nourished her, as they had her father. Now, except when she went somewhere to make a speech, she was largely tied to Delhi and her desk. Her main contact with the people was in the morning, when, before she left for her office, admirers and petitioners came to her house to meet her. This was a custom continued from the days of Nehru.

She did, she told me, talk to a number of people on the topic of forced sterilisation. 'None of them had experienced it,' she said, 'nor had any of those who were voluntarily sterilised become ill afterwards. When they talked about forced sterilisation and of people dying because of it, I asked if any of them had seen any such cases. None of them had. So how could they talk about it, I wanted to know. They would say, "*Kisi ne mujhse kaha.*"'* But asking people is not the same as actual experience of an ethos.

For example, one evening Leela and I were coming out of a cinema in Delhi. It was dark and the crowd pushed and shouted its way cheerfully out on to the pavements, when there were wild cries off to one side, and then something in the nature of a stampede of young men across to the far side of the road. The noise of the crowd swelled, no longer cheerful but with a note of terror, and people dispersed rapidly in all directions. On inquiry, I discovered that a police truck had been parked in an alley by the cinema. Somebody, having seen it, had raised the alarm that the police had been sent to seize people coming out of the cinema and drag them off to be forcibly sterilised.

Now it might have been true that none of the crowd had ever seen forcible sterilisation, but the whole crowd had obviously heard of it, and perfectly believed that the police had been sent to collect people for this purpose. Imaginary demons, perhaps, but the terror was real. It was a terror that had spread rapidly over northern India.

Throughout history, news has travelled through India, particularly in the north, by word of mouth. A rumour started at dawn in Amritsar can travel the dusty road to Delhi by nightfall: naturally enough, it picks up various embellishments and elaborations on the way. Some of these rumours have terrible repercussions: a rumour set off the Mutiny in 1857.

Had the government realised the widespread and horrific nature of the rumours about sterilisation, they could have made a determined effort to convince the people that these rumours were untrue.

* 'Somebody told me.'

Mrs Gandhi had some credibility with the masses, and moreover, the government could reach most people through the media: even very poor Indian farmers now have small transistor radios. As it was, many people believed that sterilisation was another name for castration, and that the patient was likely to die as a result of it. Bearing this in mind, the peremptory way in which the government ordered its officers to bring people in for sterilisation added to the terror. Mrs Gandhi could have travelled round the country and explained matters to the people, and they would probably have believed her, but she did not do so and many people came to think of her as an ogress, who, remote in her fastness in Delhi, had despatched her servants to destroy the most intimate part of their lives. There was nobody to tell them otherwise.

A lonely iceberg on her sea of Ministers, Mrs Gandhi had another affinity to the queens of ancient India in that she, like they, possessed disaffected relatives. The old anguish of Kamala had inhabited Mrs Gandhi's mind for years, and her relations with her aunt, Mrs Pandit, had never been outstandingly cordial. Mrs Pandit had looked down on Kamala to some extent, and made her miserable, but jealousy may in part have motivated this behaviour, for Jawaharlal, thirteen years older than his sister, had pampered and cossetted the child, and the arrival of Kamala on the scene presented the youthful Swarup Rani with a rival for the attentions of her idol. Swarup Rani married, and became Vijayalakhshmi Pandit, but her possessive attitude towards her only brother remained the same. Jawaharlal seems to have asked her advice about the adolescent Indira. He wrote to her from Dehra Dun prison in 1932, complaining that his daughter never wrote to him or to her mother. 'I know that Indu is fond of me and of Kamala,' he said. 'Yet she ignores us and others completely. Why is this so? Indu, I feel is extraordinarily imaginative and selfcentred or subjective. Indeed, I would say that, quite unconsciously, she has grown remarkably selfish. She lives in a world of dreams and vagaries and floats about on imaginary clouds, full probably of all manner of brave fancies. Now this is natural in a girl of her subjective nature and especially at her age. But there can be too much of it and I am afraid there is too much of it in her case ... I feel she requires a course of field or factory work to bring her down from the clouds ... She will have to come down and if she does not do so early she will do so late, and then the process will be painful ... ' Mrs Pandit kept this letter for over forty years, but it was recently published. I asked Mrs Gandhi about it, and she smiled rather dryly. 'After all,' she said, 'you must remember I was only fifteen years old.'

There were periods of truce between the two. In September 1942, when Indira was imprisoned for the first and only time by the British, she shared a sort of cottage with Mrs Pandit and her eldest daughter Chandralekha. They received special treatment and lived a reasonably comfortable life, the details of which Mrs Pandit recorded in a prison diary. 'The jail cat named by Indu — Mehitabel — has had four kittens and Indu and Lekha are quite excited ... The girls have a habit of giving names to everything: the lantern, table, bed, even the bottle of hair oil which has recently lost its top as the result of a fall. It is now referred to as Rupert the headless earl. The lantern is Lucifer ... ' The three women seem to have been very cheerful in their captivity, though Mrs Gandhi's recollections of it seem to have been considerably affected by the years. In 1969 she told an interviewer, 'I was regarded as so dangerous that I wasn't even given normal prison facilities.' The vivid imagination Nehru deplored when she was fifteen had persisted beyond her adolescence.

It was perhaps when independence came that the relationship between Mrs Pandit and her niece really showed a decline. Mrs Pandit was still fiercely possessive towards Jawaharlal, and the fact that Mrs Gandhi now lived with and looked after her father may have irritated his sister somewhat, despite the high diplomatic posts to which she was appointed. She was the Indian plenipotentiary successively in Washington, Moscow, and London, the three most important postings any Indian diplomat could aspire to. After all this, in the early 1960s, she was appointed Governor of Bombay, and, her term over, was elected to the Lok Sabha. Meanwhile Mrs Gandhi had entered politics, and the two women regarded each other with some disfavour from their respective seats in Parliament. It was the presence of Nehru, loved by both, that prevented open hostility, and in 1964 Nehru died.

An eyewitness told me about the scene when Nehru's body was laid out in Teen Murti House. It was laid out on a bed, small under heaped flowers, and Mrs Gandhi sat beside it. She was grey with grief, and her head was bowed. Mrs Pandit was also there, with other members of the family, people who had come to pay their final respects, and television and press reporters. 'What struck me,' said my informant, 'was that it was only Mrs Gandhi who sat by the corpse. She kept Mrs Pandit well away.'

Two years later the ugly duckling had become Prime Minister, Cinderella had become a princess. Mrs Pandit appears to have observed this with horror and disapproval. She is said to have felt that the only person worthy to replace her brother as Prime Minister was herself. Mrs Gandhi and she were openly opposed, and in 1968 Mrs Pandit retired from politics to the small town of Dehra Dun, at the foot of the Himalayas.

She had three daughters. The second of these, Nayantara, I had known since my adolescence in Bombay, when she and her husband were friends of my father. She was a bright and beautiful young woman, who had written an autobiography, slight but charming, and went on to write a number of novels. When I met her as an adult, she had suffered from many personal sorrows and had become much more silent than before. She now lived in Delhi, and though she had always been interested in politics, she now had specific political views. She expressed them mainly in a column which she wrote for my father's newspaper, the *Indian Express*. Nayantara was very close to her mother, and she appeared to resent Mrs Gandhi's treatment of Mrs Pandit: in any event the tone of her articles was sharply against the Prime Minister. Indeed, while supposed to write broadly on politics, she wrote, almost always, specifically against her cousin. Her articles were stopped when the emergency came, but she did not cease, verbally, to criticise Mrs Gandhi which, at the period, people less courageous or less obsessed never dared to do. Mrs Pandit was also, in private, vocal against the Prime Minister and her son. She is a very witty woman, her tongue touched delicately with malice, and her attacks upon Indira and Sanjay were considerably more personal than her daughter's. Nayantara was also an admirer of J.P., and immediately before the emergency had taken to writing for his publication, *Everyman's Weekly*. In view of the fact that many people who had said and done less than Mrs Pandit and her daughter had been put into prison, it was surprising that they had not. This might have been construed as a desire on the part of Mrs Gandhi to spare her relatives imprisonment: It could also be construed as a slightly feline move, an indication by a green glint of the eyes that they were simply not important enough to be imprisoned. Whichever it was—or perhaps it was a mixture of both—Mrs Pandit and Nayantara remained free, though both were certainly under police surveillance and their phones were tapped.

Mussoorie, 6,000 feet up in the Himalayan foothills, a little way above Mrs Pandit's retreat at Dehra Dun, is a place not unfamiliar to Mrs Gandhi, since in her youth she holidayed there. It is a pleasantly cool town after Delhi in the summer, and feathers of snow float down on it in winter. Here I met the former Princess Sita of Kapurthala, who lives in a cottage on top of a hill for six months of the year. I was on a sort of working holiday: Mussoorie is a small place, and the Princess a friend of Leela's: it was inevitable that we should meet. Her cottage is near trees and the noise of water, and is filled with the photographs and souvenirs of a full life: she herself is small, with white hair and excellent features, and was considered a great beauty in her youth. She told anecdotes of her past in the sharply edged, rather precise English most educated Indian women use: and the more I talked to her the more I kept trying to think of whom she reminded me. It was not long before I arrived at the obvious discovery.

To borrow the American sociologist, Jacques Barzun's phrase about America, most rich Indian families have made the leap from barbarism to decadence in a very short space of time. This applies to the family of any industrialist in the country, but most of all to the princes. The first of the princes of Kapurthala, Jassa Singh, fought the Moguls in the eighteenth century, his tall Sikh horsemen thundering out of the hills to destroy the trade caravans that came down from Kabul. In the twentieth century, Jit, one of his descendants, had a château in the south of France where the fountains in the courtyard spouted champagne. Harold Acton, in his *Memoirs of an Aesthete** refers, rather surprisingly, to the excellent taste of this prince.

Curiously enough, though the men of rich Indian families seem to become progressively less suited to any kind of understandable way of life, some of the women become more civilised by wealth. Princess Sita, now in her sixties, had a dry humour and a kind of amusement at the life that once led her: at the same time, she seems very proud of the history of Kapurthala (she married into the family, her father being the ruler of the hill state of Kumaon). Near her quiet, simple house stands what is known as 'The Château', the

* Methuen, 1948.

summer palace of the Kapurthala princes, a monument to uncertain taste. Amidst the rubble left by generations (it was built in 1896) it does contain some books and family records of interest. Princess Sita seldom visits Kapurthala: she says she does not like it any more.

She is, in fact, rather what Mrs Gandhi might be like were she to do what she says she has always wanted to, and retire to a house in the hills, near streams and among trees. Mrs Gandhi now does not much like Allahabad, exactly as Princess Sita does not like Kapurthala, but she has the same fierce pride in her family history as the Princess, perhaps with better reason. A retirement from public life would probably loosen her up: she might flicker her right eyelid and tell anecdotes to people who came to tea. I imagine she would like to have a neighbour like Princess Sita: she would be far happier in such company than in the company of servile and devious men with whom she has nothing in common except a political party. But to keep the company she does is perhaps part of Mrs Gandhi's need for martyrdom. Moreover, despite her similarities to someone like Princess Sita, she is different in her dedication, in her desire and pursuit of the whole. I cannot really see her playing bridge in the afternoons: I do not ever see her in the cottage of her dreams. Her whole life, since her childhood, has taken her to an eyrie from which she will never be able to escape.

Mrs Gandhi's social life, during the emergency, was as it had always been after the death of her father: it hardly existed. She does not smoke or drink, though unlike Desai she does not object to other people doing so: she is not gregarious: she prefers not to escape from herself. She occasionally dined with a close friend, such as Pupul Jayakar: otherwise she saw few people on a personal level. One of these few was Swami Dhirendra Brahmachari, a tall, bearded *yogi* clad in white samite, mystic, wonderful. He owned a foreign car and a private aeroplane. The Brahmachari (the word means 'one who has forsaken the world') teaches *yoga*. He taught Mrs Gandhi *yoga*, but he seemed to many people who thought well of her an undesirable acquaintance, and his visits to her house created numerous silly rumours.

Gossip and rumours are the stuff of Indian conversation, and the tongue always a viable weapon. After Mrs Gandhi had fallen from office, one of the many rumours about the Gandhi household was that Sanjay had formed what writers described as 'a caucus' with

Bansi Lal, the Haryana Chief Minister, who had become Defence Minister under the emergency, V. C. Shukla, the Information Minister who had replaced Inder Gujral, and other members of Mrs Gandhi's staff, including Yashpal Kapoor, who had been involved in the election at Rae Bareilly. 'A caucus?' Mrs Gandhi remarked sardonically when I once asked her about it. 'Tell me, what exactly is a caucus? Sanjay knew Bansi Lal, Shukla was one of my Ministers, and Yashpal had been my private secretary long before the emergency. Why shouldn't he have known these people?' What the caucus did was never made quite clear by those who alleged it existed, but the main accusation was that it influenced Mrs Gandhi unduly in her policy decisions. Such was the atmosphere of Delhi politics at this time that several journalists told me there was a rumour that the members of the caucus held unholy orgies in a Delhi hotel, and took photographs of each other in compromising positions, so that each of them had a hold over the others. In this way rumour without foundation is spread in India.

When the emergency was over I talked to Shukla. He is a dapper, quietly spoken youngish man, intelligent, and with excellent taste in painting. 'What caucus?' he inquired. 'Of course I know Sanjay, but he is a much younger man than I am, and with that gap in age, we could never be close friends. Of course I know Bansi Lal, but he is an oaf, he has no eye for painting, no ear for music. He is,' added Shukla, after a moment's thought, 'the kind of man who, if he saw a beautiful sunset behind a field of wheat, would be preoccupied calculating how much the wheat in the field was worth.'

The enervation of living in India is spectacular, especially if you have nothing to do anyway. During 1976 I had nothing whatever to do, because the government said it had no funds available for any satellite television films. The entire purpose of my mission had been defeated: all I did was plead with Ministers for funds. They all asked why the U.N., having sent me to India as an expert, did not finance my films. One day I said to Leela that I was fed up, and that we were going back to New York. I felt a sort of slackness in my mind, a lack of response in my body. I hated the heat. I wanted cold weather, winds that were arctic rather than composed of melted chocolate, voices that contained the iron and leather of English rather than the soft, perennial, erosive lilt of Indian voices speaking English. I wanted to return to a world I knew, to which, holding its hand, I could say, 'My wife doesn't understand me,' India being in a sense a wife I did not understand. My own wife, Leela, beautiful, scatty, and, at least mentally, courageous, said, 'Why give up now? Why not ask Mrs G.?'

Grumpy in the heat, I said, 'What on earth do you think she could do?' Leela said, 'Think of my Harijans.' I thought about it, and eventually telephoned for an appointment. When I went to see Mrs Gandhi and explained my problem, she lowered her spectacles a little and looked at me in a thoughtful sort of way over the rims. 'But do you *want* to stay here?' she inquired. I said that after all I had been sent by the U.N. to do some work, and I had not done it because I had received none of the agreed financial assistance from the government. She frowned over her spectacles. 'Why not?' she asked, and I, much emboldened, said, 'Ma'am, ask your Ministers.' To this she did not reply, but flickered an eye at Sharada Prasad, her Press Secretary, who was usually present at our official interviews, and said, 'Try and find out if the Health Ministry has any funds. Family planning films come under it.' A few days later the funds were paid to an independent producer, for him to execute the scripts which had been lying, mouldering like me in India, in files on my desk for months.

In her own peculiar, understated way Mrs Gandhi had given me a sort of belief. In 1961, following the invasion of Goa by Indian forces, I had attacked the action of the government in the English press and on television. I had asked whether anyone had bothered to ask the Goan people what they wanted: they might have wanted to get rid of the Portuguese, but did they want the Portuguese to be replaced by Indians? I never realised what commotion this sort of (it seemed to me) fair comment would cause in India. My father phoned me in London and said, 'Nehru is very angry. If I were you, I would change your passport. Otherwise I think your Indian passport will be impounded, you will have to come back, and it'll be difficult for you to leave again.' I had been thinking for some time of obtaining a British passport, for the simple reason that I felt I belonged to Britain, in terms of language and culture (I was, at twenty-three, much more preoccupied with culture than with people) and not to India.

I obtained my British passport. Two years before this, Nehru in Delhi had asked me, mildly, where I intended to spend the rest of my life. I had said England: he, in that gentle, slightly discursive way he had, explained that young men of some intelligence were needed in India. He had said that there would always be something I could do. I myself did not see what I could possibly do, as a writer, in a country that did not speak English, but when I said this he smiled a little and said rather tiredly, '*I* would have liked to have been a writer.' I have never forgotten the particular tone of this remark, or those beautiful eyes looking away from me through the window at a military march of tulips in the garden outside his office: it was only years later that I realised what a selfish remark mine had been, at least when made to him. In any event, in 1961 I was furious with Nehru and India.

Now, fifteen years later, Mrs Gandhi, with a shift of her eyes, had indicated that I was, in some sense, useful to the country, or at least could be. I thought of her remark, 'But do you *want* to stay here?' as far more immediate to me than the gentle arguments of her father. Whatever my allegiances and nationality, I suddenly looked over the rims of her spectacles into her totally uninterested eyes, and realised that she had given me something back which I had completely lost: she had given me roots. She may not have intended to do so: but to me a quietness is more important than words.

The United Nations and I left each other on December 31 1976. I had been asked by the Karnataka government to write a book on the state, and had done so. The book had been a success, and I thought up an idea around it. Since there are a number of states and union territories in India, I imagined each state could subsidise one such book. It was a very complicated scheme, and Air India and the state governments came into it. Leela said, 'Ask Mrs G.,' so I did.

My appointment at her office was in the morning. Sharada Prasad welcomed me in the outer room. Outside the windows a winter Delhi lay quietly: all over the streets there were posters and hoardings displaying the lady I was about to meet, and her supposed sayings. The area around the great mosque, which her ancestors had known, lay in ruins, destroyed by her son. The students chattered in the coffee houses, but the office was quiet. Sharada Prasad told me to go in. Since I was more or less unannounced, I obtained the most vivid visual image of Mrs Gandhi that I have ever had: she had her feet tucked up under her on her chair behind her immense desk and was tossing a rubber eraser from hand to hand, lips pursed in a soundless hum. She was not for that moment Mrs Gandhi any more, but the gawky, lonely child whom everyone called Indu.

I coughed: Sharada Prasad coughed: she suddenly rearranged herself, looking far from pleased. Once Sharada Prasad and I were seated, I explained, rapidly, my proposition. Mrs Gandhi had meanwhile assumed an administrative pose. She leant her elbows on the massive desk and rested her chin on her hands. Having listened, blinking a bit, she said to Sharada Prasad, 'Sounds good.' Sharada Prasad, stiff behind his notebook, said 'Yes, madame.' She then said to me, 'Is it feasible?' I said I did not know. It was a very complex operation. She said, 'All right. You will have to meet the Minister of Tourism. Arrange it, Sharada.' Sharada Prasad did so. One of the most awful moments of my life was when the Minister, a South Indian, said, almost before hearing what I said or reading what I had written, 'If the Prime Minister wants it, it will be done.' I thought of that small figure seeking comfort as children seek comfort, behind that great desk, humming to herself, tossing the eraser from hand to hand. 'It will be done,' said the Minister, gobbling his words as turkeys and South Indians do. 'Please to present proposal in actual writing and three copies.'

By the time I had done this, Mrs Gandhi had gone.

❧ 17 ❧

The Hollow Crown

THE EMERGENCY WAS by necessity a time-bound situation. Mrs Gandhi could not continue it indefinitely without being accused of dictatorship: indeed, she had already been, not only verbally by Indians but in print in a number of foreign countries. She had stated in public that the emergency would be lifted and elections held when the country had been restored to a stable condition. But you cannot have elections without a choice of people to elect, and the main opposition leaders were all in prison, or, in the case of J.P. in hospital. As time passed and there was no sign of their release, people became rather cynical about the prospect of there ever being elections.

The emergency had worked in that there was more order in the country than there had been for some years. The rumbles of unrest had not yet become volcanic in their volume. But Mrs Gandhi many people said, should do what she had promised: release her prisoners and call elections. She, meanwhile, remained enigmatic. There were to be elections in Pakistan, which she had often referred to as a dictatorship, and in Sri Lanka, but no signs of elections in India, until, on January 18 1977, Mrs Gandhi spoke.

She did so over the radio, which disseminates news to more Indians than any other arm of the media. She had decided, she told the people, to dissolve the Lok Sabha and to hold elections. The opposition leaders were to be released from prison, and the emergency would be lifted slowly. The elections were set for the end of March. Most people were amazed by these announcements: certainly nobody had expected them, and there was considerable speculation as to why they were made. Since her political moves had always been perfectly planned and timed, a hawklike series of strikes that turned her opponents into her prey, this latest move

would obviously succeed: or so the oracles whispered in the capital:
for she must be sure of success to have made it.

It was simple, the oracles said: her intelligence reports must have
reassured her that her charisma still worked and an avalanche of
votes, as in 1971, would sweep her back into elected power. The
developments in Pakistan and Sri Lanka must have made her feel
that she must keep up with the Bhuttos and Bandaranaikes, and
present the world with an image of herself as a popular leader, whose
people had accepted the necessity for the emergency and brought
her back as soon as there were open elections. Furthermore, she had
so timed her fiats that the opposition leaders, who had no party
solidarity, who in their prisons had been unable to confer or
formulate any kind of manifesto, and who were as far as was known
without money to finance a new party, had been left with two months
in which to prepare themselves for the polls.

Most of the opposition leaders were now released, none the worse
for wear and started as most Indians do at the drop of a *dhoti*, to
talk. An exception who stayed in prison, and was brought to court in
chains, was the excitable labour leader George Fernandes, who had
surrendered to the police before Mrs Gandhi declared that the
elections would be held. Fernandes was charged with having
conspired with others to assassinate Mrs Gandhi with a bomb when
she travelled to Benares in 1976. He and his alleged confederates
had been arrested at Baroda, a small town in western India, with a
large quantity of explosives. Fernandes was to stand for election
from prison, and it would make it awkward if, having won, he had
to continue in his cell for some length of time still to be defined.
However, the whole situation being so confused between the recently
released leaders, one confusion more or less did not really appear
to matter.

The released leaders meanwhile described their lives in prison.
Piloo Mody who had been with two right-wing parties in his time,
and who has the most immense stomach, had put on even more
weight in his prison, which he called 'The Arizona Motel'. His main
complaint was that the prison doctor, concerned for this colossal
captive's health, had insisted that he walk a little every day. Mody,
grumbling, walked, but he also ate: hence his increase in size.
Other leaders talked of the terrified and tortured prisoners whose
screams had continually disturbed their nightly rest, though nothing
else seems to have done so. These reports on the martyrdom of the

opposition chiefs were much publicised by a press now free to say what it wanted, and it had started to say plenty.

Satish Gujral, the painter, brother of Inder Gujral who had been removed from the Ministry of Information and Broadcasting shortly after the emergency was declared, talked to me once, in these days of bewilderment, about the elections to come. 'What do you think will happen in these elections?' Satish inquired. I replied, as most observers of the Indian scene would have done at the time, 'She'll come back, but she may come back with much less of a lead.' Satish is a highly intelligent man, with a very sharp nose for politics, surprising in a painter. 'You think so?' he said. 'No. I think not. I think the Janata will win.' I thought I had misheard him. By this time the opposition had roughly reformed itself under a Janata banner, but I did not think they had a chance.

'You did not visit the Janata rally in Delhi recently?' asked Satish. 'No, I thought not. Do you know there were 100,000 people there: mostly poor people, who were those who supported Mrs Gandhi in the past? Do you know that they pledged their support to the Janata, and, though they were poor, they gave all the money they could to the Janata in a collection made on the spot?' I said many people in Delhi supported the Jan Sangh, and the scaffolding that supported the Janata was Jan Sangh. There was no significance in the support for the Janata in Delhi. 'You wait,' Satish said. 'You will see it happen all over the country, and particularly where Sanjay has been active in the north.' I did not believe it, and shook my head at him. 'She was mad to call for these elections,' Satish said. 'This will be her political suicide.'

I think now that all the Delhi oracles had considerable misconceptions about why Mrs Gandhi would be so successful in the elections she had called. Firstly, she may have been informed by her intelligence officers that the whole country was behind her, but anyone with any awareness could have told her that to a considerable extent her intelligence officers would try to protect themselves from her wrath by not telling her the whole unpleasant truth about her loss of support. She never seems to have heard the real truth about the state of the country from anyone. Secondly, she had antagonised a number of rich and powerful people who were more than delighted to open their coffers to her opponents.

Months after the election I asked Mrs Gandhi if the elections declared in Pakistan and Sri Lanka had been a factor which influenced her in calling the election in India. She ruffled her feathers indignantly and said: 'Why should what Pakistan, or Bangladesh, or Sri Lanka, decide to do have any effect on what India wants to do? India is their largest neighbour. *They* should be influenced by what we do: what they do can't influence *us*.' I asked about the image of herself she wanted to project to the rest of the world: someone supported by her people to the extent that even after she had declared what could politely be described as a suspension of democracy, they would vote her back to power in a democratic election? 'That's not a very intelligent question,' Mrs Gandhi said, chillingly.

I have tried to establish her reasons more than once. From what I can gather from her various replies, none of the factors mentioned by supposedly expert observers in Delhi and elsewhere, had anything to do with her declaration of elections. She has a kind of inward feeling, she says, as when she warned Mujibur Rehman, shortly before his death in Dacca, that something awful would happen to him if he returned home. She had this feeling when she decided to suspend the emergency and declare elections: something awful would happen unless she did. 'To you, ma'am?' I inquired. 'No,' she said. 'Not to me. To the country. I had this sense that more and more foreign influences were seeking for excuses to disrupt, perhaps even to destroy, this country.' She has been saying this for years, however, and she has never clarified what she meant.

Mrs Gandhi may have had a kind of contempt and suspicion for the Ministers around her, but she also probably felt that she could keep them at heel indefinitely. In this she was greatly mistaken, for Jagjivan Ram, the Harijan Minister, having felt himself slighted by her, seems to have sniffed the air of January 1977, scented a possible success for the Janata, and then decided to break away from Mrs Gandhi. Taking a leaf from his leader's book, he failed to inform her of his intentions before he formed another new party, the Congress for Democracy or C.F.D. The press knew before Mrs Gandhi did. Jagjivan Ram then issued a statement deploring the many excesses of the emergency, though nobody asked him why he had not only put up with them but as a senior Minister, implemented them for the previous year and a half without so much as a mutter of protest. What was known as the Janata was actually a very loose coalition of parties, the Congress (O), Morarji's party: the Socialists: the B.L.D., controlled by the bitter, ruthless Charan Singh, formerly Chief Minister of Uttar Pradesh: and the Jan Sangh, most powerful of all the parties in the Janata coalition. The C.F.D. was now added to this assembly.

The defection of a very senior Minister hit Mrs Gandhi where it hurt. Very naturally, it had a tremendous effect on the voters, particularly those of the Harijan community, so that the pack she had ordered to heel for so long, was now snapping at her heels and falling over itself to savage her. The visible attraction of northern voters towards the Janata, as demonstrated in the Delhi rally Satish Gujral had attended, was a further source of disquiet. These voters were not exactly supporting the Janata, as yet not a party in the proper sense, and as yet without any sensibly formulated policy (indeed, some members, in their campaign speeches, often proposed policies opposed to those stated by other members), but they were opposing Mrs Gandhi, and in particular Sanjay Gandhi. These were the voters, the people, to whom things had been done. Sanjay had been in full cry under the Himalayan foothills and on the Gangetic plain, but his sterilisation campaign had not operated south of the holy river. The Dravidians had not been touched by it.

I call these people Dravidians because of another curious point about these elections. In the southern states, people spoke Dravidian languages, the gutturals of Tamil, Kannada, and Telugu rolled off their tongues, expectorated like the areca nuts they commonly chew: but they also spoke English rather than Hindi, and by and large, despite a peculiar accent when speaking it, they understood English and its nuances better than people in the north. Most of the Janata leaders spoke Hindi, and nearly all were from the north. Not only did they not speak, or want to speak, any of the southern languages but, nearly without exception, few of them were comfortable in English. Desai was better at the language than backwoodsmen like Charan Singh and Raj Narain, but his English left much to be desired. He is voluble but not easily understandable, and nobody can talk convincingly to crowds, or indeed to anybody, in a language he speaks badly. The Janata leaders were in a sense the first truly indigenous political leaders of India, and unlike Nehru and Mrs Gandhi they were from and of the people: but they exemplified the difficulties of being indigenous to a given part of India: none of them could communicate verbally to a large part of the country. Mrs Gandhi and Nehru could speak to large sections of Indian society in English: the Janata leaders could not: the Congress expected victory in the south.

In the north, Mrs Gandhi was campaigning from her own constituency, Rae Bareilly, which had been held before her by her husband. In addition, Sanjay was supposed to campaign from the nearby constituency of Amethi. The newspapers commented gleefully on the fact that on one occasion, when Maneka and he arrived on a campaigning tour, there was nobody to meet them.

To produce Sanjay for election to the Lok Sabha, in an area where he was unpopular because of the way his sterilisation campaign was said to have operated, and to produce him in a constituency so close to his mother's at a time when people were still willing to believe in her but did not believe in him, was a frightful mistake. Raj Narain was to fight Mrs Gandhi once more from Rae Bareilly, and he was already reminding people of the Allahabad High Court decision, of what Sanjay was supposed to have done during the emergency, and of the obvious fact that she intended him to continue and indeed intensify his political life by getting him voted into the Lok Sabha from a constituency she considered safe.

The Congress (R) symbol was that of a cow and a calf. It was easily recognisable for a peasant who might be illiterate, and a comforting one. Large numbers of rural voters in India opt for the symbol of a party rather than for its stated programme, and this cow and calf symbol conveyed an idea of the party's interest in peasant welfare, at least to the peasants. Someone with a bitter wit said to me in Delhi, when it was announced that Sanjay would stand from Amethi, 'The cow and the calf are fine in proximity on a poster. But when the calf is adult, it should be separated from its mother. If they browse in pastures next to each other, the slaughterers, when they come, will not only take one: they will destroy both.'

Chaos had been restored with the announcement of elections. Often, after a night when people told me what they wanted done to Mrs Gandhi after the Janata had won (hang her, they said, put her in a cell with prostitutes as she did to Snehalata Reddy and the dowager queens of Gwalior and Jaipur, make her confess her sins before the world) I awoke to a Delhi also full of anger. Even the taxi-drivers talked of what would happen after the Janata won. 'Very much difficulty,' one said to me. 'Who knows what these new men will be like? There will be a war in the country.' I, like most people, was convinced Mrs Gandhi would win, but amidst these weird febrile conversations, trapped amidst sudden processions of white-clad workers screaming hoarsely amidst banners and dust, some for Mrs Gandhi, some for the Janata, two lines of William Empson's kept coming into my mind: 'The talk will talk and go so far aslant,' and, 'You can't have madhouse and the whole thing there.' The second line seemed to me in its way an explanation of the emergency.

The peculiar and perhaps undesirable kind of sanity that had existed during the emergency was now replaced once more by the total madness which had preceded it. There were numerous allegations about the rigging of votes which would become possible when the elections took place. Each person who votes is marked on the hand with ink that takes days to fade, to show that he or she has already voted. However, the application of a certain chemical will remove this ink, so theoretically a party member with a supply of this chemical could visit every polling station in a district and cast a vote in each. Since there are about ten polling stations to a district, one man could be worth ten votes to his party. This, said the Janata was what the Congress would do in this election, and had done in the last one. The Congress replied that the Janata were certainly low enough to do it but the Congress was not. Accusations and insults flew to and fro. This was certainly not an amiable contest: it was fought out in an atmosphere of bitterness and hysteria. The Janata leaders sped round the country on their campaign, and so did Mrs Gandhi. I heard her speak at a rally in Delhi, an enormous rally in a public park. The white-clad crowds who had come to hear her spread back towards the dusty horizon, by no means silent: scuffles and shouts were frequent, and it was clear that the audience was not entirely composed of wellwishers. Mrs Gandhi and a few other Congress leaders spoke from a canopied platform high above the multitude: around the platform were pictures of Mrs Gandhi herself, and Sanjay. Mrs Gandhi had repeatedly asserted, in answer to accusations of nepotism, that her son had no official role in the Congress: if so, there was no reason for his portrait to be displayed on a Congress platform, the more so because he himself was not among those present. Additionally, anyone aware of the emotions of the masses towards Sanjay Gandhi would have kept any reminder of his existence far away. The conclusion to be drawn was that either the Congress workers who organised the occasion were entirely unaware of popular feeling, which was difficult to believe, or that they were aware of it and simply wanted to please Mrs Gandhi by publicising her son. In either case, Mrs Gandhi must herself have been either unaware of, or contemptuous of, the antagonism many people felt towards Sanjay: otherwise, in the interests of the party, she would have forbidden the display of the portrait. Its prominence at the rally was an indication of the way the Congress party seemed now to function, on a principle of blind and thoughtless faith in its own invincibility and a desire to please the Prime Minister at all costs. The party workers expected the Congress to win the election because it had won every election since independence. It was not a good basis to work from.

Mrs Gandhi, when she spoke, said nothing new. This may have been because now there was nothing new to say. She enumerated the past achievements of the Congress, promised that the future would see the eradication of poverty if her government was re-elected, made a passing reference to her father, and several contemptuous references to the opposition leaders. Her main point was that the Janata was not, properly speaking, a party, but an unformed conglomeration of different political interests which would never be able to function properly as a whole. It had no leader as such, no shared values, and no policy. This was all quite true, of course, and in normal circumstances nobody would have thought the Janata had the faintest hope of victory at the polls. But these were not normal times and when Mrs Gandhi stared down upon her opponents with aristocratic disdain she made a serious mistake.

Serious mistakes were made by other people, too, in those weeks before the election, and not the least of these was made by Jagjivan Ram. Here was a politician whom Mrs Gandhi had often protected in the past. On one occasion, when a question was asked in Parliament as to why he had filed no tax returns for the previous decade, Mrs Gandhi had replied in an indulgent fashion that he had probably forgotten. Nevertheless, Jagjivan Ram felt Mrs Gandhi undervalued him, that she did not consult him enough, and that the top Ministerial posts had never come his way despite his unarguable seniority. Moreover, he is an ambitious man, and he almost certainly wanted to be Prime Minister. He was aware of the temper of the country during the emergency, though he does not seem to have tried to tell Mrs Gandhi, and probably knew that the Janata might come in purely because they were the alternative to the Congress, and the people had come to resent and distrust the Congress. It was probably also true that, looking at the ragtag composition of the Janata, he saw huge opportunities rising over the horizon. There was no proper leader: the nearest thing to one was Desai, who was eighty-two, and though Desai was as tough as old boots he could not continue to function for ever, and the Janata would probably want a younger man as leader. Who, then, would be more suitable than he, a powerful name, the Moses of a downtrodden community, experienced in administration, able to explain to the less knowledgeable the intricacies of the files left in various Ministries by Mrs Gandhi's government?

The Janata welcomed him with joy. This was someone they could publicise as a fugitive from Mrs Gandhi's chain gang. His defection, in fact, was to play a vital role in the Congress collapse. But nobody in the world, as, on a higher level, the case of Solzenitsyn has proved, eventually loves a defector. The Janata leaders, themselves skilled in the art of deviousness, knew perfectly well why Jagjivan Ram had come over to them: they knew even better that he had not defected on a matter of principle. They decided that though he was a highly desirable acquisition for the present, he would probably prove a liability in the end. Jagjivan Ram very probably became aware of this immediately after his defection: but there was no way back, and he was trapped in the situation he had created. What he did for the Janata image by his disloyalty to Mrs Gandhi was to be the most the Janata would ever allow him to do for it.

Desai was another experienced administrator, but his age was against him, and with Jagjivan Ram probably untrustworthy, the Janata needed others who had some experience of the way a country is run. They had rabble rousers such as George Fernandes, still in prison, and Raj Narain, whose sole claim to importance was his having won his case over Mrs Gandhi at Allahabad: they had people such as Charan Singh, who had been Chief Minister of a state: but they did not really have many who could be expected to swing themselves into ministerial chairs and perform there with ability. This was something which should have been discussed

within the party before elections: but there was no time for discussions before the ides of March came upon India.

Therefore the Janata went into the elections without a policy,
without a shadow cabinet, without anything but a desire for victory,
which constituted in itself a vengeance upon Mrs Gandhi. There
were already Janata snarlers, Charan Singh being the foremost, who
vowed that hellfire should fall upon her head and that of her son
when the Janata came marching in. In this atmosphere, with not one
of the Janata leaders trustful of another, they prepared for the final
battle, in which that unlikely dragon, Mrs Gandhi, should go down
before their lances. A more ludicrous set of Saint Georges could
hardly be imagined, bickering over what would happen to the dragon
and what favours each would receive when the battle was over,
before those eminently frangible lances had been so much as
couched.

On March 22 1977, the weather having inclined from winter
towards the days of drought, the largest democracy in the world went
to the polls. The people went quietly, often carrying their victuals
for the day with them since the queues at the polling stations were
likely to be immense, prepared to be stamped with ink, like some
government file, to prove that they could not be passed on from one
ballot box to another. Large numbers of these people were illiterate,
and their forms had to be filled in by irritable, sweaty officers in the
polling stations, before the voters could press their thumbs down
on paper to validate their votes. This, it is alleged, is another way
of rigging votes: if the officers are bribed by one party or another,
a man may vote for a candidate he does not want.

The quiet people at the polling stations were rapidly bringing the
Janata into power in the north. Southward, the people stayed with
Mrs Gandhi and her party (it must be noted that most people voted
for her and not the party). But Sanjay lost at Amethi, which was to
be expected, beaten by somebody no one had ever heard of: and
then, the truly surprising news, Mrs Gandhi started to lose Rae
Bareilly. Pupul Jayakar has told me how she received the news
that she was losing. 'She was in Delhi,' Pupul said, 'and she asked
me to dinner. She was not emotional. She said, "I think I've
lost." Dinner was duly laid. Mrs Gandhi said, "I have lost." Her
family sat around her, their eyes red. They toyed with their
food.' According to Mrs Jayakar, her hostess ate dinner without any trace of emotion, 'soup, salad, and sweet', answered

telephone calls, talked to visitors and behaved exactly as she usually did.

Her conqueror in Rae Bareilly, Raj Narain, was naturally excited over his victory. Nevertheless, of all the saints who had set out to destroy a dragon, he was the one who had succeeded. The Janata now had to include him in their cabinet: like Mrs Gandhi, they had little choice within the talent available. With Desai now supposed to be the main Janata leader, it became obvious that not only were Mrs Gandhi and the Congress losers in the election, but the 600 million people of the country. 'Father, forgive them,' Mrs Gandhi could have said to the unforgiving Delhi sky, 'for they know not what they do.'

The Janata leaders squabbled, after victory. It was not until May, in fact, that they were officially proclaimed to be a party. Piloo Mody, who was probably the most intelligent and perceptive of all the opposition leaders Mrs Gandhi imprisoned, was dropped by the Janata: perhaps because he was intelligent, perceptive, and now able to see what chaos the Janata Government would lead to.

Raj Narain became Health Minister. The first thing he did was to refuse to answer queries made in English in the Lok Sabha: he wanted them asked in Hindi. He also wanted people to drink their own urine, like Desai, for breakfast. Furthermore he changed the name of the Family Planning programme, recommended that women eat herbs to prevent pregnancy, and wrecked whatever progress workers, both Indian and foreign, had made in trying to slow down the Indian population growth rate for the sake of national survival. He was vociferous, but then so were all the other new Ministers: Charan Singh, now Home Minister, was screaming for the heads of Mrs Gandhi and her son, and commissions were formed to inquire into the alleged crimes committed by the family during the emergency.

Jagjivan Ram had abandoned her before the elections: after her defeat most of the other Congress leaders, who had been with her since 1966, did so too. Chavan became the official Congress (R) leader, since Mrs Gandhi was without an electoral seat or a title, and Brahmananda Reddy, a notoriously inept man who had been Chief Minister of Andhra Pradesh in the south and was then brought to Delhi as Home Minister, perhaps because Mrs Gandhi felt he could do less damage under her own sharp eye, Congress President. Chavan became verbose about his former leader's misdeeds.

What amazed me about her at this point, in the summer of 1977, was how very much better she looked than I had ever seen her in the past. The pouches under her eyes, endemic in her since I first met her in 1968, had disappeared. She now had very bright eyes, and she looked younger and smiled more. It was the old instinct to fight anyone who was horrid to her, which had first manifested itself with her stepmotherly aunts. She likes a fight. Moreover, whenever I went to see her, there were always a number of Congressmen waiting on the verandah outside the reception room. There were also a large number of people not in the Congress costume of white *khadi* clothes and cap. I once said to her that most of these people looked very stupid. 'Of course they are not,' she snapped. 'These are the people who tell me news from small towns, from villages, people I want to hear from. How else do I keep in touch with what's going on?'

D. P. Singh was nearly always there, and I started to have an idea of my own about what was going on: that for the second time, Mrs Gandhi was planning to split the Congress party, and create a party of her own. I mentioned this idea to several foreign correspondent friends: they published it in their papers as a possibility: Mrs Gandhi denied it: my friends' editors berated them: my friends consequently berated me. I was certain of what would happen, and did not, at the time, answer the indignant accusations of my friends. I thought of a comment my agent had made when I first took him to meet Mrs Gandhi. 'When she first came through the door into that room,' he said, 'with the sunlight behind her and that white streak in her hair, I swear in all honesty, I thought she was wearing a crown.'

The point was that, once more, she intended to acquire one.

18

Upon a White Horse

MRS GANDHI MAY have been talking to politicians of her own party, but she had not yet addressed herself to the public at large, except to say that she accepted total responsibility for anything that had happened during the emergency. In the days that followed her defeat she was often to be seen at diplomatic parties in Delhi, functions which she had previously seldom attended, since she had never had the time. When politics re-entered her life, her social activity subsided once more. She was neither seen nor heard except by those who flocked to 12 Willingdon Crescent. This made the government nervous as to what she was up to. The elaborately casual loiterers on the dusty pavement outside her house were very conspicuous as Central Bureau of Intelligence officers. They obviously reported back to their new masters to say that Mrs Gandhi was busy in conferences related to her political future. That was really enough in itself to frighten the already unsettled Janata.

Also, since the expressed attitudes of the government somewhat resembled the attitudes of the French urban proletarians in 1789 towards the Bourbons subsequent to the revolution, it was intelligent of her not to speak to the people until a few months after her defeat. She must have been sure that the Janata would make a mess, and it did: it was when the first symptoms of this mess manifested themselves in shortages, increased prices, and increased crime rates, that Mrs Gandhi first started to come out and fight the people who were braying for her head. She mounted, metaphorically, the white horse of St Joan, and rode forth.

It was in the middle of 1977. After three months of sun-fire and dust from April, the sky loosens itself towards July and there is rain, normally a sparse and occasional scatter, sometimes preceded by a dust-storm. This particular July saw torrential rain, changing the countryside: the western part of Delhi, low ground cut into by canals, flooded: brown water ran happily about in the fields, gurgling and spitting like an infant harpy, sucked its way into village houses, placed itself in a loose coil around the waists of the peasants, and spewed itself upward, since it was a long way to the sea. Mrs Gandhi's people said she would visit the area. I asked if I could follow in a taxi. They said I could.

There was a train of cars and Land Rovers at Willingdon Crescent as dawn broke damply over the Himalayas and India. The door and window handles of my taxi had been stolen by some previous, needy, passenger and consequently the windows would not close, neither would the doors open except from outside. Mrs Gandhi saw me, answered my wave, climbed into a Land Rover, and started the caravan. The rain began again, having taken the night off, and I wondered if this trip was a good idea. Once we had entered the flood area we drove between acres of brown water, lapped by the wind. The rain fell harder and harder, driven by the wind through the unshuttable windows of my taxi until the floor was awash with mud and water. In this belligerent downpour, I lost all sight of the flotilla of cars ahead.

Presently, however, my taxi-driver stopped. I climbed out into knee-deep water which smelt as though every latrine in the area had disgorged its contents into the flood (since the villages of the area use their fields as latrines this was not surprising). Mud, or something glutinous, was under my feet, and because of the current, which kept deepening and widening as more rain fell and more and more canal banks collapsed, whatever I was standing on kept moving to and fro. In the distance I saw Mrs Gandhi surrounded by villagers. More villagers made exclamation marks above the scummed brown water with their black umbrellas, walking towards her Land Rover from all directions: some men, numerous women, and a few children. I thought I might also try and reach her. 'Sahib,' said my taxi-driver, who had been a soldier, 'it will not be possible for us to reach her in this taxi: it is not equipped for such situations.' I said I would walk. 'If you think you can walk in this mud and water for a quarter of a mile,' said the driver, 'you are mad, Sahib. It would take me an hour, and I have been a soldier. You are not a soldier.' He smiled delicately. 'You might even drown,' he said, 'on the way there.' The flood had now started to surge a bit, with the impetus of water from the broken canals, and the changing movement of the wind. I saw Mrs Gandhi, neat and composed, as the Land Rover beat up water like a sounding whale on its way to the horizon. She was an awfully long way ahead. Numbers of wet umbrellas crowded round me: I looked at the peasant faces, carved from warped brown wood, under them. Many of these faces belonged to women. I then discovered a schoolteacher who spoke a kind of English, and through him found out that most of these people thought that Mrs Gandhi was still the Prime Minister, and had never heard of Desai or the Janata party. 'Who else will help us?' said an elderly woman. 'I have not heard of Desai: he has not come here. She has come. She has seen. She will help.'

Some days later, a friend of mine, a Family Planning officer from Karnataka, arrived in Delhi for a conference. Through no fault of mine he calls me 'boss', having accompanied me through two trips in his state where I was, for my sins, in command of the expedition. 'Boss,' he said over lunch in our house, 'how will the programme for family planning succeed now the big boss has gone?' He meant Mrs Gandhi. I said, 'I don't know, I don't work for the U.N. now.' He said, 'Is all the work that we have done to mean nothing?' I said, 'I truly don't know.'

I told him I had to see Mrs Gandhi next morning. He said, 'Can I come with you? I mean, I will not interrupt, but I simply want to say to her that I extend my best wishes.' I had thought that Mrs Gandhi would possibly like this meeting, and also it would be a great occasion in my friend's life. Next day, therefore, I took him with me. He came into the reception room with his eyes full of tears. He did the southern *namaskar*, in which you bend deeply over your folded hands: the Aryan people of the north do it standing up straight. Mrs Gandhi blinked, and smiled, and did her *namaskar* in the southern style. I inquired where, if anywhere, she was going to appear in public next. She replied that she was going to visit her old constituency, Rae Bareilly. I asked if I could come. 'If you can get a train ticket,' she said. 'Otherwise come by plane. That's too expensive for me.'

Afterwards, my friend said to me, 'She is a lady like her father.' I replied, slightly amused, that her father had not been a lady. 'Yes, I am sorry, boss,' he said, 'she is a gentleman like her father. This Desai is not a lady or a gentleman.'

Mrs Gandhi set off for Lucknow by train, accompanied by a small and ferocious secretary, Miss Deshpande, who absolutely worships her employer, and a number of Congress workers. The purpose of her trip was avowedly simply to say hello to the people of Rae Bareilly, about two hours drive from Lucknow. At Delhi Airport, on my way out, I ran into a foreign correspondent who agreed to share my taxi from Lucknow to Rae Bareilly and back. Mrs Gandhi had told me she would be arriving at Lucknow railway station around 8 a.m.: since our plane came in around the same time, I told the driver to take us straight to the railway station. Neither my friend nor I could see much of the station, since it was a heaving mass of cheering people, impatient to see Mrs Gandhi. Having forced our way past them and the police barriers we saw her fly by, with D. P. Singh in attendance, and numerous other persons whom I did not know behind her. D. P. Singh had asked me to bring the morning papers from Delhi: I had left them on the plane: I apologised, and asked where she was off to at the moment. 'She will have breakfast,' said Mr Singh, pronouncing the word as most Indians do, in two words. 'Then we shall proceed to Rae Bareilly. You may come after her, you will soon catch us: there are rallies all down the road.' Meanwhile the crowd at the station was roaring like a sea, arms pumping up and down, banners flapping: Mrs Gandhi slipped into a car and the car slid through the people who stood with arms lifted and mouths open to cheer, live flesh frozen into Soviet statues. My correspondent friend and I breakfasted in the hotel we had booked into: we were in what had once been Oudh, the *talukdar* territory where Motilal had made his money.

After breakfast we started out through dun country, the trees slowly starting to lift their heads after the arrival of the rains. The road ran empty for many miles, until we saw ahead of us a stalled caravan of cars, and a flowered arch beyond them, at the entrance to the small town that awaited Mrs Gandhi, and we caught up at last, and there she was on a platform, shouting loudly because the microphone did not work, villagers all round her, the smell of dust and armpits and rotten fruit around us as we pushed into the crowd towards her. She shouted for five minutes, then disappeared amidst Congress volunteers and re-emerged in her car, which whipped off into the dusty road with heat haze floating on the macadam. Five minutes later there was another village where the microphone did work; later another and another: and in all of them the villagers crowded in to listen to her, mainly men, but also women. She floated past each flowered arch in her car: she climbed on the platform, pulled impatiently at the microphone: great stains of sweat appeared under her *choli*, dust fastened itself to her face, and she talked and talked, unfaltering, though I did not know what she was saying. The driver obliged with a translation. 'She is only asking, sirs, what has the Janata government done since they were elected? What did her government do?' The people stood in the roadway and cheered, threw flowers, and waved, as this strange cavalcade swept by towards Rae Bareilly, the constituency which had first accepted her husband, then her, and then, of all people, Raj Narain. The dust wrapped itself round the cars like a shroud.

Rae Bareilly itself has become an industrial town, a small one: factories smoke on the outskirts. Mrs Gandhi was awaited by thousands of anxious people: she shouted at them under the afternoon sun: then she went and had lunch. She had another meeting to come: meanwhile my friend and I lunched off chicken sandwiches, hard-boiled eggs and whisky, which Leela had providently packed, in a sort of government hostel next to the place in which Mrs Gandhi had lunched. 'Do you think,' my friend asked, 'we should stay on for the next meeting?' I said it might be as well to return to Lucknow and sleep, and then catch the plane back to Delhi, because, I thought, everything here would be a repetition of what had happened before. Meanwhile, I arranged for him to see Mrs Gandhi, to whom I introduced him, and she dustily blinked, muttered something, dashed off to wash, and returned, cool and capable once more, to finish the interview. We returned to Lucknow: Mrs Gandhi meanwhile trotted off into other areas of Uttar Pradesh.

I returned to Delhi to discover that more or less every important Indian newspaper had said that Mrs Gandhi had been met at Lucknow railway station by a widespread black flag demonstration (the production of a black flag in India indicates disapproval). Since Simon Winchester, who represented the *Guardian*, and I, who always represented myself, had been present while the crowds roared approval of Mrs Gandhi, I spoke to a number of editors and reporters in Delhi, saying that this kind of journalism was neither true nor fair: they drank my liquor and replied that the kind of journalism enforced on them by the emergency was not true or fair either: what did I expect them to do: they were paid little more than domestic servants. The implication was fairly obvious. I did not query it: slaves earn, at least, one's sympathy.

At about this point, I asked Mrs Gandhi and her family to dinner. She came, and it was obviously a release for her, in the sense that nobody discussed politics, and Leela, who is partly French, cooked a French dinner, and everybody liked it. Next day, one of the leading papers published, in a front page box, a story which said that Mrs Gandhi had been asked to dinner by us, that she had demanded numerous French dishes, that I had been so unnerved by these requests that I had asked a French diplomat for the services of his chef, that at the last moment I received a demand from Mrs Gandhi that I should not serve a certain kind of pudding, and this had led to the total disorganisation of the dinner. When I saw this item in the newspaper, I phoned Mrs Gandhi and said I would write a disclaimer, which I did. The editor would not publish it in full, but enough of it appeared to show that the original story had been a lie. Meanwhile, Mrs Gandhi, before she saw my disclaimer, wrote me a small, cold letter: I would not have believed that she thought I would have betrayed her with a lie but she, I knew, was accustomed to betrayal, though I was sorry to think she equated me with her political colleagues.

The difficulty, the delicacy, of dealing with such a person, so often hurt, so often betrayed, was compounded at the time by her alertness about everyone who surrounded her, her reluctance to be further hurt, further betrayed. It was not helped by the fact that innumerable people started to bring out books written in a few days and rushed into print, condemning her for numerous actions, some of which took place before the emergency. These books had instant rapid readerships, and were instantly forgotten: not by their authors, who piled up, by Indian standards, instant fortunes for their instant books. One was written by a handsome lady called Uma Vasudev, who a few months earlier had published a book in praise of Mrs Gandhi. Another by a Delhi reporter, Janardan Thakur, was unashamedly called *All the Prime Minister's Men*, after the Watergate best seller, *All the President's Men*. Shortly after that extraordinary volume was released upon the market, Thakur decided that he needed more ready cash or more publicity or both, and since the Janata had lost its credibility, produced a book called *All the Janata Men*. Badly documented, enormously exaggerated, hideously printed, the books came pouring out of every impecunious and untalented reporter who had ever been as much as spoken to by a policeman during the emergency.

'I never read any of it,' Mrs Gandhi once told me, but I am sure she does. When I have quoted accusations and allegations from these books, she appears to know where the quotations come from, her brows draw down, her lips purse, and she is not amused, though much of what I have to quote is very funny. Somebody with a sense of humour, probably, will one day write a book about all the books published in India about the emergency.

The Janata splits had meanwhile become more and more obvious. Not only was the government doing nothing except try to bring Mrs Gandhi to court, but within itself it fought sad, useless battles. Charan Singh, now Home Minister, was a Jat, and the Jats are a kind of tribe of farmers: Charan Singh therefore felt that the future of the country lay in rural improvement. Raj Narain, Health Minister, felt the same way. They said so. George Fernandes in the Industry Ministry, Jagjivan Ram, lonely and betrayed in the Defence Ministry, and other minor Ministers, felt, like Nehru and his daughter, that the future of the country lay in industry. These Ministers said so. Desai, the ambition of thirty years achieved, talked about nothing except urine therapy and prohibition. Some of these Ministers were so angry with one another that they refused to enter into any kind of conversation which was not abusive.

Mrs Gandhi, much more intelligent than any of them, curled up and waited.

'I am going to Kashmir,' she told me in the reception room. I asked if I could come. 'Yes,' she said, 'if you can get seats: this time bring Leela,' smiling rather brightly. 'Last time you came to Lucknow you looked miserable. It's a nice time of year for a young couple.' I said that with my fortieth birthday not far off, I did not think of myself, at least, as young. 'Humph,' she said (it is one of her characteristic noises), but I cannot reproduce it accurately in print.

A few days later we found ourselves savouring the autumn air in Kashmir. We attended a performance of local dances which was held in Mrs Gandhi's honour at a Srinagar school. She was perched on an unsteady platform with her own people and Kashmir notables, while the children cavorted formally in front of her. Leela and I were seated on chairs to the left of the platform. I kept looking back at Mrs Gandhi to see how she reacted to the performance: if it bored her, she would certainly show it. It obviously did not: say

smiled and applauded, and at one point beckoned Leela up on to
the platform and whispered to her. '*Those* costumes,' she said,
pointing, 'are typical of Muslims in Kashmir, and *those* are typical
of Kashmiri Brahmins.' I watched all this from afar, mystified by
this sudden summons of my wife, wondering if something awful
had happened, especially when I saw them with their heads together, whispering, Leela pointing at an old lady of harmless and
dignified appearance in the crowd, Mrs Gandhi nodding solemnly.
When we eventually left, I said to Leela, 'What was *that* all about?'
She explained about the costumes, and added, 'Did you see the old
lady? I thought she looked exactly like Motilal's wife, Mrs G's
grandmother you know, Swarup Rani, and I told Mrs G. that, and
she had a look and agreed with me.'

Between all these feminine confidences, Mrs Gandhi made a small
speech, the rainclouds overhead lifted, and a rush of women and
children nearly lifted her off her feet. For someone who I had always
thought did not like to be touched, she responded to their awestruck,
small caressive hands with an enormous and captivating smile. The
smile reappeared when, one wet afternoon, waiting at her guest
house for her to emerge, I received a summons to come up. On the
balcony, looking out over the weeping flowers on the lawn, Mrs
Gandhi stood with her secretary and two slightly unkempt Kashmiri
men. 'You know,' she said, 'you should talk to them.' They turned
out to be hirers of horses from the nearby valley of Pahalgam,
Nehru's favourite holiday resort, a father and son, who had come
down by bus to pay their respects. 'I've known them since the
children were small,' said Mrs Gandhi, 'and we all used to come up
to Pahalgam when my father had the time for holidays.' The men
had to leave in a few minutes to catch a bus back, so I suggested I
should come to Pahalgam and meet them in a day or two.

I hired a car to climb the steep roads, between mountains hairy
with enormous stands of pine, and ravines littered with rocks, to
Pahalgam. The horsemen awaited us, and escorted us to a rift in the
valley, where there were trees, bright water over rocks, and a certain
air of solitude. 'Here,' they said, 'we used to pitch the tents when
Jawaharlalji and his family came. We knew the boys when they were
small: we taught them how to ride. Indiraji would ride, but she
liked to walk better. She liked to walk long distances. She is a great
lady: when we heard she had lost the elections we wept.' The whole
place, apart from its silence, had its smell, of grass, stone, water,

flowers, trees. I saw where Mrs Gandhi had acquired her idea of a solitary cottage in the mountains. But as we turned away, vans came, bearing the advance unit of an Indian feature film crew, and the high crisp air filled with loud voices, the dewed turf was strewn with cigarette stubs. Soon a simian film hero and his hugely, though perhaps synthetically busted heroine would be capering amidst rocks and trees. Though younger than Mrs Gandhi, I could have told her that all dreams are meant to be destroyed. But she had been happy in Kashmir, with her dream.

D. P. Singh, according to his own version, was steadily intent on bringing Mrs Gandhi back to the political peaks after her sojourn on lower levels. In Delhi, she made her first formal public appearance since her defeat in a large hall, where senior members of the Congress were present on the platform with her. These people, who included Brahmananda Reddy, the Congress President, had been openly debating what they should do about her expulsion from the Congress. They felt it was the penalty she should pay for having brought the party to such a total defeat. I was in the front row with my friend Jag Parvesh Chandra: the TV cameras were massed in front of the platform and there were newspaper cameramen and reporters all over the place. The hall, which seated about a thousand people, was packed, with many standing spectators. The platform was also packed with nervous Congressmen. Mrs Gandhi, obviously wanting to let them sweat, arrived late. Charan Singh had been shouting for her blood, and her first remark, when on reaching the platform and the microphone, and being instantly surrounded on all sides by walls of cameramen and reporters, was that thus enclosed, she felt herself to be in prison already. This evoked laughter and cheers, the tone of which was sympathetic: and now, having made herself comfortable at the microphone as a great batsman shakes his pads comfortable when he comes to the crease, she launched herself at the audience, her shots in front of the wicket perfectly timed, bringing a laugh or a cheer, but her cuts perfectly timed too, when she whipped round like a viper at the fat and seedy Congressmen seated tremulously on the platform, each strike of her tongue bringing a cringe and shudder. Not only did she, as usual, accuse the Janata government for lack of performance, but she lashed the party men for stupidity and disloyalty. I realised once more that I had been right in what I had said to my correspondent friends earlier: she intended to build a new party, and because of this she had no scruples in breaking the old.

My wife went off to visit her parents in Bombay, and I asked Mrs Gandhi to dinner. Since I thought she would like to relax, my other guests were friends from the British Council, and an Indian poet who writes in English with immense promise, Arvind Kumar Mehrotra. The others arrived some while before she did. We were all sitting around, a bit uneasily, though we were all friends, when suddenly the bearer pulled open the door of the drawing room and said, in Hindi, 'Madamji has arrived.' None of my guests had ever met her before, hence the initial unease: they expected a huge presence: what they never expected was a small presence, neat and a little nervous, in the doorway, saying, 'I'm sorry if I'm late.' She took a little time to settle, then she started to talk to Muriel Gunton about the extraordinary price of fruit in the Delhi markets. Arvind Mehrotra showed her his latest book of poems which she read expressionlessly and returned without comment, but then she entered into a discussion with Dennis Gunton, Arvind Mehrotra and myself about the difficulties of Indian poets who write in English. We came to no conclusion: I remembered that addressing a rally in Kashmir she had had some difficulty in translating English phrases into Hindi. But that evening she was Indu, and not Indira: a tired child when she left, not a harassed woman.

It was now quite obvious that the Congress (R) party would break. Those months of talk in the reception room had led only one way. When Brahmananda Reddy announced in December 1978, that Mrs Gandhi had been expelled from the Congress party (Chavan approved heartily) she announced that *she* was the Congress party. Then Congress (I) I for Indira, or as one sardonic commentator said, I for myself, was formed. This meant there were now three Congress parties: Desai's which though merged into the Janata, still existed: Chavan's: and Mrs Gandhi's. The famous election symbol of the cow and calf, after some acrimonious discussion, remained with Chavan's party: Mrs Gandhi adopted the symbol of an up-raised hand. In India, visually understandable symbols are important since the voters are mainly illiterate, which is why Mrs Gandhi was chagrined at the loss of the cow and calf. The hand, as someone said to me, would only remind the voters of a traffic policeman. Be that as it may, Congress (I) immediately began to make a political impact, for by now the people were becoming rather tired of the Janata. Not only had the government done nothing, but its members were in such conflict that it was unlikely that anything would ever be done.

When they had done something it turned out to be a colossal blunder. Charan Singh, the Home Minister, the most vociferous of those who wanted to put Mrs Gandhi in prison, was the person responsible. I was ill and in bed on the evening of October 2 1977 when a friend phoned to say that she had passed by Willingdon Crescent and it was full of policemen: her own impression was that Mrs Gandhi had been arrested. I tried to reach the house by telephone but the line seemed to have been cut: then I phoned Jag Parvesh to ask if he had heard anything about an arrest. He had not, but shortly afterwards called me back to say it was true. He was going to the house, would I like to come? I was too ill, but Leela went instead. By the time they arrived Mrs Gandhi had been taken away, followed by her family. The grandchildren had been left in the house, weeping and demanding of the servants who the horrible people were who had taken their grandmother away. Among the others present was Rukhsana Sultana, making phone calls to all her friends.

It was a pity Jag and Leela had not arrived earlier: for there can seldom have been a more comical scene in modern India than that of Mrs Gandhi's arrest. The house was surrounded by the police: a very embarrassed senior officer went into the reception room to inform her of the situation. He apparently did not have a certain document which was necessary to make the arrest, and Mrs Gandhi demanded, justifiably, that he should produce it; also that she should be allowed time to pack. It took the police some time to obtain the document, and it took Mrs Gandhi some time to pack. In fact these two separate activities between them occupied five hours, which meant that she had plenty of time to call in the press and the radio and television people. According to an eye witness who worked in the house, the time was also used to despatch a driver to a Ministry to collect certain files. These were brought, though why the police did not observe their arrival does not seem to me very clear. When the files came, if my informant is to be believed, another highly comic scene was enacted. Sonia, Rajiv's wife, possesses a small machine for cutting noodles, which she brought from Italy. The

papers from the files were placed in the noodle machine and sliced
up by two members of the household, then hastily conveyed to the
back of the house to an area where the gardeners burn dead leaves,
and destroyed. Meanwhile, Mrs Gandhi was in her bedroom with
Usha Bhagat, her former social secretary, who was helping her to
pack, and the police were in the front of the house. When the press
arrived, Mrs Gandhi came back to the reception room.

Mrs Pandit has recorded that while they were together in prison
in 1942–3, Indira and her own daughter Chandralekha amused
themselves by acting in plays which they made up. Now, more than
three decades later, Mrs Gandhi mounted the boards once more.
She appeared in her favoured persona of Joan of Arc, and, once the
cameramen were in position, stretched her arms out to the police
officers and said, 'Handcuff me.' The police officers were reluctant
to do so: she insisted that it should be done. After a great deal of
kerfuffle, the police finally refused. By this time the media had
obtained a lot of copy. Mrs Gandhi then, obligingly, said she would
leave with the officers, and drove off with them, followed by her
family in a van. The police apparently intended to take her across
the border into Haryana, the state she had helped to create. It is
not very far from Delhi proper, but the family did not feel she should
be taken there. A couple of miles from the border, therefore, Sanjay
swerved the van across the road to block the police car which
contained his mother and her secretary, the indomitable Miss
Deshpande. A long altercation followed between members of the
family, lawyers they had brought with them, and the rather pathetic
policemen, who had no idea what to do. Mrs Gandhi, meanwhile,
stepped delicately out of the police car, sat on the culvert, and
admired the beauty of the evening sky. Eventually it was decided to
convey her back to Delhi and put her in a police station there. This
was done. Mrs Gandhi and Miss Deshpande were put into a room
in the station, where, taking a leaf out of Desai's book, she refused to
eat or drink anything not provided by the family. She read for most
of the night.

In the morning she was supposed to be produced at Tees Hazari
Court, which is near my bank in Delhi. I thought I should be
present. I needed some money: I thought I would drop in at the
bank and then cross the road to Tees Hazari. In the taxi, my
temperature still high, I closed my eyes: then awoke to a thunderous
roar of voices. The entire road leading to the court and my bank was

full of a high tide of screaming people with banners, and with riot
police. No traffic, as my driver informed me, could enter it. There
were Janata banners and Congress banners, and the members of
each party were yelling their slogans. The Janata people were
shouting '*Indira Gandhi murdabad*', that is to say, 'Death to Indira
Gandhi.' The Congress were shouting '*Indira Gandhi zindabad.
Indira Gandhi desh ka neta*': 'Long live Indira Gandhi, leader of
the nation.'

I got out of the taxi. I had forced my way through the crowd to
the doors of the bank when the police made a baton charge. I found
myself lifted on an enormous wave of people: it lifted me through
the doors of the bank, which was fortunate as the police started
using tear gas. The grilles of the bank doors were dropped. Outside
the crowds were running from the police, who were apparently in
one of their more ferocious moods. I asked my bank manager, who
was standing with me at a window, what all this was about: he said,
'They've released her.'

Not only had the court released her, but, having asked the
government lawyers what the charges against her were, and having
been told it would take some months to formulate them, it had
released her unconditionally. She went home with her suitcase,
Miss Deshpande, and her family. When the grilles were opened, I
went into a street that stank of gas and people, rediscovered my
frightened taxi-driver, and went to Willingdon Crescent to see how
she was. The garden was packed with people but in India you get
used to crowds. Jag Parvesh was there too. 'So many people were
wounded this morning,' he said. 'Mrs Gandhi is leaving tonight for
Karnataka, but I have asked her to come to the hospital to meet them.
She is coming.' At this point Mrs Gandhi appeared on the balcony
and smiled at me.

'How do you feel, ma'am?' I said. 'What's it like to spend a night
in prison?' She said, 'Oh, it wasn't really prison. I know what real
prison is like.' I do not think she does, assuming that what Mrs
Pandit says of Mrs Gandhi's prison life is true. Yet there she was,
with that alternate frown and smile, with the crowds shouting on
the lawn.

At one point, Uma Vasudev came in. As I have said, she first
wrote an extremely complimentary book about Mrs Gandhi, and
after the 1977 elections a very uncomplimentary one which made a
lot of rupees. I have seldom seen a more extraordinary sight, outside

tribal Africa, than what happened that day in the garden. There were people dancing, screaming slogans, their arms waving, all dressed in simple cotton clothes. Into this came Miss Vasudev clad in a red silk sari. There was an enormous rush of people towards her, shouting '*Uma Vasudev murdabad*'. I saw this from the balcony and said to a Congress worker, 'Shouldn't we go out and help her?' He asked if I wanted to be killed by the Congress people. She was lifted up by some of these Congress people, pushed into her car, and told to leave. I pointed out to Mrs Gandhi, standing nearby, that Miss Vasudev might come to some harm. Mrs Gandhi did not reply. She smiled.

Miss Vasudev departed, dishevelled but unhurt. Mrs Gandhi then climbed into her own car. She drove to the hospital to talk to her wounded workers. There were so many cheering spectators at the hospital that I could not follow her in. But I was at the gate when her car came out, to take her to the airport. A mass of people surrounded me, all shouting, '*Indira Gandhi zindabad*'. She was looking out at them in a rather uninterested way, but nobody could doubt that she had made a triumphal return.

The Indian public has a curious respect for people who have been political prisoners. It does not seem to matter who actually imprisoned them, nor does it seem to matter what sort of people they actually are. Congressmen imprisoned by the British who later became important officials could be accused, and rightly, of corruption and nepotism, but the length of their prison sentences seemed to mitigate their offences in the public eye. This also operated in the case of the Janata. The fact that the opposition leaders had all been imprisoned by Mrs Gandhi brought them considerable public sympathy. Now that they had arrested Mrs Gandhi on charges which they had not even drawn up properly, the sympathy of the public was with her. The government, as usual, had achieved the exact opposite of what it had set out to do. It had brought Mrs Gandhi back.

It now proceeded to do other silly things. The passports of the entire family were impounded, on the grounds that no citizen could have a passport if a court case was pending against him or her: though no official charges had been brought against any member of the family. The flying licences of Sanjay and Maneka were suspended, presumably in case Sanjay tried to fly his mother out of the country in a Cessna: Rajiv, who was an airline pilot and therefore far more likely to be able to export Mrs Gandhi illegally, was not deprived of his licence since his livelihood depended on it. Sonia could not fly anyway. Mrs Gandhi innocently sat in Willingdon Crescent and asked where the government thought she would go. Actually she did want to go to France, where the O.R.T.V. had asked her to appear in a series of television programmes. The French Ambassador in Delhi and his wife had expressed their eagerness to meet her. I conveyed this message to her one morning. She said, without replying to the invitation, 'If you know people at the Embassy, tell them to telex O.R.T.V. and say I can't come.' I thought it peculiar that she could not do this herself, but, since I was not going to the Embassy anyway, trotted home to telephone. It was lunchtime, nobody was at the Embassy: I suddenly received a call from Mrs Gandhi. 'Have you telephoned?' she inquired, and when I said not yet, replied, 'Good. There's no need to. Thank you.'

I hung up. Then I reflected on my relationship with Mrs Gandhi, and why I felt, deep within myself, the need to present her with books and flowers: why, when she issued crisp instructions, I felt, deep in myself, the need to follow them. I decided I was not unlike the political people who had followed her for years. The books and flowers were motivated by her smallness, her frailty, her apparent helplessness: when the orders came, one carried them out because they were so decisively delivered, by someone accustomed to power, even though they were small orders. Nearly all those who had carried out her large orders had become Judases. If you pick up a songbird and it suddenly shouts at you, the shock must be really traumatic: you must want to throw it down and trample on it: perhaps I would not, but given the temperament of most of the Congress politicians, I am sure they would.

D. P. Singh said to me, at one point, 'You see, you see.' They arrest her and they must release her. The party is winning all over the country. How can you say she will not come back?' We were having a drink in his house and I had never said she would not come back, but Indians are addicted to rhetoric. The commissions of inquiry had started: I asked what Mr Singh thought would happen to her. 'Nothing. Nothing,' he said.

What later interested me deeply was what happened to D. P. Singh himself.

19

Sins of Commission

JUSTICE J. C. SHAH had at one point been the Chief Justice of India. He was a somewhat irascible old man with a particularly virulent dislike of Mrs Gandhi, and he was appointed in May 1977 to be the Chairman (since he was the only member, the title did not seem to be strictly necessary) of a Commission which was to investigate any excesses committed during the emergency, and to allocate the blame for them to specific individuals. Numbers of former Ministers and officials appeared before him in a series of court sittings. They testified against one another: they blamed Sanjay: they blamed Mrs Gandhi. Some wept on the witness stand. Most of the former Ministers denied knowledge of the arrests, the sterilisations, the demolitions: Sanjay and Mrs Gandhi, they said, should bear all responsibility. The name of R. K. Dhavan, the Assistant Private Secretary to the former Prime Minister, cropped up continually. Mrs Gandhi meanwhile refused absolutely to testify before the Commission. The questions the Commission wanted to ask her about were relatively minor matters: appointments she had made and unmade, a handful of detentions, and the events that had taken place between June 12 and 25 1975, that is in the fortnight before she declared the emergency. Compared to what Charan Singh, Raj Narain, and other Janata spokesmen had accused her of, these eleven inquiries seemed exceptionally mild. Three times Justice Shah called on Mrs Gandhi to appear and answer: three times she refused. On the occasion of the third postponement, she released a statement to the press, through a lawyer, which was the cause, not unnaturally, of much comment.

In it she referred to 'a continuing process of character assassination and political denigration' against her. A former Minister of hers, T. A. Pai, who had testified against her, came in for a severe attack, somewhat below the belt. She referred to his statement as 'wholly incorrect', then added, 'in fact, I had received complaints of corruption against Pai himself and members of his family and on the repeated insistence of the complainants had referred them to the C.B.I. for discreet inquiries.' She wound up by saying, 'I feel that no useful purpose will be served by my participation in these proceedings. If [the Commission] decides, however, to hold the inquiry in accordance with law and in the course thereof summons me as a witness, I shall abide by its directive.'

Pai replied that Mrs Gandhi refused to appear before the Commission because she did not dare to. Justice Shah cogitated over her statement, then said if there turned out to be *prima facie* evidence against any persons for commission of excesses during the emergency, he would summon them: at this point in the hearings their presence was not necessary. But this protracted refusal on her part to appear led to a certain amount of agreement, by the public, with Pai's statement: so eventually, in early January 1978, she did appear, in a court packed with people, of whom I was unfortunately not one. Her counsel started out by saying that the whole inquiry had been caused by a political vendetta. Justice Shah asked Mrs Gandhi if she would file a statement. She replied that she was not legally bound to. He asked her a second time, and she refused. She later said the oath of secrecy she had taken as Prime Minister forbade her to divulge anything connected with the internal processes of her government. She also said she was not constitutionally bound to file any kind of statement either. Furthermore, she said, when she had nationalised the banks and certain judges were opposed to this move as unconstitutional, there had been a move among the M.P.s for impeachment of these arbiters of the law, and it had been she alone who stopped it. This was a typical veer into an offensive position, though what this had to do with the Commission as such she did not state. Justice Shah, surprisingly, leapt to the bait. 'I never was a shareholder of any bank,' he said, 'at the time that case was heard.' He added, 'Some people have made that allegation. It is a false allegation.' Mrs Gandhi having won the round, murmured, 'But I never mentioned you at all.' Justice Shah, unwisely for a lawyer, continued to defend himself against charges she had not made.

On January 19 she appeared a second time, more aggressive now, and said that she would not answer any further questions, which made her appearance seem rather a waste of everybody's time. The whole court had taken on the aspect of a circus, and because of the unintentionally comic statements made by witnesses and lawyers, there was constant mirth amidst the spectators. An example of this was when Mrs Gandhi first appeared. Her lawyer, Frank Anthony, an ancient and famous person of Eurasian descent, decided to tell a story. He said that in British times, a judge had once mildly chided him for taking on the defence of a notorious criminal. 'I replied,' said Mr Anthony, 'what decent person would come to me for his defence?' The whole audience looked towards a frozen Mrs Gandhi and exploded into laughter.

The cases before the Commission were many and curious. Obviously the arrests and the erstwhile beautification programme, which had involved so much demolition of slums, and the sterilisation programme, were exceptionally important to the Commission. But a number of other murky corners of Mrs Gandhi's government were having their contents swept out into public view. There was the business of Maruti. There was also a matter of the systematic persecution of a textile firm called Pandit Brothers, which belonged to the family of P. N. Haksar, once the best adviser Mrs Gandhi ever had, later in disfavour. It was also alleged that a feature film called 'Kissa Kursi Ka', which means 'The Story of a Chair (or throne)', which was supposed to be a political allegory on the emergency, was seized by V. C. Shukla, then Minister of Information, and burnt by Sanjay. There were numerous other allegations, but they seemed to build up less against Mrs Gandhi than against her son.

The one case in which there seemed to be a cloud of witnesses was that of the burnt film. It was not supposed to be a particularly marvellous film, but since it had been made (and paid for) its producers naturally felt some ire at its total destruction. Sanjay, with a host of cases against him, was first and most importantly confronted by this one. Charan Singh, grimly pleased, but disappointed in the non-event of Mrs Gandhi's arrest, watched, through his small, almost Chinese eyes, from the Home Ministry. Sanjay's sentence, on one charge or the other, was sure. Mrs Gandhi, however, seemed once more to have slipped the hook and swum out into an open sea, borne outward from the seines in which she had been trapped. 'Aren't you admiring?' Miss Deshpande asked me once, as I stood on the balcony outside the reception room, wedged between the enormous aircooler festooned in wire and a number of Congressmen, 'aren't you admiring?' Yes, I said, I was admiring.

Presently an old friend of mine, James Cameron, arrived from London with his Indian wife to make a television film for the B.B.C. about thirty years of Indian independence. He interviewed Desai and the others in the government and asked Mrs Gandhi for an interview, which she declined. Jim sat on a chair in my flat with that known wry smile, the pacemaker acquired after his accident in the Bangladesh war doubtless fluttering his heart, sipping vodka and being funny. 'I'd like to see her,' he said. Though I was not, and had never represented myself to be, a sort of bridge between other writers and Mrs Gandhi, I phoned and asked. Mrs Gandhi said rather crossly, 'The B.B.C. has always been hostile to me.' I said, 'Ma'am, James Cameron is a very great journalist, he was a friend of your father's: he isn't actually the B.B.C.' Presently, grumpily (I had disturbed her at dinner) she said, 'Oh, all right. Someone will phone you.' Someone did. They said, 'Madamji will see Mr Cameron at seven in the morning. She would like you to come.' I didn't know if the B.B.C. would like me to, but Jimmy, the bottle of vodka nearly finished, said, 'Oh, my dear boy, do.' His director, Tony Isaacs, seemed less happy about my accompanying the team, but eventually we all got to Willingdon Crescent. Chairs were arranged on a side lawn: the crew stumbled about the dew-moist turf with heavy equipment. Jimmy arrived, seated himself in one of the two chairs arranged for the interview, and Mrs Gandhi came out of the house in a pink sari.

She smiled. Tony Isaacs asked if I could sit in her chair so that the cameraman could position the shot: I pointed out that I was a lot taller than she was. The shot was positioned, fixed, and the cameras started to run: meanwhile, I went and looked at the flowers. Presently Tony Isaacs said, 'Cut,' and came to me and said, 'Can you tell me what the hell is happening?' I said that he should know. 'They seem,' he said unbelievingly, 'to be talking about Indian folk art. This programme is about Indian politics. Sit behind them when I next start the cameras. You wouldn't be seen, but listen and tell me.' I squatted behind the chairs, where the cameras would not catch me, and listened. They *were* talking about Indian folk art. This went on for many minutes. Presently Tony said, 'Cut' once more, and that was all the B.B.C. collected from Mrs Gandhi. However, when she doesn't want to speak, she doesn't speak: she makes her rapid, elusive and evasive movements, unpredictably.

At about this time she gave David Frost a long interview: she talked freely to him without, apparently, realising that a man devoted to this sort of work was probably more elusive and evasive than she could ever be. Knowing Frost, I later told her that she was probably ill-advised to have allowed the interview. She did one of her 'Humphs', then subsided into silence, which clearly meant it was none of my business, and indeed it was not.

The reason I had made my comment was because of an affection I had always had for her, which was turning into a close care, an anxiety that she should come through unhurt. She has had this effect, not only on men but on women, through most of her life. It is an effect not only charismatic but hypnotic, inexplicable in a way. That is why, when she suddenly puts on her hard outer carapace, those who throw themselves at her with good advice and sympathy tend to ricochet so far that they are the ones who are hurt.

At one point in the middle of 1978 I saw a piece in the morning paper saying D. P. Singh had announced that he was about to abandon Mrs Gandhi. We met that evening, and I forgave him all the small difficulties he had caused me in the past because his eyes were red and full of tears. This was in his house, which he once told me he occupied with forty-two members of his family, though I never met any of them. We sat in his bedroom because, he said, we could not drink anywhere else. He was a Congressman and he could not be seen drinking alcohol. Here he opened a bottle of Scotch. 'You know,' he said, 'she was in the gutter after the elections. It was I who lifted her up, and by my advice I made her rise to where she is now. I have gone, and she will fall. She is a woman with a mediocre mind, and she does not know good from evil.' He was sweating a lot, and, in his emotion, stuttering. He is normally a man of exceptionally suave manner. I inquired the reasons for his break with Mrs Gandhi.

Apparently there was a vacant seat in the Rajya Sabha. It would, said Mr Singh, have required no more than a word from Mrs Gandhi to enable him to obtain the party nomination and capture this seat, a safe one. She had refused to speak the word. 'After all I have done for her,' he said. 'After all I have done for her!' We were back in the medieval courts, and the vizier had not been awarded due recognition. Of course, in the medieval courts, he might by this time have been trampled by an elephant rather than be sitting with me lamenting and consuming Scotch. I said, 'If you think she has a mediocre mind, and she doesn't know good from evil, why did you work for her so long?' He only shrugged.

A little later I mentioned Mr Singh to Mrs Gandhi. She was curled up in her chair in the reception room, and smiling, but at the mention of D. P. Singh the smile froze and her eyelid flickered. 'He was not a suitable person,' she said, 'for me to nominate to a seat.' Once more, but the other way round, I inquired why, if D. P. Singh had served her for a long time, she should not have offered him some recompense. Why wasn't he suitable? She said icily, 'He was simply not suitable.' A few days later, on Mrs Gandhi's verandah, I encountered Mr Singh once more. He clutched one of my rather sweaty hands in both his. 'I am waiting for an interview,' he said. 'She has kept me waiting for some time. Let us meet tonight and drink some whisky.' At this moment I turned my head and saw, at the far end of the verandah, Mrs Gandhi, who had come out of the reception room. There were about fifty other people on the verandah, but her eyes were riveted on D. P. Singh and myself, clutching each other's hands, and her eyes under their kestrel hoods were like ice and fire.

Pantnagar is a small town about four hours drive from Delhi. Here there is a kind of agricultural college, which employs a large number of local workers in its fields. These workers were not overpaid, and in late April of 1978 there was some agitation among them for higher wages and overtime. The government of Uttar Pradesh, where this place is, moved in a Jat battalion of the P.A.C.—the armed police— from Meerut. The Jats are traditional enemies of everyone but the Jats—Charan Singh, incidentally, is a Jat—and the P.A.C. opened fire upon the discontented workers. According to press reports, the number killed was around 300. According to Charan Singh, who was not there, and who, when invited to inspect the spot, came as far as Lucknow, where he remained, the number killed was twelve. He then returned to Delhi: meanwhile local people reported that the P.A.C. had burnt a number of corpses in the fields of the agricultural college. The charred bones were recovered, and since they were unidentifiable, they were sent away for identification and analysis as to the cause of death. These remnants of living things unluckily disappeared: and Charan Singh, from Delhi, declared them to be the bones of hyenas killed in the accidentally ignited fields. There were two dubious aspects to this statement: the fields were open on

all sides, and no animal would have stood still awaiting its cremation:
also, even more cogent, there are no hyenas in the area. The Home
Ministry said Charan Singh had meant foxes: but sadly, there are
no foxes there either. When, eventually, the Home Ministry said he
meant jackals, the bones had disappeared, but Charan Singh's lack
of English or zoology had caused a considerable delay. The Pantnagar
students were begging for help.

Upon this scene of violence, Mrs Gandhi decided to descend.
She set off from Delhi in an air-conditioned blue Mercedes, alone
in it, followed by the usual cavalcade of cars, which included a red
Fiat full of Sikhs with rifles, and a large Matador van which held,
among others, my wife and myself. We shook and roared along the
by no means excellent roads into Uttar Pradesh. I have the habit of
watching what passes me, as I travel, through eyes which appear to
be asleep: on the road, apart from several dogs and other animals
crushed into unidentifiable tatters of red flesh, there were two overturned lorries, and at one point a dead woman. There was blood all
over the road, but someone had been kind enough to cover her
face with her sari. Presently we arrived at what appeared to be the
entry village into the Pantnagar area, and a government bungalow
where Mrs Gandhi was supposed to stop for brief refreshment.

Here there were large, noisy crowds cheering with a sound like
Niagara Falls. Mrs Gandhi was ushered inside. We tried to force
our way through the roarers after her. We were not allowed to, by
stern Congress workers, until we had proved our identity. While we
were doing this, I observed a young man, almost in tears, begging
one of the Congress workers to allow him to see Mrs Gandhi, to
whom he had something to say: only she could help. The Congress
worker said, 'No,' he certainly could not. The boy cried, 'It's
people like you who destroyed her in the elections. You are the ones
who wouldn't let her listen to what we were trying to say.' I was too
preoccupied with my own problems of getting to her to help him
get to her: but having eventually mounted the stairs, Leela and I
found her, small and irate, amidst a crowd of Congress workers.
She smiled faintly, and to my surprise, when I held out my right
hand to shake hers, responded with the little finger of her left hand.
'I have hurt my fingers,' she said, answering the astonishment in
my eyes. We then sat down at a long table covered in tea-pots and
oranges in dishes and surrounded by Congress workers. Mrs Gandhi,
who was opposite me, her head held sideways in her hand, continued

to seem unpleased with matters. 'I have better oranges in my car,' she told somebody. 'Get them.' When these were produced, she said to me, 'Will you have one?' I replied that I only ate oranges in liquid form, and she humphed. She then said to my wife, who was asking for the bathroom, 'There's only a tiny piece of soap, but I have some somewhere.' My wife said thanks but no, on this kind of trip she always carried her own. She disappeared. Mrs Gandhi sat amidst the Congressmen looking not only more and more irate, but, which I had reason to know was a worse sign, more and more sleepily bored. Maneka was somewhere around, covering the whole business for her magazine *Surya*. Mrs Gandhi kept inquiring in a bored voice where she was.

A small boy then appeared, hung a garland on her, and knelt to touch her feet. Her irritation was not improved by this. He was given the benefit of a long lecture on why nobody should touch other people's feet: it was a sign of degradation from which Indians must recover. Afterwards she fiddled with an orange. Trying to lighten the atmosphere clouded by the Congress workers around (it was obviously with them, and the slowness of her progress to Pantnagar proper, that she appeared so exasperated), I said, 'That was an awful road, wasn't it? The dead woman, and those animals which had been run over, and the overturned trucks?' She smiled suddenly, and said, 'I always sleep in cars. It's the only time I have. Where is Maneka? Where's Leela? Can't we leave?' Since I had no answer to any of these queries, I went and asked various people, none of whom had any answer either. Presently I discovered Maneka and my wife on the balcony looking down at the huge crowd beneath, who were all shouting, '*Indira ki jai!*'

I went back and told her, and the whole caravan set off afresh.

In Pantnagar we were invited to inspect a coagulated pool of blood and brains, fed on by many flies, which had been preserved so that Mrs Gandhi could see it: to look at the bullet-marks in walls, which were not wildly exciting: and to talk to various people who had witnessed the firing. Mrs Gandhi, as usual, sped around in her sandals like Hermes, almost too fast to follow. She paused only to make a speech which was noisily cheered by an audience of students, professors, and peasants. She berated the government, also as usual. What seemed remarkable was how quickly her quietness changed into violent noise, once she was up on a dais with a crowd in front of her. With us on this trip was a friend of ours, the writer Bruce Chatwin, who was doing a long piece about her for the London *Sunday Times*. He expressed his amazement to me, not only about how very shrill the lady could be when confronted by a crowd, but also because she left herself so open to assassination. The Sikhs with their rifles, in the red car, were apparently none of hers: they had been provided by the state government, anxious lest she should be killed in their manor. That afternoon I said something about this to Mrs Gandhi, who, eating an orange with considerable relish, failed to reply, except to say what I took to be 'Um-ah', a tribute, surely, to the fruit. However, it was interpreted to me: she had said 'Azamgarh', a constituency in the U.P., where there was another by-election. Her new party had won in the south: if it could now start to win in the north, there was every reason for the Janata leaders to tremble in their *dhotis*. I could not, for various reasons, accompany her to Azamgarh, but Bruce arranged to, with his photographer, the famous Eve Arnold.

Before the Azamgarh trip, Bruce and Eve went south with Mrs Gandhi. She had stones hurled at her car, none of which hit her, but one of which hit Bruce on the shoulder. This event made him even more surprised that she should leave herself so open to possible assassination. Azamgarh came next, a dusty little town in the full blaze of the north Indian summer: a boil of heat and correspondents. Eve, suffering from the heat, was at one point accommodated by Mrs Gandhi in an air-conditioned room, the only one for miles, which at that moment had been reserved for Mrs Gandhi herself. Eve returned to Delhi, svelte in her slacks. 'I don't know what she may or mayn't have done as a politician,' she said. 'I only know that she's a very nice woman and I like her a lot.' On the plane back from Benares, Mrs Gandhi had invited Eve to sit beside her: they had talked a lot over the asthmatic roar of the engines, Mrs Gandhi mainly about the current problems of Sanjay.

Meanwhile, certain other problems had surfaced about the son of another Indian Prime Minister: this was Kantilal, the son of Desai. Kantilal was by no means a young man, and even in the years when Sanjay was at school, the offspring of the man dedicated to prohibition had been attacked because of his alleged alcoholic attachments and his allegedly questionable attitudes towards money. Desai had now made Kantilal abandon his business interests and appointed him a personal secretary. Kantilal was now under his father's eye, supposedly a model of rectitude: but the accusations made against him in the past had never been refuted, because they had never been pressed. Desai had interposed himself between his son and the army of accusers. In his autobiography he attempts to defend Kantilal, and what he says is rather significant.

It is a common experience in India that many people indulge in character assassinations right or wrong, against people whom they dislike or whom they consider hostile or whom they want to harm. One sees a deep-rooted tendency in many people to believe in false stories spread against others. This is a result of the want of freedom in this country for centuries. This also makes the work of the people who want to malign others easy …

It is noteworthy that Desai himself did little to malign Sanjay, or indeed, Mrs Gandhi. The probable reason was that he feared that the lady had information about Kantilal: and that if he attacked her son, she would do the same to his. When asked about this, Mrs Gandhi is said to have responded with one of her disdainful 'humphs', the general implication of which was that she would not take the trouble. Unluckily, Charan Singh, Raj Narain, and the others attempting to force Desai to bring Mrs Gandhi to trial, also had information about Kantilal's alleged activities, and were said to be more of a threat to him in this respect than Mrs Gandhi herself. Jagjivan Ram, leering darkly from the distance to which he had been despatched, had been in politics since 1946 and a colleague of Desai's not only under him, but under three other Prime Ministers, and if anyone knew about the allegedly scandalous behaviour of Kantilal, it was probably this fat, grinning man.

Desai's nerves were obviously, therefore, not of the best as the Shah Commission went endlessly and somewhat comically on, and the 'Kissa Kursi Ka' case involving Sanjay was forced towards trial. The point about this case was that by this time the government was visibly falling apart, and Mrs Gandhi was even more visibly pulling her new party into an entity. The witnesses who had agreed to testify for the prosecution started to withdraw their testimonies, and to become witnesses hostile to the government: they, too, were courtiers, and what would they do if the queen returned in her spendour, and they were found to have defamed the prince? Justice

Shah, alarmed by this new twist, said that Sanjay had been tampering with the witnesses. In May 1978 Sanjay was sent to Tihar for 30 days, so that, Justice Shah said, he could not affect the course of truth.

Sanjay was put into a room at Tihar which had previously been occupied by the police chief employed in Delhi by the administration under Mrs Gandhi. This officer vacated the room, politely, for Sanjay, who was provided with an electric fan (it must be recalled that this was the Delhi summer), a television set, and, by the family, with books and food. So loud a scream of protest was raised in Parliament that the fan and television set were taken away. The family was allowed two visits weekly, a half hour for each visit: Mrs Gandhi usually went, but when she was away electioneering, it was Maneka who carried Sanjay's meals to him in the blue Matador van: dishes of food and a thermos flask; Maneka took them to Tihar, delivered them, waited for the empty dishes to be returned, hopped back into the Matador and went home, to wait until the next delivery was ready. Before Sanjay was put into Tihar he had asked to be isolated from others in the prison, since he feared that they might cause him bodily harm. In fact Sanjay came out all right: it was Maneka who was nearly hurt. On one occasion, it not being visiting day, she was waiting with some of the chief prison officers and policemen in an office, until a warder arrived to collect the dishes and thermos flasks. Suddenly two convicts burst into the office, seized a heavy thermos flask full of water, and swung it at Maneka. It might have killed her, had it hit her, but it did not: large numbers of bulky constables lumbered through the doorway, seized the convicts, and dragged them away.

Meanwhile, Azamgarh had fallen to Congress (I). It was a foreordained result, though the Janata had sent some of their top men, including Vajpayee, to campaign in the district. Mrs Gandhi's candidate was a Muslim woman, and, as Bruce Chatwin said to me, it was extraordinary how much one, in her mannerisms, followed the other: the candidate was a somewhat sturdily built lady, but when Mrs Gandhi flickered her eyelid, the candidate did so too: when Mrs Gandhi rested her chin on her hand and stared Medusa-like into space, so did the candidate: the occasional marvellous smile produced by Mrs Gandhi was duplicated by the candidate, who won in a trot. This was Mrs Gandhi's most important victory since she had started her own party. Victorious in the south during the 1977 elections, but defeated in her stronghold of the north largely because of the sterilisation programmes carried out there under the behest of Sanjay, she had now demonstrated that her party could still win seats in the north. This was partly because her name still stood, amidst millions of people, especially women, in the north, as a symbol of India: no Janata name did: and partly that the people were already becoming slowly but certainly aware that the Janata party had done nothing to help them and was already starting to fragment. Charan Singh, who wanted Mrs Gandhi's head on the block as soon as possible, was being frustrated in this, partly because Desai, for reasons aforementioned, did not want to pursue the matter, and partly because however long the C.B.I. floundered about, no proof of any indictable misdemeanour seemed available against the lady.

Sanjay came out of prison, and went off on a holiday with Maneka: summer still, the *loo** occasionally whirling down from the northern desert, and numerous mirages afloat on the heat-shimmered roads of the capital. Mrs Gandhi continued to revolve around the country, though the speeches she made seemed increasingly repetitive: it was as though she had nothing more now to say, except that her government had tried to make the people rich and the Janata was visibly making the country poor. The Janata, revengeful, tried little bandilleros out on her. The government, under her, had buried a time capsule with the history of independent India in it, amongst other things. Putting this capsule into the red earth of New Delhi had cost an immense amount. It cost even more for the Janata to dig it up, declare that the historical details within it left out numerous great Indian leaders and praised the Nehru dynasty, and start to produce its own time capsule. By the time the next government has dug this one up and reformulated it in suitable terms, the cost of these capsules is likely to be equivalent to the cost of feeding the entire population of India for several years.

Meanwhile, Charan Singh had a heart attack and retired to hospital. This enabled his Sancho Panza, Raj Narain, to express the views of his seniors in a way that Charan Singh, though a somewhat intolerable but at least a sensible man, would not have wished them to be. Charan Singh, daily visited by Janata leaders trying to effect a reconciliation amidst the warring elder statesmen of the party, first

* A wind similar to the *sirocco*.

resigned as Home Minister, then was prevailed upon to return. Jayaprakash Narayan, who had continually expressed himself as being much disillusioned by the performance of the Janata in over a year in power, and another elder statesman, Acharya Kripalani, were called upon to try and put the bits of the party together.

Desai meanwhile departed on a tour of the West. During his absence Raj Narain made a number of speeches berating his own colleagues in the cabinet for not putting Mrs Gandhi and her family into prison. From his sick-bed Charan Singh suddenly came forth with the statement that she should not only be imprisoned, but incarcerated under worse circumstances than the ladies of the royal blood of Gwalior and Jaipur whom she had caused to be cast into Tihar. Desai seems, from some foreign shore, to have sent a message of disapprobation regarding all these antics in his absence. When he flew back to New Delhi, an abject Raj Narain was at the airport, carrying in his hand a bottle of *attar*, an extremely sickly sweet scent, with which it was the custom of Indian courtiers to smear the clothing of their rulers as a sign of respect. Narain did this to Desai as soon as he alighted from his plane: Desai, no hedonist anyway, snapped: 'Leave me alone! When I return, you cover me with *attar*: in my absence, you have done nothing except emit a foul stench.' He said this in the hearing of newspapermen, who very naturally quoted the remark next day. Following a short and hasty series of conferences between the top echelons of the Janata leadership, both Charan Singh, who had recovered sufficiently to be back in circulation, and Raj Narain were asked to resign. They did so, Charan Singh in a typically dry, bitter and concise note, and Narain in an equally typical epistle of self-defence and counter-accusations. Next day, when Charan Singh held a rally of his B.L.D. supporters, at which Narain was present, he advised Narain, who wanted to make a speech, to shut up. Meanwhile, he himself brought two powerful weapons forward against the Prime Minister. Charan Singh was a Jat, a farmer, and he stood for the farmers and opposed economic policies tending towards industrialisation. He therefore threatened to hold a *kisan* rally, or a rally of poor peasants, to say how much they opposed the Janata policies as they stood at present. Secondly, and perhaps more frighteningly from the Prime Minister's point of view, he demanded that an inquiry be held at a Parliamentary level, and a Commission appointed, to look into the past misdeeds of Kantilal, Desai's son. The Prime Minister, who had

continually, if in a milder way than Charan Singh, been saying that
Sanjay Gandhi could never evade the consequences of his misdeeds,
promptly stated that there was no necessity to pursue Kantilal, and
that he would see that no Commission was held to inquire into what
Kantilal was supposed to have done.

These matters hung fire as the parleys at the top continued. They
provided Mrs Gandhi with new material for her speeches, which
she needed, since many people, even her sympathisers had started
to feel that the lady did protest too much. She was now further
assisted by two new events, by the first of which, as a woman of
sensibility, she cannot but have helped being saddened. Towards the
end of the Delhi summer of 1978, two young people, Geeta, a girl
aged 17, and Sanjay, a boy of 15, were trying to hitch a ride into
town. They were picked up by a car driven by two known and
wanted criminals, who took the teenagers, despite their struggles,
to a deserted area near the city limits, where they raped the girl and
killed both her and the boy. The boy, who was not only a brave but
an athletic youth, fought the killers so hard in defence of his sister
and himself, that when the decomposed bodies were discovered
three days later, his bore the marks of twenty-six stab wounds. Only
five had been needed to dispatch his sister. Ever since the outbreak
of lawlessness which had followed the suspension of the emergency,
people all over India had been complaining about the re-emergence
in city life of malefactors who raped, stole, and killed. This case,
however, caused a national scandal. The children had been fairly
rich, the offspring of a senior naval officer and his wife, but the
murder was without motive: though both Geeta and Sanjay had
money on them, none was taken: it was a totemic exercise, blood for
the sake of blood. I now heard it often said that if the emergency had
still been on, nothing of this kind would have happened, and though
the murderers were eventually captured, both the cities of Delhi,
where the murders were committed, and of Bombay, whence the
killers came and to which they fled after the murders, were in a
state of terror bordering on pandemonium. This was due in part to
accusations that the police, before the bodies of the teenagers were
discovered, had been remarkably lax in their investigations: during
Mrs Gandhi's time, it was said, they had to be on their toes. It
was another black mark against the Janata, though perhaps not
entirely the fault of the party, since ill-paid Indian policemen do
not put themselves to trouble about very much. But a further blow

now fell upon the antediluvian shoulders of Desai, a man unused
to dealing with such matters as were now raising hydra heads at
him.

Jagjivan Ram's personal life could scarcely be called a highly
praiseworthy one. He had allegedly evaded taxes for ten years,
which Mrs Gandhi had tactfully overlooked. Unfortunately, like
Mrs Gandhi and Desai, Jagjivan Ram had a son. This son had
married young, though he was more or less estranged from his wife,
allegedly because of his licentious behaviour. One morning the
Delhi papers released a front-page story stating that he and a young
college girl with whom he had a platonic friendship had been
drugged, kidnapped, and eventually abandoned in a car. While in
this drugged state, his friend and he had been undressed and
photographs had been taken of them in compromising situations,
though since they did not know what was happening to them,
nothing had actually taken place between them of any immoral
nature. A little later, it transpired, firstly that the car in which they
had been found belonged to a Defence Ministry official and was said
to have contained top secret files. Secondly, a large number of
photographs were not merely compromising: they depicted the
couple in a whirl of positions and actions, and from the faces of the
two it is evident that they were not only not doped, but were deriving
considerable satisfaction from each other. A small number of these
photographs came into the possession of various M.P.s, who were
said to be showing them furtively to other M.P.s in the corners of the
Parliament lobby, until they were warned by guards that there was
a time and place in which such photographs could be looked at, and
the lobby of Parliament in session was neither the place nor the
time. Maneka Gandhi obtained some of these pictures, which she
published in her magazine *Surya*. Since the photographs were very
blurred and the more relevant portions obscured, it was hard to tell
who was doing what to whom: but certainly both of the parties concerned were doing numerous things to each other. Since Jagjivan
Ram's son looks very much like his father, the pictures were
decidedly anaphrodisiac. Ram's son, perhaps not with a very
astute sense of the occasion, promptly sued his wife for divorce on
the grounds of desertion and mental cruelty. But the country was
now afire with rumours. Mrs Gandhi's son had certainly made
mistakes, but with or without him she had run the country. Not

only was the Janata Party *not* running the country, but the sons of no fewer than two ministers, one the Prime Minister himself and the other Jagjivan Ram, had had serious charges brought against them. In the case of Kantilal Desai, his offences were allegedly criminal: in the case of the younger Ram, the Indian public, which has not been in the habit of perusing the *Kama Sutra* for some centuries, the allegations were of sheer immorality, and the fact that a third person was obviously present, taking photographs by invitation, presumably compounded the matter. What Desai thought of it all has not yet been made public, and one doubts if it ever will be: anyway he had Kantilal to bother about, and was stubborn in his refusal of a Commission to look into his son's various ventures into business. What the bewildered public was to think, nobody dared consider.

Whatever the three parents might or might not have done, there was no doubt that Mrs Gandhi had been a more positive influence on the country, and a by far better influence, than Desai or Ram. Defectors from the Congress (O) and from the Janata, who had previously themselves defected from Mrs Gandhi, started to drift back towards her, and gossip in the Press Club (now usually much de-populated since the coming of Desai and the removal of its bar licence), was all about the possibility of the two Congresses uniting once more to make the Janata position even more embarrassing than it had previously been. There were discussions between the two parties, but they ended in a stalemate. Quite clearly, if the two Congresses became one Mrs Gandhi would insist upon her right to lead. Moreover, those in Congress (O) such as Chavan, Brahmananda Reddy, and Karan Singh, would obviously be in a most uncomfortable position if she did become the leader. As it was, Mrs Gandhi clearly saw possibilities in this: but in order to become the opposition leader, she would have to become a member of the Lok Sabha. She could not lead a party if she was not herself a Member of Parliament. This involved further long discussions amongst the top brass of Congress (I). She would have to contest a safe seat, and the whole campaigning force of the Janata and of other parties like the C.P.M. (Communist Party, Marxist) would be out to stop her, for a second electoral defeat would be a disaster. The Congress (I) waited for a by-election in a safe seat, preferably in the south, which had accepted her during the national elections, though the north had let her down. It took a while to come.

Meanwhile, the Janata, in two minds as usual, announced on the one hand that the cases against her were nearly complete and that she would stand trial at the end of the year. On the other hand, they offered her a passport so that she could visit England, where she had been invited in November 1978. In the past her travel documents had been impounded because there were court cases pending against her. If she was really to come to trial in December, there was all the more reason to withhold her passport, but the government now issued it. Admittedly it was a passport which allowed her to travel to the United Kingdom and nowhere else: but it was a valid passport, and, most curious of all, a diplomatic passport. The Janata were becoming more difficult to understand with every day that passed.

The Congress (I) found her what they were certain was a safe seat. A by-election was being held at a small town in Karnataka, Chikmagalur. The Karnataka Chief Minister, Devraj Urs, was one of the few from the older Congress to remain Mrs Gandhi's man. The Janata put their big guns into the field. George Fernandes went to campaign at Chikmagalur before Mrs Gandhi even reached it. He complained that the road that took him there had been 'strewn by villagers with dead fish, emitting a foul smell'.

❧ 20 ❧

Naked to Mine Enemies

GEORGE FERNANDES WAS so incensed by the fact that his car and escort had to drive squishily over a red carpet of rotten fish spread in his honour by the supporters of Mrs Gandhi, that in one of his first speeches as campaign manager of her Janata opponent, he referred to her as 'an incarnation of the devil'. Another candidate, who had stood for and lost twenty-seven previous campaigns over the long and devious years since 1947, began his new campaign by herding a flock of sheep ahead of him through the villages of the Chikmagalur constituency. This, he announced, was a symbol of the sheeplike attitude of those people who followed Mrs Gandhi where she led them. Yet another candidate complained bitterly that since Mrs Gandhi's crimes during the emergency had not yet been brought to court, he could not tell the voters about them. *The Voice of Millions*, a sort of newspaper printed in New Delhi, called Mrs Gandhi 'Bloody Mary', though few of its readers, who probably number a couple of thousand, could have understood the reference. However, as usual since 1975, Mrs Gandhi had made her mistakes, and these were uncovered by the press with tremendous delight on October 25 1978 a few days before the campaign in the hot—and at this time of the year, wet—southern climate of Chikmagalur. Her mistakes were largely to do with the election laws.

The election laws clearly state how people can become voters within a constituency or state. 'One who ... is ordinarily resident in a constituency shall be entitled to be enrolled a voter within the constituency, he or she is entitled to nominate a certain number of members to the Central Upper House, the Rajya Sabha, on the votes of the state assembly. It appears that in May, though Mrs Gandhi at the time was constantly telling me that she did not want to stand for any kind of election, she thought it might be worthwhile entering the Rajya Sabha through a safe ticket in the Congress (I)

II

state of Karnataka. On May 24, she applied to have her name included in the electoral roll for a constituency in Karnataka called Doddaballapur. She gave her address as 'The Vishnu Ashram in Bangalore District'. Now another of the electoral laws states that if a person has previously been a voter in another area of the country, his or her name should be deleted from the electoral roll of the previous district in which he or she had been a voter. Mrs Gandhi did not do this: up to October 26 1978 she was registered as a voter from New Delhi, her address being 1 Safdarjang Road, that is, the house she occupied as Prime Minister, which Desai now occupied. The usual change of mind took place: she withdrew her application for a place on the electoral roll at Doddaballapur, having apparently decided that after May 1978 she would be more of a threat to the Janata from the Lok Sabha than from the Upper House. Nevertheless, she had allegedly committed two offences, first of all by stating that she was an ordinary resident of Karnataka in the Vishnu Ashram, a place which her spokesman declared that she 'had visited', though her normal residence was in New Delhi: secondly, by not deleting her name from the electoral roll in New Delhi.

To be voted into the Lok Sabha, a man or woman need not come from any particular part of India. The incumbent M.P. of Chikmagalur was induced to resign, so as to cause a by-election in which Mrs Gandhi could stand for the Lok Sabha. The Janata Party, who controlled the press to the same extent as Mrs Gandhi did during the emergency, had all the editors obedient to it. On October 25 1978 as the Chikmagalur campaign started to swing, the news of Mrs Gandhi's fritillary flirtations with the election laws was released. They naturally caused some consternation in Chikmagalur, especially since the Janata stated that her supporters had made various attempts to seize and destroy the papers, signed by her, relevant to her application to become a voter on the electoral roll at Doddaballapur. She had thrown herself naked into the arms of her enemies.

As she moved with her entourage through the hot, rainy district of Chikmagalur, she was pursued by many people. The Janata had appointed Fernandes the campaign manager for the party candidate. Urs, Chief Minister of Karnataka, had announced that Desai had made an open exhortation to the Janata Party in the state, saying that Mrs Gandhi must be prevented an election victory by fair means or foul. The Janata sent what big guns they could to

Chikmagalur: Desai, after many tangles with the lady in the past, did not appear: Vajpayee, probably the most intelligent man and best speaker in the Janata, was too ill to travel (Indian Ministers and government officials had been forbidden by Desai to drink in public, so they made up for it on foreign trips. According to reliable sources Vajpayee retreated into the All India Medical Institute of Science in Delhi for a few days after each of his overseas trips, of which, being the Foreign Minister, he had plenty). In any event, it was announced that an intestinal inflammation prevented him from going south to cross swords with Mrs Gandhi. Another Minister, Bahuguna, was sent, and so was Jagjivan Ram. Ram, in one of his first speeches in the area, hammered away at the Doddaballapur incident. It was an attempt at deception, he said. (And that was not easy to deny.) He told his audience that if they elected Mrs Gandhi she would deceive them in the future as well. 'The lady,' he said, 'has no compunction in telling lies and making false declarations.' She had also, he said, the habit of saying one thing and doing another. (Neither Ram nor any of his colleagues could really be exonerated from the same charge, but India was India, after all.) Until a few days before she came to Chikmagalur to file her nomination, he said, she had repeatedly declared that she did not want power and would not stand for elections at any cost. Now, here she was, trying to come back to the Lok Sabha, the parliamentary institution which dealt with the affairs of the country. Why? he asked.

This was a totally rhetorical question. Everyone knew why.

When, after Mrs Gandhi lost the 1977 elections, she had said that a tremendous burden had been thrust upon her shoulders, that she was grateful that it had gone, and that she now wished to lead a normal life, I believed her, though as a reasonably intelligent person, I had some reservations about her being totally convinced about this herself. When she began to be surrounded, once more, by political people, it was obvious what would happen. First of all, there were hundreds of politicians who had neither made the switchover to Janata nor allied themselves under Chavan in Congress (O). Nearly every Indian politician or businessman I have met (and as types the two are closely allied) has an eve to the main chance. The main chance was obviously Mrs Gandhi. The Janata was likely to split in the near future, since it was composed of so many disparate nonentities. (And in fact it did.) Chavan was, in his basic essence, a country politician: a cunning, not a clever man, a man of little presence. Mrs Gandhi was still the only person who might be able to control, not only the country, but command some kind of international respect. A politician who stayed with her, and persuaded her to try for power once more, would probably be on to a good thing.

Mrs Gandhi was ready to fight in Chikmagalur. But the Janata were serious in their attempt to prevent this battle ending in a victory for her. According to Dr Chenna Reddy, Chief Minister of Andhra Pradesh, another Congress (I) state, the Janata were attempting to corrupt the voters of Chikmagalur. After a voter in India has cast his ballot, his fingers are marked with indelible ink (as I mentioned earlier, this ink is not as indelible as it is supposed to be) to show that he has voted. Dr Chenna Reddy alleged that the Janata were paying prospective supporters of Mrs Gandhi sums of money to allow themselves to be thus branded before the polling had even started. Another allegation was that Mrs Gandhi's followers were, in some areas, not even submitted to the indignity of inked fingers: the Janata paid them Rs. 50 (about $8) not to vote at all. Devraj Urs, the Chief Minister of Karnataka, and a powerful man in his own parish, issued an even more sensational statement. He said that it had come to his knowledge that on the eve of the by-election, the Janata supporters would issue Mrs Gandhi's acolytes with heavily doped liquor, and, while the innocently intoxicated Congressmen were snoring off the effect, would emboss their fingers with indelible ink. Thus, said Mr Urs, the Janata felt that most people would be unable to stagger as far as the polling booths the next day. If some, with stronger heads than others, did make an effort to reach the ballot boxes, they would not be allowed to vote because of the ink marks on their fingers. In case anybody complained about this, said Mr Urs, the Janata had offered them bribes of up to Rs. 50 for their silence. Such charges would seem incredible in any country but India: here they were at least possibly true, and it was also possibly true that Mrs Gandhi's camp-followers were doing something of the same kind the other way round. Whether Desai approved of the issue of liquor to the electorate or not, was difficult to ascertain. But he had, after all, been quoted by Urs as saying that Mrs Gandhi's victory must be prevented by fair means or foul.

It is quite possible, however, that whatever the Janata had done, were doing, and were preparing to do to prevent her victory, Mrs Gandhi was less worried by them than by a group of girls in white saris (white being the colour of mourning in India) who did nothing but, in total silence, follow her round from rally to rally. They were gentle, not unbeautiful girls from South India, and their leader was Nandana, the daughter of Pattabhiraman and Snehalata Reddy. As I said earlier in the book, I once brought the matter of Snehalata Reddy up to Mrs Gandhi (this was after Mrs Reddy had died), and she gave the impression then of being, for once, on the defensive, both fidgety and regretful. The sight of these doe-eyed, utterly silent, young women, accusing, still, a host of female Banquos, following her around the Karnataka countryside, watching her from the depths of their silence, may have shaken Mrs Gandhi more than anything else that happened to her during her campaign. She is used to rough political fighting, and there her main weapon is her silence: to have it used against her must have been a unique experience.

Mrs Gandhi may have made an enormous number of mistakes since 1975, but when she set off on her comeback trail she had a plan in mind: she had split the Congress once in 1969 and succeeded: out of office, she had split the remnants of the Congress in 1977-8 and created Congress (I). Her main aim now, if she were to be returned to the Lok Sabha, was to split the Congress (O) and come back as opposition leader. The Congress (O) Parliamentary Board, when it was announced that she was trying to return to the Lok Sabha, was thrown into a state of panic. If she won at Chikmagalur she would be a permanent nuisance to Congress (O). However, she would also be a source of terror to the Janata, which, in Chavan, had no real Congress leader to fight. The Congress Parliamentary Board (C.P.B.) now entered upon a long series of discussions as to whether or not they should throw their support and their own campaigning resources behind Mrs Gandhi in Karnataka. If Mrs Gandhi won and came back as the leader of Congress (I), Congress (O) would be strengthened by a further Janata defeat in a by-election. If, however, after Mrs Gandhi won, it was likely that many Congress (O) workers would return to Mrs Gandhi, Chavan and such others as Brahmananda Reddy would have to waddle over to the Janata: from the lady, once she was back, they could expect no mercy. Neither could Karan Singh, the Kashmiri king, once a supporter of Mrs Gandhi, now, like so many of her former supporters, an implacable enemy.

The C.P.B. talked and talked. Eventually, they pledged their full support to Mrs Gandhi in distant Chikmagalur. A. K. Anthony, the Chief Minister of Kerala, promptly resigned from the C.P.B. So did Karan Singh, who had been the main opponent of Congress (O) support for Mrs Gandhi.

Karan Singh, tall, handsome and slightly short of temper, issued a statement. He said the C.P.B. declaration was 'a sellout to her ... part of a calculated campaign to dilute the party and sap its political will.' He added that the decision would probably lead to a further number of defections from Congress (O) to Congress (I). Nothing, obviously, could have pleased Mrs Gandhi better. It is fairly certain that the 'calculated campaign' he talked about was started up by whisperers planted by Mrs Gandhi herself.

If she came back, there might once more be a united Congress. If she came back at all, that was: the Janata were obviously doing all they could to prevent it. It would be a long while before this hot, rainy, little constituency would see so many national figures insulting one another in public for their edification, which was intentional, but also for their entertainment, which was perhaps unintentional.

Mrs Gandhi might sleep in her car on the way from one rally to another, or eat oranges, or let her right eyelid flicker in irritation, or produce for certain people that enchanting and irresistible smile, but she knew where she intended to end up: on the rather uncomfortable opposition front bench at the Lok Sabha. The others seemed to blunder around in the mud of Chikmagalur: once more the bulls, once more the brilliant and elusive butterfly.

The language of Karnataka is Kannada. Mrs Gandhi, ploughing through the mud towards the makeshift platform from which she was to speak, made it a point to have a crash course in Kannada, in which she spoke her first few sentences at each rally, apologising for delays caused by rain and bad roads, welcoming the audience, telling them that she was in the process of learning Kannada, and then, explaining that she had learned little more than this and switching into English. What she said in English was basically that she would support the poor and downtrodden, minority castes and women, if she were to be elected: whereas, she said, the Janata would sell the country to other countries and what she referred to as 'multi-nationals'. Fernandes, somewhat of a physical as well as mental lumberer, chased her cavalcade over the muddy roads, but always seemed to arrive at a rally at the precise moment that she had departed. He flexed his verbal muscles, on each occasion, and demanded that Mrs Gandhi should share a platform with him to debate the successes and failures of both her government and the Janata. She was always a little too far ahead of him on the road for this to happen. It was also peculiar that the actual candidate of the Janata Party, a rather insignificant former Chief Minister named Veerendra Patel, seldom actually spoke: the big boys did it for him. Jagjivan Ram, George Fernandes and Bahuguna asked Mrs Gandhi to compare the results of her eleven years as Prime Minister with the achievements of the Janata government over a year and a half. Apart from the emergency period, Mrs Gandhi, a practical dreamer, had in fact done slightly better for the country than her own father, and the Janata party, by contrast, had achieved little. The exception perhaps was that Desai had made an enormously publicised speech in the U.S.A. recommending urine therapy and stating that while meat eaters could consume alcohol without ill effects, vegetarians, which 84 per cent of all Indians were, could not: hence his policy of prohibition. A friend who listened to this speech told me that the audience imagined he was trying to be witty in some obscure oriental way, and laughed: Desai, whose sense of humour is on a par with that of John Calvin and Dean Inge, was much displeased by this.

My acquaintance with Mrs Gandhi had by this time spread over a decade, and it had always been a friendly one. Since her defeat in the elections, as I have said before, it had turned into a relationship, at least on my part, of closeness and care. The questions I asked her were always answered a little evasively except when she was in a good mood. Sometimes, even when she was in a bad mood, she answered, if she thought the question of interest, cohesively and clearly. People tend to be cyclical in their behaviour: they have a night and a bright day. To me, she is a good and gentle woman who lost part of her heart on the way to wherever she now is.

People call her a liar. I would rather say she prevaricates, evading the definite statement in conversation, but, when she acts, she is not a liar to herself. She has been called ruthless, and she is: this is also because she trusts nobody. She saw her mother scorned by other members of the family: she saw her father betrayed by those in whom he placed his chief trust. She is something of an intellectual, but her lack of trust has led her to believe that the sword is mightier than the pen. She is a remarkable woman as it is, probably the most remarkable woman I have ever met: but she could have been equally remarkable as a completely different sort of woman, if her childhood, her adolescent loneliness, her broken marriage, and her long watch over the dying days of her father, could be replaced and made into one. The absence of trust, the frequency with which she has been betrayed, contribute to this. It has led to temporary dependence on bad advisers, sycophants who tell her what she wants to know, because she believes they tell her the truth. Even during the emergency she believed those who told her how much the people loved Sanjay. It has also led her to suddenly throwing good advisers out, because they have told her the truth. Pilate had the right line written for him in the New Testament: truth is not an exactitude: it varies from person to person. Pilate was not being sardonic when he asked what truth was, and Mrs Gandhi does not ask what truth is, so long as it is what she, against all evidence, believes.

I still believe that she was correct in her declaration of the emergency, which came at a time when the country was about to be plunged into a chaos from which it would probably not have recovered. The freedom of the media under the Janata is as restricted as it was during the emergency months. To give an example, there is a government film, recently released, which is supposed to be a description of India in the year 1977. It starts in March, after the Janata had won the elections.

Three cuts were made in this film. One is of a long shot of Dr Jonas Salk receiving the Nehru Peace Prize. Since Mrs Gandhi is shown in the background this shot was cut out. Another, once more in long shot, shows V. C. Shukla, Mrs Gandhi's Information Minister during the emergency, at the back of a crowd. This was cut. The most unkindest cut of all was when, while taking a sequence in a government office, a calendar with Mrs Gandhi's face on it appeared in the frame. This sequence was taken out too.

Things work this way in India, more than in some other places: a mixture of cynicism and cruelty pervades Indian life. Once defeated, the previous ruler does not attract pity so much as contempt. Mrs Gandhi had known and suffered as a child the experience of not being accepted into her own family. Then the cruising years came, when she floated under the wing of her father. Until Chou En-Lai,

Nehru's friend, shattered his heart in 1962, Indira was able to stay in the shadows and was anxious to remain there. She was dependent on her father in a psychological sense, that is to say she was protected by him. At the same time she had the feeling that she protected him, alleviating his tiredness, keeping bores off his back, feeding him properly. After 1962 Nehru became dependent on her to a much greater extent than she had ever been on him, and she saw his agony and once more felt how much betrayal hurt.

Then came the years of power, when she fought, manipulated, and overrode the people around her, so that she should not herself be betrayed. Simultaneously, she surrounded herself with people, good and bad advisers, to ensure within herself the sense of acceptance within a world she had created. What she had herself created, she could herself destroy: with a sweep of the hand, a flicker of the eye, she could dismiss people from her presence forever. In a sense, as a psychological study, she was not unique, but certainly rare. She had been made lonely as a child, and she needed to be accepted: yet, once in a world where she was accepted, she suddenly seems to have felt a compulsion towards loneliness, and swept aside those who had accepted her. One of the effects on those she cast aside, for in a way her acceptance world was theirs as well, was to make them feel how it was to be lonely and betrayed. The unanimity with which former friends and relatives have attacked her, verbally and in print, after her overthrow in the 1977 elections, says a lot about this.

But after the defeat, she could not bear total loneliness: she came back into politics, she collected new people around her, created new worlds to destroy: D. P. Singh, for example, once very close to her, was picked up in her hand and thrown away. Moreover, the knowledge that she had been rejected in 1977, not simply by relatives of her youth and the political enemies of later years, but by the people of India as a whole, threw her far back into the interstices of her own mind. From this rejection came the endless and repetitive speeches about foreign powers anxious that she should fall from power. From it also came the continual outcries against the Janata as the persecutors of a lonely and defenceless woman: the Janata certainly followed a policy of persecution towards her, but the constant insistence on her part that she was being made a martyr of, (shades of the schoolroom where she first read about Joan of Arc), became a little wearisome after a while. 'Methinks the lady

doth protest too much', a British diplomat in Delhi once remarked
to me: it was a general feeling.

Then the third theme of her speeches was the nonsense made of
government by the Janata. This was also true, but too often repeated
in the same way: the basis of each speech was a denial of misdeeds
during the emergency, a recital of the persecutions she had been
put to by the Janata, and a condemnation of Janata rule. This was all
very well: but as the newspapers reported the same speech, with
minor alterations, from every corner of the country she visited,
people ceased to be interested: for she said nothing new, and there
was in fact nothing new to say. But if the reports in the newspapers,
when she spoke, became shorter and shorter, the public still massed
to see her and hear her: she was, after all, a kind of legendary figure,
and the presence of crowds reassured her once more.

Her visit to England would obviously be a further reassurance:
she likes England, and, having been invited there by a section of the
Indian community, must have looked forward to her visit, but, under
the overcast sky of autumn England, a new storm blew up. A large
section of Indians resident in England, who had had nothing to do
with the original invitation, formed themselves into an association
to oppose Mrs Gandhi's visit. They would not boycott her public
appearances: far from it, they said, they would be present, and would
cause as much trouble as they could to a 'dictator' and 'murderess'.
They also asked the then British Prime Minister, James Callaghan,
in view of the improved relations between the United Kingdom and
India, to ban her from entry into Britain. 'The more you are
criticised,' Mrs Gandhi had once said to me, 'the stronger you should
become within yourself.' This is a statement I accept with some
reservations: if you are criticised by people you know, it perhaps
strengthens you, but the sense of innumerable hostile hordes who
not only criticise you but actively hate you must shake a person,
even one as normally impassive as Mrs Gandhi.

The uproar in England about her proposed visit arose at about
the time Mrs Gandhi started to campaign in Chikmagalur. As the
election drew near, another incident occurred. Nandana Reddy,
with her silent companions, had followed Mrs Gandhi all round the
district. At a small town about 30 miles from Chikmagalur proper,
on October 31, Nandana, a black scarf wrapped round her face as a
token of her silence, was carrying a placard which inquired 'Who
is responsible for my mother, Snehalata Reddy's death?' A police

inspector tried to arrest her and hustle her into a van, but she put up some resistance. Thereupon a number of constables made a *lathi* charge swinging their knobkerrie-like clubs. Eleven people were hurt, but Nandana was selected for particular attention. Two policemen seized and held her, while several others belaboured her with their *lathis* (she is a pretty, slight young woman who had already been much disturbed mentally by the death of Snehalata). Eventually, when she was unconscious and covered with blood, the constables decided it would be wiser to stop. They therefore dumped her in a ditch and left her there. She was found by some reporters, who carried her to their car and drove her, still unconscious, to the nearest doctor, some distance away.

Next day newspapers all over the country carried the story on the front page. Nandana was said to be seriously hurt but no details had clearly emerged as yet. There was, however, a lot of speculation. Mrs Gandhi had apparently seemed to pay no attention to Nandana and her friends when they came to her rallies. On October 30, however, Nandana had broken her silence in a sort of press conference, in which she repeatedly asked who was responsible for Snehalata's death, and implied that Mrs Gandhi was. From the reports, she sounded a little hysterical: in any event, it seemed curious that the attack upon her should have been made the day after her statement to the press. The rumours started, as they were bound to. The Janata had no interest in stopping Nandana's activities: indeed, it was quite the opposite: a grieving girl who blamed Mrs Gandhi for the death of her mother obviously attracted the sympathy of the villagers who would eventually vote.

Now the police who attacked Nandana were part of the Karnataka state force, an appendage of the government, which was a Congress (I) government. The implications, to some people, seemed obvious: Nandana had been pointed out to the police as someone who required special treatment. The attack upon her and the attempt to arrest her which preceded it, were entirely unprovoked, since neither she nor the people around her were doing anything that could possibly be construed as illegal or violent. Someone had clearly issued instructions about Nandana, and these instructions had been carried out, perhaps in excess of orders. The Congress (I) promptly said that the attack had been instigated by the Janata so that Mrs Gandhi would be blamed for it. Since the state police worked under a Congress (I) government, it was difficult to see how the Janata could have done this. The police themselves said that they had specific orders from the Centre to protect Mrs Gandhi from the crowds (presumably because the government did not want Mrs Gandhi to be murdered or hurt, and the blame placed on it). It is possible that these instructions were taken too seriously by the police but admittedly this is not likely.

What enraged most people in the country, including Mrs Gandhi's own supporters, was the statement that Nandana, a truthful young woman, made from a hospital bed in Chikmagalur on November 1. According to Nandana, she and her followers turned up at Kakkinge, the small town where the incident took place, on the evening of October 30. Mrs Gandhi was supposed to address a rally there at 4 p.m. It was raining heavily, but Nandana and her followers stood under the weeping sky and awaited the arrival of the lady. There were, according to Nandana, more policemen around than usual, but an Inspector identified by her as Mr Iqbal, told her, 'They are here to protect you.' At 7.40 in the darkness and rain, Mrs Gandhi's cavalcade of cars arrived. 'There was nobody in the audience,' Nandana said, 'at least, only a few. They shouted slogans praising her. She began her speech. Someone signalled to the police from the dais ... then the attack began ... a dozen of them pounced on me and rained down *lathi* blows. Mrs Gandhi looked on.' I recalled the incident at Willingdon Crescent when Uma Vasudev had been attacked by Congress workers, and Mrs Gandhi, asked whether she should not intervene, stood in silence, and very faintly smiled.

Some months before she won at Chikmagalur, on a hot dusty July afternoon, I received a telephone call from Mrs Gandhi's office, asking for my exact address, since Mrs Gandhi had written me a letter. This was not normal procedure: her officials knew my telephone number and my address already, and Mrs Gandhi did not usually write to me: she had someone telephone if she wanted to see me or speak to me. Our last meeting, a few days before, had been very friendly: but the peculiar circumstances, and the tone of the secretary on the telephone, made me feel that something important, indeed momentous, had happened in the few intervening days. I hate to wait for things to happen, so I said I would come and collect the letter. I drove round to Willingdon Crescent, where a usually smiling secretary nodded coldly at me and handed it over. Standing in the dusty sunlight on the lawn, I opened it and read it. The sand-wind made the letter shake in my hands, ribbing the fold with brown dust. I looked up from it at the balcony, where several secretaries were now apparently on sentry duty. I inquired if Mrs Gandhi was available, since I would like to speak to her. 'It is the afternoon,' they replied in a kind of Gregorian chant. 'She is asleep.' So I left.

I re-read the letter on the way back. It was polite and civilised, but too civilised, too polite: it was also very vague in its terms, and from my knowledge of Mrs Gandhi, such as it was, I interpreted it as a severance of relationship, especially since it did not require an answer. At first I experienced the kind of dull shock that many others must have done during their contact with Mrs Gandhi. Barely a week ago, my friendship for her and trust in her had been, apparently, mutual. Now, because of rumours of un-specified stories I had written about, brought to her by unnamed people, this period was obviously over. I had started by wanting to be an eye that watched her and an ear that listened: I had ended by feeling strong sympathy for her as well as friendship, the two being not always inseparable: now the friendship had gone, drifted away on a wind of distrust, for all the good wishes she conveyed at the end of the letter.

When I started the book, I had asked her to read the chapters, since numerous interpretations of fact arose from the many inter-views I had had with other people. I had said at the time that I wanted her corrections on facts, not of any opinions I might form during my research on those facts. 'It wouldn't be right for me to read a book written about me,' she said. That was all right by me.

Back home, I sat down and wrote her a letter. If she thought, I said, that I had misquoted her and perpetrated untruths, I was sorry. But since she had not read the book, nor had anyone in India except Leela, I wondered what her sources of information were.

A day later I telephoned one of the secretaries to ask if Mrs Gandhi had received the letter. 'Oh, yes,' he said like Hurree Babu, 'letter is at present in front of Madamji herself. She is reading it.' I inquired when I could see her. 'Oah, she wants to see you too much,' said the secretary, 'but do not worry yourself to call us, we will call you.' That meant what theatrical agents say, and I did not believe it: no-body ever called me, and what was even more to the point, Maneka, who usually rang me every so often to ask for a contribution to her magazine *Surya*, ceased to do so.

Epilogue

I DID SEE Mrs Gandhi again, eventually, but in circumstances completely different from those which existed while I was writing the body of this book.

After our disagreement, or whatever one chooses to call it, I watched with sorrow while not only the Janata but her own followers piled humiliation after humiliation upon her. The Chief Minister of Karnataka, the southern state in which she won the by-election at Chikmagalur, was a plump pipe-smoker of 64, Devraj Urs. He was the President of the Congress (I) and had been one of Mrs Gandhi's most powerful and faithful supporters since her fall in 1977. But he now demonstrated some acerbity towards his leader. On October 12 1978, after Mrs Gandhi's victory at Chikmagalur, Urs remarked, in a widely reported speech, that this was *his* victory, not hers. Without him, he implied, she would have lost.

Whether this was true or not, Mrs Gandhi was now implanted in the Lok Sabha, from which, predictably enough, she began to launch violent verbal assaults upon the Janata, who were terrified. Mrs Gandhi in the political wilderness, making offensive remarks about the government, was one matter: the lady vocal in parliament was another. The Janata high command, divided within itself, was united in opposition to Mrs Gandhi, and the leaders resolved that they ought to stop all this.

In 1977 two Janata M.P.s, Madhu Limaye and Kanwarlal Gupta, had brought a privilege motion against her. They obviously anticipated her coming back into politics, and wished to bring about another arrest. They alleged that in 1975 she had been directly responsible, as Prime Minister, for the harassment of certain officials who had been attempting to collect information about Maruti, and the lodging of false charges against them. This, they said, was a breach of parliamentary privilege. The privilege Committee of the House thereupon went into session.

After Mrs Gandhi's victory, this Committee, in a fashion timely for the Janata, produced its findings. Desai promptly moved a resolution in parliament for Mrs Gandhi's expulsion from her seat, and her arrest. On December 19, a warrant for her arrest was sworn. Mrs Gandhi's thespian sense now came to the fore. She insisted that her arrest should take place on the floor of the House. When proceedings for the day were over, she seated herself on a bench, surrounded by friends and foes alike, and, while awaiting the arrival of the police, held a press conference. During the course of this, she scribbled down a piece of verse on a scrap of paper, which was circulated among her followers and the press. This said, 'Wish me well as you bid me goodbye/With a cheer, not a tear, in your eye./ Leave me a smile/I can keep all the while/That I am away.) The Congress (I), or some of them, claimed that she had written it, suddenly inspired by the muse. Some pressmen, however, reported that the lines came from a popular song written during the Second World War.* Speculation ceased, though, when the police arrived to make the arrest. It was made: she did not, this time, demand handcuffs. She left parliament amidst waves of Congress (I) workers trying to impede the constabulary. This time she spent a week in prison, and on December 26 was released.

However, the Janata were still adamant that she should be expelled from the Lok Sabha. On January 5 1979, the irrepressible George Fernandes said she had accepted colossal bribes from multinationals. On January 15 the Chief Election Commissioner said that he had looked into the case and Mrs Gandhi, having been expelled from the Lok Sabha, had automatically to vacate her seat. She was once more in the wilderness and this time it must have been more bitter than before. She had been insulted, imprisoned, and flung out of the parliament where she had sat for so many years. She started to campaign around the country. On February 10 she was back in Karnataka, where she was cheered by many, but also picketed by opponents with black flags. Her relations with Urs were by now rather strained. They had had differences, and these were notably over the fact that Urs wanted to unite all the various factors within

* Mrs Gandhi's was an inaccurate version of 'Wish me luck as you wave me goodbye', sung by Gracie Fields in the film *Shipyard Sally*, 1939.

the Congress and make them one party. He may have started to doubt that Mrs Gandhi carried enough power, now, to return by herself. If so, Mrs Gandhi, more astute and supple a person than Urs, must have been aware of this and have been annoyed.

Besides, Urs had been accused of corruption, and a body known as the Grover Commission had been set up to look into the accusations. It may have seemed to him an excellent time to make friends with the Janata. On May 3 1979 he went to Delhi to meet Charan Singh, and in the same month the Grover Commission found him culpable of eight charges of corruption. On June 8 the working committee of Congress (I) ordered Urs to resign from the presidency of the party. A week later the Congress Committee in Karnataka was dissolved, and Urs was replaced as its leader. He was by no means deflated, however. The very next day, he re-formed the Committee, threw out his successor, and broke away from Congress (I).

This performance, though it had its comic aspects, split the Congress once more. It also meant that Mrs Gandhi had been deprived of the important support of the Karnataka leader. If the Congress was in some chaos, however, so was the Janata. Charan Singh and Desai had been on a collision course for some time. At one point Desai had made Charan Singh resign. Charan Singh's faction had then made such protests that the Prime Minister had to eat humble pie. Charan Singh came back to the cabinet, and was named a Deputy Prime Minister. This was a post he coveted, for he was an ambitious man, and wanted to lead the country. He evidently thought that Desai, at 83, could not last, and would soon either retire or die, leaving the throne empty for takeover. Charan Singh was himself 76: and he had had two heart attacks. There was little time for him either. He began to manoeuvre.

He did so with remarkable success, and split the Janata. On July 9 1979 Raj Narain left the party and formed a new one, though it could hardly be called powerful, since its sole membership consisted of 13 M.P.s. Six days later, on July 15, Desai, lonely and embittered, resigned. If he had genuinely believed that he had come to power as a messiah, what happened to him must have hurt him terribly, for he is a proud man. On July 28 Charan Singh became Prime Minister with a coalition of what was now called Janata (S), his branch of the ill-conceived party, and Congress (S), the opponents of Mrs Gandhi, who were so called because their temporary chief was Swaran Singh,

Foreign Minister under Mrs Gandhi. This government suffered from even more internal friction than the previous one, and collapsed on August 20, after 24 days in power. Prior to this a no-confidence move was passed in parliament. Charan Singh went to the President and asked for midterm elections. These were announced for January 1980.

On August 21 Raj Narain proposed that Charan Singh should form a new party. On September 25 he did so by the simple expedient of renaming the Janata (S) the Lok Dal, or People's Party. But he was now no more than a caretaker.

For the people had watched the activities of the governments they had brought to power after Mrs Gandhi for two and a half years, and they had watched with increasing cynicism. Prices had risen tremendously, and many commodities such as diesel oil, kerosene, gas cylinders, and firewood were virtually unobtainable. The lorries which ply, fuelled by diesel, from the capital to other cities, lay like stranded whales, in endless lines, around the petrol pumps. Many people found it impossible to cook for days at a time. I observed all this in Delhi, but there were shortages all over the country. Moreover, the population was fully aware of the ambitions that had prevailed and dogfights which had taken place among the leaders of the country since 1977. They realised that these leaders cared for power, not the people. The small figure of Mrs Gandhi, so remote for months, now came sharply into focus in the eyes of the masses.

She was busy. She meant herself to be seen and heard all over the country, and she was. She meant to draw loyalties to herself from the members of other parties, and she did. When the elections came, she meant to be prepared. She was to stand from her old consti-tuency Rae Bareilly, where she had been so unexpectedly defeated by Raj Narain in 1977. Her new opponent, Mrs Scindia, the dowager maharani of Gwalior, whom she had once cast into Tihar prison, was also exceptionally busy. She had personal reasons for wanting to defeat Mrs Gandhi. But Mrs Gandhi this time was determined not to be defeated.

In September Urs formed the Congress (U), named after himself. Amateur humorists now talked of the Congress (I) and the Congress (You). Congress (O) melded with Urs's party, but nevertheless there seemed to be a medley of parties in conflict. Apart from the two

Congresses, there were the Janata, now under Jagjivan Ram, the
Lok Dal, the Communist parties, and small parties like the Akalis,
the Sikh party, which were all in the fray. It looked as though there
would be a very fragmented vote. The Delhi political writers, so
often at Mrs Gandhi's throat in the past two years, now predicted, a
little nervously, that she would come in by a very small margin.
However, they added hopefully, Sanjay had helped her considerably
towards her defeat in the last election. Had she not had him around
her neck, she would have won in 1977. And she had still not shed
him. He was to stand for the Lok Sabha from Amethi, not far from
Rae Bareilly, where he had lost heavily in the previous election. As
long as he was around, wrote these experts, she would be in trouble,
before, during, and after the coming elections. Somehow I thought
them wrong. It seemed to me that the fury of the people against
Sanjay had been forgotten.

In Delhi, winter was on its way. The whole city was full of loudspeaker vans praising one party or another, causing dogs to bark and
householders to be awoken from their Sunday afternoon siestas.
There were processions and huge dusty rallies, party banners
streaming from the platforms. The same thing continued all over
the country, for week after week. The politicians shouted themselves
hoarse: though this time the Janata were somewhat on the defensive.
The election was the usual topic whenever friends or even strangers
met, and one heard the same remarks and prediction made over and
over — sometimes by oneself. The weather became colder: men and
women wrapped themselves in shawls. In some parts of the country
people died of exposure. It was forecast that the cold in the north
would adversely affect the turnout of voters there: they would not
want to come out in frosty weather, and queue up for hours, with
nothing to show at the end of it but a Prime Minister. Anything that
could be predicted about the elections was. But, curiously enough,
none of the forecasts I heard came anywhere near the final truth.

The first votes were cast on January 3 1980. The pundits had
predicted violence at the polls. What sharply struck me, as I moved
around Bombay, where I happened to be, was not only that there
was no violence, but there seemed to be hardly any people. The
early morning, I was told, was when most of the population voted.
However, when the first counts came, they revealed, surprisingly,
that a low proportion of voters had turned out, and observers

reported that the electorate had shown a curious apathy towards the elections. Considering the amount that everyone from professors to peons had told me about the future of the country, and the importance of the elections, I wondered if there had been some kind of miscount. But this inexplicable indifference was real.

What was also real, I discovered, as the results came in, was that not only was there no fragmented vote, but the Congress (I) was winning everywhere. Mrs Gandhi was coming back, not with a small lead, but a huge one: it was going to be a landslide, and in the end it was, something nobody had predicted. At one point it looked as if the Congress (I) would finish with 75 per cent of the contested seats. Due to a few scattered Janata and Lok Dal victories at the end of the count, it did not. But it collected 351 seats of a total 524 (though due to terrorist trouble in Assam, the contest for a handful of constituencies was delayed). The next most successful party was the Lok Dal, with 39 seats. It was an even more massive victory than that of 1971, when she had become a heroine after her triumph in Bangladesh.

Several writers outside India commented, when the results were published, that hers was not a positive but a negative victory: that it was asininity and incompetence on the part of the Janata leaders that turned the people away from them, and that when the people turned away, the only person they could see was Mrs Gandhi. I think this is partly true, but the magnitude of her victory indicates that there was much more to it than that. Those who voted brought her back for numerous reasons: foremost amongst them, with the country in crisis, was that they thought she was the only leader who could outface the crisis. This, at least, was what many people told me in the days of the Janata rule. They came from all classes of society, but most of them came from the poorer classes, that is to say from the mass of the Indian population. It was therefore not the rich or intellectual, but the bulk of her people, who brought her home once more.

I have said that after our trouble in 1978, I had not seen her, though I had followed her activities in the press. Leela and I sent her a Christmas card in 1978, and she sent us a New Year card back with a friendly inscription. She must have been deeply depressed at the time, one of the worst periods of her life, and I thought it exceptionally kind of her. During much of 1979 I was in England, but towards the end of the year, considering all wounds healed, I took some flowers to Willingdon Crescent to wish her luck in the elections. She did not speak much, since we were surrounded by her followers, but she smiled. The atmosphere amidst her followers was one of some anxiety. The elections were due very shortly. In November, in Patna, JP's home town (he had died the month before of a heart attack, which, much weakened by age and kidney trouble, he could not overcome), a gang of men had attacked Mrs Gandhi's car. She escaped unhurt, but one of her companions, a Congressman named Mishra, was badly injured. Her aides told me about the incident, which anyway I had read of in the press. 'I think,' said one, 'it had something to do with the death of JP. These people blamed her for it.' A second aide said, 'Possibly the Janata put these people up to it. With the elections coming, they want her out of the way, and', he added, 'those are not scrupulous people. We must be careful with her life.'

A few weeks later, on the day that her total victory was declared, I returned to Willingdon Crescent in the winter sunshine. It was crisp weather, with a wind flowing past me. The garden was packed with people, and there were hundreds outside the house. Drums thumped, bugles blared, flags clattered overhead. There were continual shouts of '*Indira Gandhi ki jai*' and '*Indira Gandhi, desh ka neta*', cries I had heard before in very different situations. I struggled through the crowd to the front steps. For me they had numerous memories. I had come up them in all weathers, and I had seen Mrs Gandhi in this house in a variety of moods. Now the balcony was full of supporters, not all of whom had been supporters in the two years of her political exile.

Fortunately, one of her aides saw me. He took me by the arm and piloted me through the dense mass of bodies into the reception room, also full of people. Some sat, most stood. I stood, there being no more room to sit. At one point Sanjay appeared at the door, draped, like a young Caesar, in a purple shawl. He exchanged a few words with one of the Congressmen near the door, apparently to the effect that his mother would soon appear. Then he disappeared himself. The drums went on outside. Suddenly Mrs Gandhi, in a sari of pastel colours, framed herself in the doorway, slight and with a smile on her face. The Congressmen and women present folded their hands to her. When some had left, and there was more room, others knelt on the floor and touched her feet. I had heard her reprimanding people in the past for this habit, but today she did not, possibly because there were so many people and there was no time for lectures. Finally the room was empty except for her and me. She looked different from the way she had looked for two years: somehow taller.

Standing there, facing her, the echoes of the thousands of words we had exchanged in this room resounded in my ear. I recalled her sadnesses and silences, the brief time of her triumph when I had met her after her first arrest and release. 'Congratulations, ma'am,' I said. 'Could I –' The words 'see you sometime?' were cut short on my lips. 'Not now, Dom,' said Mrs Gandhi, 'I haven't *one* minute to spare.' She kilted up her *sari* and flew out of the front doorway. I watched her disappear into the sunshine and the cheering crowds.

On January 14 1980, Mrs Indira Gandhi was sworn in for the fourth time as Prime Minister of India.

Index